# Educational Governance Research

Volume 6

# Educational Governance Research

## Aims and Scope

This series presents recent insights in educational governance gained from research that focuses on the interplay between educational institutions and societies and markets. Education is not an isolated sector. Educational institutions at all levels are embedded in and connected to international, national and local societies and markets. One needs to understand governance relations and the changes that occur if one is to understand the frameworks, expectations, practice, room for manoeuvre, and the relations between professionals, public, policy makers and market place actors.

The aim of this series is to address issues related to structures and discourses by which authority is exercised in an accessible manner. It will present findings on a variety of types of educational governance: public, political and administrative, as well as private, market place and self-governance. International and multidisciplinary in scope, the series will cover the subject area from both a worldwide and local perspective and will describe educational governance as it is practised in all parts of the world and in all sectors: state, market, and NGOs.

The series:

- Covers a broad range of topics and power domains
- Positions itself in a field between politics and management/leadership
- Provides a platform for the vivid field of educational governance research
- Looks into ways in which authority is transformed within chains of educational governance
- Uncovers relations between state, private sector and market place influences on education, professionals and students.

More information about this series at http://www.springer.com/series/13077

Mustafa Yunus Eryaman • Barbara Schneider
Editors

# Evidence and Public Good in Educational Policy, Research and Practice

Springer

*Editors*
Mustafa Yunus Eryaman
College of Education
Çanakkale Onsekiz Mart University
Çanakkale, Turkey

Barbara Schneider
College of Education
Michigan State University
East Lansing, MI, USA

ISSN 2365-9548 ISSN 2365-9556 (electronic)
Educational Governance Research
ISBN 978-3-319-58849-0 ISBN 978-3-319-58850-6 (eBook)
DOI 10.1007/978-3-319-58850-6

Library of Congress Control Number: 2017943970



Printed on acid-free paper

This Springer imprint is published by Springer Nature
The registered company is Springer International Publishing AG
The registered company address is: Gewerbestrasse 11, 6330 Cham, Switzerland

# Acknowledgments

We would like to thank friends and colleagues who have supported our editing endeavor. So many people have contributed that we will undeniably leave out some important ones. Nevertheless, we would like to give special thanks to the series editors, Lejf Moos and Stephen Carney, for their excellent work reviewing contributions and assisting us and chapter contributors with their recommendations.

Producing an edited book requires substantial amounts of feedback, which were provided by a distinguished panel of expert reviewers. Among others who provided helpful remarks, we would like especially to acknowledge Ingrid Gogolin, Alistair Ross, Bertram Bruce, and Martina Riedler.

We would like to extend our thanks and appreciation to the editorial board members and reviewers of the *International Journal of Progressive Education*, *International Journal of Educational Researchers*, and *Educational Policy Analysis and Strategic Research* for providing their insights, thoughts, and suggestions that have helped make the book as it is today.

We would also like to thank the University of Hamburg, Canakkale Onsekiz Mart University, the German Academic Exchange Service (DAAD), and the Scientific and Technological Research Council of Turkey (TUBITAK) for supporting Mustafa Yunus Eryaman in his visit to Germany in 2015, 2016, and 2017 which facilitated work on the book.

# Contents

# Contributors

**Jeffrey S. Brooks** is professor of educational leadership in the Faculty of Education at Monash University. He is a J. William Fulbright Senior Scholar alumnus who has conducted studies in the USA and the Philippines. His research focuses broadly on educational leadership, and he examines the way leaders influence (and are influenced by) dynamics such as racism, globalization, distributed leadership, social justice, and school reform.

**Tracey Burns** is a project leader in the Centre for Educational Research and Innovation of the OECD. She leads the Governing Complex Education Systems Project and is also responsible for the OECD work on Trends Shaping Education, which looks at how trends outside of education could have an impact on education in the future. Previous to this, she worked on social determinants of health and on education and social inclusion issues both at the OECD and in Vancouver, Canada. Tracey holds a BA from McGill University, Canada, and a MA and PhD from Northeastern University, USA. Relevant publications include Burns et al. (eds.) (2016). *Modern Educational Governance: The challenge of complexity*; Fazekas, M., and T. C. Burns (2011), "Exploring the complex interaction between governance and knowledge in education," *OECD Education Working Papers*, No.67; and OECD (2007), *Evidence in Education: Linking research and policy*. T. Burns and T. Schuller (eds.).

**Mustafa Yunus Eryaman** is the vice president of the World Education Research Association and professor of curriculum and instruction at Çanakkale Onsekiz Mart University. He has served as associate dean in the Faculty of Education and as the interim chancellor at Çanakkale Onsekiz Mart University. He is currently a visiting DAAD professor at the Institute for International Comparative and Intercultural Education in the University of Hamburg. He serves as a council member in the European Educational Research Association and World Education Research Association. He received his MEd from the University of Missouri-Columbia and his PhD from the University of Illinois at Urbana-Champaign. He is the author of

*Teaching as Practical Philosophy* (2008) and editor of the *International Handbook of Progressive Education* (2015) and *Peter McLaren, Education, and the Struggle for Liberation* (2009).

**Elizabeth Farley-Ripple** is associate director and assistant professor in the School of Education at the University of Delaware. She is an experienced policy researcher, with expertise in mixed methods. She also has experience with a range of quantitative methods such as multilevel modeling, longitudinal analysis, and social network analysis and has worked extensively with surveys and qualitative methods, conducting and analyzing data from hundreds of interviews, documents, and observations. Her research interests focus on policy analysis and evidence-based decision-making, and she has worked on a range of educational and social policy issues including administrator mobility, school and teachers' use of data, teacher quality and effects, and issues of equity in a variety of student outcomes such as dropout, educational attainment, teen fertility, and postsecondary access. Dr. Farley-Ripple has published research in top journals such as *Educational Researcher*, the *Journal of Educational Administration*, *Educational Policy*, the *American Journal of Education*, *Educational Management Administration and Leadership*, and *Urban Education*. She has served as principal investigator, or Co-PI, on grants funded through the Institute of Education Sciences and the Spencer Foundation and was a lead researcher on two prior studies of administrator mobility and turnover in Delaware.

**Jonathan W.P. Goh** is an associate dean (research quality) at the Office of Education Research (OER) and associate professor in the Policy and Leadership Studies (OER) Department, National Institute of Education (NIE), Nanyang Technological University, Singapore. He obtained his PhD (with distinction) from the University of Western Australia in 2001. Jonathan currently supports the OER in developing research capacity at the institute and helps oversee OER grant management processes. His teaching and research interests include data analysis techniques (including Rasch analysis, hierarchical linear modeling, and structural equation modeling), student learning approaches and assessment, educational leadership and management, educational marketing, and cross-cultural aspects in leadership and management. Jonathan has been actively engaged in consultancy work with various industries including finance (e.g., Citibank Australia), consumer products (e.g., Smith's Crisps and Leeuwin Winery), hospitality (e.g., Sheraton Perth Hotel, Duxton Hotel, and Thomas Cook Travel), and education (e.g., several private and public schools in Singapore, the Ministry of Education (MOE) of Singapore, and the Ministry of Education of the Kingdom of Bahrain).

**Gonzalo Jover** is a professor at the Faculty of Education at Universidad Complutense de Madrid, where he currently holds the position of associate dean of research. He was previously the head of the Department of Educational Theory and History of Education and coordinator of the master's and PhD programs. He is a visiting research fellow at a number of universities in Europe and North, South, and Central America. He is vice president of *Sociedad Española de Pedagogía* and member of the boards of the *European Educational Research Association* (EERA) and the *World Educational Research Association* (WERA). His lines of research focus on the development of theoretical knowledge of education, political philosophy, and professional ethics, subjects on which he has published numerous articles. Two of his recent books are *Ética profesional docente*, with R. García López and J. Escámez (Madrid, 2010), and *Democracy and the Intersection of Religion: The Reading of John Dewey's Understanding of Democracy and Education*, with R. Bruno-Jofre, J. S. Johnston, and D. Tröhler (Montreal, 2010).

**Allison E. Karpyn** is the associate director of the Center for Research in Education and Social Policy and assistant professor of education. For more than 15 years, Dr. Karpyn has developed and led research and evaluation efforts in education and the social sciences, particularly in low-income communities. As associate director of the Center for Research in Education and Social Policy and assistant professor of education, Dr. Karpyn often works to guide and support the implementation and execution of high-quality research, both qualitative and quantitative.

**Derya Yılmaz Kılıçoğlu** received her BA from Middle East Technical University and her PhD in educational sciences from Eskişehir Osmangazi University. With the scholarship provided by the Council of Higher Education, she visited the University of Cambridge in 2014 as a visiting scholar. Dr. Yılmaz Kılıçoğlu's teaching and research interests include leadership in education, educational policy, organizational change, organizational behavior, and research methods in education. She has published a range of articles and book chapters about organizational change, organizational behavior, and leadership in education. Dr. Yılmaz Kılıçoğlu also presented papers at regional conferences and at national conferences conducted by the American Educational Research Association, European Educational Research Association, and International Society of Educational Planning. Yılmaz Kılıçoğlu joined Eskişehir Osmangazi University in 2010 and currently is an assistant professor in the Department of Educational Sciences.

**John Benedicto Krejsler** is professor at the Danish School of Education, Aarhus University, Denmark. His research interests include school, teacher education, and university reform as well as education policy in a transnational perspective, evidence and new conditions for producing "truths" about "what works," and social technologies (e.g., comparative surveys and rankings, appraisal interviews). His work draws on poststructuralist theory and critical theory among others. J. B. Krejsler has seats on the boards of the *Nordic Educational Research Association* and the *European Educational Research Association* and was a visiting scholar at the University of California Los Angeles (UCLA) (2015) and a visiting professor at Kristianstad University (Sweden) in 2009 and 2010.

**Ong Kim Lee** is currently an adjunct faculty of the College of Education of Ohio University, USA, in the area of educational statistics and educational research methods, where he started from August 2013. Prior to that, he was an associate professor at the National Institute of Education (NIE), Nanyang Technological University (NTU), Singapore, for 12 years from 1 January 2000. He was appointed chair of the Department (Academic Group) of Policy and Leadership Studies from 01 July 2005, and for his last 1 year at the university, he was concurrently appointed as associate dean for research. In February 2012, he was elected to be the next vice president of the World Educational Research Association (WERA) starting on 01 July 2012 for a 2-year term. Ong Kim Lee obtained his PhD from the University of Chicago in 1992, specializing in measurement, evaluation, and statistical analysis (MESA). His areas of interest include testing and measurement which cover test item construction and calibrations, test equating, and the construction of latent variables for research through the use of Rasch measurement. He has conducted training programs for education officers from the Maldives, Vietnam, Indonesia, Pakistan, and Malaysia.

**Sarah-Kathryn McDonald** is a principal research scientist in NORC's University of Chicago-based Academic Research Centers. Since 2002, she has collaborated with faculty, clients, and staff at NORC on projects and centers funded by organizations including the National Science Foundation, US Department of Education, National Research Council, and Alfred P. Sloan Foundation. From October 2012 to December 2014, she was on leave from NORC, serving at the National Science Foundation—first as a program director and then (acting) division director of the Division of Research on Learning in Formal and Informal Settings in the Directorate for Education and Human Resources. Academic institutions with which she has worked include the University of Chicago (as associate director for policy outreach at the Consortium on Chicago School Research), the University of London's Birkbeck College (on the faculty, as a member of the college's board of governors, and as an honorary research fellow attached to the Department of Management), London School of Economics and Political Science (instructor on the International Business in the International System course), Oxford University's Nuffield College (research officer on the British General Election Study), and Northwestern University (a fellow of the Center for Urban Affairs and Policy Research and adjunct faculty in the Kellogg Graduate School of Management).

**Kalyn McDonough** is the research project coordinator at the Center for Research in Education and Social Policy. She graduated with a master's degree in social work from the University of Pennsylvania School of Social Policy and Practice in May 2015. She earned her undergraduate degree in urban affairs and public policy from the University of Delaware in June 2012. During her time as an undergraduate, she conducted an independent research study in the Criminal Justice Department and served as a legislative fellow in the Delaware State Legislature.

**Hannele Niemi** is professor of education in the Teacher Education Department in the University of Helsinki. Hannele Niemi's experience at the University of Helsinki includes her roles as the vice rector for academic affairs (2003–2009), the dean of the Faculty of Education (2001–2003), the head of the Department of Education (1998–2000), and the vice dean (1998–2000) of the Faculty of Education. Prior to working at the University of Helsinki, Niemi served as a professor of education in the Teacher Education Departments of Oulu, Turku, and Tampere Universities in Finland (1987–1998). She also served as a visiting professor at Michigan State University (1989) and as a visiting scholar at Stanford University (2010, 2013, and 2015, 7 months in total). She was selected as the most influential person in education in 2013 by the Finnish Teachers' Union and was invited to become a member of the Finnish Academy of Science and Letters (Academia Scientiarum Fennica) in 2004. Niemi has contributed to many European Union (EU) and Organisation for Economic Co-operation and Development (OECD) projects as an expert or researcher. Her main research interest areas are teachers' professional development, quality of teacher education, moral education, and technology-based learning environments. Niemi has contributed to many international education research publications and has published books in more than ten languages.

**Enric Prats** is associate professor of international pedagogy at the Faculty of Education at the University of Barcelona. He is the secretary of the Faculty Improvement and Innovation Program fostered by the universities and regional government of Catalonia and the coordinator of the editorial board of the open journal *Temps d'Educació* (published in Catalan, Spanish, and other languages). He serves as the head of the Education and Community Section of the Educational Sciences Institute at the University of Barcelona. His lines of research focus on educational theories, the pedagogies of values, and the analysis of international educational policy and planning. Some of his recent publications include *L'educació, una qüestió d'estat* (Barcelona, 2013) and *Teorizando en educación: entre erudición, poesía y opinionitis* (Barcelona, 2015).

**Mark Rickinson** is an associate professor and associate dean (engagement) in the Faculty of Education at Monash University in Australia. His research focuses on the role of evidence in educational practice and policy and the role of learning in environmental and sustainability education. He is currently leading a collaborative study with the Victorian Department of Education and Training on the use of evidence in education policy development.

**Rien Rouw** is currently seconded to the OECD from the Dutch Ministry of Education, Culture and Science. Prior to this, he was deputy head of the division for knowledge relations and knowledge economy at the ministry. Besides that, he worked as research fellow at the Netherlands School for Public Administration and at the Scientific Council for Government Policy, doing research on evidence-based policy making in Dutch government. Some recent publications include "Policy analysis in practice: reinterpreting the quest for evidence-based policy." In: Van Nispen, F., and Scholten, P. (eds., 2014). *Policy Analysis in the Netherlands: Institutionalization and Performance*. Bristol: Policy Press, *Gevoel voor bewijs* [*Sense of evidence*] (2011), and *Bewezen beleid in het onderwijs* [*Evidence based policy in education*] (2009).

**Hairon Salleh** is an assistant professor with the Policy and Leadership Studies Department at the National Institute of Education, Nanyang Technological University, Singapore. His research interests center on school leadership and teacher learning communities, mainly in the areas of distributed leadership, teacher leadership, professional learning communities, teacher professional development, and action research. He is currently the principal investigator for a funded research project entitled "Leadership for Collective Learning: A Distributed Perspective." His recent publications include "Pursuing the elusive construct of distributed leadership: Is the search over?" in *Educational Management Administration and Leadership* (EMAL) and "Teacher leadership enactment in PLCs: Towards a better understanding of the phenomenon" in *School Leadership and Management* (SLM).

**Barbara Schneider** is the John A. Hannah chair and distinguished professor in the College of Education and Department of Sociology at MSU. She is the principal investigator of the College Ambition Program (CAP), a study that tests a model for promoting a STEM college-going culture in high schools that encourages adolescents to pursue STEM majors in college and occupations in these fields. She worked for 18 years at the University of Chicago, holding positions as a professor in sociology and human development and senior researcher at the National Opinion Research Center (NORC). She remains a senior fellow at NORC, where she is the principal investigator of the Center for Advancing Research and Communication in Science, Technology, Engineering, and Mathematics. She uses a sociological lens to understand societal conditions and interpersonal interactions that create norms and values that enhance human and social capital. Her research focuses on how the social contexts of schools and families influence the academic and social well-being of adolescents as they move into adulthood. Professor Schneider has published 15 books and over 100 articles and reports on family, social context of schooling, and sociology of knowledge. She recently served as editor of *Sociology of Education* and as president of the American Educational Research Association (AERA).

**Katherine Tilley** is a doctoral student in education specializing in evaluation, measurement, and statistics at the University of Delaware. She graduated from the University of Delaware with a BA in psychology in January 2014. She has several years of experience working as a research assistant. She worked as a research assistant in the Psychological and Brain Sciences Department at the University of Delaware as an undergraduate. After graduation, Kati worked as a research associate in the Center for Training, Evaluation, and Community Collaboration (CTECC) conducting a mixed methods evaluation study. Currently, she has a research assistantship with the Center for Research in Education and Social Policy in the College of Education and Human Development.

**Selahattin Turan** received his BA from *Ankara University* Faculty of Educational Sciences in 1990 and PhD from *Ohio University* from the School of Applied Behavioral Sciences and Educational Leadership in 1998. He joined Eskişehir Osmangazi University in 1998, where he is a professor of educational leadership.

He was past president of the International Society for Educational Planning (ISEP) and a past chair of the Division A (Administration, Organization and Leadership) Ad Hoc International Committee of AERA. His primary professional interests are theory in leadership, educational policy, and sociology of technology and alternative perspectives in education. Dr. Turan has coauthored many book chapters and books. He is also on the editorial boards of many national and international journals. Dr. Turan has published widely in a variety of scholarly journals and presented papers at the annual meetings of AERA, ISEP, NCPEA, and UCEA. Mr. Turan was the past president of the ECO Educational Institute and dean of the College of Education at Eskişehir Osmangazi University.

**Jan van Tartwijk** is professor of education at Utrecht University where he chairs the university's graduate school for teacher education and the Educational Consultancy and Training Group of the Faculty of Social and Behavioural Sciences. He is involved in a number of research projects, which all have in common that they aim to contribute to the quality of teaching and teacher education.

**Patricia Villamor** is associate professor of the Faculty of Education at Universidad Complutense de Madrid. She has been a visiting researcher at several universities abroad, including at the Faculty of Education at Queen's University (Ontario, Canada) and the School of Education, Department of Administration, Training, and Policy Studies, at Boston University (Massachusetts, USA). Her lines of research focus on the theory of education and educational policy, particularly on international comparison of educational policies, which are subjects she teaches in conjunction with other universities. She has taken part in several different research projects, privately and publicly funded alike.

**Jane Wilkinson** is an associate professor of educational leadership at Monash University, Melbourne, Australia, and an adjunct researcher with the Research Institute for Professional Practice, Learning and Education (RIPPLE) at Charles Sturt University, Wagga Wagga, NSW, Australia. Jane has published widely in the fields of practice theory, praxis and leadership, gender and leadership, and refugee education. Jane is coauthor of *Changing Practices, Changing Education* (Kemmis, Wilkinson, Edwards-Groves, Hardy, Grootenboer, and Bristol) (Springer, 2014) and with Tanya Fitzgerald of *Travelling Towards a Mirage?: Gender, Leadership and Higher Education* (Post Pressed, 2010). Jane is an assistant editor of the *International Journal of Leadership in Education;* an editorial board member of the *Journal of Gender Studies* and *Journal of Educational Leadership, Policy and Practice*; and a convenor of the Australian Association for Research in Education's Leadership Special Interest Group.

**Theo Wubbels** is professor of education at Utrecht University, former associate dean of the Faculty of Social and Behavioural Sciences, Dutch national coordinator for the innovation of university teacher education, and president of the European Educational Research Association. His research focuses on interpersonal relationships in education, social climate in the classroom, and teaching and learning in higher education.

# Introduction: Evidence and Public Good in Educational Policy, Research, and Practice

**Abstract** The demands about the quality and relevance of educational research to inform the policy and practice have been growing over the past decade in response to the evidence-based education movement; however, the literature is yet to tackle the question of the interrelationships between evidence, research, policy, and practice in education for the public good in an international context. In this introductory chapter, the authors first explore the literature on the evidence-based and evidence--informed education movements and then introduce a new term, *evidence-free*, that is, actions of some policymakers who disregard or misuse evidence for their own agenda. Furthermore, the authors provide several guiding questions of the edited work and explore the implications of the contributions in the book for further research and theory development alongside policy implications.

## Evidence and Public Good in Educational Policy, Research, and Practice

When the developed and emerging economies went into their global economic downturn from the beginning of the 1990s onward, many governmental policies on the education sciences centered on their inappropriateness for the requirements of today's and future international labor markets. Education and the social sciences have either undergone or are under pressure to adopt policies based on neoliberal economic indicators such as efficiency, standardization, testing, and accountability. Some of the changes educational institutions face today include the closing of teacher education programs at higher education institutions, proliferation of test--based evaluation, standardization of curriculum and assessment, unidirectional push for the marketization of educational programs, and budget cuts for the funding of education and social science research. Arguably, the social and education sciences have never been under greater pressure than today.

In March 2014, together with four social science and humanities (SSH) associations, the European Educational Research Association (EERA) sent a letter to the EU commissioner to indicate their concern with the low budget for SSH in the Horizon 2020 Work Program (letter from the SSH scientific community to the commissioner 2014). In another statement, the executive committee of the EERA (2014) criticized European policymakers for not mentioning SSH or educational research as challenges in the Europe 2010 document and in the draft Horizon 2020. The statement indicates that "…the current EC strategic policy preferences will push the social and behavioral sciences and humanities, including educational research, to the margins of the research arena. This is not problematic as such, but because we read this as a sign indicating a dehumanising of the European society."

A similar policy development occurred in Japan recently. Hakubun Shimomura, the minister of education in Japan, sent a letter to all of 86 national universities in the country to call them to take "active steps to abolish [social science and humanities] organisations or to convert them to serve areas that better meet society's needs" (*Times Higher Education* 2015). Twenty-six universities out of 60 national universities which offer courses in these programs have confirmed that they will either close or scale back their social science and humanities faculties as a response to the directive of Japan's government. Takamitsu Sawa, the president of Shiga University, stated that "if Japan is serious about getting 10 of its universities into the world's top 100, it will be far more cost-effective and advantageous to promote, rather than abolish or curtail, education and research in the humanities and social sciences" (*The Japan Times* 2015).

In Australia, Graham and Buckley (2014) demonstrated that the proportion of national research funding spent on education is tragically small: "educational researchers were the recipients of 1.33% of the entire funding pool for ARC Discovery Projects in 2014 and 1.94% of the total ARC Linkage Projects budget for 2015" (AARE 2016; p. 2).

In Chap. 1 of this edited book, Krejsler documents the ways in which the evidence discourse launched into the field of education by external stakeholders in mostly top-down moves across the Nordic countries has served the demands of the competitive global knowledge economy.

In Chap. 4, Farley-Ripple, Karpyn, McDonough, and Tilley discuss how three major government policies in the USA, *the Improving America's Schools Act of 1994, the Goals 2000: Educate America Act, and the No Child Left Behind Act of 2001 (NCLB)*, were fueled by a neoliberal interest in maintaining US economic competitiveness in the world. The authors argue that when the NCLB became law in 2002 as the federal government's biggest intervention into education in the history of the country, it promised to grow financial and educational productivity in an increasingly globalized economy, to increase objectivity in evaluation and assessment, and to reduce educational inequality. In response to an OECD report, the secretary of education of the time, Rodney Paige, connected NCLB's aim of educational efficiency with the nation's international economic competitiveness:

> This report documents how little we receive in return for our national investment. This report also reminds us that we are battling two achievement gaps. One is between those being served well by our system and those being left behind. The other is between the US and many of our higher achieving friends around the world. By closing the first gap, we will close the second. (US Department of Education 2003)

George W. Bush also made a similar statement regarding the role of international economic competitiveness in educational policymaking:

> NCLB is an important way to make sure America remains competitive in the 21st century. We're living in a global world. See, the education system must compete with education systems in China and India. If we fail to give our students the skills necessary to compete in the world in the 21st century, the jobs will go elsewhere. That's just a fact of life. It's the reality of the world we live in. And therefore, now is the time for the United States of America to give our children the skills so that the jobs will stay here. (US Department of Education 2006, p. 2)

The education secretary of the Obama administration, Arne Duncan, also shared similar ideas: "The fact is that we are not just in an economic crisis; we are in an educational crisis," he says. "We have to educate ourselves to a better economy" (US News 2009). Today, the passage of the new US federal education policy, Every Student Succeeds Act (ESSA; 2015), continues the emphasis of earlier legislation, modifying provisions for standardized testing of all students and reinforcing the importance of educating all children with the knowledge and skills for the twenty--first century.

Even though research institutions and policy circles are losing ground against a discourse that considers education a commodity, there is a growing interest among educational NGOs and research circles in understanding and reframing education and educational research as public good that signifies a common commitment to social justice and democratic equality and "involves complex moral and political judgments regarding what constitutes the good for the polity as a whole" (Nixon 2011; p. x). For example, in its mission statement, the American Educational Research Association identifies the promotion of the use of research to serve the public good as the fundamental responsibility of the association. In order to accomplish this task, the AERA provides "scientific evidence on the benefits of diversity and affirmative action in legal briefs submitted to the Supreme Court; hold[s] Capitol Hill briefings on research issues of importance to the public and policymakers; and issu[es] research-based positions on educational issues of public concern" (AERA 2016). The Australian Association for Research in Education (AARE) (2016) identifies its vision as to enhance the public good by promoting, supporting, and improving research and scholarship in education to generate high-quality educational research. The British Educational Research Association (BERA 2016) is another NGO "committed to working for the public good by sustaining a strong and high quality educational research community, dedicated to advancing knowledge of education." The lobbying effort of the European Educational Research Association to influence the policymakers in the European Commission in order to make educational and social science research more visible in the Horizon 2020 Work Program is another important example of serving the public good.

One of the key concerns of these educational research organizations today is that the quality and relevance of educational research help to build scientific evidence to improve education practice and serve the public good. In fact, the demands for raising the quality and relevance of educational research can be found within the educational research community itself. In 1996, Hargreaves blamed educational research of not having generated the cumulative body of applicable knowledge that would facilitate teaching to become a research-based profession (Hargreaves 1996, 1997, 1999). Hargreaves (1996) noted that:

> In medicine, as in the natural sciences, research has a broadly cumulative character. Research projects seek explicitly to build on earlier research – by confirming or falsifying it, by extending or refining it, by replacing it with better evidence or theory, and so on. Much educational research is, by contrast, non-cumulative, in part because few researchers seek to create a body of knowledge which is then tested, extended or replaced in some systematic way. A few small-scale investigations of an issue which are never followed up inevitably produce inconclusive and contestable findings of little practical relevance. Replications, which are more necessary in the social than the natural sciences because of the importance of contextual and cultural variations, are astonishingly rare. p.2

Hargreaves' criticism further proposed that educational research should be a matter of centralized agenda setting so that it can turn into more practically relevant endeavor. He also suggested that educational practice should not be left to the opinions of educators but that their work should be based upon research evidence. Hargreaves advocated a reformation of educational research so that educational practice could be transformed into an evidence-based practice (Biesta 2007). Around the same time as Hargreaves was calling for evidence-based practice, Bob Slavin in the USA was urging public schools to spend their money on evidence--based approaches. The mutual transformation of both educational practice and research was the central principle of evidence-based movement (Davies 1999; Fox 2003; Biesta 2007).

In Britain, the drive for evidence-based research and practice in education rather came with the reports commissioned by the Department for Education and Employment and the Office for Standards in Education (Ofsted) (Tooley and Darby 1998; Biesta 2007). These reports expressed big concerns about the value and relevance of educational research, stating that educational research did not deliver answers to the questions the policymakers request in order to develop educational policy (Biesta 2007). Furthermore, the reports suggested that educational research did not provide clear guidance to the educational professionals for their professional practice and that educational research was methodologically inconsistent, fragmented, politically motivated, and noncumulative (Pring 2000). The call for reforming educational research and practice in Britain has led to a series of initiatives intended to reduce the gap among policy, research, and practice (Evans and Benefield 2001; Hammersley 2001; Coe 2002; Biesta 2007). In these reports and initiatives, there was a strong drive for randomized controlled trial (RCT) which, according to some advocates of evidence-based movement, is the only method that can deliver scientific evidence about "what works" (Hargreaves 1999; Oakley 2002; Cutspec 2004; Biesta 2007). More recently, Goldacre (2013) argued that education profession is still far from evidence based, despite the range of programs and initiatives established during the 1990s and 2000s.

Evidence-based education movement is mainly questioned by its opponents in regard to its suitability for the field of education. Some of the opponents have criticized the attempts to equate the fields of education and medicine (Davies 1999; Pirrie 2001; Simons 2003; Gee, 2005; Biesta 2007) and have indicated different implications of evidence in these fields (Nutley and Davies 2000). Others have scrutinized positivistic assumptions forming the notion of evidence-based education and have questioned the narrow definition of research advocated in evidence-based movement (e.g., Atkinson 2000; Elliot 2001; St. Pierre 2002; Erickson and Gutierrez 2002; Oliver and Conole 2003; Gee 2005; Eryaman 2006; Biesta 2007; Bruce and Eryaman 2015). Others have critiqued its top-down, linear approach to educational achievement (e.g., Hammersley 2001; Ridgway et al. 2000; Davies 2003; Fox 2003; Olson 2004; Eryaman 2006; Biesta 2007, 2010a) and the lack of appreciation of the vital role of values in educational policy, research, and practice (e.g., Davies 1999; Hammersley 2001; Elliot 2001; Willinsky 2001; Sanderson 2003; Oliver and Conole 2003; Gee 2005; Eryaman, 2006; Biesta, 2007, 2010b).

As a result of ongoing debates on evidence-based approach in education, more nuanced approaches to the link between research, policy, and practice emerged, using concepts like "evidence-informed" (Hargreaves 1999; Barnett 2001), "evidence-influenced," and "evidence-aware" practice (Nutley et al. 2002). In this context, Barratt and Hodson (2006) defined the conception of the evidence-informed practitioner as follows:

> The evidence-informed practitioner carefully considers what research evidence tells them in the context of a particular child, family or service, and then weighs this up alongside knowledge drawn from professional experience and the views of service users to inform decisions about the way forward. p. 14

While criticizing the evidence-based "what works culture" that threatens to reduce education to a technique and teaching to an instrumental intervention, Godfrey (2014) further explored the notion of the evidence-informed practitioner in the context of the *research-engaged school*:

> One understanding of the term 'evidence-based practice' envisages schools as organisations whose practices are largely or entirely dictated by externally generated, top-down knowledge. By contrast, in a research-engaged school, teachers should be free to use professional judgement based on a combination of tacit and explicit knowledge… Thus, judgement, intuition and instinct, gained through experience, as well as research-based data should all be called upon to inform practice. As many have argued, the term 'evidence-based practice' too often suggests an uncritical engagement with supposedly incontrovertible research evidence, based on a prescriptive 'what works' model (e.g. Biesta 2007). Therefore, in a research-engaged school, the 'evidence base', should be viewed not as a body of finite knowledge to be prescribed and imposed on teachers, but rather as a living process built around practical experience in classrooms, developed from and adapting to particular teaching and learning settings. p. 10

Maynard (2006) pronounced three reasons why policymakers and teachers frequently disregard the evidence-based decision-making: (a) they identify the evidence as lacking credibility; (b) they perceive the evidence as impractical to their context; or (c) the evidence is poorly synthesized. Consequently, educational practitioners and policymakers have long employed numerous forms of evidence that fall outside of the scope formed by policy. Defined as "practitioner knowledge" or "local knowledge," this type of evidence includes student questionnaires, parent surveys, or classroom observations to collect data on instructional practices (Honig and Coburn 2008).

While these new approaches suggest an alternative conception of the complex ways in which research might inform policy and practice (Greenhalgh and Worrall 1997; Eraut 2003; Biesta 2010b), many advocates of the evidence-based movement still support the idea that the only way toward a meaningful progress in education is to employ the "gold standard" of the RCT as the experimental methodology that can prove the efficiency of interventions "beyond reasonable doubt" (Slavin 2002, p. 16).

We introduce in this book a new term, *evidence-free*, that is, actions of some policymakers who disregard or misuse evidence for their own agenda. This idea is built on earlier work by Weiss (1991) who also suggested that policy often is implemented without evidence. However, the notion of *evidence-free* seems to underscore the discontinuity between what some have argued as fundamental for reform and what others have ideologically supported as reform irrespective of evidence. In Chap. 7, Burns and Rouw provide a more in-depth look at the notion of *evidence--free* by introducing three distinct categories of incorrect use of data developed by Schildkamp, Karbautzki, and Vanhoof (2014): *nonuse*, *misuse*, and *abuse*:

1. *Nonuse*: data is not collected or capacity is lacking to allow for its use. This also includes actors choosing not to use data that is contrary to their argument or beliefs.
2. *Misuse*: data is poorly collected (quality concerns), is incorrectly interpreted (analysis or capacity issues), or does not provide adequate answers to be useful for decision-making.
3. *Abuse*: sample or data are manipulated to yield particular results, or the data results in unintended consequences (e.g., narrowing the curriculum to improve student scores on tested subjects).

In Chap. 11, Turan and Kilicoglu document how different political parties in Turkey throughout its history imposed evidence-free and opinion-based policies, which merely depend on selective use or nonuse of evidence with ideological standpoints, prejudice, or speculative conjecture of interest groups. The authors further provide evidence-based recommendations for Turkish educational policymakers and practitioners to serve the public good.

In Chap. 4, Jover, Prats, and Villamor demonstrate the ways in which the international assessments were (mis)used as instrumental evidence resource by neoliberal and neoconservative politicians in Spain to justify their ideologically motivated reform agendas. The authors argue that both ideological tendencies radically transformed the notion of the public good in Spain, "a notion that does not fit comfortably in either one."

Several research studies provided case examples of the notion of *evidence-free*. For instance, Coburn and Talbert (2006) demonstrated how some school district staff viewed evidence as a way to justify an existing program or to gather support among other stakeholders for a specific decision. Sometimes referred to as "strategic" (Huberman 1990), this way of use defines the process of using evidence to make political advances or gain political support (Corcoran et al. 2001). Honig and Coburn (2008) found district office administrators sometimes used evidence to support opinions they had already formulated, purposefully aligning the evidence with a position that furthered their own agendas. Knorr (1977) described this appropriation of evidence for predetermined ends as "symbolic," since the decision-maker is most concerned with advancing a particular idea. Likewise, in a review of literature, Farley-Ripple (2012) noted that evidence is often used after a policy decision was already made.

This edited book is timely, given current debates about the purpose and form of educational policy, research, and practice in an era of post-truth, globalization, efficiency, standardization, evidence-based decision-making, testing, and accountability. The demands about the quality and relevance of educational research to inform the policy and practice have been growing over the past decade in response to the evidence-based education movement; however, the literature is yet to tackle the question of the interrelationships between educational research, policy, and practice for the public good in an international context. In this edited book, professors and policymakers from the OECD, the USA, Denmark, Belgium, Sweden, Finland, Singapore, Australia, Spain, Turkey, and the Netherlands present their own conception of the evidence-based/evidence-informed education as well as a justification for why particular examples or issues chosen fit within that conception for the sake of public good. Thus, unlike the current literature focusing merely on evidence-based education in the USA and Britain, this book takes a truly international perspective. Furthermore, by drawing together interdisciplinary approaches from political philosophy, social work, medicine, psychology, and sociology and by bringing academicians, policymakers, and practitioners together to discuss the theoretical underpinnings and practical examples of evidence-based and evidence-informed educational policy, research, and practice for the public good, this book fills a much-needed gap in the literature addressing the complex relations between the theory, research, evidence, policy, and practice in education.

## Focus of the Book

In this edited book, we aim to take an analytic perspective on the theoretical underpinnings and practical examples of evidence-based and evidence-informed educational policy, research, and practice in an international context. Our commitment to serve the public good as the scholars and professionals of education and educational research sets the terms of our critical and analytic endeavor in this work. As Schwandt (2015) pointed out, although occupational fields of education and social sciences may require high levels of knowledge and skill, they cannot be considered professions unless they are centrally conceptualized as serving some essential part of the public good. We argue that analytic thinking and reflective practice are necessary capacity for professionals who want to go beyond the application of formulaic procedures to serve to the public good (Schön 1987). We call for a new epistemology and axiology of practice that stresses analytic thinking, reflection, and intellectual discovery as central components of the professional inquiry and judgment.

In this context, this work aims to foster wonder or appreciation of the complexity and interconnectedness of ideas in educational research, policy, and practice, and goals such as critical thinking, the development of engaged citizenship, understanding the perspectives of others, serving the public good, or ethical life in general are central to the notion of this endeavor. Our critical commitment in this work is not about being against or for the evidence-based or evidence-informed approaches. As indicated above, our purpose is to demonstrate how the diverse discourses (such as evidence based and evidence informed) inform the interrelationships among educational research, policy, and practice for the public good in an international context. What makes this work unique is its openness to the diversity of voices/discourses to the extent that these discourses provide a sound argument regarding the issue of public good in policy, research, and practice. The chapters provide contextual and case-based analysis of serving the public good through the democratic contestation and deliberation that we welcomed on all sides of the conversation in this work.

## Guiding Questions of the Book

Across a wide range of topics, assessment and evaluation, educational administration and school governance, teaching and teacher education, area of the curriculum, and policy, the chapters in this edited work ask, "What have we learned from the discourses of evidence on educational policy, research, and practice that can support democratic, humanistic, and morally responsible development for individuals and societies?" The main focus of this work is, thus, to explore the ways in which the discourses on evidence have informed and transformed the relationships between research, policy, and practice for the public good in different international contexts. The chapters will demonstrate how the discourse on evidence in education has evolved. They will address guiding questions such as:

1. What constitutes evidence and the public good?
2. How are evidence and public good defined in different international contexts?
3. How does evidence serve the public good in educational policy, research, and practice?
4. What kind of role should the discourses on evidence and public good play in professional practice?

5. How are the discourses on evidence informing and transforming the relationships between educational research, policy, and practice for the public good?

## Chapter Contributions in the Book

By focusing on the guiding questions mentioned above, some chapters in this edited book explored the particular approaches as exemplars of challenges or opportunities for the education for the public good. Others focus on the historical or philosophical basis for understanding the ways in which the discourses on evidence have evolved. The chapters consider both the past successes and failures of discourses and policies of evidence-based and evidence-informed education, as well as current work and future possibilities for the sake of the public good. The contributors present their conceptions of the relationship between evidence and public good grounding their discussions within practical case examples from their national and/or international contexts.

In Chap. 1, "Understanding Public Good in the Context of Evidence Discourse in Education," Mustafa Yunus Eryaman provides a systemic analysis of the literature on the concepts of "public good" and "scientific evidence" in order to develop an understanding of what these concepts imply and demands of researchers, policymakers, and practitioners in the field of education. Eryaman further explores the studies on practitioners' and policymakers' definition and the use of evidence in educational policy and practice and provides nine guiding principles for educational researchers to generate scientific evidence that can promote a shared democratic vision of public good and recognize the plurality of goods and multiple principles of educational practice.

In Chap. 2, "Capturing the 'Evidence' and 'What Works' Agenda in Education: A Truth Regime and the Art of Manoeuvring Floating Signifiers," John Benedicto Krejsler from Denmark critically examines the evidence-based discourses by locating the Danish examples within larger transnational agendas. Krejsler further argues that the field of education and its professions may profit from adopting evidence as a floating signifier by proposing three analytical distinctions that may help educational researchers or professionals maneuver within current evidence and what works discourse and serve public good:

1. A distinction between *evidence-based* and *evidence-informed* knowledge
2. A distinction between *global* and *local forms of evidence*
3. A distinction between *external* and *internal forms of evidence*

In Chap. 3, "What Is Evidence Required for and Who Generates That Evidence in the Finnish Educational System?," Hannele Niemi from Finland analyzes major opportunities as well as difficulties in providing and applying research- and evidence-based knowledge in the Finnish educational system. Niemi questions what purposes evidence is required for and who provides that evidence by providing case examples from the Finnish educational system. The author further introduces the Finnish enhancement-led evaluation policy and its main principles relating to evidence production. Niemi concludes that in the case of Finland, interrelations between equity in education and evidence for improvements in the whole system go toward understanding what is a public good for the whole society.

In Chap. 4, "Educational Policy in Spain: Between Political Bias and International Evidence," Gonzalo Jover, Enric Prats, and Patricia Villamor from Spain analyze the type of political reading in Spain made from the results of the *Programme for International Student Assessment* (PISA) assessments by focusing on the three general laws on education that have been passed in Spain in the last 20 years. Their analysis reveals the submission of the political debate under the pressure to achieve a more internationally competitive system. The authors demonstrate the ways in which the international assessments were (mis)used as instrumental evidence resource by the right- and left-wing politicians in Spain to justify their ideologically motivated reform agendas. They further discuss that both ideological tendencies radically transformed the notion of the public good in Spain, "a notion that does not fit comfortably in either one."

In Chap. 5, "Defining How We Get from Research to Practice: A Model Framework for Schools," Elizabeth Farley-Ripple, Allison E. Karpyn, Kalyn McDonough, and Katherine Tilley from the USA explore the context of US national education policy regarding research evidence use and analyze the recent efforts which seek to better understand and motivate the use of research in American schools to inform the public good. The authors further discuss that the types of research privileged by policy are not essentially prioritized by policymakers and that a focus on the instrumental role of research in educational policymaking significantly underestimates the extent to which research can and does serve the public good. As their discussion reveals problematic assumptions and solutions, the authors describe a proposed bi-directional model for understanding the relationship between research and practice and highlight current efforts to support the use of research evidence in schools and districts to serve public good.

In Chap. 6, "Assessing Students' Growth in Mathematics and English Language in Singapore: The Practice, the Evidence and the Perceptions," Jonathan W.P. Goh, Ong Kim Lee, and Hairon Salleh from Singapore investigate the students' growth in mathematics and English language by examining evidence generated from Grade 5 students' performances in 28 elementary schools in Singapore. The authors provide a discussion on the assessment practices of a sample of teachers in these schools and contrast the findings with accepted theoretical concepts of the measurement tools required for valid assessments. The authors further argue that the chapter contributes to the justice and equality as public good in Singapore education system by demonstrating how the use of an alternative assessment strategy provides more accurate comparisons and hence better understanding of student performance based on meritocratic educational system that provides students with equal opportunities to succeed in life and, in the long run, to create a just society.

In Chap. 7, "Evidence Informed Innovation of Education in the Netherlands: Learning from Reforms," Theo Wubbels and Jan van Tartwijk from the Netherlands provide a critical analysis of the three major reforms in the history of Dutch secondary education by grounding their analysis on the discourses of evidence and the public good. The authors demonstrate how the failures of the government initiated innovations in these reforms led to the conclusion that innovations should be evidence informed and initiated by teachers themselves in a way that they would be able to use empirical and theoretical knowledge that has been developed in educational research and combine this knowledge with their practical wisdom, experiences, and insights in their local context. The authors further argue that the link between education and educational research as means to strengthen the common good in these reforms was evidently missing. They further criticize the reforms for not paying attention to the potential effects of the innovations on promoting the public good.

In Chap. 8, "The Evidence Agenda in Education: An International Perspective," Tracey Burns and Rien Rouw from the OECD examine the role of "evidence" in educational policymaking and explore some of the main trends and themes that have emerged internationally in the last decade. The authors look at the remaining gaps in the knowledge and the biggest challenges countries face as they move to building the capacity and processes necessary. They further discuss the major opportunities as well as the challenges of the use of evidence in educational policymaking and evaluation by analyzing two cases of the use of evidence in action: Sweden and Flanders (Belgium). Their comprehensive analytical framework of governance and knowledge for rethinking research use as evidence in educational policy and practice with its challenges provides a sound argument for bridging the gap between educational research, policy, and practice to serve public good. The authors conclude that the use of evidence in educational policymaking is vital to ensure efficient and equitable school systems that work to serve the public good.

In Chap. 9, "School Principals and Evidence Use: Possibilities and Problems for Preparation and Practice," Jeffrey S. Brooks, Mark Rickinson, and Jane Wilkinson from Australia review and critique the literature on school leadership preparation and evidence use in three sections. In the first section, the authors explore distinctions in the ways that scholars and practitioners have come to conceptualize evidence use and consider the implications of various definitions for leadership practice. In the second section, they examine various ways that programs around the world approach training prospective or sitting school leaders in preservice programs. In the third section, the authors review and interrogate research that investigates principals' use of evidence in decision-making processes, paying special attention to effective and ineffective strategies. The authors conclude with providing recommendations for preservice and in-service development with regard to leadership and evidence use for the public good.

In Chap. 10, based on their insights from their work with two national initiatives designed to reform educational practice in the USA, Sarah Kathryn McDonald and Barbara Schneider present seven guiding principles of evidence-based/evidence--informed educational policy and research to lay the foundation for making rigorous and comprehensive judgments about what evidence and scientific research designs should be taken into account when scaling up educational reforms to serve the public good. The authors further provide case examples from the USA with a clear potential to both utilize and generate evidence in the public interest including educational research studies that seeks to support underrepresented groups in preparing for and achieving successful transitions to postsecondary education and careers, in STEM and other fields.

In Chap. 11, "Evidence-Based Policy and Practice in Turkish Education System," Selahattin Turan and Derya Yılmaz Kılıçoğlu from Turkey scrutinize Turkish education policies with their lack of contributions to the public good through an evidence-based analysis. The authors argue that there is a culture of disconnectedness in research, policy, and practice in Turkish education system. They evaluate the performed national changes, projects, and reforms between the years 2000 and 2015 by the Ministry of National Education in regard to the evidence of effectiveness. The author further recommends evidence-based policies by considering the linkage between research and practices in education in order to improve well-being for schools and education.

Çanakkale Onsekiz Mart University
Çanakkale, Turkey
e-mail: yunuseryaman@gmail.com
Mustafa Yunus Eryaman

Michigan State University
East Lansing, MI, USA
e-mail: bschneid@msu.edu
Barbara Schneider

## References

American Educational Research Association (AERA). (2016). *Research and the public good statement*. Availability: http://www.aera.net/Education-Research/Research-and-the-Public-Good

Atkinson, E. (2000). In defence of ideas, or why 'what works' is not enough. *British Journal of Sociology of Education, 21*, 317–330.

Australian Association for Research in Education (AARE). (2016). *Submission to the productivity commission inquiry into the National Education Evidence Base*. Availability: http://www.pc.gov.au/__data/assets/pdf_file/0008/199574/sub022-education-evidence.pdf

Barratt, M., & Hodson, R. (2006). *Firm foundations: A practical guide to organisational support for the use of research evidence*. Dartington: Research in Practice.

Bennett, W. (1986). *What works: Research about teaching and learning*. U.S. Department of Education.

Biesta, G. J. J. (2007). Why 'what works' won't work. Evidence-based practice and the democratic deficit of educational research. *Educational Theory, 57*(1), 1–22.

Biesta, G. J. J. (2010a). *Good education in an age of measurement: Ethics, politics, democracy*. Boulder: Paradigm Publishers.

Biesta, G. J. J. (2010b). Why 'what works' still won't work: From evidence-based education to value-based education. *Studies in Philosophy and Education, 29*(5), 491–503.

British Educational Research Association (BERA). (2016). *Mission statement*. Availability: https://www.bera.ac.uk/

Broekkamp, H., & Van Hout-Wolters, B. (2007). The gap between educational research and practice: A literature review, symposium, and questionnaire. *Educational Research and Evaluation: An International Journal on Theory and Practice, 13*(3), 203–220.

Bruce, B. C., & Eryaman, M. Y. (2015). Introduction: Progressive impuls in education. In M. Y. Eryaman & B. C. Bruce (Eds.), *International handbook of progressive education* (pp. 1–52). New York: Peter Lang.
Clegg, S. (2005). Evidence-based practice in educational research: A critical realist critique of systematic review. *British Journal of Sociology of Education, 26*(3), 415–428.
Coburn, C., & Talbert, J. E. (2006). Conceptions of evidence use in school districts: Mapping the terrain. *American Journal of Evaluation, 112*(4), 469–495.
Coe, R. (2002). *Finding out what works: Evidence-based education*. Durham: Durham University School of Education.
Corcoran, T., Fuhrman, S. H., & Belcher, C. L. (2001). The district role in instructional improvement. *Phi Delta Kappan, 83*(1), 78–84.
Cutspec, P. A. (2004). Bridging the research-to-practice gap: Evidence-based education. *Centerscope: Evidence-Based Approaches to Early Childhood Development, 2*(2), 1–8.
Davies, P. (1999). What is evidence-based education? *British Journal of Educational Studies, 47*, 108–121.
Davies, B. (2003). Death to critique and dissent? The policies and practices of new managerialism and of 'evidence-based' practice. *Gender and Education, 15*(1), 91–103.
Davies, T. O., Nutley, S. M., & Smith, P. C. (Eds.). (2000). *What works. Evidence-based policy and practice in the social services*. Bristol: The Policy Press.
Donaldson, S. I., Christie, C. A., & Mark, M. M. (2009). *What counts as credible evidence in applied research and evaluation practice?* Thousand Oaks: Sage.
EERA Statement. (2014). *Re-humanising research. Public Service Europe*. Available online at: http://www.eera-ecer.de/fileadmin/user_upload/Documents/E27_L_Moos_ATL.pdf
Eisenhart, M., & Towne, L. (2003). Contestation and change in national policy on 'scientifically based' education research. *Educational Researcher, 32*(7), 31–38.
Elliott, J. (2001). Making evidence-based practice educational. *British Educational Research Journal, 27*(5), 555–574.
Eraut, M. (2003). Practice based evidence. In G. Thomas & R. Pring (Eds.), *Evidence-based policy and practice*. Milton Keynes: Open University Press.
Erickson, F., & Gutierrez, K. (2002). Culture, rigor, and science in educational research. *Educational Researcher, 31*(8), 21–24.
Eryaman, M. Y. (2006). Traveling beyond dangerous private and universal discourses: Radioactivity of radical hermeneutics and objectivism in educational research. *Qualitative Inquiry, 12*(6), 1198–1219.
Eryaman, M. Y. (2007). From reflective practice to practical wisdom: Toward a post-foundational teacher education. *International Journal of Progressive Education, 3*(1), 87–107.
Eryaman, M. Y. (2008). *Teaching as practical philosophy*. Saarbrücken: VDM Verlag Dr. Müller.
Eryaman, M. Y. (Ed.). (2009). *Peter McLaren, education, and the struggle for liberation*. Cresskill: Hampton Press.
ESSA. (2015). Every Student Succeeds Act of 2015, Pub. L. No. 114–95 § 114 Stat. 1177 (2015–2016).
Evans, J., & Benefield, P. (2001). Systematic reviews of educational research: Does the medical model fit? *British Educational Research Journal, 27*, 527–541.
Farley-Ripple, E. N. (2012). Research use in central office decision-making: A case study. *Education Management, Administration and Leadership, 40*(6), 784–804.
Feuer, M., Towne, L., & Shavelson, R. (2002). Scientific culture and educational research. *Educational Researcher, 31*, 4–14.
Fox, M. (2003). Opening Pandora's box: Evidence-based practice for educational psychologists. *Educational Psychology in Practice, 19*(2), 91–102.
Gee, J. P. (2005). It's theories all the way down: A response to scientific research in education. *Teachers College Record, 107*(1), 10–18.

Godfrey, D. (2014). Leadership of schools as research-led organisations in the English educational environment: Cultivating a research-engaged school culture. *Educational Management, Administration and Leadership*. doi:10.1177/1741143213508294.

Goldacre, B. (2013). *Building evidence into education*. London: Department for Education.

Graham, L., & Buckley, L. (2014). Ghost hunting with lollies, chess and lego: Appreciating the 'messy' complexity (and costs) of doing difficult research in education. *The Australian Educational Researcher, 41*(3), 327–347.

Greenhalgh, T., & Worrall J. G. (1997). From EBM to CSM: The evolution of context sensitive medicine. *Journal of Evaluation in Clinical Practice, 3*(2), 105–108.

Hammersley, M. (1997). Educational research and a response to David Hargreaves. *British Educational Research Journal, 23*(2), 141–161.

Hammersley, M. (2001). *Some questions about evidence-based practice in education*. Paper presented at the "Evidence-based practice in education" symposium at the annual conference of the British Educational Research Association, September 13–15, 2001. Retrieved November 30, 2016, from http://www.leeds.ac.uk/educol/documents/00001819.htm

Hammersley, M. (2009). What is evidence for evidence-based practice? In R. St. Clair (Ed.), *Education science: Critical perspectives* (pp. 101–111). Rotterdam: Sense.

Hargreaves, D. (1996). *Teaching as a research-based profession*. Teacher Traning Agency Annual Lecture.

Hargreaves, D. (1997). In defence of evidence-based teaching. *British Educational Research Journal, 23*(4), 405–419.

Hargreaves, D. (1999). Revitalising educational research: Lessons from the past and proposals for the future. *Cambridge Journal of Education, 29*(2), 239–249.

Huberman, M. (1990). Linkage between researchers and practitioners: A qualitative study. *American Educational Research Journal, 27*(2), 363–391.

Knorr, K. D. (1977). Policymaker's use of social sciences knowledge: Symbolic or instrumental? In C. H. Weiss (Ed.), *Using social research in public policy making* (pp. 165–182). Lexington: Lexington Books.

Letter_from_SSH_scientific_community_to_the_Commissioner. (2014). Available online at: http://www.eera-ecer.de/fileadmin/user_upload/Documents/Letter_from_SSH_scientific_community_to_the_Commissioner_Copy.pdf

Maynard, R. A. (2006). Evidence-based decision making: What will it take for the decision makers to care? *Journal of Policy Analysis and Management, 25*, 249–265.

Mosteller, F. & Boruch, R. (Eds.). (2002). *Evidence matters: Randomized trials in education research*. Washington, DC: Brookings.

Nutley, S., & Davies, H. (2000). Making a reality of evidence-based practice. In H. T. Davies, S. M. Nutley, & P. C. Smith (Eds.), *What works? Evidence-based policy and practice in the public service*. University of Bristol, Bristol: The Policy Press.

Nutley, S. M., Davies, H. T. O., & Walter, I. (2002). *What is a conceptual synthesis?* Briefing Note 1, University of St Andrews: Research Unit for Research Utilisation.

Nutley, S., Walter, I., & Davies, H. T. (2007). *Using evidence: How research can inform public services*. Bristol: Policy Press.

Oakley, A. (2002). Social science and evidence-based everything: The case of education. *Educational Review, 54*(3), 277–286.

Oliver, M., & Conole, G. (2003). Evidence-based practice and e-learning in higher education: Can we and should we? *Research Papers in Education, 18*(4), 385–397.

Olson, D. (2004). The triumph of hope over experience in the search for "what works": A response to Slavin. *Educational Researcher, 33*(1), 24–26.

Pirrie, A. (2001). Evidence-based practice in education: The best medicine? *British Journal of Educational Studies, 49*(2), 124–136.

Pring, R. (2000). *Philosophy of educational research*. London: Continuum.

Ridgway, J., Zawojewski, J. S., & Hoover, M. N. (2000). Problematising evidence-based policy and practice. *Evaluation and Research in Education, 14*(3&4), 181–192.

Riedler M., & Eryaman M. Y. (2016). Complexity, diversity and ambiguity in teaching and teacher education: Practical wisdom, pedagogical fitness and tact of teaching. *International Journal of Progressive Education, 12* (3), 172–186.
Sanderson, I. (2003). Is it "what works" that matters? Evaluation and evidence based policy making. *Research Papers in Education Policy and Practice, 18*(4), 331–347.
Schön, D. (1987). *Educating the reflective practitioner*. San Francisco: JosseyBass Higher Education Series.
Schwandt, T. A. (2015). *Evaluation foundations revisited: Cultivating a life of the mind for practice*. California: Stanford University Press.
Schildkamp, K., Karbautzki L., & Vanhoof, J. (2014). Exploring data use practices around Europe: Identifying enablers and barriers. *Studies in Educational Evaluation, 42*, 15–24.
Simons, H. (2003). Evidence-based practice: Panacea or over promise? *Research Papers in Education, 18*(4), 303–311.
Slavin, R. E. (2002). Evidence-based educational policies: Transforming educational practice and research. *Educational Researcher, 31*(7), 15–21.
Slavin, R. E. (2004). Education research can and must address "what works" questions. *Educational Researcher, 33*(1), 27–28.
St. Pierre, E. A. (2002). 'Science' rejects postmodernism. *Educational Researcher, 31*(8), 25–27.
The Japan Times. (2015, September). *Humanities under attack*. Available online at: http://www.japantimes.co.jp/opinion/2015/08/23/commentary/japan-commentary/humanities-attack/#.VgGL_vmqqkp
The Times Higher Education. (2015, September). *Social sciences and humanities faculties 'to close' in Japan after ministerial intervention*. Available online at: https://www.timeshighereducation.com/news/social-sciences-and-humanities-faculties-close-japan-after-ministerial-decree
Thomas, G., & Pring, R. (Eds.). (2004). *Evidence-based policy and practice*. Milton Keynes: Open University Press.
Tooley, J., & Darby, D. (1998). *Educational research: An OFSTED critique*. London: OFSTED.
US Department of Education. (2003). *Education review international report*. Available online at: www.ed.gove.nclb
US Department of Education. (2006). *President Bush discusses No Child Left Behind*. Available online at: www.ed.gov/news/releases/2006/10/20061005-6.html
US News. (2009). *What Arne Duncan thinks of no child left behind*. Available online at:
Weiss, C. H. (1991). Policy research as advocacy: Pro and con. *Knowledge & Policy, 4*, 37–56.
Willinsky, J. (2001). Education and democracy: The missing link may be ours. *Harvard Educational Review, 72*(3), 367–392.

# Chapter 1
# Understanding Public Good in the Context of Evidence Discourse in Education

Mustafa Yunus Eryaman

**Abstract** Even though the evidence-based movement and the concept of public good have been thoroughly discussed and from a range of perspectives in the literature, there is no general consensus on the definitions and nature of these terms and concepts. In this chapter, the author conceptualizes what is meant when educators speak of the concepts like *public good* and *scientific evidence* in order to develop an understanding of what the concepts imply and demand of us as researchers, policy makers and scholars in the field of education. The author also analyzes the studies on practitioners and policymakers' definition and use of evidence in educational policy and practice. Furthermore, the author provides nine guiding principles for educational researchers to generate scientific evidence that can promote a shared democratic vision of public good and recognize the plurality of goods and multiple principles of educational practice. At the end of the chapter, the author analyzes how the chapter contributors in this edited volume contribute to the literature on evidence and public good, and provides recommendations for the future studies.

## Introduction

The role and importance of scientific evidence in educational research, policy, and practice has been under discussion in many academic publications last few decades and has also been the focus of policy-level discussions in many countries. One of the key concerns of the educational policy makers and researchers in these countries is that the quality and relevance of educational research helps to build scientific evidence to improve education practice and serves the public good.

Even though the evidence-based movement and the concept of public good have been thoroughly discussed and from a range of perspectives in the literature, there is no general consensus on the definitions and nature of these terms and concepts. For instance, someone could argue that all research, no matter how large or small in

M.Y. Eryaman (✉)
College of Education, Çanakkale Onsekiz Mart University, Çanakkale, Turkey
e-mail: yunuseryaman@gmail.com



M.Y. Eryaman, B. Schneider (eds.), *Evidence and Public Good in Educational Policy, Research and Practice*, Educational Governance Research 6,
DOI 10.1007/978-3-319-58850-6_1

size and scope, is conducted in the interests of the public good, but, of course, that does not mean that it is automatically a public good, or that it serves all groups in the public sphere in the same way or in equal measure (O'Donoghue 2014). Further, someone could state that there is prevalent public trust that academicians will carry out research and generate scientific evidence for the public good; as Lynch (2006) says, "there is a hope and expectation that those who are given the freedom to think, research and write will work for the good of humanity in its entirety" (p. 11), although the questions then becomes, 'which public' and 'whose good', both of which are very contested terms?

In the next section, I conceptualize what is meant when educators speak of the concepts like *public good* and *scientific evidence* in order to develop an understanding of what the terms and concepts implies and demands of us as researchers, policy makers and scholars in the field of education.

## What Is Evidence? and What Constitutes Scientific Evidence?

In order to understand the nature and notions of evidence-based policy, research and practice, it is important to clarify what the literature means by 'evidence.' The notion of evidence originates from legal documents in the Western world. In legal studies, evidence comes in the form of witness testimony, police reports, expert opinions, and forensic research files (Brownson et al. 2009). In policy-related fields, evidence can be categorized under three approaches for the purposes of policy making: political, professional, and scientific (Head 2008). Nutley et al. (2007) argue that what counts as evidence is a complex and contested issue:

> The attaching of labels such as 'evidence' or 'research' to particular types of 'knowledge' are in fact political acts. [...] Assessing 'what counts as evidence' or 'what counts as research' involves not just technical objective judgements but also subjective and contextualised assessments. p. 25

It appears that the term evidence reflects philosophical and methodological differences across professional and academic disciplines in terms of identification and utilization (Hammersley, 2009; Hargreaves, 1999). In academic and research circles, more quantitatively oriented researchers contend that credible evidence is generated from rigorous methodologies, such as the randomized control trial (RCT), and other approaches such as systematic reviews, meta-analyses, quasi-experimental designs, or observational studies. Particularly, the RCTs have dominated the evidence movement in US, with the Cochrane Collaboration (2014) as a representative of the field of medicine and the Campbell Collaboration (2014) of the social sciences (Biesta 2010a; Hansen and Rieper 2010). Some quantitative researchers proposed a methodological hierarchy in which RCTs serve as the gold standard. For instance, Jin and Yun (2010) have called for the development of an evidence hierarchy by expert scholars, whereby methods were ranked from most-credible to least-credible. I take a somewhat different approach; while recognizing the value of the

RCT for producing the credible statistical evidence for estimating causal effects, other forms of evidence are also valuable for advancing the public good. Moreover, increasingly scholars have come to rely on a variety of methods when conducting their research. The perspective of the editors of this book more closely aligns with that of Bouffard and Reid (2012) who propose that instead of developing hierarchies of evidence, researchers should develop evidence-informed practices that are sensitive to different individual and professional perspectives and contexts. Rather than classifying which source of evidence is universally superior, efforts should be made towards identifying the sources of evidence that are contextually relevant, empirically supported, rigorous, systematic and scientifically credible, and translated to a language practitioners will understand. To promote the use of scientific evidence among practitioners, researchers should continuously engage with local contexts and present their work in a more accessible and digestible manner.

Schalock and Verdugo (2012) identified scientific evidence as information acquired from credible sources that employed valid and reliable methods based on an evidently articulated and empirically supported rationale. In accordance with the definition in the Education Sciences Reform Act of 2002, Schalock et al. (2011) conceptualize scientific evidence as research that (1) uses rigorous, systematic, valid and reliable methods to generate knowledge relevant to education activities, programs or practices; (2) presents findings and/or makes claims that are sustained by the methods that have been employed; and (3) is published in a peer reviewed academic journal or approved by a panel of independent experts through a comparably rigorous, objective, and systematic review.

In organizing an international volume of diverse points of view on what constitutes evidence in advancing the public good, other perspectives on evidence ought to be considered. Biesta (2010b), for example, conseptualized a framework for value-based education as an alternative to the evidence-based education. Biesta underlined the "democratic deficit" of evidence-based practice, arguing that evidence-based practice often supersedes professional judgment and wider deliberations surrounding educational practice. Biesta proposed three different deficits of evidence-based practice that raise vital issues about the viability of the idea of evidence-based or evidence-informed practice: (1) knowledge deficit, (2) efficacy deficit, and (3) application deficit. Knowledge deficit emerging from representational epistemology relates to the notion that evidence of what worked does not guarantee that it will work in future interventions unless practitioners are able to "encapsulate all factors, aspects and dimensions that make up the reality of education" (p. 494). From an ontological perspective, effectiveness or efficacy deficit refers to the principle that educational interactions function as open, recursive semiotic systems, and so, causal relations can never be entirely determined. Finally, in the praxeological domain, application deficit concerns the idea that practices can change through the application of scientific knowledge, and applying scientific knowledge in the social domain misses important aspects of what enables the application of such knowledge. Biesta (2007) further proposed that research can only provide an "understanding of possibilities" and of "what the problem might be", not prescribe practitioners what to do (p.16).

Broekaert et al. (2010) provide three distinct categories of understanding evidence: the empirical–analytical, the phenomenological–existential, and the post-structural. These three categories conceptualize different frames of reference to understand the use of evidence in policy and practice. For instance, the empirical–analytical perspective emphases on experimental evidence as the basis for evidence based policy and practice. The phenomenological–existential perspective views intervention success as based on the "practitioner knowledge" or "local knowledge," which includes field-notes, interviews, surveys, or classroom observations. From the post-structural perspective, the assessment of evidence is based on principles of public policy such as inclusion, participation, self-determination, and empowerment.

## Practitioners and Policymakers' Definition and Use of Evidence

Understanding how practitioners and policymakers define and integrate evidence into their practice is a complex process mediated by personal knowledge, beliefs, inspirations, and the work environment (Coburn and Turner 2011). Pre-existing opinions and socio-cultural factors are integral to how practitioners and policymakers interpret and organize the evidence (Eryaman 2007). How practitioners and policymakers interpret new information is largely determined by what they know and believe; they will integrate new information into their preexisting opinions rather than engage with evidence that could alter their existing cognitive and socio-cultural frameworks (Greeno et al. 1996). Practitioners and policymakers' knowledge level can also play a crucial role in their engagement with evidence.

### *Practitioners Definition and Use of Evidence*

There are several studies investigated what practitioners count as evidence (Cousins and Leithwood 1993; Eryaman 2008, 2009; Finnigan et al. 2012; Riedler and Eryaman 2016; Zeuli 1994). In Chap. 8 of this edited work, Brooks, Rickinson and Wilkinson provide a review of literature to demonstrate the distinctions in the ways that academics and practitioners have come to conceptualize evidence use, and analyze the implications of various definitions for educational practice from three categories of evidence use: *instrumental, conceptual* and *symbolic*. Zeuli (1994) further documented in his study that all participant teachers paid special attention to evidence that fits with their professional experiences and could be directly translated into classroom practices. The teachers exceedingly preferred qualitative evidence resulting from (a) real-world case studies that exemplify in-class teaching and learning, and (b) interviews with students. For Zeuli (1994), purely quantitative assessment results like test scores do not provide adequate evidence to support or disprove the effectiveness of an educational intervention. Furthermore, Zeuli (1994) and Leithwood (1993) revealed that the degree to which teachers perceived evidence as practical or responded to their local needs was important in their judgments of its value. In contrast to these studies that depicted practitioners' comprehensive understanding of evidence, Finnigan et al. (2012) depicted that practitioners sustained a narrow understanding of evidence. Particularly, they revealed that many practitioners equated evidence almost entirely with student test scores.

A number of empirical studies demonstrated that practitioners mostly rely on information they deem trustworthy, accessible, and easily usable (Carnine 1995). Educational practitioners found research studies published in scholarly journals trustworthy. Accessibility means the easiness with which educational practitioners can acquire and comprehend research data. Usability refers to the possibility that educational practitioners apply the scientific evidence they obtain into their classrooms (Carnine 1995).

Nevertheless, educational practitioners commonly contest educational research, debating that its findings can hardly be applied to their unique classroom context. Consequently, practitioners lean towards avoiding educational research and select sources of information that are more relevant to their needs (Zeuli 1994). For instance, Landrum et al. (2003) revealed that educational practitioners frequently rated scholarly journals and university coursework as less usable and accessible than evidence gathered from more informal sources including discussions with colleagues and workshops.

Tan and Gilbert (2014) proposed that educational practitioners are more willing to change their conceptions and practices if they are personally dissatisfied with their current situations and practices as well as external societal or policy demands to change, and if they realize that the research evidence is *accessible, plausible* and *feasible. Accessibility* refers to physical access to research evidence (ability to retrieve research data) and cognitive access to research (intelligibility of the research findings to practitioners). *Plausibility* means that the research context and the school environment are similar, that the research evidence is credible as well as relevant to the cultures, experiences, expectations and primacies of teachers, and that the research evidence can be used to solve problems. *Feasibility* refers to incorporability of research evidence into current practices/conditions with the available resources and expertise, and whether it is worth the time and energy in doing so.

Taken together, the literature demonstrates that practitioners have varying beliefs about what counts as credible evidence. As the arduous debate persists and policies pushing for "evidence-based" practices continue to emerge, the practicing community is expected to oblige. This obligation forces practitioners to modify the current ambiguous definition of evidence to fit their environmental, social, and organizational needs. Rather than allowing practitioners to accept all information sources unquestioningly, the research community must engage with practitioners to develop a mutual understanding of credible evidence (Nicholson-Goodman and Garman 2007).

## *Policymakers and Administrators' Definition and Use of Evidence*

Several studies investigated what educational policy makers and administrators count as evidence. Honig and Coburn (2008) demonstrated that educational policy makers and administrators use the term *evidence* to encompass a wide range of information. Nelson et al. (2009) revealed that when asked to provide the sources of information on which educational leaders rely, the respondents identified "evidence" broadly as local research, personal experience, gut instinct or intuition, personal communication, local data, the experience of others, along with research-based evidence. Nelson, Leffler, and Hansen indicated that no one kind of source of evidence was preferred over the others, and the educational leaders did not differentiate research evidence from evidence generated from other sources. They also demonstrated that policymakers favored evidence that was "practical, real-life, or pragmatic" (p. 19). Based on the preferences of policymakers, it seems that they identified the value of evidence based on the degree to which it corresponded to the local context and expectations.

In the literature, there are three major ways that evidence is used to inform policy-making processes: instrumental, conceptual, and symbolic/political (Beyer 1997; Coburn and Talbert 2006; Coburn et al. 2009; Johnson 1999; Malen 2006). Beyer (1997) described these three categories of evidence use as follows:

> Instrumental use involves applying research results in specific, direct ways. Conceptual use involves using research results for general enlightenment; results influence actions but more indirectly and less specifically than in instrumental use. Symbolic use involves using research results to legitimate and sustain predetermined positions. p. 17

By conducting research on 204 upper-level governmental officials to analyze the gap between scientific research and policy decisions, Caplan (1979) demonstrated that 90% of self-reported instances of evidence use was related to "day-to-day policy issues of limited significance" (p. 462). Caplan named this way of decision-making as "micro-level decision" (p. 462), which others have labeled as *instrumental use*. Within the educational setting, educational policymakers and administrators involve in instrumental way of evidence use to inform policy and program decisions. Coburn and Talbert (2006) demonstrated four instrumental uses of evidence in a school district: monitoring student development to make placement decisions; complying with accountability demands; informing policy decisions; and assessing student progress to recommend instructional practices. Weiss (1979) identified the notion of instrumental research utilization as the "problem-solving model" it as follows:

> The decision drives the application of research. A problem exists and a decision has to be made, information or understanding is lacking either to generate a solution to the problem or to select among alternative solutions, research provides the missing knowledge. With the gap filled, a decision is reached. p. 427

Several scholars criticized the instrumental model as over-simplified or unrealistic (Amara et al. 2004; Caplan 1979; Weiss 1986). They argued that research evidence is more often used conceptually by policymakers, influencing policymaking processes less directly and specifically than instrumental use. With conceptual use, research evidence is used in tandem with other forms of information to influence decisions. In these cases, evidence served the function of 'enlightening' decision-makers (Coburn et al. 2009). In their research study, Caplan et al. (1975) revealed that almost 60% of government policy makers used research evidence in a way that was consistent with the conceptual model.

In addition to the instrumental and conceptual uses of evidence, several scholars have argued that policymakers also use research evidence symbolically to endorse the policies they wish to promote. Sabatier (2007) discussed that given the high stakes of the policy process, "most actors face enormous temptations to present evidence selectively … and generally to distort the situation to their advantage" (Sabatier 2007, 4). Coburn and Talbert (2006) demonstrated that some district administrators did not see research evidence to inform policy decisions as only instrumental, but rather as a way to justify an existing program or to gather support among other stakeholders for a particular decision. Sometimes referred to as "strategic" (Huberman 1990), the *symbolic/political* model defines the process of using evidence to make political advantages or build political support (Corcoran et al. 2001). For instance, Honig and Coburn (2008) demonstrated that district administrators intermittently used evidence to support opinions they had already articulated, deliberately aligning the evidence with a position that promoted their own agendas. Similarly, Farley-Ripple (2012) argued that research evidence is often used after a policy decision was already made.

Even though use of scientific evidence is required for policymaking by federal and state educational policies, Maynard (2006) indicated three reasons why policymakers often disregard the findings of research studies in their decision-making processes: (a) they perceive the research evidence as lacking credibility; (b) they recognize the research evidence as impractical to their local context; or (c) the findings of the research studies are poorly synthesized. As a result, educational policymakers and administrators have long used other forms of evidence called "practitioner knowledge" or "local knowledge" (Honig and Coburn 2008).

In Chap. 9 of this book, Brooks, Rickinson and Wilkinson conclude that educational leadership and evidence use should be seen as a continuum of knowledge and skills that spans the whole range of preparation and practice. They argue that if school administrators attained foundational skills and knowledge in pre-service training programs and were informed by a critical perspective on evidence use that encompassed more than simple input-outcome relationships, their decision-making processes would be greatly enhanced, and would serve the public good by facilitating a more equitable education for all students.

## Understanding Public Good in the Context of Evidence Discourse

The concept of the public good is never static as it continually is restated by various discourse communities (Calhoun 1998; Mansbridge 1998; Pusser 2006). Whereas the concept private good is most closely related to personal gain and individual rights, the public good is much more associated with the commonwealth and the interconnected well-being of the society. To address the issue in political terms, the public good is concerned with concepts like majority control, political equality, and democratic justice, and it entails a type of mutual commitment and collaborative action that is absent in a purely private good realm. With regard to education then, a public good commitment necessitates a mutual understanding concerning the common goal of public education, an obligation to social justice and equality, and a focus on that which provides learners with the skills needed for a meaningful role as a citizen in a participatory democracy. The public good effects how individuals partake in their democratic system and if they participate at all. Therefore it is vital to understand how educational policy and research can inform and transform the public good.

George H. Mead (1964) rightly argued that "to be interested in the public good we must be disinterested, that is, not interested in goods in which our personal selves are wrapped up" (p. 355). Following the Mead's maxim, Borman et al. (2012) proposed that to involve in educational research that serve public good, the researcher needs to conduct inquiry that is beyond individual self-interest. Likewise, Nixon (2011) identified the public good as "a good that, being more than the aggregate of individual interests, denotes a common commitment to social justice and equality" (p. 1), even though he further argued that the public good "involves complex moral and political judgments regarding what constitutes the good for the polity as a whole" (p. x). For research outputs to be a public good, they need to directly contribute to the solution of existing problems by offering 'relevant' and 'useful' knowledge for the purpose of solving such problems (O'Donoghue 2014).

However, there is no assurance that useful knowledge of a problem is an end to itself. Bassel (2013) argues that, "more information and better understanding would not simply make the problem go away when research is disseminated and goes public" (n.p). This reservation is motivated in part by her interest in how these terms 'public' and 'good' get constituted and deployed in the service of research. For her, it is a matter of whose public and whose good ultimately informs research. From a different disciplinary standpoint, Ingold (2013) also suggested that, "The mere provision of information holds no guarantee of knowledge, let alone understanding" (p. 1).

Jenson (2006) identified some of the most important challenges of doing research in the interest of the public good as "designing and implementing investigations that are compatible with the goals of public service; applying rigorous research designs in real-world settings; creating university–community partnerships; and disseminating the results of investigations." (p. 195). This includes creating partnerships with groups other than and in addition to research participants before conducting research, and entails a strong sense of the conditions of the nature of the research to be conducted and its methodologies. To conduct research for the public good, O'Donoghue (2014) argued, is "to engage in research that is expected to do something, something that is recognizable and intelligible through current systems of recognition and reward. It is, one might say, problem and solution driven research" (p. 8).

In Chap. 9 of this book, McDonald and Schneider introduce seven guiding principles of evidence-based/informed educational policy and research to lay the foundation for making sound judgments about what evidence and rigorous research designs should be taken into account when scaling-up educational reforms to serve the public good. These principles are:

1. Gauging the impact on learning,
2. Knowing what to measure,
3. Employing standards of scientific design,
4. Recognizing magnitudes of change,
5. Judging the evidence for scale-up,
6. Accumulating knowledge for generalizability,
7. Conducting research for the common good

The UNESCO report *Rethinking Education,* on the other hand, draws attention to the weakening of the concept of the public good under the alliance of scienticism and neo-liberalism as the most worrying symptoms in contemporary education systems, and recommends a recovery of the notion with the concept of common good:

> The notion of common good goes beyond the instrumental concept of the public good in which human well-being is framed by individualistic socio-economic theory. From a "common good" perspective, it is not only the "good life" of individuals that matters, but also the goodness of the life that humans hold in common. It cannot be a personal or parochial good. It is important to emphasize that the recent shift from "education" to "learning" in international discourse signals a potential neglect of the collective dimensions and the purpose of education as a social endeavour. This is true both for the broader social outcomes expected of education, and for how educational opportunities are organized. The notion of education as a "common good" reaffirms the collective dimension of education as a shared social endeavour (shared responsibility and commitment to solidarity). (UNESCO 2015, p. 78)

A majority of the criticisms of evidence-based practices and policy focus on limitations related to the instrumental, neoliberal, and non-contextual factors associated with evidence-based movement (Kemm 2006; Lincoln and Cannella 2004a; Greenhalgh and Russell 2009). Additional criticisms address the lack of integration of ethical, moral and political considerations (Sanderson 2009). For instance, as the largest evidence-based intervention by a federal government into education in the history, No Child Left Behind (NCLB) Act has received heavy criticism from the academic circles. In February 2015, more than 500 education researchers in US have signed an open letter to Congress and the Obama administration about how the NCLB law should be reconsidered, stating that they "strongly urge departing from test-focused reforms that not only have been discredited for high-stakes decisions, but also have shown to widen, not close, gaps and inequities" (Washington Post 2015).

The letter references a policy report written by Kevin Welner and William J. Mathis, discussing how the debates about the reauthorization of the NCLB disregard the harm to the public good caused by the law's test-based reforms. Welner and Williams (2015) argues in the report that:

> Today's 21-year-olds were in third grade in 2002, when the No Child Left Behind Act became law. For them and their younger siblings and neighbors, test-driven accountability policies are all they've known. The federal government entrusted their educations to an unproven but ambitious belief that if we test children and hold educators responsible for improving test scores, we would have almost everyone scoring as "proficient" by 2014. Thus, we would achieve "equality." This approach has not worked. Yet over the past 13 years, Presidents Bush and Obama remained steadfastly committed to test-based policies. These two administrations have offered federal grants through Race to the Top, so-called Flexibility Waivers under NCLB, School Improvement Grants, and various other programs to push states, districts, and schools to line up behind policies that use these same test scores in high-stakes evaluations of teachers and principals, in addition to the NCLB focus on schools.

The NCLB law further required public schools to ground their educational programs in Scientifically Based Research (SBR). With the NCLB law, the 'gold standard' of randomized controlled field trials became the preferred methodology for educational research (Eryaman 2006). With the invitation of the Department of Education, the National Research Council (NRC) developed a set of narrowly defined criteria of scientific research in a report (NRC 2002). Gee (2005) argued that "the principles about what is science offered by SRE (NRC) are relatively vague generalities and dangerous as such since they can be applied in so many different ways based on the political interest of the person or agency applying them" (p. 9). St. Pierre (2002) critiqued the NRC report for being too narrow and for denying diverse methodological and theoretical approaches of educational research. Eryaman (2006) supported the idea of keeping educational research open to diverse traditions of scholarship so as not to inhibit the knowledge sharing and generation in academia. Erickson and Gutierrez (2002), and Lincoln and Cannella (2004a, b) also criticized the report for its exclusive focus on what works and for not paying enough attention on advancement of a critical stance toward science. They further questioned the principles of the NCLB and the NRC report for producing a conservative Right discourse in which neo-conservative fundamentalism produced regulatory and disciplinary powers that reinforce and allocate resources to Eurocentric, universalist, and objectivist educational research, policy and practice (Bruce and Eryaman 2015; Eryaman 2006).

Eryaman (2007) urges educational policy makers and practitioners to look at educational research for practical examples of how to create and shape well-formed human lives to serve public good and to explore who we authentically are and who we would like to become. The view of educational research implied in evidence discourse simply focuses on "what works" in regard to neo-liberal economic indicators: efficiency, standardization, testing, and accountability. For Eryaman (2006),

> What is needed for educational research, however, is a view of educational practice that acknowledges the non-causal, social, practical, moral, and political nature of educational

> inquiry that helps individuals to acquire the knowledge, attitudes, and skills needed to function effectively in a pluralistic democratic society and to interact, negotiate, and communicate with peoples from diverse groups in order to create a civic and moral community that works for the common good. What is needed, in other words, is an acknowledgment that education is a moral and political accomplishment rather than a mere technical or technological activity. The most important question for educational researchers is therefore not about mere technical and procedural efficacy of their research but about the potential social, moral, and political value of what they do. p. 1211

In order for educational researchers to generate scientific evidence that can promote a shared democratic vision of public good and recognize the plurality of goods and multiple principles of educational practice, I provide them with nine guiding principles:

1. Ontological: How do we continually challenge our presuppositions and subjectivities while continuing to conduct research? How do we eliminate our prejudices that preclude openness to other ideas and worldviews without losing our critical commitment to serving public good?
2. Epistemological: What should count as knowledge and as knowing in educational and social inquiry? How do we validate the way we describe knowledge and knowing without falling into objectivism and ethnocentrism?
3. Political: Who shall control the selection and distribution of knowledge in the communities of educational and social inquiry? Through what discursive practices? What responsibilities do we as educational inquirers have to ensure that the selection and distribution of knowledge promote a democratic vision of good education at both the institutional and practical levels?
4. Economic: How is the control of language and discursive practices linked to the existing and unequal distribution of power, goods, and services in the communities of educational and social inquiry?
5. Ideological: What knowledge, techniques, and methodologies are most worthy of teaching and learning? Whose knowledge, techniques, and methodologies are they?
6. Technical: How shall technical, methodological, theoretical, and practical knowledge be made accessible to the communities of educational, political, and social inquiry? Which types of distribution techniques and strategies should be used to serve public good?
7. Aesthetic: How do educational and social inquirers link moral, political, practical, and technical knowledge to the discursive practices of their own and other communities without falling into objectivism and ethnocentrism? How do they act "aesthetically" as inquirers in doing this?
8. Ethical: How shall educational and social inquirers treat others responsibly and fairly? What is the link between moral responsibility and discursive practices of educational and social inquirers? How do we pursue social justice without imposing our presuppositions about emancipation and social-political transformation?
9. Historical: What ongoing and historical conversations and discourses in the field of educational and social inquiry already exist on methodological, political, theoretical, and practical issues of educational and social research? (revised version of Eryaman 2006, p. 1213)

Schwandt (2005) further argued that educational researchers ought to join the political and public (not just the academic) discourse about the role of educational research in society and about how research evidence is both implicated in and confronts the politics of what counts as knowledge:

> Who does an educational science serve and how? Who stands to gain and who to lose from the appeal to or disregard of scientific findings? How is a science of education implicated in a political agenda? Under what circumstances is an endorsement of educational science a simultaneous expression of disrespect for difference and diversity in perspective and understanding? p. 304

## Conclusion and Recommendations

The chapter contributors in this edited volume joined the public and academic debate on evidence and public good by exploring the ways in which the discourses on evidence have informed and transformed the relationships between educational research, policy and practice in different international contexts.

One of the major reoccurring thoughts throughout all chapters is about the nature, types, and properties of evidence as well as several controversies surrounding what constitutes the best evidence. The consensus position is that evidence is important but there is considerable disagreement about what counts as externally valid sources of evidence for policy decisions. A distinction is made by several authors regarding distinctions between evidence-based and evidence informed knowledge; global versus local evidence and external versus internal evidence, these ideas are best summarized in the Chap. 1 by Krejsler. Essentially here the position is grounded in the assumption that the knowledge base upon which researchers are grounding their designs are often not informed by professionals in the field resulting too often in a rush to judgement about what works and does not work and the identification of a culprit for these differences. The solution of John Benedicto Krejsler is an argument for conceiving of evidence as a floating signifier; in which he makes a strong argument about the value and importance of understanding the context in which education reforms are implemented and a question about who has the executive authority to act upon the knowledge that is produced. Taking this perspective he concludes that in order to serve the public good, not that evidence should be discarded but rather understood accounting for the values and purposes of the political and social context in which education reforms and activities are enacted.

Support for evidence informed rather than evidence based education can be found in the Chap. 7 by Theo Wubbels and Jan van Tartwijk from the Netherlands, who take the position that it is doubtful that research can ever produce definitive answers to what and how to teach. Moreover, that educational research will never be closely connected to practitioners so that incorporating variations in context can never be fully explored or justified enough for policy decisions. They support the position that to advance the public good, that practitioners should combine the work of researchers into their practice. Their position is grounded in a deep history of education reform and the infrastructure that the Netherlands has used to implement change in practice and policy. Most recently, the government has taken a multi-structural approach working on a new pilot that collaboratively works with schools and universities to design and implement education reforms. However, these reforms while promoting diversity of views may fall short of promoting the public good without paying particular attention to the needs of students from different socioeconomic classes especially those from disadvantaged communities.

Echoing to some extent many of questions asked in the Netherlands chapter, regarding the purposes of evidence, what it will be used for, and who is providing it; the Finnish narrative by Hannele Niemi, in Chap. 3, highlights the some of the international and national data sources often used to generate evidence regarding the effectiveness of the Finnish educational system. While not taking issue with the desire for robust evidence, Niemi also supports practitioners being directly involved in the creation of evidence. However, she takes that ideas one step further by calling for multidisciplinary and multi-professional perspectives. In suggesting the inclusion of practitioners, Niemi underscores the research training that pre- professionals in Finland receive in their education system and how these experiences prepare them to become willing and informed decision-makers in the production of evidence. She raises yet another problem that is determining based on the evidence, what messages deserve priority among policymakers given their intent to produce a population of lifelong learners. For the past 60 years or so, Finland has promoted the connection between educational policy and the public good embracing equity—free education for all from preschool through higher education and viewing public service as a source of pride and appreciation. Evidence of its educational system is derived for purposes of improvement rather than hierarchical ordering and potential sanctions for inadequate performance as found in many accountability systems. This deep connection between the value of education and its relationship to advancing the public good helps to support the types of evidence Finland uses in constructing different educational policies.

In Spain, the sources of evidence that policy makers use are typically extracted from international assessments is described by Gonzalo Jover, Enric Prats, and Patricia Villamor in Chap. 4. Supporting the concept that data on educational access and performance need to be collected for advancing the public good; they show how evidence has been used to open-up greater divisions between the politic right and left. While both parties have at different times endorsed a similar message about the need for education to advance the public good, from the authors' perspective, how this should be accomplished has yet to materialize into policies that reflect either party. Both parties use empirical data but for different political purposes. This suggests that data although on its face may be seen as scientifically accurate how it is interpreted and used brings with it unexpected and unintentional consequences especially in contentious political environments.

Singapore, with its strong central Ministry of Education serves as a stark contrast to the Spain example. Citing the long Chinese history that has relied on various data systems to assess the quality of candidate for different positions in the government, the authors Johnathan WP Goh, Ong Kim Lee, and Hairon Salleh in Chap. 6, explain that the educational assessment system in Singapore is situated in this tradition. The authors contend that the assessment system in Singapore is used for the public good in multiple venues including employment as well as education. Distinguishing between formative and summative assessment, both of which are used in Singapore, the authors show how mathematics teachers use formative assessments to modify their instruction for purposes of improving student performance. Summative evaluations they view as a tool for promotion and reward purposes. The critical difference here from the concerns of Krejsler, is that the researchers and their government have a more bounded view of specific types of evidence for various purposes. It could be that in this smaller country that a more unified system of evidence can foster consensus between practitioners, evaluators, and government officials. One strong relationship between evidence use, interpretation, and policy practice can be traced to a meaningful purpose in the service of a discrete question for gaining information for an explicit answer. In contrast to Singapore, one might expect that in more porous political environments along with social media and other sources for disseminating evidence, how information is used to promote a position is unrestrained.

Selahattin Turan and Derva Yilmaz Kihcogu's Chap. 11 on the Turkish education system and how it uses data to support the public good draws attention to the disconnection between the evidence and its actual implementation. To facilitate a closer tie between evidence and practice the authors offer several recommendations that have relevance to other nations as they create a legitimate space for evidence based reforms. As researchers of policy implementation have shown, decision makers often ignore evidence and are often caught in the will of their constituencies. The authors call for decision makers to embrace the evidence and to do so by systematically compiling evidence that is relevant and meaningful to the decisions at hand. And then, to work with the government to take the evidence seriously in their deliberations, policy agenda-setting, and implementation in collaboration with the researchers and analysts. To facilitate the development and use of evidence-based decision making, the authors make the case for additional resources to be funneled to independent research think tanks and centers. For evidence to be taken seriously it needs to be rigorous, independent, and amply funded especially if the end-game is evidence-based knowledge in the service of the public good.

The Chap. 5 by Elizabeth Farley-Ripple, Allison Karpyn, Kalyn McDonough and Katherine Tilley, focuses on the uses of evidence and how it can motivate the public good. These forms of use include: (1) instrumental, documenting how evidence is used in decision-making; (2) conceptual, altering understanding of the issues and solutions; and (3) political, manipulating evidence for a particular goal. Categorizing these distinctions, the authors move on to describing what is known about research use in the schools, focusing on who, what, and how. From their perspective they question the value of implementing a top-down approach to research use, emphasizing instead the importance of building wide communities of professional learners and filling current gaps between the incentives, relevance, and contextual differences between researchers and practitioners. By bringing together a more singularly focused goal regarding the nature and quality of research aided in part by philanthropic and government supported efforts, research findings have a better opportunity to influence and work in support of the public good.

Another U.S. chapter by Sarah Kay McDonald and Barbara Schneider sets out a list of principles for making sound judgments about research quality and what evidence should be taken into account interventions designed for scale-up. In the Chap. 10, the authors explicitly detail what needs to be considered before evidence based decisions can be made to advance the common good. These principles with specific examples of each include: what are the factors need to be considered when gauging the impact of an intervention on learning; how outcomes of interest should be measured; why employing randomized control trials (RCTs) for purposes of scale-up are appropriate and useful; why it is important to establish causal inference; what contextual variations and subpopulation factors need to considered in studying specific outcomes; when and how to extend the study findings to the broader population; and why we need to conduct work that advances the public good for all students.

In the Chap. 9 on school principals' use of evidence, Jeffrey S. Brooks, Mark Rickinson and Jane Wilkinson argue that evidence needs to be understood in broad terms that contain but go beyond 'research evidence' on the one hand, and is not limited only to 'performance data' on the other hand. The authors discuss that the field of educational leadership needs to reframe its orientation toward evidence use to serve public good, and school leadership and evidence use should be considered as a continuum of knowledge and skills that spans the whole range of preparation and practice. The authors further propose that if school administrators developed fundamental abilities and knowledge in pre-service preparation programs and were educated a nuanced view on evidence use that encompassed more than simple input-outcome relationships, their practice would be greatly enhanced.

Tracey Burns and Rien Rouw, in the Chap. 8, shifts from a specific country perspective to a more global one, relying on their experiences working at OECD. The first proviso they make is that performance data is only one source of evidence. Second, that there is not a hierarchy of quantitative data in which randomized trials sit at the top. Their position, one that is fairly uniform in the research field, is that the question being asked determines the design and data base. Recognizing that there are challenges to both the production and use of evidence, they describe the challenges and limitations of autonomous models—where researchers have control of major aspects of the design and the questions of impartiality and objectivity that arise in this situation. On the other hand, studies designed through multiple partnerships require a good deal of negotiation and sometimes when too abundant can make it unusable by its sheer magnitude and uninformative about specific situations. The authors then detail two different case studies of how evidence was used in Sweden and Belgium concluding with a set of questions that combine many of the points regarding evidence discussed throughout all of the chapters in this volume.

By demonstrating how the diverse discourses inform the interrelationships among educational research, policy and practice for the public good in an international context, all chapter contributors in this edited book support the notion that educational policymakers, researchers and practitioners ought to work toward advancing a more equitable and just society by serving as a critical voice in social, political, academic and cultural environments ineradicably marked by significant inequalities, cultural complexities, power disparities, and political uncertainties.

In conclusion, the research design, data collection and analysis depend on what the evidence will be used for, and who will have the primary responsibility for its collection and dissemination. Several key questions emerged from this volume including: What are the incentives for different types of data collection efforts and to what extent can they inform local contexts and or generalize to larger populations? How can researchers and others help to create an appetite for evidence that is safe from the predilections of particular ideological leanings and unbiased accountability evaluation systems? And most importantly, what is the nature of evidence based or evidence informed data that can advance the needs of the public good both within and across different levels of the education system? How can evidence discourse help us answer the questions of what kind of society we should have and what directions we should take? The aswers? Found in the rich and informative chapters by the contributors of this book.

## References

Amara, N., Ouimet, M., & Rejean, L. (2004). New evidence on instrumental, conceptual, and symbolic utilization of University Research in Government Agencies. *Science Communication, 26*, 75–106.

Bassel, L. (2013). Making research work as a public good requires a mutually reinforcing process of engagement. Available Online: http://blogs.lse.ac.uk/impactofsocialsciences/2013/06/05/making-research-work-as-a-public-good/. Accessed 30 Nov 2016.

Beyer, J. M. (1997). Research utilization: Bridging the gap between communities. *Journal of Management Inquiry, 6*, 17–22.

Biesta, G. J. J. (2007). Why 'what works' won't work. Evidence-based practice and the democratic deficit of educational research. *Educational Theory, 57*(1), 1–22.

Biesta, G. J. J. (2010a). *Good education in an age of measurement: Ethics, politics, democracy.* Boulder: Paradigm Publishers.

Biesta, G. J. J. (2010b). Why 'what works' still won't work: From evidence-based education to value-based education. *Studies in Philosophy and Education, 29*(5), 491–503.

Borman, K. M., Danzig, A. B., & Garcia, D. R. (2012). Education, democracy, and the public good. *Review of Research in Education, 36*(1).

Bouffard, M., & Reid, G. (2012). The good, the bad, and the ugly of evidence-based practice. *Adapted Physical Activity Quarterly, 29*, 1–24.

Broekaert, E., Autrique, M., Vanderplasschen, W., & Colpaert, K. (2010). The human prerogative': A critical analysis of evidence-based and other paradigms of care in substance abuse treatment. *Psychiatry Quarterly, 81*, 227–238.

Brownson, R. C., Chriqui, J. F., & Stamatakis, K. A. (2009). Understanding evidence-based public health policy. *American Journal of Public Health, 99*(9), 1576–1583. http://doi.org/10.2105/AJPH.2008.156224.

Bruce, B. C., & Eryaman, M. Y. (2015). Introduction: Progressive impuls in education. In M. Y. Eryaman & B. C. Bruce (Eds.), *International handbook of progressive education* (pp. 1–52). New York: Peter Lang.

Calhoun, C. (1998). The public good as a social and cultural project. In W. Powell & E. Clemens (Eds.), *Private action and the public good* (pp. 20–37). New Haven: Yale University Press.

Caplan, N. (1979). The two-communities theory and knowledge utilization. *American Behavioral Scientist, 22*(3), 459–470.

Caplan, N., Morrison, A., & Stambaugh, R. J. (1975). *The use of social science knowledge in policy decisions at the national level*. Ann Arbor: Center of Research on Knowledge Utilization, Institute for Social Research, University of Michigan.
Carnine, D. (1995). Trustworthiness, usability, and accessibility of educational research. *Journal of Behavioral Education, 5*(3), 251–258.
Coburn, C., & Talbert, J. E. (2006). Conceptions of evidence use in school districts: Mapping the terrain. *American Journal of Evaluation, 112*(4), 469–495.
Coburn, C., & Turner, E. O. (2011). Research on data use: A framework and analysis. *Measurement: Interdisciplinary Educational Change, 9*(4), 173–206.
Coburn, C. E., Toure, J., & Yamashita, M. (2009). Evidence, interpretation, and persuasion: Instructional decision making at the district central office. *Teachers College Record, 111*(4), 1115–1161.
Corcoran, T., Fuhrman, S. H., & Belcher, C. L. (2001). The district role in instructional improvement. *Phi Delta Kappan, 83*(1), 78–84.
Cousins, J. B., & Leithwood, K. A. (1993). Enhancing knowledge utilization as a strategy for school improvement. *Knowledge: Creation, Diffusion, Utilization, 14*(3), 305–333.
Erickson, F., & Gutierrez, K. (2002). Culture, rigor, and science in educational research. *Educational Researcher, 31*(8), 21–24.
Eryaman, M. Y. (2006). Traveling beyond dangerous private and universal discourses: Radioactivity of radical hermeneutics and objectivism in educational research. *Qualitative Inquiry, 12*(6), 1198–1219.
Eryaman, M. Y. (2007). From reflective practice to practical wisdom: Toward a post-foundational teacher education. *International Journal of Progressive Education, 3*(1), 87–107.
Eryaman, M. Y. (2008). *Teaching as practical philosophy*. Saarbrücken: VDM Verlag Dr. Müller.
Eryaman, M. Y. (Ed.). (2009). *Peter McLaren, education, and the struggle for liberation*. Cresskill: Hampton Press.
Farley-Ripple, E. N. (2012). Research use in central office decision-making: A case study. *Education Management, Administration and Leadership, 40*(6), 784–804.
Finnigan, K., Daly, A. J., & Che, J. (2012). Mind the gap: Learning, trust, and relationships in an underperforming urban system. *American Journal of Education, 119*(1), 41–71.
Gee, J. P. (2005). It's theories all the way down: A response to scientific research in education. *Teachers College Record, 107*(1), 10–18.
Greenhalgh, T., & Russell, J. (2009). Evidence-based policy making: a critique. *Perspectives in Biology and Medicine, 52*(2), 304–318.
Greeno, J. G., Collins, A. M., & Resnick, L. B. (1996). Cognition and learning. In D. Berliner & R. Calfee (Eds.), *Handbook of educational psychology* (pp. 15–41). New York: Macmillian.
Hammersley, M. (2009). What is evidence for evidence-based practice? In R. S. Clair (Ed.), *Education science: Critical perspectives* (pp. 101–111). Rotterdam: Sense.
Hansen, H. F., & Rieper, O. (2010). The politics of evidence-based policy making. The case of Denmark. *German Policy Studies, 6*(2), 87–112.
Hargreaves, D. (1999). Revitalising educational research: Lessons from the past and proposals for the future. *Cambridge Journal of Education, 29*(2), 239–249.
Head, B. W. (2008). Three lenses of evidence-based policy. *Australian Journal of Public Administration, 67*(1), 1–11.
Honig, M. I., & Coburn, C. (2008). Evidence-based decision making in school district central offices: Toward a policy and research agenda. *Educational Policy, 22*(4), 578–608.
Huberman, M. (1990). Linkage between researchers and practitioners: A qualitative study. *American Educational Research Journal, 27*(2), 363–391.
Ingold, T. (2013). *Making: Anthropology, archaeology, art and architecture*. London: Routledge.
Jenson, J. (2006). Research and the public good. *Social Work Research, 30*(4), 195–197.
Jin, J., & Yun, J. (2010). Evidence-based practice in adapted physical education. *Journal of Physical Education, Recreation & Dance, 81*(4), 50–54.

Johnson Jr., B. L. (1999). The politics of research-information use in the education policy arena. *Educational Policy, 13*(1), 23–36.

Kemm, J. (2006). The limitations of 'evidence-based' public health. *Journal of Evaluation in Clinical Practice, 12*(3), 319–324.

Landrum, T. J., Tankersley, M., & Kauffman, J. M. (2003). What is special about special education for students with emotional or behavioral disorders? *The Journal of Special Education, 37*, 148–156.

Leithwood, K. A. (1993, October). *Contributions of transformational leadership to school restructuring*. Paper presented at the Convention of the University Council for Educational Administration, Houston.

Lincoln, Y. S., & Cannella, G. S. (2004a). Dangerous discourses: Methodological conservatism and governmental regimes of truth [Special issue]. *Qualitative Inquiry, 10*(1), 5–14.

Lincoln, Y. S., & Cannella, G. S. (2004b). Qualitative research, power, and the radical right. *Qualitative Inquiry, 10*(2), 175–201.

Lynch, K. (2006). Neo-liberalism and marketisation: The implications for higher education. *European Educational Research Journal, 5*(1), 1–17.

Malen, B. (2006). Revisiting policy implementation as a political phenomenon: The case of reconstitution policies. In M. Honig (Ed.), *New directions in education policy implementation: Confronting complexity* (pp. 83–104). Albany: State University of New York Press.

Mansbridge, J. (1998). On the contested nature of the public good. In W. Powell & E. Clemens (Eds.), *Private action and the public good new* (pp. 3–19). Haven: Yale University Press.

Maynard, R. A. (2006). Evidence-based decision making: What will it take for the decision makers to care? *Journal of Policy Analysis and Management, 25*, 249–265.

Mead, G. H. (1964). National mindedness and international mindedness. In A. J. Reck (Ed.), *Selected writings: George Herbert Mead* (pp. 355–370). Chicago: The University Of Chicago.

National Research Council. (2002). *Scientific research in education*. Washington, DC: National Academy Press.

Nelson, S. R., Leffler, J. C., & Hansen, B. A. (2009). *Toward a research agenda for understanding and improving the use of research evidence*. Portland: Northwest Regional Educational Laboratory.

Nicholson-Goodman, J., & Garman, N. B. (2007). Mapping practitioner perceptions of "It's research-based": Scientific discourse, speech acts, and the use and abuse of research. *International Journal of Leadership in Education: Theory and Practice, 10*(3), 283–299.

Nixon, J. (2011). *Higher education and the public good: Imagining the university*. London/New York: Bloomsbury.

Nutley, S., Walter, I., & Davies, H. T. (2007). *Using evidence: How research can inform public services*. Bristol: Policy Press.

O'Donoghue, D. (2014). Doing arts-based educational research for the public good: An impossible possibility? *International Journal of Education & the Arts, 15*(SI 2.3). Retrieved from http://www.ijea.org/v15si2/

Pusser, B. (2006). The role of public spheres. In G. Tierney (Ed.), *Governance and the public good* (pp. 1–20). Albany: State University of New York Press.

Riedler, M., & Eryaman, M. Y. (2016). Complexity, diversity and ambiguity in teaching and teacher education: practical wisdom, pedagogical fitness and tact of teaching. *International Journal of Progressive Education, 12*(3), 172–186.

Sabatier, P. A. (2007). *Theories of the policy process* (2nd ed.). Boulder: Westview Press.

Sanderson, I. (2009). Intelligent policy making for a complex world: Pragmatism, evidence and learning. *Political Studies, 57*, 699–719.

Schalock, R. L., & Verdugo, M. A. (2012). A conceptual and measurement framework to guide policy development and systems change. *Journal of Policy and Practice in Intellectual Disabilities, 9*, 63–72.

Schalock, R. L., Verdugo, M. A., & Gómez, L. E. (2011). Evidence-based practices in the field of intellectual and developmental disabilities: An international consensus approach. *Evaluation and Program Planning, 34*(3), 273–282.

Schwandt, T. A. (2005). A diagnostic reading of scientifically based research for education. *Educational Theory, 55*(3), 285–305.
St. Pierre, E. A. (2002). Science rejects postmodernism. *Educational Researcher, 31*(8), 25–27.
Tan, K. C. D., & Gilbert, J. K. (2014). Chemistry teaching: Impact of educational research on the practices of chemistry teachers in Singapore. *Chemistry Education Research and Practice, 15*, 207–218.
UNESCO. (2015). Rethinking education. In *Towards a global common good?* París: UNESCO.
Washington Post. (2015, February). *More than 500 researchers sign NCLB letter to Congress: Stop test-focused reforms*. Available online at: https://www.washingtonpost.com/blogs/answer-sheet/wp/2015/02/14/more-than-500-researchers-sign-nclb-letter-to-congress-stop-test-focused-reforms/
Weiss, C. H. (1979). The many meanings of research utilization. *Public Administration Review, 39*, 426–431.
Weiss, C. H. (1986). Research and policy-making: A limited partnership. In F. Heller (Ed.), *The use and abuse of social science* (pp. 214–235). London: Sage.
Welner, K. G., & Williams, J. M. (2015). *Reauthorization of the elementary and secondary education act: Time to move beyond test-focused policies*. Available online at: http://nepc.colorado.edu/publication/esea
Zeuli, J. S. (1994). How do teachers understand research when they read it? *Teaching and Teacher Education, 10*(2), 39–55.

# Chapter 2
# Capturing the 'Evidence' and 'What Works' Agenda in Education: A Truth Regime and the Art of Manoeuvring Floating Signifiers

**John Benedicto Krejsler**

**Abstract** Education has moved higher up on the policy agenda and serving the public good has acquired new meanings. This entails demands to provide policy and market with instruments to enable evidence-based or at least evidence-informed choices in a so-called competitive global knowledge economy. This has, not surprisingly, led to a struggle about 'evidence' and the right to decide how 'what works' can be defined in education, which has consequences for school, professionals and educational research.

The chapter explores this issue by means of Danish examples located within larger transnational agendas. Evidence discourse was initially a bottom-up professional strategy within the medical field. It was, however, reworked and launched into education in a more top-down move that has largely bypassed professionals.

From this perspective, the author argues that the field of education and its professions may profit from adopting evidence as a floating signifier. This is, admittedly, a difficult endeavour as the evidence discourse is currently at odds with a majority of mainstream paradigms and understandings of school and teaching within the teaching profession and educational research. Taking the approach of the floating signifier could, nonetheless, be strategically useful in the struggle to expand the meanings of evidence to also reflect the experiences of professionals and the span of contemporary educational research. Three analytical distinctions are proposed in order to facilitate manoeuvring evidence as a floating signifier: evidence-based vs evidence-informed knowledge; global vs local evidence; and external vs internal evidence.

J.B. Krejsler (✉)
Danish School of Education, Aarhus University, Copenhagen, Denmark
e-mail: jok@edu.au.dk



M.Y. Eryaman, B. Schneider (eds.), *Evidence and Public Good in Educational Policy, Research and Practice*, Educational Governance Research 6,
DOI 10.1007/978-3-319-58850-6_2

## Introduction

This chapter takes as its point of departure the ascendant position of the evidence discourse within education. In stark contrast to its genesis within the medical field, the evidence discourse has been launched into the field of education by external stakeholders in mostly top-down moves that have largely bypassed professionals within the field (Hammersley 2007; Krejsler 2013). Danish examples will serve to illustrate the argument; the trend, however, can be seen across the Nordic countries (e.g. Bergmark and Lundström 2006; Oscarsson 2006; Telhaug et al. 2006; Utdanningsforbundet 2008) and beyond, globally (Furlong et al. 2009a, b; Henry et al. 2001; Hopmann 2008; Meyer and Benavot 2013; OECD 2007; Rizvi and Lingard 2010; Wells 2007; Krejsler 2017 (forthcoming)).

I shall argue that the evidence discourse mirrors a cultural struggle that currently rages about how key areas within modern societies are to be defined (Biesta 2007, 2010; Gibbons 1994; Hammersley 2013). How we perceive evidence for what works has significant implications regarding how a hospital or a school may conceive of their visions, targets and practices, and what kinds of research and research paradigms are considered legitimate in the production of knowledge. A too strict focus on Randomized Controlled Trials (RCT tests) in the health services and education will tend to marginalize other and 'softer' professional practices of validation. In other words, discourses about the population's health and education proliferate in close reciprocity with the criteria for verification that such knowledge is subjected to. Health and educational issues must be conceived of in ways that somehow satisfy the criteria for producing evidence which mandate powers funding those activities demand.

On this background, I shall argue that evidence may be conceived of as a floating signifier with great advantage, and support this claim by introducing three distinctions to analytically qualify critique of, and challenge the current dominant regime of, evidence: By introducing (1) the distinction between *evidence-based vs evidence-informed* knowledge, I wish to exploit an already fruitful approach to distinguishing between issues that merit so-called 'hard' and others that merit 'soft' evidence approaches to evaluating what works. By introducing (2) the distinction between *global vs local forms of evidence* I wish to highlight that some issues merit knowledge that is valid regardless of context, whereas intervention in other contexts requires forms of knowledge that are highly responsive to the particular context of intervention. By introducing (3) the distinction between *external vs internal evidence* I want to problematize the question about who has the right – or more precisely the executive powers – to make decisions about which forms of evidence count as knowledge that works. This points to the tensions between the considerable production of knowledge and documentation for what works by professionals and educational researchers, which function as supplements or contesting knowledge to the forms of evidence that powerful external stakeholders currently impose on education.

In total, this chapter is an argument that serving the *public good* in a democratic society requires tools for producing 'evidence' and knowledge about 'what works' that reflect the diversity of values and purposes that members of this society strive to accomplish. And education in particular cannot be dissociated from the visions of the good life and the good society that give education direction, unless you accept an instrumental and objectivist vision of knowledge and education. Consequently, the term of the floating signifier is not a license that any 'evidence' goes, but a reflection that truths about what works in education can seldom be dissociated from the perspectives, values and purposes that give direction to educational activities (e.g. Biesta 2007, 2010).

## Discourses, Genealogies and Floating Signifiers

A Foucauldian approach allows us to make evidence discourse problematic as a particular truth regime that makes some ways of speaking and acting possible while excluding others (Foucault 1971). Like any other discourse, it is constituted as a pattern of interconnected statements which reciprocally refer to one another, thereby continually reinforcing the totality of the discourse. The immanent logic thus construed forms a strategic space wherein a number of different subject positions emerge to be occupied by willing individuals. Obviously, one must subject one's self to the discursive regime in question in order to be included as a legitimate subject within this regime.

Foucault argued that the power-knowledge effects of a given discourse must be measured by the extent to which it matches and mirrors the dominant configuration of dominant and less dominant discourses that set the boundaries for how individuals can think and act at a given time and space in history (Foucault 1993, 1997). Foucault considered it his task to chart, via a genealogical method, the topological contours of the battlefields with which subjects within different discursive fields struggle to come to terms (e.g. the fields of madness, reason, imprisonment, subjectivity, sexuality and so forth).

Drawing on insights from Foucauldian genealogy, I shall sketch major threads that appear to have coalesced, making evidence discourse an increasingly dominant voice which cannot be ignored when considering what works in education. Or, formulated as a question in a Foucauldian genealogical vein: How has it come about that researchers, policy-makers and practitioners today make education problematic in terms of 'evidence' and 'what works'?

In order to explore potentials for expanding what evidence and what works may mean, I shall introduce 'floating signifiers' as a useful thinking tool. This entails an analytical concept coined by Ernesto Laclau (1993) in order to capture a category of open empirical concepts that have become increasingly prevalent in modern societies, producing meaning and consensus at a sufficiently general level in order to cover the diversity of lifeforms at play when various subject positions negotiate what shall count as legitimate truths within different policy areas. The current political climate abounds with dominant floating signifiers such as 'quality', 'efficiency' and 'excellence'. They set new agendas and dislocate established truths by expressing flexibly the interests of dominant configurations of stakeholders.

A particular consensus-producing feature of the floating signifier is that it makes it difficult to disagree until you require specifics about how it is intended to be operationalized. You cannot disagree with 'quality' as such. Similarly, it is hard to disagree that evidence and what works approaches to dealing with reality are desirable. As documented in this chapter, the dominant version of evidence performs exactly that operation. It appears open to interpretation at a surface level while being simultaneously already coded with meaning and woven into powerful genealogies of possible meanings by virtue of lengthy negotiations among powerful stakeholders. In medicine as well as education, evidence for what works is thus established by linking particular perceptions of science to the pragmatic powers and agendas of dominant stakeholders within policy, science and market.

Observing evidence as a floating signifier thus assists us in mapping dominant policy agendas and, hopefully, challenges us to experiment, looking for new interpretations in the ruptures and inconsistencies that appear from the maelstrom of highly charged political contexts (Deleuze and Guattari 1994; Krejsler 2016). Overall, this chapter represents a thinking technology for researchers and professional groups within education in their struggle to produce knowledge and practices that gain legitimacy by exploiting the interstices and possible loopholes in current dominant policy configurations to which they are subjected. As a hybrid technology, it represents potential pitfalls as well, as engaging in the dangerous struggles around dominant policy practices entails the risk of being co-opted into negotiations that may well narrow the room for manoeuver, giving legitimacy to an evidence consensus that may disregard useful knowledge and practices which educational researchers and professionals have built up over decades. That is the risk taken when entering this game. However, the costs of staying out of it may well be considerably higher, as it leaves the space entirely to others. As such, this chapter claims to do service to the public good by supplying a conceptual apparatus that may expand what counts as 'evidence' and 'what works' knowledge, and thus may assist more groups in entering the struggle about education and how it may be thought and organized.

## The Genealogy of 'Evidence' and 'What Works' Discourse in Education

In this section I shall clarify how the evidence discourse became a dominant regime of knowledge in education by mapping how major sources from medicine coalesced with agendas of school effectiveness research and transnational agencies like the OECD and its focus upon optimizing human capital. This would eventually transform conditions for producing knowledge about education (Bhatti et al. 2006; Hammersley 2007; OECD 1996, 2007; Rieper and Hansen 2007).

Historically, the concept of evidence has many sources, ranging from everyday common sense discourses to judicial and economy discourses. From the late 1980s onwards, however, the concept of evidence has mainly – albeit not exclusively – been associated with a resurging neo-positivist paradigm and its procedures for producing knowledge about what works in relation to particular interventions (Alvesson and Skjöldberg 2000; Hammersley 2007; Krejsler 2013; Pawson 2006; Rieper and Hansen 2007; Sackett et al. 1996).

The evidence discourse that has gained pre-eminence in relation to producing knowledge about what works is rooted within the medical field (Bhatti et al. 2006; Browman 1999; Rieper and Hansen 2007; Sackett et al. 1996). In 1972, Archie Cochrane (1909–1988) published "Effectiveness and Efficiency – Random reflections on health services" (Cochrane 1972), the groundbreaking book that was destined to achieve an almost mythical position. Cochrane argued that public resources are scarce, and therefore it is important that they are spent on practices with a proven record of effectiveness. He argued that a systematic base of scientifically tested knowledge of what works should be accumulated, preferably based on Randomized Controlled Trials (RCTs) or similar experimental designs that aim at testing well-defined causal relations. He was convinced that this approach would supply reliable knowledge to the health services with greater probability than other approaches to evidence. A substantial element to Cochrane's argument was that the universality and objectivity of evidence produced by RCT would contribute to continually ensuring equal access for all to effective treatment. Cochrane's simple suggestion, and the fact that RCTs were becoming mainstream in medical research, contributed to a breakthrough within the health services. By 1990, *The Cochrane Collaboration* (www.cochrane.org) was established, which has since then been under continuous expansion and is today an international and highly influential collaboration of professionals, with considerable impact on policy. These events gave momentum to the efforts to elaborate so-called *systematic reviews* of international research about what works in relation to particular medical substances and treatments. The evidence ladder here serves as a methodological device to rank the quality of studies according to an ideal of objectivity, validity and reliability that celebrates the Randomized Controlled Trial as its golden standard (e.g. http://www.controlled-trials.com/). This development has been facilitated by the fact that in the 1980s, *meta-analysis* developed into an independent field of research. Meta-analysis is the methodological basis of this review form designed to statistically calculate and synthesize what primary studies say about what works according to rigorous standards privileging the evidence ladder. The emergence of the evidence discourse, Cochrane's initiative and its repercussions mainly arrived 'bottom-up', i.e. from the profession of medical doctors themselves. This truth regime signifies a neo-positivist, quantitative and experiment-oriented approach to doing science.

Inspired by the work of the Cochrane Collaboration, the Campbell Collaboration was established in 2000 with the ambition to make social welfare, crime prevention and education as evidence-based as medicine (Bhatti et al. 2006; Petrosine et al. 2001). The Campbell Collaboration upholds basically the same review procedures as the Cochrane Collaboration, including the evidence ladder that places at its top systematic reviews conducted as meta-analyses of primary studies that place RCTs as the golden standard.

In relation to social welfare, crime and education, the evidence discourse is considerably more directed by the agendas of policy-makers and administrators. In part, this can be explained by the fact that these fields differ from the medical field in crucial aspects (e.g. Bhatti et al. 2006; Hammersley 2007; Pawson 2006). Among other issues, these fields are more diverse in terms of professionals' levels of education, lack of unified professional identity and questioned public status and state authorization. Further, their knowledge base refers to a number of competing scientific paradigms, largely social sciences and humanities paradigms that are often more difficult to convert into regimes that produce so-called 'certain knowledge about what works' which is measurable and can be standardized.

One could argue that education constitutes the field that has been impacted most severely by the evidence discourse understood as a pressure that has largely come from external stakeholders representing discursive regimes which resonate poorly with most existing discourses among professionals and researchers in education (Ball 2007; Bhatti et al. 2006; Borgnakke et al. 2006; Krejsler 2013). It should be added, though, that established traditions among researchers and professionals within education have since long adopted evidence discourse. The latter often engage in close collaboration with policy-makers and administrators in an effort to develop and implement evidence-based or evidence-informed policy, with many researchers gathering in or referring to the well-established International Congress of School Effectiveness and Improvement (e.g. http://www.icsei.net/).

This intensified focus on education is hardly surprising in a period when national governments and transnational bodies like the OECD, EU and the Bologna Process are increasingly occupied with discourses of Knowledge Economies and Life-Long Learning (Henry et al. 2001; Meyer and Benavot 2013; Nóvoa and Lawn 2002; Prewitt 2012; Rizvi and Lingard 2010). The OECD has increased attention to improve the role and efficiency of educational research as a background for decisions made by policy-makers, in addition to the ongoing efforts of practitioners to make educational institutions more result and efficiency oriented and more evidence-based (Burns and Schuller 2007; OECD 2007). An increasing number of comparative surveys, statistics and country reports have thus been developed as aids to policy and practice advice.

In 2004, one of these country reports was accomplished at the request of the Danish government (OECD/CERI 2004). It came to the main conclusions that Danish educational research (R&D) was characterized by too little focused research on key areas, and that links were too weak between educational research and the needs of practitioners and policy-makers. It was within this context that the OECD made the recommendation that a Clearinghouse for Educational Research should be established, drawing on the accomplishments of the British Evidence for Policy and Practice Information and Co-Ordinating Centre (EPPI) as well as the American What Works Clearinghouse (WWC) (http://ies.ed.gov/ncee/wwc/). WWC was established in close collaboration with the Campbell Collaboration (Boruch and Herman 2007). This was done in continuation of the *No Child Left Behind* School

Act (U.S. Department of Education 2002), with the explicit purpose of making school practice more evidence-based (Coalition for Evidence-Based Policy 2003). EPPI and – even more so – WWC have drawn extensively upon inspiration from, and collaboration with, the Campbell Collaboration. To illustrate the impact of these developments in terms of what counts as evidence and knowledge about what works, it should be noted that legislation following the NCLB act requires schools to rely on scientifically based research for programs and teaching methods. The act defines this as "research that involves the application of rigorous, systematic, and objective procedures to obtain reliable and valid knowledge relevant to education activities and programs" (Hamilton et al. 2008; Zucker 2004). This means scientifically based research results in "replicable and applicable findings" from research that uses appropriate methods to generate persuasive, empirical conclusions. Non-scientific methods – according to this discourse – include following tradition, personal preferences, and what is claimed to be non-scientific research such as research based on case studies, ethnographies, personal interviews, discourse analysis, grounded theory, action research and other forms of qualitative research . The latter are no longer seen as an acceptable basis for making decisions about teaching children under the act, which makes them ineligible for federal funding.

The Danish Clearinghouse for Educational Research applies a broader definition of evidence than the one represented by the Campbell Collaboration, WWC and the evidence ladder. It explicitly mentions EPPI as a key inspiration. In addition, it should be mentioned, however, that very few RCT-primary studies have been carried out in Danish or Scandinavian contexts, which for a considerable time to come would make systematic reviews relying on such studies dubiously reliant on American studies in particular. And, judging from existing reviews, the Danish Clearinghouse approach appears to be closer to the more inclusive and narrative approaches to synthesizing reviews of what works that thrive among scholars like Hilbert Meyer (2004) and Brophy and Good, who for decades have represented alternative approaches to synthesizing evidence for what works in education (Brophy and Good 1986; Good and Brophy 2003). Currently, the approach to conceiving of evidence represented by John Hattie and his best-seller *Visible Learning* is gaining considerable ground (Hattie 2009). This approach mimics the Campbell approach in some aspects by carrying out quantitatively based reviews from thousands of primary studies – albeit not adopting the evidence ladder as such – in order to identify correlations that enable statements about what works in relation to facilitating learning.

It will thus be interesting to observe in the years to come which strategies for determining what counts as evidence will be adopted by the Danish Clearinghouse for Educational Research. Will this clearinghouse succeed in bridging the gaps between policy-makers, practitioners and the research community, in terms of ideas about what works, and thus gain broad legitimacy? Or will it rather be looked upon as an unbearable attempt to reduce the multi-paradigmatic features of existing educational research in order to elevate more mono-paradigmatic quantifiable measuring to the legitimate standard for producing truths to teachers and pre-school teachers (e.g. Borgnakke et al. 2006; Christensen and Krejsler 2013; Lihme 2005;

MandagMorgen 2004; Moos et al. 2005; Thorslund 2005; Utdanningsforbundet 2008)? Or will it be ignored?

In summary, we observe that the evidence discourse is subtly transformed as it travels from a medical context to an education context. The educational research community and professionals appear to have less of a say than policy-makers and administrators. Human capital and knowledge economy discourses visibly intervene, carried forth by strong transnational players, the OECD in particular. A truth regime that often resonates poorly with existing discourses and regimes for producing truths about what works among the bulk of professionals has to be accommodated (Ball 2007; Biesta 2007, 2010).

## 'Evidence', 'What Works' and the Reconfiguration of Dominant Policy

The expansion of the evidence discourse from the medical field to education signifies the establishment of a dominant discursive formation that cannot be ignored. Thus, in a Danish context, Nordic Cochrane, Nordic Campbell Centre and the Danish Clearinghouse for Educational Research were all established in alliance with dominant players in Danish society such as the National Board of Health, the Ministry of Health, the Ministry of Social Welfare, the Ministry of Education and the Ministry of Science, Technology & Innovation (Bhatti et al. 2006; Moos et al. 2005). Nordic Cochrane and Nordic Campbell Centre received substantial supplementary funding from the Ministry of Health and the Ministry of Social Welfare, which, however, was not the case with the Danish Clearinghouse for Educational Research. In England, the Evidence for Policy and Practice Information & Co-Ordination Centre (EPPI), the Campbell Collaboration and other key evidence-producing institutions succeeded in elevating this truth regime into a dominant discourse by joining forces with New Labour and its interest in legitimizing policy choices with reference to evidence-based or, at least, evidence-informed scientific backing (e.g. Furlong et al. 2009a, b; Oakley 2007; Wells 2007).

As already argued, the evidence discourse is furthermore closely aligned with dominant players on the global stage such as the OECD and EU, as knowledge economy discourse surges (e.g. Henry et al. 2001; Krejsler et al. 2014; Pawson 2006). It is part of a global regime of knowledge that standardizes knowledge production across national boundaries and academic disciplines (Larner and Walters 2004; Nóvoa and Yariv-Mashal 2003). Comparisons and rankings of countries gain ground as education and the competitiveness of nations are increasingly linked discursively (Henry et al. 2001; Hopmann 2008; Meyer and Benavot 2013; Nóvoa and Lawn 2002).

New Public Management strategies are employed to implement the idea of a market of public services, which presupposes a market of competing suppliers of services that are comparable and transparent to consumers (Hood 1995;

Sahlin-Andersson 2001). Here, the evidence discourse expediently offers a methodology that makes services measurable and comparable with the explicit purpose of exposing what works (Hammersley 2013; OECD 2007; Pawson 2006; Prewitt 2012; Rieper and Hansen 2007). A seductive imagery of standards and transparency is produced, which comes in handy for policy-makers and practitioners who need simplified criteria for prioritizing choices in a complex world abounding with information and possible choices. Floating signifiers like 'freedom', 'quality', 'choice' and 'evidence' profoundly influence health services and education as consumers are allotted tax-financed vouchers to choose among public services made comparable in order to optimize what they believe will provide the best treatment or learning environment.

In light of the battles with positivism in the late 1960s and the rise of social constructivism since the 1980s, it is noteworthy that the evidence discourse drawing, as it does so explicitly, on neo-positivist ideals, succeeds in gaining such momentum within the hitherto largely humanities and social sciences dominated fields of education (Alvesson and Skjöldberg 2000; Gibbons 1994; Habermas 1971; Hammersley 2013; Lyotard 1999/1984).

## Thinking 'Evidence' and 'What Works' Differently: Exploring the Potentials of a Floating Signifier

The rise of the evidence discourse as a dominant truth regime draws attention to the fact that over time, different academic and professional fields have developed different criteria for producing truths, in basic research as well as applied research (Clarke 2006; Gibbons 1994; Habermas 1971; Hammersley 2007). They exercise different functions, serve different stakeholders, and produce, consequently, different knowledge bases that represent different approaches to what works. This, however, is no argument for not continuously scrutinizing whether already established criteria for scientific practice are unduly taken for granted. Nonetheless, it brings into question whether the RCT-based or similar criteria for evidence may be ascribed universal validity across academic and professional boundaries. Among many educational researchers and practitioners, contestation is rising against an evidence discourse that is experienced as largely disregarding the 'nature' and particularities of the educational field as they understand it (Ball 2007; Biesta 2007, 2010; Hammersley 2013).

Nevertheless, it is recognized that the field of education is under increasing pressure from external stakeholders to document what works according to particular formats, as public debate increasingly takes direction from what counts as evidence in large-scale international quantitative comparisons. This is largely driven by a pressure to produce so-called certain knowledge which, allegedly, makes it easier to prioritize interventions with a proven track record in education and thus make more efficient use of limited tax revenue. The OECD PISA surveys have been particularly influential in shaping national agendas in that direction (Hopmann 2008; Meyer and Benavot 2013). It is still highly disputed, however, among educational researchers and professionals whether the breakthrough of the evidence discourse in the form of quantitative measuring, statistics, rankings, benchmarking and so forth actually increases the overall quality of education (Biesta 2010; Hammersley 2013). A strong critical voice, Stephen J. Ball (2007), warns that educational studies should not be reduced to a mere technician's approach to finding tools that work, thereby potentially excluding the role of the intellectual's theoretically informed approach to research.

In order to manoeuver within the opportunities and pitfalls of this new – and at times treacherous – discursive landscape, I suggest that we enter into a struggle to expand the meanings of evidence and ideas of what works in ways that link constructively to the long genealogies of producing truths within different professional languages and academic disciplines in education. In claiming to serve the public good, I do this to emphasize that evidence and what works should be dealt with as means to an end: better education. Education – as well as other professional fields – first and foremost needs professionals who can exercise professional judgment according to the educational situation to be dealt with. Obviously they need knowledge about what works, but the question about which knowledge that works, many would argue, can seldom be decided in advance and independently of the educational situation in question. Consequently, it becomes evident – in my mind – that it would be a tactical blunder of considerable dimensions to voluntarily surrender the right to define the floating signifiers of evidence and what works too quickly and conclusively to the dominant evidence discourse and its particular staging of how one produces evidence about education. What counts as evidence about what works in relation to a given issue thus appears to merit – more often than not – a rigorous appraisal of the 'nature' of the professional field and the influence of the particular context involved.

Working with evidence as a floating signifier requires careful appreciation of the actual strategic spaces available in current policy and scientific discourse and their associated contexts. Nonetheless, by engaging in constantly challenging the limits of the actual possible one may find spaces and opportunities to expand and – possibly – loosen bits of meaning of evidence from the currently dominant evidence discourse (Deleuze and Guattari 1994; Krejsler 2006, 2016).

In this light, I suggest that we introduce three analytical distinctions into the evidence discourse to sharpen the gaze when the educational researcher or professional manoeuvers within current evidence and what works discourse:

1. A distinction between *evidence-based* and *evidence-informed* knowledge allows for distinction between 'hard' and 'soft' evidence issues;
2. A distinction between *global* and *local forms of evidence* enables distinction between a global form of evidence that is valid among all within a well-defined group of intervention across contextual particularities and a local form of evidence that primarily makes sense with reference to the particularities of the context involved;

3. A distinction between *external* and *internal forms of evidence* makes visible the distribution of power relations concerning who owns the right to produce legitimate knowledge about what works.

## *Evidence-Based or Evidence-Informed Knowledge and Professional Discretion*

Following the genealogy of evidence discourse closely will reveal that as it moves from medicine towards 'softer' areas such as education, the need for a distinction between evidence-based and evidence-informed knowledge about what works gradually develops (e.g. Hammersley 2013; Hammersley 2007). In medicine, it often – but not always – makes perfect sense to talk about *evidence-based* knowledge about what works, i.e. causal or quasi-causal knowledge. In education, however, contextual factors often – but not always – become so important that it makes sense to talk more humbly about *evidence-informed* knowledge. In relation to a pill for headaches, it usually makes sense to talk about evidence-based knowledge; however, when doing counseling in relation to a child at school whose parents are in the process of being divorced, it is mostly difficult to speak of what works in a strong sense. This does not mean, however, that choice of interventions cannot be informed by knowledge about what works although decisions will often require close and careful reference to the particular context, the ones involved as well as appreciation of and dialogue about the issue as it evolves.

Even strong proponents of dominant evidence approaches, like Ann Oakley, previous director of EPPI (2007) and David H. Hargreaves (2007) concede that in softer, multi-paradigmatic policy-fields it makes sense to speak more tentatively about *evidence-informed policy and practice* rather than employing a more rigorous *evidence-based* approach like the one within the medical field. Further, as mentioned, the similar but broader approaches to looking for correlations based on large quantitative systematic reviews, like those carried out by researchers such as John Hattie, are gaining considerable momentum (Hattie 2009). Already existing approaches to synthesizing knowledge about what works offer potential alliance partners in challenging the dominant evidence discourse in ways that resonate better with understandings among professionals and researchers of various paradigms. For instance, the strong German tradition represented by Hilbert Meyer and Andreas Helmke among others has attempted to make more inclusive and narrative syntheses of what research claims works in education (Helmke et al. 2008; Meyer 2004). For instance, in *Was ist guter Unterricht?* (What is good teaching?) Hilbert Meyer concludes that research shows considerable agreement that there are traits which characterize good teaching across contexts, including: it is well structured; the teachers know their subject; methods cannot be chosen independently of context; and teaching that works takes into consideration the individual differences and learning needs of students. Syntheses of the latter kind have been criticized for being so general that they do not offer much guidance to teachers in relation to concrete instruction. They do not capture the causal or quasi-causal relations that the dominant evidence regime is looking for, and they do not isolate particular methods, ways of organizing class and so forth in manners that are valid across contexts as global evidence. The counterargument is that this level of generality reflects the contextually dependent 'nature' of most educational issues.

## *Global Versus Local Forms of Evidence: Which Kind of Knowledge Is Relevant?*

Here, focus is on the features of the knowledge base that is applied to deal with professional issues (e.g. Moos et al. 2005). *Global evidence* represents knowledge that is valid with large probability for all within a well-defined group of intervention, for example taking a particular medicine against a certain type of symptoms, or the application of a particular reading method to deal with particular pronunciation problems. Most dominant evidence-discourse aspires for knowledge about what works that represents global evidence. *Local evidence* points to the importance of contextual knowledge for deciding whether a given intervention is likely to work.

Local evidence should not be confused with what is called internal evidence in the following section, which rather refers to the aspect of who demands that a particular kind of knowledge shall be applied, be it external or internal stakeholders. Local evidence refers to a kind of knowledge production that is sensitive to local contexts and may or may not be relevant in other contexts. Production of this kind of – often qualitative – knowledge often employs other research paradigms, such as action research that directly involves students, teachers and other stakeholders in producing knowledge about what works, or ethnographic qualitative approaches that are sensitive to the particularities of a given school and classroom culture located within a particular local, social, ethnic and national culture. What counts as evidence and what works as best practice for a nurse in their care for a particular patient is often hard to settle without reference to the particular context, i.e. local evidence: is it a cancerous patient overwhelmed by fear of death? Is the patient a child, an elderly spouse or a single and lonely patient without relatives? Is the patient religious or an atheist? Here, it hardly makes sense to apply methods that fit all. The same would often apply to the teacher dealing with a child in crisis, and so forth.

Since the 1960s and 1970s, individualizing discourse has developed into a particularly strong regime for producing concepts and technologies that resonate with local evidence and context sensitivity. Over the decades, this discourse has highlighted a plethora of terminologies about the academic, social and personal competences to be developed by students in each their individual way, be it the self-realization, project-oriented, unique individuality or the lifelong learner version (Gardner 2011; Gartenschlaeger and Hinzen 2001; Rogers 1969). Here, demands for evidence that particular interventions work refer more to professionals' and students' process evaluation within the institution, i.e. local forms of evidence. The social technologies employed to produce evidence of student achievement would be project work, log books, portfolios, social contracts, formative evaluation and so forth. Attention is directed at dialogue, supervision and other process technologies that reflect interaction between teacher and students. At an organisational level, appraisal interviews with teachers and teams of teachers, and dialogue with parents are employed (Krejsler 2006, 2007). When society increasingly demands that individuals learn to document their particular academic, social and personal competences, obviously school will be required to produce evidence that students acquire such competences (Undervisningsministeriet (Danish Ministry of Education) 1996, 2003). It may be reasonably assumed that a host of knowledge and practices developed and practiced by the teaching profession for decades qualifies as evidence for best practice, be it project work, log books, portfolios, self-appraisal or social contracts. Concerning educational research, Stephen Kemmis argues that participatory action research, which involves teachers and students, is an indispensable approach to producing knowledge and practices, i.e. an alternative understanding of evidence for what works (Kemmis 2007). Obviously, even local forms of evidence should be scrutinised for their potentials and pitfalls, as has been done extensively by, among others, Foucault-inspired educational research (e.g. Krejsler 2006; Popkewitz 1998; Rose 1999/1989).

Most educational situations, however, tend to call for interventions that make use of both global and local forms of evidence. Even within contextually very particular situations there are plenty of partial aspects that may benefit from reference to global evidence. For the nurse, this could be knowledge about and access to pain-relieving medicine. For the teacher, it could be knowledge about and access to methods for learning links between sound and letters, knowledge about physiological development for children of particular ages and ensuing learning barriers, and so forth. Exercise of professional discretion here demands that professionals have significant mastery of various theories and methods representing both global and local forms of evidence that can be brought into play when a given practice must be dealt with. Global and local forms of evidence are here exposed as 'just' the means – or the repertoire of knowledge – that professionals draw on when performing the art of exercising professional judgment in situations of application. *Blind evidence* refers to situations where global or local forms of evidence are applied blindly by virtue of habit, dogmatism or tradition, i.e. where professional judgment is suspended when it comes to determining whether one or the other form of evidence should be applied to a concrete situation.

Even strong proponents of the dominant evidence and what works truth regime, such as Professor Robert E. Slavin, director of the Center for Research and Reform in Education at Johns Hopkins University, shows considerable understanding for employing the distinction between global and local evidence, albeit from a narrower epistemological perspective than argued in this chapter:

> However, there is a big distinction between two kinds of good evidence that I think it is useful to make … One kind of good evidence relates to proven programs … A hallmark of proven programs is that they are designed for replication … The other type of good evidence, local evidence, is derived internally to a given school, district, city, or state. Such evidence helps policymakers and educators understand their own situation, opportunities, and problems, and to evaluate policies or practices already underway or being considered. Such data may be particularly valued by the local leadership, because it addresses problems they care about, but it is not intended to produce answers to universal problems, except perhaps as a byproduct … Of course, proven programs and local evidence can overlap, as when a given district or state implements and evaluates a replicable program that responds to its own needs … Because the local leadership was involved all along, they may have greater commitment to obtaining good data and then acting on it. Local evaluations exist in a particular context, which may make the findings of interest in that context and in other places with similar contexts … As we build up stronger and broader evidence of both kinds (i.e. proven programs and local evidence (JBK)), it will be important to learn how each contributes to learning about optimal practice in education. (Slavin 2016)

## *External or Internal Evidence: Who Has the Decision-Making Powers to Require Which Knowledge Should Be Applied?*

Whereas the above distinction between global and local forms of evidence focuses on differences in the forms of knowledge that the professional may employ, the distinction between external or internal evidence asks who has the right to make the decisions about which forms of evidence should be applied. External evidence refers to requirements that external stakeholders such as politicians, officials, administrators or external experts impose upon a given professional area, its organizations and professionals. Internal evidence refers to knowledge and evidence for what works that professionals and associated researchers choose to develop and apply based on research, development and practice within their field, be it global or local forms of evidence.

*External evidence* typically refers to situations where policy-makers or national and municipal funding bodies require that professionals use special methods or approaches when it comes to documenting that there is evidence showing that applied interventions have effects that work better than other available interventions. When such external evidence demands are linked to funding or specific municipal or national quality assurance measures, they usually have the effect that professional practices are aligned to satisfy such requirements. Here, one may find that external evidence tends to impact on educational practice by enhancing attention towards fulfilling the demands that are required. This may produce positive effects in that students know which well-defined demands to achieve. It may even ensure that most students achieve some basic literacy and numeracy skills. Further, it may encourage professionals to become more systematic and stringent in conceptualizing and implementing interventions that may previously have been conducted with less reflection, relying more on tradition and habits. This may ensure that systematic methods are applied, and that obligations are honored to measure and compare individuals' behavior before and after a given intervention in quantitative terms, across organizations, municipalities and nations. This may lead to development of a reservoir of knowledge to provide overview of the multitude of possible interventions, and potentially develop global evidence that may qualify professional judgment. When professionals know that they are expected to abide by relatively well-defined requirements, they may actually enhance performance due to having tangible demands to live up to. This may provide some certainty in working procedures to ensure that all clients/users meet some basic requirements in relation to social skills, job readiness or other demands.

Inversely, however, it may produce negative effects in terms of undermining trust-based relationships between external stakeholders and large sections of professionals and the educational research community. The latter may experience a loss of ownership and professional autonomy in relation to the practice they are required to exercise professional judgment within or produce knowledge about. When professionals experience that, first and foremost, they are expected to abide by a given manual, they may – as a consequence – lose attention to all the other potential solutions to the problem which their professional repertoire might otherwise have sensitized them to activate. This could mean that interventions that do not fit into an experimental and quantifiable design are likely to be excluded; not because they do not work, but because their effects cannot be made comparable or measured in Randomized Controlled Trials or similar formats. Interventions based on qualitative methods that seek to adapt approaches to the particular context will not be chosen – e.g. an approach that seeks to involve, by means of explorative dialogue, the clients whose resources are assumed pivotal to engage in order to make real and long-lasting changes in habits and lifestyle. The imposition of external evidence measures may result in substantial washback effects on interpretation of curricula and on teaching (e.g. Graham 2006). If demands are primarily directed at literacy, numeracy and science subjects – as is currently the case in Denmark and in the PISA surveys – it may be at the expense of other subject areas such as history, music, arts and physical education. It may turn much social and educational work unnecessarily instrumental. There is a risk that the cultural heritage may lose some of its features of having a value in its own right – in contributing to developing 'the good life' and 'the good society' – if students experience that they come to school mainly to get good grades and do well in tests (Biesta 2007, 2010; Hammersley 2013).

In contrast, *internal evidence* points to knowledge and practice which professionals and/or associated researchers choose to develop and apply within their organizations, and which simultaneously works to qualify their knowledge base and professional practice. Such practice involves various mixtures of global and local forms of evidence. In order to qualify such a concept of internal evidence, it must be linked with procedures regarding how local practice may be continuously qualified on a scientific basis. If one blindly exalts local traditions and knowledge of what we usually do to 'knowledge about what works', one's knowledge base is in imminent danger of becoming provincialized. As an example, the Norwegian educational philosopher Erling Lars Dale spent much of his career developing a scientific and systematic approach to conceptualizing how internal evidence about what works can be qualified – an approach aimed at integrating global forms of evidence with local forms of evidence. Dale developed the notion of 'didactic rationality', built on pedagogy as a scientific discipline and as a criterion for adequate scientific justification of educational practice (e.g. Dale 2008). The main idea is that an educational practice can only count as rational if there is a systematic link between three levels of competence and the corresponding role expectations: K1 (to carry out teaching/educational practice), K2 (to construct teaching/educational programs) and K3 (to communicate on the basis of and construct didactic theory). At the K1 level, the professional teacher exercises the role of teaching and is subject to immediate demands to act. At K2 level, the professional exercises the role of being a team colleague, and plans instruction and class activities for the immediate future. Here, they are under suspended demands to act within the context of a compelling local school culture, a particular mix of students and given local, municipal and national frameworks. At competence level K3, the professional exercises the role of researcher in their own professional practice. Here, the professional is freed from the demand to act which everyday school life and its context usually impose upon them. And the practice levels K1 and K2 can be questioned and discussed in relation to the larger societal contexts which frame them. To the extent that the professional can build up systematic coherence between the three levels of competence on a scientific base, their practice acquires the potential to qualify and develop evidence, i.e. 'knowledge about what works'. Other approaches that resonate with such an understanding of developing internal evidence would draw on concepts such as the reflective practitioner, the transition from novice to expert, tacit knowledge, communities of practice and so forth (Dreyfus and Dreyfus 1986; Polanyi 1967; Schön 1983; Wenger 1998).

## Join the Struggle to Expand 'Evidence' and 'What Works'!

As education and other public service areas are linked to global knowledge economy discourse (e.g. Henry et al. 2001; Larner and Walters 2004; OECD 2007; Rizvi and Lingard 2010), a growing need is produced for instruments to prioritize an increasing number of possible interventions in education to optimize learning within a framework of limited tax resources (Prewitt 2012; Sahlin-Andersson 2001). This state of affairs has facilitated the advent of a particular dominant evidence discourse for producing knowledge about what works which tends to reduce the kinds of knowledge and approaches that will be deemed legitimate and funded by states under pressure. This is done to reduce the public services expenditure and to better their perceived rankings among competing knowledge economies (Hammersley 2013; OECD 2007; Wells 2007). Consequently, the need to enable evidence-based or evidence-informed choices about what works is growing (Prewitt 2012). This chapter has had the double purpose of (1) mapping the genealogy of this discourse in order to (2) enable the reader to constructively join the cultural struggle about defining and, hopefully, expanding how knowledge about what works can be defined.

Establishing the regime of truth regarding what counts as evidence about education and other public services is obviously a high-stakes endeavour that includes dominant players in society and has serious implications for what may count as public good. Recognizing this pressure, this chapter argues that a fruitful strategy for educational researchers and professionals may be to adopt the concept of evidence as a *floating signifier* (Laclau 1993). It is argued that this may prove helpful in their struggle to expand the meanings of evidence to also cover substantial parts of their professional knowledge and experience. In the long run, this may prove beneficial also to students, citizens, consumers, policy-makers and others, as a considerably broader knowledge and experience base will come to inform how education – but also health and social welfare – practices are carried out. And thus public good will be served!

Viewing and dealing with evidence as part of a cultural struggle is, as argued in this chapter, no easy endeavour. If one aspires to be taken seriously, it requires up-to-date knowledge about, and proficiency in, how to play the complex constellations of subject positions among policy, market and professional players who compose the game to be mastered.

From the point of departure of understanding evidence as a floating signifier whose meanings can be expanded, the reader is incited to venture into the struggle with aid and inspiration from three analytical distinctions:

- Between evidence-based and evidence-informed knowledge;
- Between global and local forms of evidence; and
- Between external and internal evidence.

This serves the purpose of enabling professionals and others to think differently as they struggle to come to terms with the potentials and pitfalls of the pressure from the evidence discourse (Krejsler 2016). This chapter thus constitutes an encouragement to engage in the battle about what *public good* may be and become in terms of defining *what works* in public services, recognizing the particular challenges posed by the advent of *the evidence discourse*.

## References

Alvesson, M., & Skjöldberg, K. (2000). *Reflexive methodology: New vistas for qualitative research*. London: Sage Publications.

Ball, S. J. (2007). Intellectuals or technicians?: The urgent role of theory in educational studies. In M. Hammersley (Ed.), *Educational research and evidence-based practice* (pp. 106–120). London: SAGE. (in collaboration with Open University Press).

Bergmark, A., Lundström, T. (2006). Mot en evidensbaserad praktik? Om färdriktningen i socialt arbete [Towards and evidence-based practice? On the direction of social work]. *Socialvetenskaplig Tidskrift* (2/2006), 99–113.

Bhatti, Y., Hansen, H. F., & Rieper, O. (2006). *Evidensbevægelsens udvikling, organisering og arbejdsform: En kortlægningsrapport [The evidence movement, its development, organization and work form: A mapping report]*. Copenhagen: AKF-Forlaget.
Biesta, G. (2007). Why 'what works' won't work: Evidence-based practice and the democratic deficit in educational research. *Educational Theory, 57*(1), 1–22.
Biesta, G. (2010). Why 'what works' still won't work: From evidence-based to value-based education. *Studies in Philosophy and Education, 29*(5), 491–503.
Borgnakke, K., Hauberg Mortensen, F., Rasmussen, P., Salling Olesen, H. (2006). Evidens – hvad kan det bruges til? [Evidence: What is it good for?]. *Forskerforum*, 17–19.
Boruch, R. F., & Herman, R. (2007). What works clearinghouse: United States. In T. Burns & T. Schuller (Eds.), *Evindence in education: Linking research and policy* (pp. 53–62). Paris: OECD/CERI.
Brophy, J., & Good, T. L. (1986). Teacher behavior and student achievement. In M. C. Wittrok (Ed.), *Handbook of research on teaching* (3rd ed.). New York: Macmillan Publishing Company.
Browman, G. P. (1999). Essence of evidence-based medicine: A case report. *Journal of Clinical Oncology, 17*(7).
Burns, T., & Schuller, T. (2007). The evidence agenda. In T. Burns & T. Schuller (Eds.), *Evidence in education: Linking research and policy* (pp. 15–32). Paris: OECD.
Christensen, S., & Krejsler, J. B. (2013). *Evidens: Kampen om viden der virker [Evidence: The struggle about knowledge that works]*. Copenhagen: FOA.
Clarke, A. (2006). Evidence-based evaluation in different professional domains: Similarities, differences and challenges. In I. F. Shaw, J. C. Greene, & M. M. Mark (Eds.), *The SAGE handbook of evaluation* (pp. 559–581). London: SAGE Publications.
Coalition for Evidence-Based Policy. (2003). *Identifying and implementing educational practices supported by rigorous evidence: A user friendly guide*. Washington D.C.: U.S. Department of Education.
Cochrane, A. (1972). *Effectiveness and efficiency – random reflections on health services*. London: Nuffield Provincial Hospitals Trust.
Dale, E. L. (2008). *Pædagogik og professionalitet [Education and professionalism]*. Aarhus: Klim.
Deleuze, G., & Guattari, F. (1994). *What is philosophy?* New York: Columbia University Press.
Dreyfus, H., & Dreyfus, S. (1986). *Mind over machine*. New York: Free Press.
Foucault, M. (1971). *L'ordre du discours; leçon inaugurale au Collège de France prononcée le 2 décembre 1970 [The order of discourse]*. Paris: Gallimard.
Foucault, M. (1993). Qu'est-ce que les Lumières? [What is enlightenment?]. *Magazine Littéraire, 309*, 61–74.
Foucault, M. (1997). On the genealogy of ethics – an overview of work in progress. In P. Rabinow (Ed.), *Foucault – ethics, subjectivity and truth (Essential works of foucault 1954–1984)* (Vol. 1, pp. 253–280). New York: The New Press.
Furlong, J., Cochran-Smith, M., & Brennan, M. (Eds.). (2009a). *Policy and politics in teacher education: International perspectives*. New York: Routledge.
Furlong, J., McNamara, O., Campbell, A., Howson, J., & Lewis, S. (2009b). Partnership, policy and politics: Initial teacher education in England under new labour. In J. Furlong, M. Cochran-Smith, & M. Brennan (Eds.), *Policy and politics in teacher education: International perspectives* (pp. 45–56). New York: Routledge.
Gardner, H. (2011). *Truth, beauty, and goodness reframed: Educating for the virtues in the 21st century*. New York: Basic Books.
Gartenschlaeger, U., & Hinzen, H. (2001). *Prospects and trends in adult education: A selection of contemporary writing on project work*. Bonn: Institute for International Cooperation of the German Adult Education Association (IIZ/DVV).
Gibbons, M. T., Martin, & Scott, P. (1994). *The new production of knowledge: The dynamics of science and research in contemporary societies*. London: SAGE.
Good, T. L., & Brophy, J. (2003). *Looking in classrooms* (9th ed.). Boston: Allyn & Bacon.
Graham, J. (2006). The drivers of change. *Professional Voice, 4*(2), 1–10.

Habermas, J. (1971). *Knowledge and human interests*. Boston: Beacon Press.
Hamilton, L. S., Stecher, B. M., & Yuan, K. (2008). *Standards-based reform in the United States: History, research, and future directions*. Retrieved from RAND Corporation, Washington, DC: http://www.rand.org/content/dam/rand/pubs/reprints/2009/RAND_RP1384.pdf
Hammersley, M. (Ed.). (2007). *Educational research and evidence-based practice*. London: Sage. (In collaboration with Open University Press).
Hammersley, M. (2013). *The myth of research-based policy and practice*. London: SAGE.
Hargreaves, D. H. (2007). Teaching as a research-based profession: Possibilities and prospects. In M. Hammersley (Ed.), *Educational research and evidence-based practice* (pp. 3–17). London: SAGE. (in collaboration with Open University Press).
Hattie, J. (2009). *Visible learning: A synthesis of over 800 meta-analyses relating to achievement*. New York: Routledge.
Helmke, A., Walter, C., Lankes, E.-M., Ditton, H., Eikenbusch, G., Pfiffner, M., & Christiansen, J. P. (2008). *Hvad vi ved om god undervisning [What we know about good teaching]*. Frederikshavn: Dafolo.
Henry, M., Lingard, B., Rizvi, F., & Taylor, S. (2001). *The OECD, globalisation and education policy*. Oxford: IAU Press & Elsevier Science Ltd..
Hood, C. (1995). The "new public management" in the 1980s: Variations on a theme. *Accounting, Organizations & Society, 20*, 93–109.
Hopmann, S. T. (2008). No child, no school, no state left behind: Schooling in the age of accountability. *Journal of Curriculum Studies, 40*, 417–456.
Kemmis, S. (2007). Action research. In M. Hammersley (Ed.), *Educational research and evidence-based practice* (pp. 167–180). London: Sage. (In collaboration with Open University Press).
Krejsler, J. (2006). Education and individualizing technologies: Exploring new conditions for producing individuality. In T. S. Popkewitz, U. Olsson, K. Petersson, & J. Kowalczyk (Eds.), *The future is not what it appears to be – pegagogy, genealogy and political epistemology* (pp. 193–212). Stockholm: HLS Förlag.
Krejsler, J. (2007). Discursive strategies that individualize: CVs and appraisal interviews. *International Journal of Qualitative Studies in Education, 20*(4), 473–490.
Krejsler, J. B. (2013). 'What works' in education and social welfare?: A mapping of the evidence discourse and reflections upon consequences for professionals. *Scandinavian Journal of Educational Research, 57*(1), 16–32.
Krejsler, J. B. (2016). Seize the opportunity to think differently!: A Deleuzian approach to unleashing becomings in education. *Educational Philosophy and Theory*. http://dx.doi.org/10.1080/00131857.2016.1163247
Krejsler, J. B. (2017(forthcoming)). Imagining school as standards-driven and students as career-ready! A comparative genealogy of US federal and European transnational turns in education policy. In N. Hobbel & B. Bales (Eds.), *Teacher education and the common good: International perspectives*. New York/London: Routledge.
Krejsler, J. B., Olsson, U., & Petersson, K. (2014). The transnational grip on Scandinavian education reforms: The open method of coordination challenging national policy-making. *Nordic Studies in Education, 34*(3), 172–186.
Laclau, E. (1993). Politics and the limits of modernity. In T. Docherty (Ed.), *Postmodernism: A reader*. New York: Harvester.
Larner, W., & Walters, W. (Eds.). (2004). *Global governmentality: Governing international spaces*. New York/London: Routledge.
Lihme, B. (2005). Tema: måling og evidens [Theme: Measuring and evidence]. *Social Kritik – Tidsskrift for social analyse og debat*. Retrieved from.
Lyotard, J.-F. (1999/1984). *The postmodern condition: A report on knowledge* (trans: Bennington, G., & Massumi, B., Vol. 10). Minneapolis: University of Minnesota Press.
MandagMorgen. (2004). *Virker velfærden? – Et debatoplæg om evidens og velfærd [Does Welfare Work? – A discussion paper on evidence and welfare]*. Copenhagen: Huset Mandag Morgen.
Meyer, H. (2004). *Was ist guter Unterricht?[What is good teaching?]*. Berlin: Cornelsen, Scriptor.

Meyer, H.-D., & Benavot, A. E. (Eds.). (2013). *PISA, power, and policy: The emergence of global educational governance*. Oxford: Symposium Books.
Moos, L., Krejsler, J., Hjort, K., Laursen, P. F., & Braad, K. B. (2005). *Evidens i uddannelse? [Evidence in education?]*. Copenhagen: The Danish University of Education Press.
Nóvoa, A., & Lawn, M. (Eds.). (2002). *Fabricating Europe: The formation of an education space*. Dordrecht: Kluwer Academic Publishers.
Nóvoa, A., & Yariv-Mashal, T. (2003). Comparative research in education: A mode of governance or a historical journey? *Comparative Education, 39*(4), 423–438. doi:1360-0486.
Oakley, A. (2007). Evidence-informed policy and practice: Challenges for social science. In M. Hammersley (Ed.), *Educational research and evidence-based practice* (pp. 91–105). London: SAGE. (in collaboration with Open University Press).
OECD. (1996). *The knowledge based economy*. Paris: OECD.
OECD. (2007). *Evidence in education: Linking research and policy*. Paris: OECD.
OECD/CERI. (2004). *National review on educational R&D: Examiners' report on Denmark*. Paris: OECD/CERI. (http://www.vtu.dk/fsk/div/unisoejlen/NationalReviews.28.10.04.pdf).
Oscarsson, L. (2006). Evidenskravet och socialt arbete [The demand of evidence and social work]. *Socionomen* (4/2006).
Pawson, R. (2006). *Evidence based policy: A realist perspective*. London: Sage.
Petrosine, A., Boruch, R. F., Soydan, H., Duggan, L., & Sanchez-Meca, J. (2001). Meeting the challenges of evidence-based policy: The campbell collaboration. *The Annals of the American Academy of Political and Social Science, 578*(1), 14–34.
Polanyi, M. (1967). *The tacit dimension*. London: Routledge & K. Paul.
Popkewitz, T. S. (1998). Struggling for the soul: The politics of schooling and the construction of the teacher. New York/London: Teachers College Press.
Prewitt, K. S., Thomas, A., & Straf, M. L. (Eds.). (2012). *Using science as evidence in public policy*. Atlanta: National Academies Press.
Rieper, O., & Hansen, H. F. (2007). *Metodedebatten om evidens* [The method debate about evidence]. Copenhagen: AKF-Forlaget.
Rizvi, F., & Lingard, B. (2010). *Globalizing education policy*. London/New York: Routledge.
Rogers, C. (1969). *Freedom to learn: A view of what education might become*. Columbus: Charles Merill.
Rose, N. (1999/1989). *Governing the soul: The shaping of the private self*. London/New York: Free Association Books.
Sackett, D. L., Rosenberg, W. M. C., Gray, J. A. M., Haynes, B. R., & Richardson, S. W. (1996). Evidence based medicine: What it is and what it isn't (Editorial). *BMJ, 312*, 71–72.
Sahlin-Andersson, K. (2001). National, international and transnational constructions of new public management. In T. Christensen & P. Lægreid (Eds.), *New public management—the transformation of ideas and practice* (pp. 43–72). Aldershot: Ashgate.
Schön, D. A. (1983). *The reflective practitioner: How professionals think in action*. London: Temple Smith.
Slavin, R. E. (2016). *Proven programs vs. local evidence*. Retrieved from http://www.huffingtonpost.com/robert-e-slavin/proven-programs-vs-local_b_9038560.html
Telhaug, A. O., Mediås, O. A., & Aasen, P. (2006). The nordic model in education: Education as part of the political system in the last 50 years. *Scandinavian Journal of Educational Research, 50*(3), 245–283.
Thorslund, J. (2005). Evidens og pædagogik – så kom den ventede diskussion [Evidence and Education – the expected debate finally arrived]. *AGORA – tidsskrift for forskning, udvikling og idéudveksling i professioner*. No.7. September 2005. Copenhagen: CVU Storkøbenhavn.
U.S. Department of Education. (2002). *No child left behind: A desktop reference*. Washington, DC. Retrieved from https://www2.ed.gov/admins/lead/account/nclbreference/reference.pdf
Undervisningsministeriet (Danish Ministry of Education). (1996). *Udvikling af personlige kvalifikationer i uddannelsessystemet* [The development of personal qualifications in the education system]. Copenhagen: The Ministry of Education.

Undervisningsministeriet (Danish Ministry of Education). (2003). *Fælles Mål – herunder "Elevens alsidige personlig udvikling* [Common goals – including" the student's allround personal development]. Copenhagen: The Ministry of Education.

Utdanningsforbundet (Union of Education Norway). (2008). *Evidens og evidensdebattens betydning for utdanningssystemet* [The impact of evidence and the evidence debate on the educational system]. Oslo: Utdanningsforbundet, Avdelning for Utredning.

Wells, P. (2007). New labour and evidence based policy making: 1997–2007. *People, Place & Policy Online, 1*, 22–29.

Wenger, E. (1998). *Communities of practice: Learning, meaning, and identity*. Cambridge: Cambridge University Press.

Zucker, S. (2004). *Scientifically based research: NCLB and assessment*. Retrieved from Pearson Education Inc., San Antonio TX: http://images.pearsonassessments.com/images/tmrs/tmrs_rg/ScientificallyBasedResearch.pdf

# Chapter 3
# What Is Evidence Required for and Who Generates That Evidence in the Finnish Educational System?

**Hannele Niemi**

**Abstract** The article will analyze the major opportunities as well as the difficulties in providing and applying research- and evidence-based knowledge in the Finnish educational system. It asks what purposes evidence is required for and who provides that evidence. The chapter introduces the Finnish enhancement-led evaluation policy and its main principles relating to evidence production. In the Finnish system, evidence is a broad concept covering national and international evaluations, researcher contributions, and the practitioner's capacity to create evidence. In the Finnish educational system, evidence comes from different sources and is also discussed with different partners. Creating evidence is not a unidirectional process. It is a joint process where researchers, policy-makers, and practitioners work together in a complementary fashion. However, there are several challenges. Some difficulties arise from the disconnection between decision-makers at policy level. It is also very demanding to generate evidence for the whole educational ecosystem that has equity and lifelong learning as its main objectives. The third issue to overcome is how to disseminate and communicate evidence to different users.

## Introduction: Public or Common Good and Evidence in the Finnish Context

Daviet (2016) writes that in global public policy education has commonly been considered a public good. He refers to international organizations, particularly United Nations (UN) agencies and, among these, UNESCO, which have promoted the notion of a public good for decades. A "public good" has traditionally been defined using Samuelson's (1954) notion, whose remarkable criterion is that an individual's consumption of one leads to no subtractions from any other individual's

H. Niemi (✉)
Faculty of Educational Sciences, University of Helsinki, Helsinki, Finland
e-mail: hannele.niemi@helsinki.fi



M.Y. Eryaman, B. Schneider (eds.), *Evidence and Public Good in Educational Policy, Research and Practice*, Educational Governance Research 6,
DOI 10.1007/978-3-319-58850-6_3

consumption of it. In other classical definitions, such as Musgrave's, public goods are contrasted with private goods and services. Definitions of public good often assume that it is non-competitive and non-excludable, meaning that it is impossible to exclude any individuals from consuming the good (Musgrave 1969; Desmarais-Tremblay 2014). All these definitions come from economics and are rooted in neo-classical economic theories.

Recently, critical voices have emerged questioning the relevancy of these definitions in the changing educational landscape (UNESCO 2015). Daviet (2016) questions how well the economic conception of public good provides a real basis for understanding the social, cultural, and ethical dimensions of education. Daviet (2016, p. 5) warns: "The neoclassical theory, which undergirds the concept of public good in its largest sense, builds on a set of interrelated theoretical assumptions, among which are methodological individualism and utilitarianism. Methodological individualism considers a standard and abstract individual as a unit of analysis." Daviet sees how transforming governance models, the increasing involvement of civil society organizations, and the growing trend towards the privatization and commodification of education place the notion of a public good in a new situation. She asks how education can go can "beyond narrow utilitarianism and economism that is integrated with the multiple dimensions of human existence" and calls for a humanistic and holistic approach to the public good of education as an alternative to earlier economically rooted definitions. Her concept of a common good enables comprehension of the changes affecting the educational landscape by considering structures of governance and procurement that involve not only the state, but also a large variety of non-state actors. Finally, the concept of a common good, encompassing ethical and political concerns, provides a principle for rethinking the purpose of education. Daviet (2016, p. 8) defines common goods in the following way: "[T]hose [goods] that contribute to the general interest, enabling society as a whole to be reinforced and to function better, as well as individuals to live better. Therefore, common goods must benefit all. Defining what is a common good is a collective decision that involves the state, the market and civil society."

The discussion about public and common goods is very interesting from the viewpoint of the Finnish educational system. Equity in education has been a leading concept of the Finnish educational system since the late 1960s. Finnish basic education has been logically developed according to the comprehensive school model, which guarantees everyone equal opportunities in education irrespective of sex, social status, and ethnicity, among others, as outlined in the Constitution. Basic education is a basic right of citizenship. It is free of charge at the basic level and mainly also at other levels; even in higher educational settings, no tuition fees are charged for students from Finland or other European countries. Education in Finland is a public service, and the equity principle covers all educational levels from early childhood education to higher and adult education. Equity is related to the large societal issues to which education is one contributor; to other services, such as health and social welfare issues. All these contributions have the purpose of creating coherence in society. In educational services, the main point is how well the whole educational ecosystem system supports learning—not narrowly focusing on only cognitive learning outcomes, but paying more attention to the whole system's capacity to produce high quality services (Finnish National Board of Education [FNBE] 2016).

Education in Finland is publicly funded and, in fact, there are only a few private schools in the formal educational system. The private sector is also involved in adult education, and many public–private combinations exist. Even though education provided by public entities such municipals/cities, through the provision of teaching and learning materials, local facilities, and services, many connections to private companies exist. New digital learning environments also cross between the public and private spheres (Niemi et al. 2014). Finnish education fits within traditional definitions of public good in the sense that it is non-competitive and non-excludable in a wide sense. The main principle is that every school must provide a quality education so that parents need not worry about their children having access to the next level of the educational system. The Finnish system is decentralized, and the local needs of students and learners are seen as important. In this sense, the system comes close to Daviet's definition of common good because education may have different shapes and ways of being implemented depending on local conditions and communities. The understanding of a public or common good in Finland means that educational services go beyond pure economics and include the objective, or even norm, of supporting different learners for their future lives. It means common services for all, but also special support for those who have learning difficulties, including in some cases personalized learning routes that are publicly funded. This means that in certain situations public money and resources are allocated to the weakest students based on their learning difficulties. In that sense, a public good is exclusive because its consumption by some leads to subtractions from others' consumption of that good. The equity principle means that there are special support systems for those who would otherwise be in danger of dropping off later in life. We may conclude that education is public service guaranteed by the Constitution. It is publicly funded, but also has many features of a common good because its objectives include wider purposes, not only educational consumption. It aims for personal growth on an individual level, but also competence and skills that matter for the wellbeing of communities and the promotion of social coherence.

This requires that the concept of evidence for police and practice in education be seen from much wider perspectives than only economics or certain universal standards. As Luke et al. (2010) remark, the use of evidence and science to address issues of educational equity and social justice is not straightforward. They emphasize that, when defining evidence, we should see that educational systems are "profoundly troubled by complexity, diversity, and difference." In the Finnish case, the equity principle means that evidence comes not only from one source or actor. In the Finnish case, evidence is related to how the whole system works for equity and provides high quality education for all. In the Finnish discussion, having a value basis is a key issue. Evidence-based policy and practice are related to the values of education in the whole educational system (Laukkanen 2008; Niemi 2016; Sahlberg 2011). In addition to equity, the other important aim is to provide lifelong opportunities for all citizens. These objectives are connected to a decentralized educational administration and a curriculum that allows much freedom at the local level. Teachers' high standards of academic education and their professional roles create conditions that have a strong effect on evidence-based policy and practice. The special feature of evidence-based policy is enhancement-led evaluation, in which the main goal is to collect evidence for improvement, not for rankings.

In this chapter, these frames are considered and analyzed in terms of how they modify the concept of evidence in the Finnish educational system. The article has two questions: (1) What is evidence for, and (2) By whom and with whom is evidence created in the Finnish education system?

## What Is Evidence for in the Finnish Context?

The relationship between research, policy, and practice has been under discussion since 2000 in many academic publications and has also been the focus of policy-level discussions in many countries (e.g. Boaz et al. 2002; Hammersley 2004, 2005). Globally, the Organisation for Economic Cooperation and Development (OECD) has been very active in this discussion (Burns and Schuller 2007; Schuller 2006). Medicine is often referred to as a good example of evidence-based policy and practice, particularly its Cochrane system (www.cochrane.org/evidence), which provides the latest knowledge for practitioners and for public use. It is based on research work from the academic community and is transparent. In Finland, a similar open database called Good Care (*Käypä hoito*) is open to the public, providing information and suggestions for medical care via the Internet. In the international discussion there has been an active debate regarding education: Should a similar kind of database be created for education and is it possible? In this discussion, educational research and its capacity to provide evidence have often been subject to criticism. Tom Schuller (2006) notes and refers also to Angrist (2004) that educational research has been strongly criticized for its weakness in not even attempting to supply rigorous evidence on the effects of education. Some of the criticism concerns the low academic standing of educational research, and the low level of impact on policy or practice.

The OECD, CERI, and the EU Commission have repeatedly required more policy relevance and an interdisciplinary approach (e.g. Benavot et al. 2005; Greco et al. 2005). Boaz et al. (2002, p. 7) summarize the current deficiencies regarding why educational research is not serving policy or practice:

> Much research is considered less than robust, there are paradigm wars, eclectic methods competing rather than complementing, large datasets are analysed but there is relatively little true experimentation, fragmented research community, no accessible database of research evidence (but fresh initiatives underway), few systematic reviews.

Some educational researchers have proposed very experimental and controlled models for educational research in order to produce more cumulative knowledge (e.g. Slavin 2002). These suggestions have raised very controversial opinions among education researchers.

Berliner (2002) and McCormick (2003) also remark that educational research is the hardest science of all when striving for research and evidence-based policy and practice because of the enormous complexity of educational phenomena. Berliner writes:

> Our science forces us to deal with particular problems, where local knowledge is needed. Therefore, ethnographic research is crucial, as are case studies, survey research, time series, doing experiments, action research, and other means to collect reliable evidence for engaging in unfettered argument about educational issues. A single method is not what the government should be promoting for educational researchers. It would do better by promoting argument, discourse and discussion. (Berliner 2002, p. 20)

Complexity, the situational nature of education, as well as the practitioner's role are issues that make the concept of evidence very challenging in education.

Equity has been a leading principle of Finnish educational policy since the late 1960s. Equity means equal opportunities for everyone to continue their learning and education at any phase in their lives. This principle entails that everyone has sufficient learning skills and opportunities to educate and develop themselves in different learning environments (Ministry of Education and Culture [MEC]). The MEC summarizes the official educational policy thus: "The welfare of Finnish society is built on education, culture and knowledge. The flexible education system and basic educational security make for equity and consistency in results" (MEC 2016a). Flexible system and structures mean that students always have the opportunity to continue their education, even when they have failed at some point along their learning path.

In this kind of system, the required evidence must reveal how the system works. The Finnish educational system has been referred to as an ecosystem, where the different levels and sectors should function as a whole when aiming at high quality learning for all (Niemi et al. 2014; FNBE 2016).

The landscape of education and teaching is under extreme pressure in Finland, as it is everywhere. This changing environment impacts the concepts of learning, teaching, and knowledge, with new technology and rapid changes in the economy, societal structures, industrial life, and vocations requiring changes in schools and teaching. How does this Finnish system provide good education for people from different backgrounds and in its various different learning environments?

In Finland, the required evidence should be comprehensive, covering the whole system and still giving detailed information regarding the different levels of education. This is an aim and a challenge. In the international debate on evidence, research reviews and meta-analyses are often focused on a narrow theme or phenomenon. In the Finnish case, evidence does not come from any once source.

## *The National Enhancement-Led Evaluation Policy*

A quest for good learning outcomes is on the educational agenda of many countries. Globally, much controversy exists over what is the best way to use assessment as a tool through which to achieve high learning outcomes. Some countries have chosen standardized testing, which stresses competition between schools, and focuses on measurable performances. The Finnish choice has been *enhancement-led evaluation* at all levels of education (Kumpulainen and Lankinen 2016). The assessment of outcomes is regarded as an important tool through which to improve education. There is no standardized testing, nor inspection system to control the educational arrangements at schools or institutions. Instead of inspection, there is an evaluation system (FNBE 2016).

At a national level, the main actor is the Finnish Education Evaluation Centre [FINEEC] (2016). It is an independent government agency responsible for the evaluation of education. It carries out evaluations related to education including the operations of education providers from early childhood education to higher education. The key operating principles of FINEEC are the independence of evaluation and enhancement-led evaluation. Independence refers to the freedom of evaluation methods, the organization, and results from the influence of, for example, the MEC or other parties. The concept of enhancement-led evaluation means that the purpose of all evaluations is linked to improvements in the educational system. It has many similar features to the concept of communicative evaluation (Niemi and Kemmis 2012) that defines evaluation with three functions.

As a process, communicative evaluation (Niemi 1996) sets out to interrupt our usual ways of thinking and doing things with the explicit intention of creating shared frameworks of understanding about (a) where we are now (*revelation*), (b) where we are heading (*anticipation*), and (c) how we can and should move forward together (*building communication and partnerships*). Practically speaking, we see communicative evaluation as characterized in terms of three functions (Niemi and Kemmis 1999, 2012, p. 64):

- *Revelation*: helping people to understand cultural, social and interpersonal dynamics in and around programmes and settings, and to do so in a critical way;
- *Anticipation*: helping people to orientate towards the future in increasingly unsettled times; and
- *Building communication and partnership*: helping people to work together for transformation, not only at local levels but also in relation to global issues, trends and tendencies.

FINEEC (2016) expresses its principles as follows:

> Enhancement-led evaluation emphasizes participation, as well as trust between the party implementing the evaluation and evaluation participant, and the responsibility of education providers and higher education institutions in the development of the quality of their operations. In enhancement-led evaluation, the methods will be tailored according to the objectives of the evaluation and theme to be evaluated.

In its strategy, FINEEC (2016) has defined four interrelated focus areas:

1. Developing learning and competence with evaluation. Evaluations implemented with different enhancement-led methods aim at improving learning results and competence at all educational levels.

2. Evaluation activities that cover all educational levels provide information on the functionality of the entire educational system and policy. The evidence-based evaluation information forms a basis for development work. Evaluations are also targeted at the educational level boundaries and various transition phases.
3. Evaluations are targeted at societally important and critical themes. Based on an analysis of the changes in the operating environment, significant development targets in education which are not included in the Evaluation Plan, may be raised for evaluation.
4. FINEEC supports education providers and higher education institutions in developing quality management by evaluating their quality systems and producing information on good practices in quality management and development, as well as by spreading the information across different educational levels. Moreover, FINEEC supports schools, educational institutions and higher education institutions in utilizing national evaluations and self-evaluations as well as in strengthening the enhancement-led evaluation approach.

Since the mid-1990s, the Finnish National Board of Education has conducted national assessments of learning outcomes, mostly in the ninth grade of basic education. Regular assessments have been carried out in mathematics, the student's mother tongue (either Finnish or Swedish), and literature, and occasionally in other subjects as well. This task was transferred to FINEEC in 2014. These assessments have been and will be sample-based and usually cover 10–15% of the age cohort. The assessments are based on the objectives of basic education. The items and contents of the assessments are pre-tested with schools outside the sample and are designed based on teacher feedback. The assessment results are reported as summaries for the MEC, the Finnish National Board of Education, teacher education institutes, and educational providers, as well as for schools and teachers. All schools in an assessment sample receive an individual feedback report. Evaluations also consist of questions on the teaching and assessment methods in participating schools, educational resources, and on student motivation, their self-concept as learners, and on how they view the usefulness of the subject matter.

## *The Role of International Evaluations in the Finnish Context*

Finland has been part of several international evaluations (e.g. the Programme for International Student Assessment [PISA]; the Trends in International Mathematics and Science Study [TIMSS]; the Progress in International Reading Literacy Study [PIRLS]; the Teaching and Learning International Survey [TALIS]; and The Programme for the International Assessment of Adult Competencies [PIAAC]. The Finnish system has also received much attention because of its 15-year-old students' high learning outcomes in the international PISA measurements. Many researchers, such as Gert Biesta (2009, p. 1), note that in recent years, international measurements of student learning outcomes have become important sources for educational planning:

> One of these tendencies is the rise of an international 'league-table industry' which is increasingly influencing education policy at national and local level. Studies such as the Trends in International Mathematics and Science Study (TIMSS), the Progress in International Reading Literacy Study (PIRLS) and, most notoriously, OECD's Programme for International Student Assessment (PISA), generate a never-ending stream of comparative data that are supposed to tell us which educational systems are better and which are best.

However, in the Finnish case, evidence consists of much more than PISA scores. Finnish policy-makers see that the additional value of international measurements to Finland is linked to broad knowledge production and to peer viewpoints in the countries outside of the EU. These international measurements provide an opportunity to compare Finland's situation to other countries; evidence that is interesting in terms of the aims and policies of the Finnish educational system (Laukkanen and Palonen 2011). The results from the international measurements are used to identify how to improve the system. Even though Finland is still among the best educational countries in the world, many Finnish analyses of the PISA results and trends focus particularly on the weaknesses and concerns highlighted in those results. This approach is useful for finding out what the most important issues are for improving Finnish education. OECD data are used in further analyses for national purposes, as Välijärvi and Sulkunen (2016, p. 1) write:

> The decreasing trend in average performance and the increasing number of low performers have gained wide attention in the educational field in Finland, and rightly so. Moreover, it is evident that educational equality and equity which have been—and still are—in the heart of educational policy in Finland shows disconcerting development as the gender gap is widening and the impact of home background on students' reading literacy performance has increased. Particularly students from culturally disadvantaged homes are at risk and show relatively steep decrease in both reading engagement and performance. These trends show that the Finnish school has difficulties in supporting students' growth and development of key competencies in the changed context, where technologies related to literacy, textual landscapes and literacy practices are changing constantly.

Based on the recent PISA results, the researchers (Välijärvi and Sulkunen 2016) claim that the Finnish educational system needs to find new pedagogical ways to promote the development of students' reading and mathematical literacy (including digital literacy), and also to support the growing number of low-performing students who do not necessarily receive adequate support from home. These challenges have already been recognized in the earlier analysis requested by the MEC: "Measures will be taken to reduce inheritance of education and to minimise gender differences in learning outcomes, participation in education and in the completion of studies" (MEC 2012).

The recent PISA results and the other assessments have led to several further measures and national programs being launched to buck the negative trend and to update Finnish education to meet with twenty-first-century demands. Some are substantial reforms, such as the Finnish National Core Curriculum for Basic Education that was recently revised following the usual 10-year cycle, but also taking into account the results from national and international evaluations. The reform process was very interactive, involving teachers, researchers, teacher educators, and a wide range of different societal stakeholders, parents, teacher unions, and labor markets (Vahtivuori-Hänninen et al. 2014). The curriculum emphasizes a new pedagogical culture in which students will have ownership of and an active role in their learning. In addition, the Finnish MEC launched subject-specific national development programs, e.g. the Joy of Reading (*Lukuinto*), to strengthen the literacy skills of 6 to 16-year-olds and increase their reading engagement, with the special target of boys, who are overrepresented among the low performers. Another program targets mathematics and science learning for 6 to 16-year-old students and their teachers (MEC 2016b). A common aim, according to the MEC and FNBE, is to develop a new pedagogical culture to support, on the one hand, collaborative learning, and, on the other hand, individual learning.

## *Research Providing Evidence*

National evaluations use scientific methods for data gathering and analysis. They inform policy-makers, practitioners, and other stakeholders with research-based knowledge. In addition, several other research provisions come from universities. The following research bodies are located within universities:

**The Finnish Institute for Educational Research (FIER)**
(https://ktl.jyu.fi/en) is a multidisciplinary centre for educational research, assessment, and development, based at the University of Jyväskylä, Finland. Its research covers the entire educational system, from pre-school to higher education, and the links between vocational and academic education and working life. Co-operation with schools, educational administrators, workplaces, policy-makers, and the media is a key element in its operational strategy, which aims at increasing the effectiveness of research findings. The FIER collaborates extensively with the OECD, various EU Agencies and IEA publications.

**[The] Centre for Educational Assessment**
(http://www.helsinki.fi/cea/eng/) at the University of Helsinki focuses on students' competences in the curricular subjects to fostering their aptitude for learning later in life. The important theme is learning to learn as the foundation for lifelong learning. The Centre works in collaboration with schools and municipalities in the fields of educational assessment, research and development. The results of assessment are utilized for monitoring and further developing education in classrooms and at school and municipal level. Assessments implemented at different grade levels or at regular intervals offer the providers of education means to monitor educational effectiveness at municipal and national level.

**Research Unit for the Sociology of Education (RUSE)**
(http://ruse.utu.fi/home/) at the University of Turku is a research institute in the field of the sociology of education. Its mission is to produce international high quality research on the social sciences, especially on higher education, education policy, and on the relations between education and the labor market. It also develops methodological solutions for social sciences and modes of analysis for evaluating research and teaching.

In addition, eight universities have a Faculty of Education with teacher education (TE) programs. TE has committed itself to a strong research-based orientation and researchers provide research that is funded mostly by the main national research funders, the Academy of Finland and the National Agency for Technology and Innovations in Finland. The latter has supported the development of educational technology in Finnish schools in recent years with projects in which teachers, students, parents, researchers, policy-makers, and companies work together with joint aims (Niemi et al. 2014).

## *Who Should Provide the Evidence?*

The recent Finnish educational system's roots go back to the late 1960s when a comprehensive school model for all children was established. The ideology of equity and principles of lifelong learning have been the driving forces throughout the educational system. A strong principle of lifelong learning linked with equity has changed the teacher's role and TE radically. Finnish teachers are expected to work with mixed ability groups and to take care of different learners.

Basic education consisting of 9 years of comprehensive school, upper secondary education, and vocational education are financed by the state and local authorities. These educational services are provided by local authorities, which are municipalities or consortiums of municipalities. Municipalities (local authorities) and their schools write their own curricula on the basis of the national core curriculum. Local needs can be taken into consideration in these curricula. Schools can have their own profiles such as e.g., science or music education.

The national core curriculum has an important role in the Finnish system of school development as a means for enabling and managing educational change and also in terms of providing freedom to local actors for making education relevant in local contexts. The current curriculum system in Finland is based on three essential ideas (Vitikka et al. 2016):

- Management by goals given in legislation and in the national core curriculum.
- Autonomy of municipal authorities in providing and organizing education: the local curriculum as a steering document at local level.
- Utilization of teachers as valued experts who develop the school-based curriculum as a source for different approaches to schoolwork.

In the educational literature, there has been much discussion on what the real core and nature of the teaching profession is (Brandsford et al. 2005; Darling-Hammond 2010a, b; Hargreves 2003). Is it an autonomous expert profession or is it more of a craft that does not have a very independent status? In many countries, teachers also face high pressure with high-stake national testing having heavy consequences on teaching and learning in classrooms and narrowing professional autonomy. The Finnish national system provides teachers with the freedom to take into account students' needs and local conditions. It also requires a high ethical commitment from teachers to develop their teaching in such a way that all students can make progress in their learning. Assessments are mainly used to help students to learn better.

When discussing the nature of evidence in the international discussion, many voices stress the role of practitioners in assessing the relevance of evidence. When practitioners are informed through evidence, regardless of its origin (research or e.g. observations), they have the right and the obligation to assess its relevance. In the Finnish educational system, teachers are expected to be autonomous, pedagogically thinking, and critically oriented professionals who take care of different learners. Teachers and principals are both responsible for the quality of education and they also need to acquire evidence that is required for school development. The teacher's role is to translate the equity principle and LLL objectives into practice. In that work, they have much professional freedom, e.g. what teaching and learning material they use, what teaching methods they apply, and how they use assessments to promote student learning.

The Finnish system supports arguments that evidence does not only develop from systematic research. It can also develop from observations and the experiences of experts, policy-makers, and practitioners in their own fields (e.g. Issitt and Spence 2005). Hammersley (2004) argues that this evidence does not necessarily emerge from systematic investigations, but it still can be important, and perhaps even more important. There are also many voices that stress the role of practitioners in assessing the relevance of evidence. When practitioners are informed through evidence they have the right and the obligation to assess its relevance. Robertson and Dale (2007) note that users must judge what works when applying evidence in practice. There is always a specific context and they have to ask about not only what works, but for whom, under what circumstances, and so on. How to use research or evidence-based knowledge thus depends upon a mix of evidence and judgement, and this is a dynamic process, in which the teacher or policy-maker is also attuned to the effects and consequences, and uses this knowledge to loop back into the process. Policy-makers and practitioners need the capacity to understand how evidence is built up and how they are part of its construction. If teachers are expected to work as professionals who have freedom and autonomy to make decisions in changing contexts, then they must evaluate what works and what does not.

Some years ago, the European Commission prepared a staff working paper (Commission of the European Communities 2007; Niemi 2014) to promote evidence-based policy and practice in education. It invited a small working group to the table, whose task was to determine how to create, deliver, and apply evidence-based knowledge in and for education. Hannele Niemi, as a member of the group, developed a model on the basic conditions that are needed in educational policy-making and in the teaching profession to apply evidence in policy and practice. The model was introduced in the European Commission's staff working paper (Commission of the European Communities 2007; Niemi 2014). The important message is that no information source or action in itself can promote evidence-based action. If we want teachers to work as high-level professionals, they need certain basic conditions to be met for knowledge creation and agency in their work.

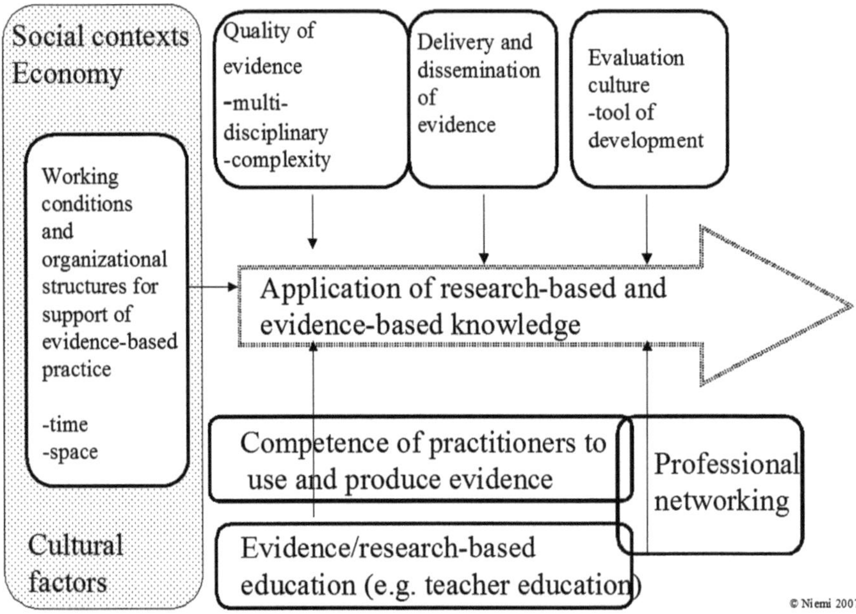


**Fig. 3.1** Evidence related to practitioners' work

The successful application of evidence and research-based knowledge depends on many factors, which are in mutual interaction. The following model (Fig. 3.1) summarizes the main components.

## Practitioners' Role in Using and Creating Evidence

The above model illustrates that no source of information in itself can promote evidence-based action. Policy-makers and practitioners need the capacity to understand how evidence is built. The more their decisions have a significant impact, the more they need critical scientific literacy to help them understand the validity and relevance of information from research and other evidence sources. Evidence should not only be used but also created by practitioners through reflection and the sharing of experiences. They need open and analytical minds to produce sound evidence and working communities that support practitioners' knowledge creation. Educational contexts and decisions are always very complex phenomena, and for this reason, the evidence-based approach must also include multidisciplinary and multi-professional perspectives.

The model also illustrates that knowledge application depends on the social, economic, and cultural determinants of each country, and its regional or local context. It illustrates that all factors influence the different phases of knowledge application. Social, economic, and cultural contexts are in a state of continuous change. Knowledge application in education is not a process of static implementation, but rather a continuous process. Teachers' pre-service education plays an important role in constructing teachers' professional identity and developing their capacity to use different evidence sources. It is an important precondition, but without opportunities to work in their work as decision-makers, creating and using evidence in schools loses its power. Teachers need professional networking, tools for gaining easy access to different evidence sources, and an evaluation culture in which they can use different methods for assessing students' learning and the effectiveness of their teaching.

To educate professionals who have the capacity to use evidence, Finnish TE for both primary and secondary schools involves 5-year programs (consisting of both BA and MA degrees), with high entrance criteria; thus, TE students are very talented and committed to the teaching profession. The aim is that teachers can internalize a research-oriented attitude toward their work. This means that teachers take an analytical and open-minded approach to their work, that they draw conclusions based on their observations and experiences, and that they develop teaching and learning environments in a systematic way. Finnish TE also has a strong research component with the aim of educating teachers to be critical knowledge creators. BA and MA degrees consist of research methodological studies and a thesis, which involves scientific studies. Students learn to read educational research reports, to acquire data, to analyze it, and draw conclusions. Research methods may vary from historical analysis to surveys and experiments. The main objective of these studies is not the completion of the master's thesis itself, but actually to further the process by which students come to see themselves as active studying and working agents. For this aspect of the degree program, the processes of active working and thinking are integrated in various complex and sometimes unexpected ways. The aim of the guiding process is to help students discover and tap into their own intellectual resources and to make them better able to utilize the resources of the study group in which they work (Niemi and Jakku-Sihvonen 2006, p. 37). An important aim of research-oriented studies is also to educate teachers who are able to study and develop their own research-based practices. The critical scientific literacy of teachers and their ability to use research methods are considered crucial. Accordingly, most of Finland's TE programs require studies of both the qualitative and quantitative research traditions.

There are studies that have analyzed teachers and student teachers' concepts and feedback on the TE research studies. Jyrhämä and Maaranen (2016, p. 104) conclude:

> Based on our results, it seems that teachers' inquiry-orientation is first and foremost an attitude towards one's work. The focus is on the development of one's self, as well as the development of the school community, alternative ways of working, reflection, dialogic, feedback etc.

Niemi and Nevgi (2014) has found very much the same kinds of experiences among student teachers. The value of research studies is focused on the following qualities:

- Critical thinking;
- Independent thinking;
- Inquiring and scientific literacy; and
- Questioning phenomena and knowledge.

The general picture is very positive. The student teachers view research studies as valuable for their teaching profession and see them as continuous developmental tasks for their future work. The pre-service TE system has been created to make teachers researchers in their work. We have evidence from research results and TALIS reviews that teachers' in-service training requires many improvements. It is not systematic, and is not based on Finnish teacher's research capacity. The change in direction toward more school-based developmental projects has been very slow. The main reasons for this are the funding system and the fact that pre-service training is provided by universities, and the arrangements for in-service training are the employers' (municipalities) responsibility. Evidence of needs to change teachers' in-service training exists but is not used for a change. Another case concerns ample evidence that in pre-service TE, student teachers need more experience gained from collaboration within school communities, as well as with partners outside the school, especially with parents. However, although we are consistently presented with the same evidence, it seems that some elements of TE culture are very difficult to change.

## Discussion

We can see that in the Finnish educational system there are many channels that provide research-based knowledge for policy and practice. Evidence is available and its meaning is discussed and reflected on in many forums. Most research and evaluation studies are conducted using multiple and mixed methods. Biesta (2007) argues that the current climate, in which governments and policy-makers seem to demand that educational research plays only a technical role, is dangerous. It is a threat to democracy itself. He claims that there is a real need to widen the scope of our thinking about the relation between research, policy, and practice, so as to make sure that the discussion is no longer restricted to finding the most effective ways to achieve certain ends, but also addresses questions about the desirability of the ends in themselves (Biesta 2007, p. 18).

In the Finnish system, there is a culture of discussion and interaction between research, policy, and practice. However, many challenges still need to be faced. Many of them are related to decision making at the political level:

*Policy-Level Disconnectedness* The problem is how to get information to the policy level and step outside the territory traditionally held by policy-makers. The educational ecosystem covers the whole life course. Most lifelong learning issues that are related to the public educational system are under the remit of the MEC, but lifelong learning and equity in education require much more collaboration. Learning in work life is becoming increasingly important. These issues are dealt with the Ministry of the Employment and the Economy. Refugees and immigrants are an increasing population in Finland, and their issues are handled in the Ministry of the Interior. The ageing population is also on the rise in Finland. Health issues are the domain of the Ministry of Social Affairs and Health, but ageing is also very much related to the capacity to learn as lifelong learners and to keep opportunities open to contribute to working life.

*Evidence for the Whole Educational System* In medicine, research can be focused on individual diseases and sometimes on a very narrow symptom. The holistic view of the human body is often missing. This often causes serious problems for patients, even though a particular pain or illness can be cured. In education, the whole educational ecosystem and the interconnecting formal and non-formal environments for lifelong learning set very demanding objectives. Even though the structure of the Finnish educational system is very flexible, transitions from basic education to secondary level, and then through to the tertiary level, consist of many dysfunctions that cause discontinuity in people's learning paths, and additional costs to society via exclusion, drop-out rates, and unemployment. Constantly changing circumstances in the labor market and in terms of societal structures mean that new evidence is constantly required.

*Disseminating and Communication* In democratic societies, there are many partners and stakeholders who need knowledge about education and who need to be made aware of the latest research and evidence. These kinds of groups are e.g. parents, partners in working life, and companies. The media forms a substantial group of actors as well as holding a large audience. How the different partners understand the quality of evidence and its complexity can vary considerably. There have been cases where the media has taken only one aspect of the evidence and created a totally different message than the one presented in the original assessment or data. We may ask whose responsibility it is to interpret the evidence and to tell the public about it. When evidence is complex and multilayered, considerable communication between the different partners in education is needed.

*Evidence Is a Continuous Process* Teachers and policy-makers need high-level analytical skills and a sound understanding of the demands of democracy. They must find, observe, and understand the complexity of educational processes, and examine the evidence from different sources. They also need to be open to acquiring and assessing local evidence. Technical and instrumental knowledge of evaluations and as well as professional culture and traditions may narrow perspectives of needs to change practices (e.g. Carr and Kemmis 1986). Scardamalia and Bereiter (2003) have examined the behavior of experts. The feature that really distinguishes experts from others is their approach to new problems. The pattern recognition and learned procedures that lead to intuitive problem solving are only the beginning. The expert invests it in what Bereiter and Scardamalia call "progressive problem solving," that is, tackling problems. That increases expertise rather than reducing problems to previously learned routines. In addition to enquiry skills and being open to different kinds of evidence, they need cultural awareness and an understanding of how democracy, research, and evidence-based policy and practice are interrelated.

*Evidence-Based Policy and Practice Demand Cooperation* The Finnish National Board of Education expresses its mission as follows (FNBE 2016):

> There is a wide-spread consensus of the main pillars of education policy and the policy is characterized by cooperation and continuity—evolution rather than revolution. Tripartite partnership among Government, trade unions and employer organisations is an integrated part of policy-making. Participation and consultation of a wide range of different stakeholders play a central role in educational reform. Teachers and the Trade Union of Education as their representative are the key players in the development of education. The main objectives and broad lines of the policy are defined at central level, but the implementation of these is the responsibility of the local level.

The recent understanding of knowledge production has revealed that knowledge is a more comprehensive concept than research or evidence. Knowledge is constructed through research (with its different modes), evidence, literature, and learning experiences. Knowledge creation needs different information sources and social interaction. When promoting evidence-based policy and practice, it is necessary to understand that policy-makers and practitioners are learners in their own work and they create knowledge in their practice. The latest research on learning considers learning as an active individual process, but increasingly we have evidence that it is also a process which is based on sharing and participation with different partners in a community (Nonaka and Toyama 2003; Scardamalia and Bereiter 2003). If we view knowledge creation as an interactive process, creating evidence and using evidence-based knowledge is no longer a unidirectional process. It is a joint process where researchers, policy-makers, and practitioners work together in a complementary way, seeking evidence for better policy and practice. In this process, networking between the different partners is necessary for the educational ecosystem to thrive.

*New Sources of Evidence Create New Requirements for Managing Evidence* In science learning, the concept and method for learning analytics is growing. New technology creates big data and the learner's pathway through the electronic system can be followed and can also connect to other data via traces left in the system. In healthcare and medicine, this approach has been possible and is in use to a higher extent. The patient as well as the doctor can follow this data. This creates new questions: what is one's own data, what kinds of data sets can be connected, who can use "my data," or how I can use my data? Students can already retrieve continuous information about their learning processes, e.g. in learning games. This data can also be connected to various brain functions. In the future, the sources and channels of evidence will increase; thus, evidence is not a static concept. It is dynamic and changes along with new methods.

## Conclusion

The landscape of education and teaching is under significant pressure. This changing environment impacts the concepts of learning, teaching, and knowledge, with new technology and rapid changes in the economy, societal structures, industrial life, and vocations requiring changes in schools and teaching. Biesta (2009), Mathison (2009), and Day and Johansson (2008) argue that the question of good education cannot be solved merely by considering instrumental aims nor resolved *without* engaging in discussions about values and purposes. The values and purposes of education also have a deep impact on the teaching profession (Campbell 2008). In the Finnish case connections between equity in education and evidence for improvements in the whole system goes towards understanding what is a common good for the whole society.

Evidence-based policy and practice are a continuous process in which different sources are needed. A particular data source does not have any objective value because the question *what for* is fundamental. The quality of the evidence must be based on transparent criteria, and part of these is values. Evidence-based policy and practice also needs a continuous discussion between different partners to overcome gaps that cause serious dysfunctions in the educational ecosystem.

## References


Angrist, J. D. (2004). American education research changes tack. *Oxford Review of Economic Policy, 20*(2), 198–212.

Benavot, A., Erbes-Seguin, S., & Gross, S. (2005). Interdisciplinary in EU-funded social science projects. In M. Kuhn & S. O. Remoe (Eds.), *Building the European research area. Socio-economic research in practice* (pp. 115–175). New York: Peter Lang. 115–175.

Berliner, D. (2002). Educational research: The hardest science of all. *Educational Researcher, 31*(8), 18–20.

Biesta, G. (2007). Why "What Works" won't work: Evidence-based practice and the democratic deficit in educational research. *Educational Theory, 57*, 1–22.

Biesta, G. (2009). *Good education: What it is and why we need it.* Inaugural lecture. The Stirling Institute of Education. 4th Mar 2009. http://www.ioe.stir.ac.uk/documents/GOODEDUCATION--WHATITISANDWHYWENEEDITInauguralLectureProfGertBiesta.pdf

Boaz, A., Ashby, D., & Ken Young K. (2002). *What have they got to offer evidence based policy and practice?* Working Paper 2. Systematic Reviews: ESRC UK Centre for Evidence Based Policy and Practice. Queen Mary. University of London.

Brandsford, J., Darling-Hammond, L., & LePage, P. (2005). Introduction. In L. Darling-Hammond & J. Brandsford (Eds.), *Preparing teachers for a changing world: What teachers should learn and be able to do* (pp. 1–40). San Francisco: Wiley.

Burns, T., & Schuller, T. (2007). The evidence agenda. In T. Burns (Ed.), *Evidence in education: Linking research and policy* (pp. 15–31). Paris: OECD.

Campbell, E. (2008). Preparing ethical professionals as a challenge for teacher education. In K. Tirri (Ed.), *Educating moral sensibilities in urban schools* (pp. 3–18). Rotterdam: Sense Publishers.

Carr, W., & Kemmis, S. (1986). *Becoming critical.* Philadelphia: Falmer Press.

Commission of the European Communities. (2007). *Towards more knowledge-bases policy and practice in education and training*. Commission staff working document. SEC (2007) 1098. Brussels. http://ec.europa.eu/dgs/education_culture/publ/pdf/educ2010/sec1098_en.pdf

Darling-Hammond, L. (2010a). New policies for 21st century demands. Interviewed by James Bellanca. In J. Bellanca & R. Brandt (Eds.), *Rethinking how students learn* (pp. 33–50). Bloomington: Solution Tress Press.

Darling-Hammond, L. (2010b). Teaching and educational transformation. In M. Fullan, A. Hargreaves, A. Lieberman, & D. Hopkins (Eds.), *Second international handbook of educational change* (pp. 505–522). New York: Springer.

Daviet, B. (2016). *Revisiting the principle of education as a public good, Education Research and Foresight Series, No. 17*. Paris: UNESCO. http://www.unesco.org/new/en/education/themes/leading-theinternational-agenda/rethinking-education/erf-papers/.

Day, C., & Johansson, O. (2008). Leadrship with a difference in schools serving disadvantaged communities: Arenas for success. In K. Tirri (Ed.), *Educating moral sensibilities in urban schools* (pp. 19–34). Rotterdam: Sense Publishers.

Demarais-Tremblay, M. (2014). *On the definition of public goods*. Assessing Richard A. Musgrave's contribution. Documents de travail du Centre d'Economie de la Sorbonne 2014.04.

FINEEC (The Finnish Education Evaluation Centre). (2016). https://karvi.fi/en/fineec/

FNBE (Finnish National Board of Education). (2016). *Education system*. Education Policy; Quality Assurance National Reference Point.

Greco, L., Landri, P., Tomassini, M., & Wickham, J. (2005). The development of policy relevance in European social research. In M. Kuhn & S. O. Remoe (Eds.), *Building the European research area. Socio-economic research in practice* (pp. 177–237). New York: Peter Lang.

Hammersley, M. (2004). Some questions about evidence-based practice in education. In G. Thomas & R. Prong (Eds.), *Evidence based practice in education* (pp. 133–149). Maidenhead: OUP/McGraw-Hill.

Hammersley, M. (2005). Is the evidence-based practice movement doing more good than harm? Reflections on Ian Chalmers' case for research-based policy making and practice. *Evidence & Policy, 1*(1), 85–100.

Hargreaves, A. (2003). *Teaching in the knowledge society. Education in the age of insecurity*. New York: Teachers College Press.

http://www.oph.fi/english/education_system_education_policy

http://www.oph.fi/english/education_development/quality_assurance_and_evaluation

Issitt, M., & Spence, J. (2005). Practitioner knowledge and evidence-based research, policy and practice. *Youth and Policy, 88*, 63–82.

Jyrhämä, R., & Maaranen, K. (2016). Research orientation in teachers' work. In H. Niemi, A. Toom, & A. Kallioniemi (Eds.), *Miracle of education: The principles and practices of teaching and learning in Finnish schools* (2nd revised ed., pp. 91–108). Rotterdam: Sense Publishers.

Kumpulainen, K., & Lankinen, T. (2016). Striving for educational equity and excellence: Evaluation and assessment in Finnish basic education. In H. Niemi, A. Toom, & A. Kallioniemi (Eds.), *Miracle of education. The principles and practices of teaching and learning in Finnish schools* (2nd revised ed., pp. 71–82). Rotterdam: Sense Publishers. Rotterdam: Sense Publishers.

Laukkanen, R. (2008). Finnish strategy for high-level education for all. In N. C. Sognel & P. Jaccard (Eds.), *Governance and performance of education systems* (pp. 305–324). Dordrect: Springer.

Laukkanen, R., & Palonen, M. (2011). OECD:n koulutuspolitiikka Suomen kannalta. Teoksessa R. Laukkanen (Toim.) *Tiedosta käytännöksi – OECD tietoon perustuvan koulutuspolitiikan tukena*. [ In R. Laukkanen (Ed.) *From knowledge to practice. OECD as support for knowledge-based educational policy*] (pp. 5–13). Reports and reviews 2011:20. Helsinki: Finnish National Board of Education.

Luke, A., Green, J., & Kelly, G. (2010). What counts as evidence and equity? In A. Luke, J. Green, & G. Kelly (Eds.), *Review of research in education: Volume 34 (what counts as evidence in educational settings? Rethinking equity, diversity, and reform in the 21st century)* (pp. vii–xvii). Washington, DC: American Educational Research Association.

Mathison, S. (2009). Serving the public interest through educational evaluation: Salvaging democracy by rejecting neoliberalism. In K. E. Ryan & J. B. Cousins (Eds.), *The SAGE international handbook of educational evaluation* (pp. 525–548). Thousand Oaks: Sage.

McCormick, R. (2003). *Reliable evidence for policy making in complex settings*. Paper presented to the EMINENT IV Conference, Geneva, 9–10 Oct 2003.

MEC (Ministry of Education and Culture). (2012). *Education and research 2011–2016. A development plan*. Helsinki: Department for Education and Science Policy, Ministry of Education and Culture.

MEC (Ministry of Education and Culture). (2016a). *Education system in Finland*. http://www.minedu.fi/OPM/Koulutus/koulutusjaerjestelmae/?lang=en

MEC (Ministry of Education and Culture). (2016b). *Key projects reform Finnish education*. http://www.minedu.fi/OPM/Julkaisut/2016/Key_projects_reform_Finnish_education.html?lang=en&extra_locale=en

Musgrave, R. A. (1969). Provision for social goods. In J. Margolis & H. Guitton (Eds.), *Public economics: An analysis of public production and consumption and their relations to the private sectors*. London: Macmillan.

Niemi, H. (1996). Effectiveness of teacher education – a theoretical framework of communicative evaluation and the design of a Finnish research project. In H. Niemi & K. Tirri (Eds.), *Effectiveness of teacher education. New challenges and approaches to evaluation*, *Research series A 6/1996. Reports from the Department of Teacher Education in Tampere University* (pp. 11–32). Tampere: University of Tampere.

Niemi, H. (2014). Teachers as active contributors in quality of education: A special reference to the Finnish context. In D. Hung, K. Y. T. Lim, & S.-S. Lee (Eds.), *Adaptivity as a transformative disposition for learning in the 21st century* (pp. 179–199). Singapore: Springer.

Niemi, H. (2016). The societal factors contributing to education and schooling in Finland. In H. Niemi, A. Toom, & A. Kallioniemi (Eds.), *Miracle of education: The principles and practices of teaching and learning in Finnish schools* (2nd revised ed., pp. 23–40). Rotterdam: Sense Publishers.

Niemi, H., & Jakku-Sihvonen, R. (2006). Research-based teacher education. In R. Jakku-Sihvonen & H. Niemi (Eds.), *Research-based teacher education in Finland – reflections by Finnish teacher educators* (pp. 31–50). Finnish Educational Research Association: Turku.

Niemi, H., & Kemmis, S. (1999). Communicative evaluation: Evaluation at the crossroads'. *Lifelong Learning in Europe, 1*, 55–64.

Niemi, H., & Kemmis, S. (2012). Communicative evaluation for improvement in education. In J. Harford, B. Hudson, & H. Niemi (Eds.), *Quality assurance and teacher education: International challenges and expectations* (pp. 53–82). Oxford: Peter Lang.

Niemi, H., & Nevgi. (2014). Research studies and active learning promoting professional competences in Finnish teacher education. *Teaching and Teacher Education, 43*, 131–142.

Niemi, H., Multisilta, J., Lipponen, L., & Vivitsou, V. (Eds.). (2014). *Finnish innovations and technologies in schools*. Towards new ecosystems of learning. Rotterdam: Sense Publishers.

Nonaka, I., & Toyama, R. (2003). The knowledge-creating theory revisited: Knowledge creation as a synthesizing process. *Knowledge Management Research and Practice, 1*, 2–10. http://dx.doi.org/10.1057/palgrave.kmrp.8500001.

Robertson, S., & Dale, R. (2007). *Comments on the pre-final version of the draft papers of the three consultants (Leney, Niemi and Rickinson) on the links between research, policy and practice.*" *Nesse*. Graduate School Education-University of Bristol.

Sahlberg, P. (2011). *Finnish lessons: What can the world learn from educational change in Finland?* New York: Teacher College Press.

Samuelson, P. A. (1954). The pure theory of public expenditure. *The Review of Economics and Statistics, 36*(4), 387–389.

Scardamalia, M., & Bereiter, C. (2003). Knowledge building. In *Encyclopedia of education* (2nd ed., pp. 1370–1373). New York: Macmillan Reference, USA.

Schuller, T. (2006). International policy research: 'evidence' from CERI/OECD. In J. Ozga, T. Seddon, & T. Popkewitz (Eds.), *Education research and policy* (pp. 78–90). London: Routledge.

Slavin, R. (2002). Evidence-based education policies: Transforming educational practice and research. *Educational Researcher, 31*(7), 15–21.

UNESCO. (2015). *Rethinking education: Towards a global common good?* Paris: UNESCO.

Vahtivuori-Hänninen, S., Halinen, I., Niemi, H., Lavonen, J., & Lipponen, L. (2014). A new Finnish national core curriculum for basic education (2014) and technology as an integrated tool for learning. In H. Niemi, J. Multisilta, L. Lipponen, & M. Vivitsou (Eds.), *Finnish innovations & technologies in schools: Towards new ecosystems of learning* (pp. 21–32). Rotterdam: Sense Publishers.

Välijärvi, J., & Sulkunen, S. (2016). Finnish school in international comparison. In H. Niemi, A. Toom, & A. Kallioniemi (Eds.), *Miracle of education: The principles and practices of teaching and learning in Finnish schools* (2nd revised ed., pp. 3–23). Rotterdam: Sense Publishers.

Vitikka, E., Krokfors, L., & Hurmerinta, E. (2016). The Finnish national core curriculum: Structure and development. In H. Niemi, A. Toom, & A. Kallioniemi (Eds.), *Miracle of education: The principles and practices of teaching and learning in Finnish schools* (2nd revised ed., pp. 83–90). Rotterdam: Sense Publishers.

# Chapter 4
# Educational Policy in Spain: Between Political Bias and International Evidence

**Gonzalo Jover, Enric Prats, and Patricia Villamor**

**Abstract** In Spain since the Constitution was ratified in 1978, eight laws have been passed regulating the education system in non-university stages, thereby subjecting education to continual upheaval. In the first laws, from the 1980s and early 1990s, the debate was primarily political, but by the year 2000, coinciding with Spain's taking part in the *Programme for International Student Assessment* (PISA), legislation had apparently become more technical in nature. The objective of this paper is to analyse the type of political reading made from the results of these international assessments. It focuses on the three general laws on education that have been passed in Spain in the last 15 years. The sources for the study are the debates that took place while the laws were being drafted, especially during the parliamentary proceedings. The analysis shows the submission of the political debate under the pressure to achieve a more internationally competitive system. In the realm of the political right this step gave victory to neo-liberalism over neo-conservativism. In the realm of the political left, it represents the rise of neoliberal socialism and the surrender to the forces of the economy. Both tendencies dramatically affect the notion of the common good, a notion that does not fit comfortably in either one.

## Introduction

In 1978 the Constitution of Spain was ratified, endowing the country with a new political system after 40 years of dictatorship. In it, Article 27 laid out the legal framework for the new education system. It became one of the most controversial articles in the new Constitution, and one that was hardest for the two main political forces at the time to agree upon: the centre-right UCD (*Unión de Centro Democrático*) party with a continuist orientation in educational matters, which gave broad leeway

G. Jover (✉) • P. Villamor
Faculty of Education, Universidad Complutense de Madrid, Madrid, Spain
e-mail: gjover@ucm.es

E. Prats
Faculty of Education, Universidad de Barcelona, Barcelona, Spain



M.Y. Eryaman, B. Schneider (eds.), *Evidence and Public Good in Educational Policy, Research and Practice*, Educational Governance Research 6,
DOI 10.1007/978-3-319-58850-6_4

to private schools (at that time, chiefly run by Catholic religious orders) and school choice, and the constellation of leftist parties that advocated a more radical break much like the Constitution of the short-lived Spanish Republic in 1931.

Since the Constitution was ratified in 1978, eight laws have been passed regulating the education system in non-university stages, thereby subjecting education to continual upheaval. In the first laws, from the 1980s and early 1990s, the debate was primarily political, but by the year 2000, coinciding with Spain's taking part in the *Programme for International Student Assessment* (PISA), legislation had become more technical in nature, in the sense that it aimed to be based on empirical evidence alone.

The use of empirical evidence to support education policies is nothing new to Spain. Its origin may be traced back to the discussions from the mid 1800s on the possibilities of idealism and positivism in education, which took form in what was known as *Krausopositivism* (in reference to the philosophy of Karl Christian Friedrich Krause), a Spanish construction meant to "reconcile the historic contradiction between empiricism and idealism without ignoring or nullifying either of the two essential elements for scientific construction" (Salmerón 1878, p. XIII). From the 1940s, the Spanish National Statistics Institute (*Instituto Nacional de Estadística*, INE) took on the task of drawing up the data on education in Spain. These statistics form the basis of the series *Data and figures on education in Spain* published yearly by the General Technical Secretariat of the Ministry of Education as of 1961. The information presented at that time was still very basic, and consisted mainly of data on enrolment and institutions at the various different levels of the education system, with a clear purpose of justifying the policies being enacted at that time (Ministerio de Educación Nacional 1961). This task of collecting and analysing the statistics was taken over by the Ministry of Education itself as of 1985, jointly with the Departments of Education of the Autonomous Communities as the latter were gradually given competencies in education. From 1995 on, the National Institute for Educational Evaluation (*Instituto Nacional de Evaluación Educativa*, INEE) has been in charge of working with the education authorities in each autonomous community to draw up the general assessment of the education system at non-university levels and to coordinate international study programmes.

The data from national and international studies are available to independent researchers. The ISOC – Social Sciences and Humanities database of the Spanish National Research Council (*Consejo Superior de Investigaciones Científicas*, CSIC) lists nearly 300 articles from Spanish journals for the keyword PISA, especially since 2006. These articles often feature the results from research projects carried out at universities. Moreover, several of the main Spanish journals on educational research have published monographic issues on this subject. One of the journals with the greatest impact according to Scopus is the *Revista de Educación*, which published the first monographic issue on PISA in 2006 (Vélaz 2006). Since 2012, the journal has included one or two articles a year on the matter. Another journal, *Profesorado. Revista de Currículum y Formación del Profesorado,* from the Universidad de Granada, published a monograph in 2009 on the PISA experience in Germany (Pereyra and Kotthoff 2009) and later, in 2013, the volume titled *PISA a examen: Cambiando el conocimiento, cambiando las pruebas y cambiando las escuelas* ('PISA examined: Changing knowledge, changing tests and changing schools') (Pereyra et al. 2013). This volume includes a set of critical articles on the validity and pertinence of international tests, revealing the division in the academic community on their relevance and the decisions to be made based on their results in the context of Spain. Practically all the major Spanish journals on social sciences and the humanities have published studies on international testing in recent years. Generally, the contents of these studies can be put into the following categories: methodological analysis of the construction or application of the tests (Fernández-Cano 2016); areas evaluated in PISA and factors related to the competences developed by students (Sáenz 2007; Serrano et al. eprint); the status of comparison of the different countries or autonomous communities that took part in the different evaluations (Gil-Flores 2014); dropout rates and the inequalities found in the evaluations (Choi and Calero 2013); critical analysis of the influence of PISA on political, educational and social decisions (Pedró 2012; Duru 2013; Fernández-González 2015).

Nevertheless, the matter of PISA has by no means been exclusive to the academic community. Starting with the *Law on the Quality of Education* (*Ley Orgánica de Calidad de la Educación*, LOCE) passed in 2002 but never actually enacted, whenever a new law has been proposed, it has been justified by appealing to the results from international evaluations. Our aim here is to analyse the type of political reading made from these results. We will focus on the three general laws on education that have been passed in Spain in the last 15 years: the abovementioned *Law on the Quality of Education*, the *Law on Education* (*Ley Orgánica de la Educación,* LOE) from 2006, and the *Law on the Improvement of the Quality of Education* (*Ley Orgánica para la Mejora de la Calidad Educativa,* LOMCE) from 2013. The main sources for the analysis are the debates that took place while the laws were being drafted, especially during the parliamentary proceedings.

## International Assessments Used as Grounds for Political Justification

The *Law on the Quality of Education* (LOCE) was passed in December 2002 under the government of the right-wing People's Party under José María Aznar and his Minister of Education, the Political Science and Administration professor Pilar del Castillo. The law was meant to correct what the Government felt had been the failure of the socialist reform from the 1980s and 1990s, mainly in regard to the participatory nature of managing schools as implemented in the *Law on the Right to Education* (*Ley Orgánica del Derecho a la Educación,* LODE) of 1985, and the comprehensive philosophy of the *Law on the General Arrangement of the Education System* (*Ley Orgánica de Ordinación General del Sistema Educativo,* LOGSE) of 1990. To illustrate the shortcomings, the LOCE appealed to measurable results from national and international evaluations:

> The evaluations and analyses on our education system carried out by national and international institutions reveal worrying differences in achievement in comparison with the other countries in our economic and cultural surroundings. These shortcomings become particularly clear in secondary education. There, one fourth of the student body drops out before attaining the lower compulsory secondary education certificate, leaving the system without any diploma or qualification. Furthermore, our students score below the European Union average in their knowledge of instrumental subjects such as mathematics and sciences, fundamental in a social and economic reality in which the scientific and technological dimension of knowledge is primordial… (LOCE, preamble)

The LOCE kicked off a cycle of invoking the standardised assessments from international organisms as an argument of political justification that continues today. When the bill was first drafted, Spain had already taken part in several of these evaluations, such as the 1988 and 1991 cycles of the *International Assessment of Educational Progress* (IAEP), on mathematics and science, derived from the *National Assessment of Educational Progress* (NAEP) of the United States, the *Third International Mathematics and Science Study* (TIMSS), with tests given in 1995, and the first study of the *Programme for International Student Assessment* (PISA) in the year 2000.

Reports written up by the National Quality and Assessment Institute (*Instituto Nacional de Calidad y Evaluación*), dependent on the Ministry of Education, indicated a decline in Spanish students, in comparison with students in other countries, in their relative rankings in IAEP and TIMSS, in sciences as well as in mathematics (López and Moreno 1997a, p. 11; b, pp. 11 and 12). Similarly, in the results from PISA, Spanish students scored lower than the OECD average on reading comprehension, mathematics and sciences. Moreover, these results also made it clear that few Spanish students scored very high or very low, but were concentrated at the average levels, with little variation in achievement between the schools and lower incidence of the family context than in most of the countries (INCE 2001).

The process of drafting the bill brought about considerable controversy. The members of the State School Council, the highest organisation of social representation in matters of education policy, who were most against the bill walked out of the proceedings in mid-debate when they found that their voices were being unduly silenced. Its passage through parliament was accompanied by several protest marches and coincided with a large general strike (Digón 2003). Finally, on December 23, 2002, the LOCE bill was passed by the Spanish Parliament. However, an unexpected political change occurred in the country in the aftermath of the terrorist bombings on March 11, 2004, which immediately halted its application and led to it being replaced by the *Law on Education* (LOE).

The LOCE is based on a neoliberal philosophy that can be summed up in five points: (a) primacy of a culture of individual effort; (b) result-oriented by implementation of various means of assessment; (c) promotion of "equal quality opportunities" by means of a dual configuration as of the age of 14, which broke from the principle of comprehensive education of the Spanish 1990 reform; (d) reinforcement of the social consideration and the initial and permanent teacher training systems, with a content that was more rhetorical than real; (e) development of the autonomy of the schools in matters of curriculum, organisation and management.

The LOCE makes no explicit formulation of the public good. In the debate on the bill the concept of "the public" appeared almost exclusively in relation to the old dichotomy between public and private schooling, and thus is identified with "the State". The idea of the public good behind the law can however be deduced from the philosophy that inspired it. In her defence of the bill in the Lower House (*Congreso de los Diputados*) of the Spanish Parliament on October 3, 2002, Education Minister Pilar del Castillo referred to this philosophy by stating that "education is not on the right or on the left, nor is it above or below the social fabric; it is at its very core" (Congreso de los Diputados 2002a, p. 9593). Education is ideologically separate from political confrontations. The line of argumentation suited to it is not that of the rationality on the desirable model of an educated person in society, but of an instrumental rationality raised on the "culture of effort, assessment and attention to results" (ibid.). Fixating on the results and their assessment, however, eclipses any discussion on the purposes of education. The measures to adopt are justified by "the shortcomings of our education system that national and international analyses have repeatedly made clear" (ibid). The direction of the improvements is not set by the citizens, nor does it come from an explicit conception of the education ideal, but from the analyses of the experts, who thereby turn into arbiters of the public good.

This instrumental rationality is consistent with a liberal political conception upheld on freedom and flexibility, sold under the slogan of "quality educational opportunities for all" (ibid, p. 9595) as the best means for the underprivileged to get ahead by their efforts, some along some routes, others along other routes. By this appeal to effort, the public good is reduced to merely the sum of the good of the individuals. No project is articulated for social good itself. González de Txabarri, a Member of Parliament from the Basque Group, rejected the bill outright on account of it lacking in social character and its deviation "toward the personal dimension by insisting that the learner is the one who has to perform more: more work, more effort" (ibid, p. 9600). He criticised the efficiency-based view of the law in its focus on results and its neglect of contextual factors. In his opinion, the concept of quality being used was overly restrictive in that it left out "democratic values such as human dignity, social justice, equal rights, freedom, participation, transparency. Overlooking these criteria, the bill centres on criteria of effectiveness and skirts the issue of attaining basic social objectives" (ibid, p. 9601). But even the political opposition, adverse to the bill, ended up buying into its logic. For example, that same Member of Parliament warned about the Government concealing the good scores attained in the Basque Country, and censured the ministry for manipulating "the analyses and results of the experts who assess the parameters of the education system" (ibid.).

Thus, in the political debate on the bill, the supposedly unbiased data from the international assessments became an instrumental resource used by advocates and detractors alike. From the political party in power the data were used to justify the inclusion of different educational options of either a more academic or more professional orientation as of the age of 14 (Congreso de Diputados 2002b, p. 19557) or cutting back on the budget for education (Congreso de Diputados 2002c, p. 19648).

Meanwhile, the opposition accused the governing party of have made "scarce use of the results from the main research done in recent decades on this matter" (Congreso de Diputados 2002b, p. 19530). The political debate turned into a game of numbers in which weight no longer went to the best argument but to the largest pile of data, normally read in different ways depending on which side of the political fence one is on. At the Commission on Education, the spokesperson for the Socialist Group in Parliament criticised the Government for not having made a serious diagnosis of the situation before proposing the new bill. She pointed out that when the previous law (LOGSE) was passed, the Ministry of Education commissioned *thirty-four specialists from the OECD* to carry out an analysis on student achievement, and she described the distressing picture they then painted. Against that backdrop, she added, the situation reached during the years the LOGSE was in effect prove to be "a giant leap forward in our country to offset the terrible dropout rate we find here" (Congreso de los Diputados 2002b, p. 19568). What for some was proof of the failings of the previous legislature, for others was proof of its success. The numbers were used to back up one side as well as the other.

## The Socialist Reform

The *Spanish Socialist Workers' Party* (*Partido Socialista Obrero Español*), led by José Luís Rodríguez Zapatero, won the elections on March 14, 2004. As the Socialists had announced in their electoral campaign, one of the first measures that they took when they returned to Government was to halt application of the LOCE. At the same time, they began to draw up a new regulation that culminated in passing the bill known as the *Law on Education* (LOE) on May 3, 2006, with María Jesús San Segundo, first, and Mercedes Cabrera, afterwards, as Ministers of Education and Science during that legislature.

The LOE is articulated along three main lines. The first line establishes the need to combine quality with social equality, i.e., to pursue the objective of quality education for everyone. This line is actually the main purpose of the law. In fact, the document by the Ministry of Education and Science in September 2004 that acted as the basis for the debate with the education community was published under the title *A Quality Education for All and among All*. The quality of education was spelled out in two aims: improve the overall scores on international assessments and reduce the high student dropout rates.

Once again, international assessments and statistics were used more as justification than any general concept of education. New effort was put into glossing over any true debate on the purposes of education, thereby turning all education reform into a set of technical modifications to teaching. In the discussion of the bill in the Lower House, Ana Pastor, the speaker from the People's Party, then in the opposition, repeated the same words used by the Minister, Pilar del Castillo, during the proceedings on the previous bill: "Education is neither on the left nor on the right of the social fabric of our country. Only partisan positions can claim otherwise.

Education is the birthright of all society and holds the very centre of society, as in fact does freedom" (Congreso de Diputados 2005a, p. 6299). Any political point of view on education is thus discredited as "partisan".

As the document published for the debate on the bill states, "quality cannot be conceived as a dimension disjointed from equality, since the two principles are inseparable" (Ministerio de Educación y Ciencia 2004, p. 18). However, social equality is also described in terms of the international assessments, which show less variance on the Spanish scores that in the rest of the OECD average. This allows giving a positive reading to the effects of the comprehensive school policy put through in the 1990s. Thus, the Spanish report on the PISA 2003 results states:

> The total variance in the math scores of Spanish students is 87%, less than the OECD average, which is desirable from the point of view of equality (…) This score is not due to chance, but to the education policies instituted for decades, which have opted to set up the Spanish education system as a comprehensive, integrating system, with a single type of secondary schools for all students, one that shies away from early tracking and other designs that end up in teaching different contents to students of the same age. (Ministerio de Educación, Política Social y Deporte 2008, p. 56)

In the parliamentary debate on the bill, the Minister of Education at the time, Maria Jesús San Segundo, defended the comprehensive school by using these arguments:

> At present, the whole of Spanish society has the conviction that the quality of education must be improved and the scores from PISA 2000 and 2003 must be raised, but also that such a benefit must reach all young people without exception. On this historic occasion, with the objectives of UNESCO and the European Union on the table, any offer of quality without equality would be a fraud that we cannot allow. In the knowledge society, exclusions are contraindicated and PISA has shown that strategies of early tracking of students do not lead to good results. (Congreso de Diputados 2005a, p. 6294)

Nevertheless, the opposition used these same data against the minister to question the concept of social equality as a homogenous distribution of scores: "The OECD, through their PISA program, and the European Union claim that our indicator scores show an early dropout rate, insufficient graduation in education and especially, Madam Minister, you cannot come here to talk of equality" (ibid, p. 6299).

The second line in the socialist education reform is the need to carry out the improvement of the system not only from the efforts of students, the academic community and the school administrators, but also from society as a whole, understanding that educating the young is a concern involving every citizen. As part of this commitment, this law is meant to ensure suitable and balanced distribution of students needing special education support among public schools and private subsidized schools. Even though the law seems to defend the autonomy of the schools and their teaching faculty in drawing up their own teaching programmes, the truth is that this idea of equitable division relies on the schools being homogeneous, with little differentiation in their curriculum and pedagogy, teaching a heterogeneous population whose social plurality is reflected in each school while also representing a model of social harmony.

The third principle underlying the socialist law consists of accepting the educational objectives set by the European Union. The LOE lends itself to the skills-based approach used in the PISA assessments and adopted by the European Union. In the base document for the law, the Ministry stated its desire to "orient the Spanish education objectives in the direction set by the European Union for the year 2010" (Ministerio de Educación y Ciencia 2004, p. 10). Thus, the experts and international politics once again are what decide on the orientation of the reforms to be undertaken.

The analysis of the three main lines of the socialist reform show that, despite their different place on the political spectrum, the type of argumentation for the LOE was much the same as for the previous law. For example, the preamble of the law states that the reform is not the product of any particular ideological or pedagogic stance, but of the results and remarks from expert organisations:

> In November 1990, the ministers of education of the nations from the Organisation for Economic Cooperation and Development met in Paris to discuss how to bring about quality education and vocational training for all. In September 2004, more than sixty ministers convened in Geneva for the 47th International Conference on Education held by UNESCO showed the same concern, which makes it clear that the challenge posed in the preceding decade still holds true (LOE, preamble).

In any case, the LOE attempted to articulate the technical language of the data with an idea of the common good. The law gave great importance to preparing students to be citizens and to participate in economic, social and cultural life with a critical and responsible attitude. To that end, it established adding a course subject to the curriculum generically called "Citizenship education", although its specific formulation varied at the different levels of education. The subject was to be present across the entire school system. Its aim was to offer every student a space for reflection, analysis and study on the fundamental features and operation of a democratic government, the principles and rights set forth in the Spanish Constitution and in the international treaties and declarations on human rights, and the shared values that constitute the underpinnings of democratic citizenship in a global context. This was one of the most controversial aspects of the bill. For most parliamentary groups, it was not necessary to add this subject, since education in values was supposed to be taught transversally throughout the entire curriculum and by all teachers. For the main opposition party, the People's Party, it was an imposition for indoctrination: "[You] impose a subject on indoctrination: Citizenship education" (Congreso de Diputados 2005a, p. 6300). This accusation was based on the lack of any scientific backing to the subject matter: "Without the support of any scientific discipline, a subject matter inexorably heads toward becoming a means for indoctrination; and science is what prevents such indoctrination" (Congreso de Diputados 2005b, p. 30). Only empirical science can set the education ideals for school.

## The Conservative Counter-Reformation

The change in political stripes that came about in Spain following the general elections of 2011 brought victory once again to the People's Party, and caused a new conservative shift in social and education matters. This turnabout now happened in an international economic context that pressured for lowering the public deficit by cutbacks on basic budget items. One of the first measures taken by the recently empowered Government was to start up a legislative counter-reformation of education led by the Minister of Education José Ignacio Wert, a lawyer and sociologist with a long background in politics. In only 9 months from his cabinet appointment, the Minister presented a draft of a bill for public opinion. That draft, from September 2012, began with the following assertion:

> Education is the motor that drives the competitiveness of the economy and the level of prosperity of a country. The level of education of a country determines its ability to compete successfully in the international arena and to face the challenges of the future. Improving the level of education of the citizens means opening the doors to highly qualified jobs, which entails aiming at economic growth and achieving competitive advantages in the global marketplace. (Ministerio de Educación, Cultura y Deporte 2012a, p 1)

In the statement above, the good for the country is predicated on economic growth and competitiveness in a global setting, limiting individual aspiration to merely fitting in with the labour market, with no further ado of a cultural, social or personal development kind. With this letter of introduction, the proposal was unlikely to drum up agreements, which later became patently clear with the constant protest demonstrations and student and trade union strikes that took place while the proceedings on the bill were underway. The *Law on the Improvement of the Quality of Education* (LOMCE) was finally passed by the Spanish Parliament on December 9, 2013, after a bitter and quarrelsome parliamentary debate that pitted the People's Party against all the other groups in the House.

The press release from the Ministry of Education on the occasion of presenting the bill to the Council of Ministers was based on data from the OECD. Namely, it held that the system was financially strong, with twice as much public spending that in the previous decade and high above that in the other OECD countries and economies. However, at the same time, it noted that the weaknesses of the system, according to the international reports, were concentrated on the high dropout rates in lower secondary education (Ministerio de Educación, Cultura y Deporte 2012b). Once again, international comparisons served to justify making the intended changes.

Actually, the use of technical data of an international nature was meant to keep any throwback to partisan politics away from the proposed reform and to convey the idea that the proposal rose above political controversy, which was blamed for the nation's falling behind in education. This discourse struck deep in the public opinion. The following paragraph appears in the final preamble to the law, which was also used in the press release;

> The objectivity of the international comparative studies, which at the least reflect the stagnation of the system, leads to the conclusion that a reform of the education system is

> needed, one that shuns the ideological debates that have hindered progress in recent years. A sensible, practical reform is needed, one that will let each student develop his or her maximum potential (LOMCE, preamble).

Further on, the text reaffirms its intention to carry out the international recommendations, stating that "the reform fostered by the LOMCE is backed up by evidence and gathers the best comparative practices" (ibid.), a litany that was used again and again in parliamentary and public speeches alike. However, its subsequent development proved not to be based on concrete evidence, and the best practices known were not in fact used. Instead, nearly the opposite happened: the repertory of reforms in fact harkened back to antiquated pedagogic and teaching devices, such as moving away from a competences-based curriculum to a contents-based approach.

The bill was quickly passed into law. From its formal proposal at the Council of Ministers to its final publication, the proceedings only took 15 months, a remarkably short period of time. There seemed to be a degree of urgency in the party that supported the Government for a quick solution to what had come to a standstill when the LOCE was repealed in 2004.

Of course, nearly every opposition party objected to the need for the new law as well as to its orientation. Meanwhile, the defence of the reform was based on the need to lower the debate on education to merely technical matters, and always using international data, thereby sidestepping any ideological confrontation. That was the position of the People's Party, whose spokesperson was quick to assert:

> The historic opportunity that the citizens have deposited in this Parliament to become champion and guarantor of the needed improvement to the quality of the education system has been replaced by a terribly ideologicalised, partisan, biased debate unbefitting the nature of the matter of discussion (Congreso de Diputados 2013a, p. 21).

By demonizing the political debate, the intention was to constrain the confrontation to technical terms with supposedly neutral, unbiased data. The spokesperson for the People's Party finished off his argument with a new appeal to what the international reports were preaching, attacking the immobility of political adversaries and their indifference to those reports: "Some people in the House are still bent on reaffirming their own mistakes, on propping up a model of education that the international reports point to every single day as being directly responsible for the ebbing, if not back moving backward, of the quality of the system" (ibid.).

The spokesperson for the Basque Group replied that more discussion was needed over the data, "which in no case justify the terms you propose in the law for the model, for the architecture of the education system" (ibid, p. 27). The representative from the left-wing Plural Left (*Izquierda Plural*) Group went even further: "You have typed out a law on a calculator rather than on the rights of the citizens" (ibid, p. 28).

In summary, the parliamentary confrontation on the LOMCE repeated and reinforced the stances that had been taken in drafting the LOCE back in 2002. The instrumental logic of the LOMCE was shored up by new international data after various cycles of PISA reports that showed Spain stably in the mid-range band of the OECD, which the mass media then portrayed as a stagnation of the education system. Furthermore, individual talent once again become a key element in the argumentation for the reform, but was only used to establish a chain of successive tests that students had to pass at the end of the stages of primary, lower secondary and higher secondary education. The law thus backed away from any approach to the common good that goes beyond the logic of individual success. Finally, the dimension of equal opportunity was buried under a conceptualization that increased segregation by means of early tracking mechanisms in the third year of lower secondary education as well as segregation for religious reasons by grouping students according to their faith, and linguistic segregation in communities with two co-official languages, with separate models proposed for each linguistic option. With segregating elements such as these, the LOMCE moved away from any integrating approach to the common good, which would require an integral look at the education act. What the LOMCE offered was a new reduction of education to the learning of particular subjects considered instrumental.

## Conclusion

In the legislative reforms of the Spanish education system since the first results from the *Programme for International Student Assessment* (PISA) appeared, the continual appeal to empirical data has played an instrumental role in concealing the political meaning of education. This instrumental use helps explain how the same results can be used to justify opposing policies. The problem is not only that of trying to get more out of the data than they can offer (Carabaña 2015); the instrumental use of these data also spurns their own value. It is not important what they indicate. In political discourse, what matters is the aura of 'scientificity' and objectivity, endorsed by the panels of experts in assessment, sometimes from an international origin, which sets the data above the political interests and discussions of their context. This use ignores the fact that international orientations in education, the priority of some objectives over others, of some assessment areas over others, are themselves political subjects.

In a recent revision, Pereira, Perales and Bakieva chose 116 empirical papers done on data from the PISA project in its various forms since the year 2000 and found in the most widely used scholarly databases in English, French, Spanish and Portuguese. As a result of the revision, the authors propose carrying out studies on the extent to which the political and the didactic recommendations made in those papers are valued and implemented accordingly by the different governments (Pereira et al. 2016). In that sense, Fernández-González recently wrote of the impact of PISA on the official discourse upholding the most recent general law on education passed in Spain (the LOMCE). Using strategies of critical discourse analysis of statements from upper-level politicians, this research shows similarities between the orientation of PISA and the reforms covered in the LOMCE. For example, it shows the coincidence between the PISA decision to focus on three specific competencies and the ministerial criticism of curricular dispersion, which leads to concentration on a few areas deemed instrumental. The study also highlights the individualist approach taken by the PISA model, which it relates to the defence made in the Spanish legal text of the need to increase personal effort and attend to individual talents, disregarding the contingencies of the context (Fernández-González 2015).

The coincidence in discourses between PISA and the LOMCE goes beyond mere ideological likeness between a supranational organism defending a particular kind of economics and a government of a political stripe close to it. In the end, what is being suggested is the validity of PISA as a tool for assessing educational policies and the difficulty in discerning its objectivity. Pedró (2012) thus distinguishes between the impact in the media and the impact in discourse in politics as a result of PISA. He concurs with Meyer and Benavot's thesis in that "the 'cloud of data' produced by PISA may easily operate like a Rorschach in which anyone can find support for any preconceived idea" (Meyer and Benavot 2013, p. 21), and points out that most politicians in office look more at the international reports than their own internal assessments. As Pedró highlights, PISA measures constructs that are not featured in national programs, thereby bestowing on the OECD the role of designers of an international curriculum, one that is hastily copied by whatever government happen to be in power and have pledged to reform their own curricula, either by adding new orientations or by concentrating on the areas measured by PISA.

However, in terms of political discourse, these analyses have fallen on deaf ears. Indeed, in the documentation on the parliamentary debates we have reviewed, references to actual researchers in education are few and far between. The source of justification seems to rest solely on data as provided by the reports from official national or international agencies. Mr. Gradgrind's words in *Hard Times* resonate here: "In this life, we want nothing but Facts, sir; nothing but Facts!" (Dickens 2001, p. 2.). From the supposed objectivity of data, any attempt to question or look beyond what the international assessments say is dismissed, as Minister Wert did, as "ideological *apriorism*" (Congreso de Diputados 2013b, p. 34), as if the reading made of the data, whether by the government or the opposition, were not also political. The alternative to that de-politisation that arose in the parliamentary debates merely amounts to converting politics into a realm of pure opinion, where, as an opposition member told the Government, "it is legitimate that you try to impose your model, but it is equally legitimate that we try to avoid it" (Congreso de Diputados 2002a, p. 9607). The political debate thus becomes a one-sided dialogue in which the only possible approach is the one of strategic agreements, or, as another congressman called them, satisfactory balances (ibid., p. 9614). What these debates often show is the eclipsing of political judgement, like the "manifestation of the wind of thought" that Hannah Arendt referred to, which is not knowledge, or stockpiling data, "but the ability to tell right from wrong, beautiful from ugly" (Arendt 1978, p. 193).

An oft-repeated phrase in this process is that education "is neither on the left nor on the right". Minister Pilar del Castillo appealed to Arendt to back up this argument (Congreso de Diputados 2002a, p. 9593). In her essay *The Crisis in Education*,

Arendt asserted that "we must decisively divorce the realm of education from the others, most of all from the realm of public, political life" (Arendt 2006, p. 192). Arendt's statement regarding political initiation addresses her conception of education as a transition between the private world, where childhood takes place, and the public or political world, where adulthood occurs. Politics should be kept outside the classrooms; to do otherwise would rob children of the chance that the radical fact of birth bestows of creating something new. Arendt thus seems to side with the opponents to including the course on citizen education in the school curriculum.

However, it has been pointed out that, in contrast to the rejection of politics in *The Crisis in Education*, Arendt's philosophy contains elements that help articulate the two realities better (Biesta 2010). For example, in the manuscripts for her *Introduction into Politics*, Arendt wrote that "politics is based on the fact of human plurality. God created man, but men are a human, earthly product, the product of human nature (…) Politics deals with the coexistence and association of *different* men" (Arendt 2005, p. 93). Politics is in the realm of diversity, of the polyphony of voices. Any attempt at removing it from education means replacing human plurality with a one-way image, in this case that of *homo oeconomicus*, which creates economic growth and is skilled at moving about on the stage of global competition.

Rejection or fear of talking about the valuative dimension of the concept of education leaves no room in the political discourse for a pedagogical concept of quality. Instead, this discourse usually focuses on the improvement of the scores on national and international assessments and on lowering drop-out rates, for example as done in the preamble to the LOE. From a less reductionist perspective, quality in education requires paying attention and valuing the intrinsic elements in the education process, such as the type of education desired, the corresponding training of the teachers, the curriculum or the teaching methods suited to that conception, etc. Furthermore, the fact that the assessment of the quality of education is based on a ranking of scores on external tests itself establishes a hierarchy of schools leading society to interiorize a single model of good schooling, and thus, of the educated person (Van Zanten 2008, p. 315).

After ratification of the Constitution of 1978, every different political party that takes office has generated a new law on education to reflect its own particular view. The top echelons of the education system have therefore been criticised for having politicised education without restraint, thereby unnecessarily complicating the life of schools and families alike. The intention of separating education from politics in each new legislative bill conceals an attempt at being free of that criticism. But the alternative to this continual roller coaster of laws is not to sell the message of a false de-politisation, but to work to achieve common ground, each from his or her political preference. Spain has made it a habit for each new legislature to call for a widespread pact on education without it ever having been achieved. Such a pact cannot mean stifling the polyphony of voices under the weight of the data, which would be tantamount to replacing the democracy of the people with a government of experts. This of course does not mean rejecting out of principle what the empirical data can offer, provided that the data are not expected to have the last word over all other arguments.

The case of Spain, which we have analysed here by looking at the three last general laws passed on the education system, is an example of the political debate being waylaid by the technical details, the explicit ideological aims by the need for an internationally more competitive system. In the realm of the new political right that arose in Spain under the Constitution of 1978, this step gave victory to neo-liberalism over neo-conservativism, with the victory meaning the submission of a vision of life based on traditional values, to a vision based on the belief that the market will transform private good into public good (de Puelles 2016). In the new left, the way of justification we have seen in the debates represents the rise of neoliberal socialism and the surrender to the forces of the economy, which Pierre Bourdieu and Günter Grass denounced in a famous conversation at the end of the 1990s (Le Monde 1999). Both tendencies dramatically affect the notion of the common good, a notion which does not fit comfortably in either one.

As the UNESCO report *Rethinking Education* has made clear, the loss of a shared valuative dimension under the alliance of scientificism and neo-liberalism is one of the most worrying symptoms in education systems today. The report draws attention to the weakening of the concept of the public good at play with the conversion of education into learning in the international discourse, and suggests correcting it by recovering the notion of the common good:

> The notion of common good goes beyond the instrumental concept of the public good in which human well-being is framed by individualistic socio-economic theory. From a "common good" perspective, it is not only the "good life" of individuals that matters, but also the goodness of the life that humans hold in common. It cannot be a personal or parochial good. It is important to emphasize that the recent shift from "education" to "learning" in international discourse signals a potential neglect of the collective dimensions and the purpose of education as a social endeavour. This is true both for the broader social outcomes expected of education, and for how educational opportunities are organized. The notion of education as a "common good" reaffirms the collective dimension of education as a shared social endeavour (shared responsibility and commitment to solidarity). (UNESCO 2015, p. 78)

Overcoming the scenario these policies have led to will require resituating education in the context of a debate that must necessarily be not only, but also fundamentally, ethical and political.

## References


Arendt, H. (1978). *The life of the mind*. San Diego: Harcourt.

Arendt, H. (2005). *The promise of politics*. New York: Schocken Books.

Arendt, H. (2006). *Between past and future*. New York: Penguin.

Biesta, G. (2010). How to exist politically and learn from it: Hannah Arendt and the problem of democratic education. *Teachers College Record, 112*(2), 556–575.

Carabaña, J. (2015). *La inutilidad de PISA para las escuelas*. Madrid: Catarata.

Choi, A., & Calero, J. (2013). Determinantes del riesgo de fracaso escolar en España en PISA-2009 y propuestas de reforma. *Revista de Educación, 362*, 562–593.

Congreso de los Diputados. (2002a). Proyecto de Ley Orgánica de Calidad de la Educación. *Diario de Sesiones del Congreso de los Diputados (Pleno y Diputación Permanente, VII Legislatura), 193*, 9593–9620.

Congreso de los Diputados. (2002b). Dictamen sobre el Proyecto de Ley Orgánica de Calidad de la Educación. *Diario de Sesiones del Congreso de los Diputados (Comisiones, VII Legislatura), 600*, 19522–19598.

Congreso de los Diputados. (2002c). Dictamen sobre el Proyecto de Ley Orgánica de Calidad de la Educación. *Diario de Sesiones del Congreso de los Diputados (Comisiones, VII Legislatura), 602*, 19630–19686.

Congreso de los Diputados. (2005a). Proyecto de Ley Orgánica de la Educación. *Diario de Sesiones del Congreso de los Diputados (Pleno y Diputación Permanente, VIII Legislatura), 118*, 6293–6314.

Congreso de los Diputados. (2005b). Dictamen sobre el Proyecto de Ley Orgánica de la Educación. *Diario de Sesiones del Congreso de los Diputados (Comisiones, VIII Legislatura), 418*, 5–44.

Congreso de los Diputados. (2013a). Dictamen sobre el Proyecto de Ley Orgánica para la Mejora de la Calidad Educativa. *Diario de Sesiones del Congreso de los Diputados (Pleno y Diputación Permanente, X Legislatura), 145*, 5–33.

Congreso de los Diputados. (2013b). Comparecencia del señor Ministro de Educación, Cultura y Deporte (Wert Ortega). *Diario de Sesiones del Congreso de los Diputados (Comisiones, X Legislatura), 323*, 1–48.

de Puelles, M. (2016). Reflexiones sobre cuarenta años de educación en España o la irresistible seducción de las leyes. *Historia y Memoria de la Educación, 3*, 15–44.

Dickens, C. (2001). *Hard times*. Mineola: Dover.

Digón, P. (2003). La Ley Orgánica de Calidad de la Educación: análisis crítico de la nueva reforma educativa española. *Revista Electrónica de Investigación Educativa, 5*(1). Retrieved March 28, 2016, from http://redie.uabc.mx/vol5no1/contenido-digon.html

Duru, M. (2013). Desde el atractivo poder de los datos de PISA a las desilusiones del Benchmarking. ¿Desafío a la evaluación de los sistemas educativos? *Revista de Currículum y Formación del Profesorado, 17*(2), 93–104.

Fernández-Cano, A. (2016). Una crítica metodológica de las evaluaciones PISA. *Relieve, 22*(1), 1–17.

Fernández-González, N. (2015). PISA como instrumento de legitimación de la reforma de la LOMCE. *Bordón. Revista de Pedagogía, 67*(1), 165–178.

Gil-Flores, J. (2014). Factores asociados a la brecha regional del rendimiento español en la evaluación PISA. *Revista de Investigación Educativa, 32*(2), 393–410.

INCE. (2001). *Conocimientos y destrezas para la vida. Primeros resultados del proyecto PISA 2000*. Madrid: INCE.

Le Monde. (1999). Pierre Bourdieu et Günter Grass: la tradition "d'ouvrir sa gueule", *Le Monde*, 02–12–1999. Retrieved May 9, 2016, from http://www.lemonde.fr/une-abonnes/article/1999/12/02/pierre-bourdieu-et-gunter-grass-la-tradition-d-ouvrir-sa-gueule_33212_3207.html

López, J. A., & Moreno, M. L. (1997a). *Resultados de Ciencias. Tercer Estudio Internacional de Matemáticas y Ciencias (TIMSS)*. Madrid: INCE.

López, J. A., & Moreno, M. L. (1997b). *Resultados de Matemáticas. Tercer Estudio Internacional de Matemáticas y Ciencias (TIMSS)*. Madrid: INCE.

Meyer, H. D., & Benavot, A. (2013). PISA and the globalization of education governance: Some puzzles and problems. In H. Meyer & A. Benavot (Eds.), *PISA, power and policy: The emergence of global education governance* (pp. 9–26). Oxford: Symposium Books.

Ministerio de Educación Nacional. (1961). *Datos y cifras de la enseñanza en España, 1960*. Madrid: Ministerio de Educación Nacional/Secretaría General Técnica.

Ministerio de Educación y Ciencia. (2004). *Una educación de calidad para todos y entre todos*. Madrid: MEC.

Ministerio de Educación, Cultura y Deporte. (2012a). *Anteproyecto de Ley Orgánica para la Mejora de la Calidad Educativa*. Retrieved May 3, 2016, from http://www.stecyl.es/borralex/LOMCE/Anteproyecto_LOMCE_septiembre2012.pdf

Ministerio de Educación, Cultura y Deporte. (2012b). *El Ministro de Educación, Cultura y Deporte presenta al Consejo de Ministros el Anteproyecto de Ley Orgánica para la Mejora de la Calidad Educativa*. Retrieved April 25, 2016, from http://www.mecd.gob.es/prensa-mecd/en/actualidad/2012/09/20120921-consejo-ministros.html

Ministerio de Educación, Política Social y Deporte. (2008). *PISA 2003. Matemáticas. Informe español*. Madrid: MEPSYD.

Pedró, F. (2012). Deconstruyendo los puentes de PISA: del análisis de resultados a la prescripción política. *Revista Española de Educación Comparada, 19*, 139–172.

Pereira, D., Perales, M. J., & Bakieva, M. (2016). Análisis de tendencias en las investigaciones realizadas a partir de los datos del Proyecto PISA. *Relieve, 22*(1), 1–18.

Pereyra, M.A., & Kotthoff, H.G. (2009). La experiencia de PISA en Alemania: recepción, reformas recientes y reflexiones sobre un sistema educativo en cambio. *Profesorado. Revista de Currículum y Formación del Profesorado*, 13(2), 6–224.

Pereyra, M.A., Kotthoff, H.G., Cowen, R. (2013). PISA a examen: Cambiando el conocimiento, cambiando las pruebas y cambiando las escuelas. *Profesorado. Revista de Currículum y Formación del Profesorado*, 17(2), 6–224.

Sáenz, C. (2007). La competencia matemática (en el sentido de PISA) de los futuros maestros. *Enseñanza de las Ciencias. Revista de Investigación y experiencias Didácticas, 25*(3), 355–366.

Salmerón, N. (1878). Prólogo. In H. Giner (Ed.), *Filosofía y Arte* (pp. VII–XXXV). Madrid: Imprenta de M. Minuesa.

Serrano, M. A., Vidal-Abarca, E., & Ferrer, A. (eprint). Decisiones estratégicas de lectura y rendimiento en tareas de competencia lectora similares a PISA. *Educación XXI.* doi:http://dx.doi.org/10.5944/educxx1.12076. Retrieved October 24, 2016, from http://revistas.uned.es/index.php/educacionXX1/article/view/12076/13471

UNESCO. (2015). *Rethinking education. Towards a global common good?* París: UNESCO.

Van Zanten, A. (2008). Reflexividad y elección de la escuela por los padres de la clase media en Francia. In M. I. Jociles & A. Franzé (Eds.), *Es la escuela el problema? Perspectivas socio-antropológicas de etnografía y educación* (pp. 307–331). Madrid: Trotta.

Vélaz, C. (2006). Programa para la Evaluación Internacional de los Alumnos. *Revista de Educación,* special issue, 13–542.

# Chapter 5
# Defining How We Get from Research to Practice: A Model Framework for Schools

**Elizabeth Farley-Ripple, Allison E. Karpyn, Kalyn McDonough, and Katherine Tilley**

**Abstract** In this chapter, the authors argue that stronger connections between research and practice in education are inherently a public good. The authors discuss recent efforts by the US Government to encourage production of better education research, and more effective application of this research to practice. The current educational policy climate, generated in large part by the 2001 passage of No Child Left Behind and reiterated through reauthorization in the Every Student Succeeds Act, places immense pressure on schools and districts to use evidence to inform their decisions regarding student learning. However, due to the complexity of these decisions, such mandates have often fallen short in ensuring that evidence is incorporated. The chapter establishes the context of national education policy regarding research evidence use and explores recent efforts which seek to better understand and motivate the use of research in schools to inform the public good. As this discussion reveals problematic assumptions and solutions, the authors propose a bi-directional model for understanding the relationship between research and practice, and highlight current efforts that support use of research evidence in schools and districts.

## Introduction to the Issue

In this chapter, we argue that stronger connections between research and practice are inherently a public good. Recent efforts by the US government have sought to better understand how to generate better research and better application of that research to practice. The current educational policy climate, generated in large part by the 2001 passage of No Child Left Behind and reiterated through reauthorization in the Every Student Succeeds Act, places immense pressure on schools and districts to use evidence to inform their decisions regarding student learning. However,

E. Farley-Ripple • A.E. Karpyn • K. McDonough (✉) • K. Tilley
School of Education, University of Delaware, Newark, DE, USA
e-mail: kaymcd@udel.edu

 
M.Y. Eryaman, B. Schneider (eds.), *Evidence and Public Good in Educational Policy, Research and Practice*, Educational Governance Research 6,
DOI 10.1007/978-3-319-58850-6_5

30 years of research (Short 1970) on knowledge utilization, organizational decision-making, and evidence-based decision-making in education suggests that incorporating evidence is almost certainly not as simple as merely mandating that it be done (Farley-Ripple 2012). Our purpose in this chapter is to establish the context of national education policy regarding research evidence use and to explore recent efforts which seek to better understand and motivate the use of research in schools to inform the public good. As this discussion reveals problematic assumptions and solutions, we describe a proposed bi-directional model for understanding the relationship between research and practice, and highlight current efforts that support use of research evidence in schools and districts.

## *Creating an Accountable U.S. Educational System*

Modern efforts to revitalize the US education system are often traced to the early 1980's when the United States Department of Education undertook a critical examination of the practice of public education (U.S. Department of Education 1983). Based on perceptions that the U.S. system was inferior to those of other industrialized nations, a landmark report, *A Nation At Risk,* articulated 38 recommendations in the areas of content, standards and expectations, time, teaching, leadership and fiscal support. In response to the report, issued by the Commission on Excellence in Education, a tidal wave of reform efforts took hold at national and local levels across the country. Reforms generally focused on the need for "rigorous and measurable standards" and kick-started a standards and accountability movement that has continued to build momentum for decades.

Under the leadership of President Bill Clinton, the emphasis on accountability and standards continued to get support including additional funding and requirements to develop state standards for academic-content and tests. Efforts were formally established with the passing of the *Improving America's Schools Act* of 1994 and the *Goals 2000: Educate America Act.* Nearly 10 years later, *No Child Left Behind Act of 2001* (NCLB), which passed with overwhelming bipartisan support in Congress, expanded testing efforts and more clearly tied penalties to poor test performance (Brenchley 2011). Again, the policy was fueled by an interest in maintaining U.S. competitiveness (Hess and Rotherham 2007). Further, the policy recognized achievement gaps between poor and minority students and their more advantaged peers, and sought to raise the bar on educational opportunities provided to all children nationwide.

As federal policy began to emphasize school standards and accountability, there were parallel efforts to ramp up education research and a renewed emphasis on bridging the gap between research-based knowledge and school practice (Biddle and Saha 2006; Blake and Ottoson 2009; Broekkamp and van Hout-Wolters 2007; Honig and Coburn 2008; Ottoson 2009; Wong and Mid-Atlantic Lab for Student Success 1998). NCLB specified new expectations for what constituted research knowledge, effectively stipulating the level of rigor of the research designs from which the evidence was derived. NCLB legislation went so far as to include in its definition of scientifically-based research "a preference for random-assignment experiments" in impact evaluations of programs or policies (NCLB 2001). Not long afterwards, *Education Sciences Reform Act* of 2002 (ESRA) established the Institute of Education Sciences (IES), which prioritized funding for randomized experiments (Viadero 2004). The U.S. Department of Education established explicit expectations for the role of research in informing decisions about education programs, policies, and practices through NCLB and reinforced by ESRA. For example, NCLB required that all federally-funded education programs, including out-of-school time programs, had to be based on research studies that met specific scientific standards.

According to NCLB, these scientific standards consist of:

1. Use of the scientific method with an emphasis on experimental control (or comparison) groups;
2. Replication of results, using multiple studies by different investigator;
3. Ability to generalize results from one sample to other children in the general population;
4. Fulfillment of rigorous standards with an emphasis on peer review; and convergence (or consistency) of results between studies (NCLB 2001).

"The primary goal of scientifically based research (SBR) is to ensure that programs for children are based on methods that have been proven effective and are therefore more likely to benefit other children, with a corollary goal of increasing the overall quality of education research" (Bouffard 2003). As a result of these policies, the landscape of education research, for the purpose of bettering the education system in the United States, began to change drastically.

The *Every Student Succeeds Act* of 2015 (ESSA) replaced NCLB as the most current reauthorization of the Elementary and Secondary Education Act, and shifted to the states more flexibility and accountability to implement educational evaluations. The legislation continues to emphasize the need for "evidence-based" programs, which is defined as "activity, strategy, or intervention that shows a statistically significant effect on improving student outcomes or other relevant outcomes" (ESSA 2015). But unlike NCLB, ESSA uses a tiered system to order the rigor of the research. The tiers span from: (1) randomized experiments, to (2) quasi-experiments, to (3) correlational studies, and finally to (4) strong theories "likely to improve student outcomes" (ESSA 2015). Additionally, ESSA returns the power to states, from the federal government, in determining the quality of evidence, and accountability now lies more clearly on the shoulders of schools and districts.

## *Research and Research Use as a Public Good*

The policies we have just described, in many ways, attend to public education as a public good, and reflect Labaree's (1997) values of both democratic equality and social efficiency. Labaree explains democratic equality as operationalized in preparing citizens, providing equal treatment, and offering equal access as a means of achieving the egalitarian goals of education. Labaree further explains social efficiency in terms of stratification and vocationalism, and that education serves as a social mechanism for enhancing economic productivity. While sometimes conflicting, both conceptualizations of education as a public good are evidenced in the political discourse leading to the aforementioned policies and in the policies themselves. However, we extend this argument a step further. Through explicit and increased emphasis on not only the production of high quality education research, but in the *use* of research to inform decision-making in the service of democratic equality and social efficiency, United States federal accountability policy promotes education research as a public good as well.

More than a decade into efforts to transform education research there are clear indications that the nature and rigor of the research produced today is quite different from that of 20 years ago (NBES 2008, 2015). Further, expectations for the *use* of this research in order to improve the educational attainment and well-being of children and society have grown dramatically. When done well, research provides meaningful, actionable and equity-supporting strategies that result in improved educational outcomes which benefit both children and society. The public good is derived from both the use of tax-payer dollars to fund the research (e.g. through grants or direct funding of institutions) and in the application of strategies derived from research in public educational settings. We offer, by way of example, ways in which education research can and has served the public good.

Reading for example is one area where the field's knowledge of how and when to teach students has grown enormously in the past 15 years. Nationally, Reading Recovery, a short-term early intervention approach designed to help the lowest achieving readers in first grade to advance their proficiency to match that of their peers, resulted in notable achievement gains across contexts and demographic categories (May et al. 2016). Further, the development of this program and its subsequent large scale evaluation were funded through the Institute for Education Sciences, a tax-payer funded institution.

Similarly, findings from a review of secondary administrative data revealed that students who are unable to read on grade level by grade 3 are far more likely to fail to graduate on time from high-school (Hernandez 2011). This new evidence shifted benchmarking for children nationally, generated new conversations about early intervention strategies, and resulted in widespread development of early warning systems that help to reach at-risk youth before they drop out.

A pivotal 2011 study, *Breaking Schools' Rules,* examined school discipline as related to students' success and juvenile justice involvement among one million Texas students and found the following: nearly six in ten public school students were suspended or expelled at least once between their seventh- and eighth grade school years, African-American students and those with educational disabilities were disproportionately more likely to be removed from the classroom for disciplinary reasons, and students who were suspended or expelled for a discretionary violation had a significantly higher likelihood of being in contact with the juvenile justice system (Fabelo et al. 2011). The discipline policies negatively impacted students' lives far beyond the classroom, and disproportionately impacted groups of students who historically have faced discrimination, students of color and students with disabilities. The study exposed the damaging effects of policies and practices that are not driven by data and research. These alarming findings ushered in a number of initiatives by federal agencies and private entities. The U.S. Department of Education and U.S. Department of Justice launched the Supportive School Discipline Initiative targeted at building consensus for action among a variety of stakeholders, investing in research and data collection needed to inform programs and policies, ensuring school policies align with the nation's civil rights laws, and promoting knowledge around evidence-based practices on the topic. The initiative has ignited a nationwide movement on restorative justice (U.S. Department of Education 2011).

From the premise that education research is a public good, then a primary concern is to ensure strong, enduring connections between research and practice. Though federal policy demands a significant role for research in educational decision-making, as Honig and Coburn (2008) note, there are implicit assumptions underlying federal efforts to bridge research and practice, including the presumption that particular forms of evidence (e.g. "what works" research) are more appropriate than other forms, that the resources available to review and utilize research results are adequate, and that mechanisms are in place to stimulate research that is timely and relevant. Concerns for the underutilization of social science research in social policy have further resulted in studies that investigated the barriers to use in policymaking and local decision processes. The findings of these studies consistently reveal weak ties between researchers and practitioners (Backer 1993; Broekkamp and van Hout-Wolters 2007; Davies and Nutley 2008; Landry et al. 2001), that the characteristics of research evidence may present challenges for uptake (March 1994; Hannaway 1989; Birkeland et al. 2005) and that the characteristics of both educational organizations and decision-makers may constrain or support research use (see Farley-Ripple 2012 for a discussion).

Reflecting on the history of education research and policy, efforts of national legislation to influence research use in schools are based on a particular theory of action that may not accurately reflect decision-making in schools and districts. In order to fulfill the role of research as a public good, we need a framework for understanding and improving the relationship between research and practice. Our purpose in this chapter is to offer one. We begin by exploring what we know about the use of research in education.

## What Do We Know About Research Use in Schools?

We start with examining *how* research is used in schools. There are three forms of research use commonly examined in the literature: instrumental, conceptual, and symbolic/political.

***Instrumental use*** describes a situation in which individuals are able to cite or document specific ways in which evidence was used in decision-making processes (Caplan 1979; Rich 1977). This form of use is consistent with guidance in U.S. accountability legislation and emphasizes the use of research evidence in program or intervention adoption decisions. Research does indeed find that this is an important role for research. In Coburn and Talbert's (2006) study, for example, researchers found four different types of goals for research use which included meeting accountability demands, informing program and policy decisions, monitoring student progress to inform placement decisions, and monitoring student progress to inform instructional practices (Coburn and Talbert 2006). Examples are frequent in the literature and are reiterated in a recent report from the National Center for Research, Policy and Practice which found that instrumental use may be the most commonly reported type of research use, primarily involving designing professional development and directing resources to programs (Penuel et al. 2016).

***Conceptual use*** refers to gradual shifts in decision-makers' consciousness and an adaptation of their basic perspectives. This means that use can occur even if direct application of evidence does not because research can expand or challenge people's understanding of issues and potential solutions. This 'enlightenment' function (Weiss and Bucuvalas 1980) of research "contributes to the policymaking process indirectly and over time by shaping more general interpretations and understandings of issues and gradually altering the working assumptions and concepts of policymakers" (Porter and Hicks 1997, p. 34). This form of use is not evident in current accountability policy, but is an important way in which research may impact education policy and practice. Farley-Ripple (2012) noted that conceptual use of research played a significant role in three decisions made in response to growing accountability pressures, including the need to improve professional development, the strategic planning process, and textbook adoption. In a recent blog, Farrell and Coburn (2016) elaborate on the power of conceptual use to introduce new ideas, broaden or narrow understanding, and to provide organizing frameworks for improvement efforts. These are notably *not* adoption decisions but represent important connections between research and practice.

***Symbolic or political use*** of research refers to the manipulation of evidence in order to reach particular profit or power goals. Several studies provide examples of how district central office administrators used evidence to justify or corroborate opinions they have already formulated (Corcoran et al. 2001; Hannaway 1989; Honig and Coburn 2008). Symbolic use also includes behavior in which users believe the perception of evidence-based decision-making is important, but are not engaging with or applying the evidence in meaningful ways (Knorr 1977; Feldman and March 1981). Though there is significant evidence of instrumental and conceptual use of research evidence in education, attention needs to be paid to political and symbolic use as well. This may be particularly true under the current logic of federal accountability policies in which mandates and contingent funding are used to motivate research use.

In addition to *how* research is used, we also must understand *what* research is used. Federal accountability policy privileges a specific definition of scientifically-based research and has promoted it through significant investments, described earlier. However, it is unclear whether there is shared understanding about what constitutes research evidence (Bransford et al. 2009) and studies have consistently identified a gap between what is privileged and what is actually used. Educators hold a variety of definitions of what counts as evidence, with research identifying formats ranging from empirical studies, to local evaluation reports, and to expert opinion to popular press (Coburn et al. 2009; Behrstock-Sheratt et al. 2011; Farley-Ripple 2012; Finnigan et al. 2013; Davies and Nutley 2008; Penuel et al. 2016). It is important to note that most of the literature on evidence use typically focuses on identifying what research educators consider, not necessarily *all* the information sources that might constitute evidence in decision-making, which include the broad range of data available to schools and districts, as well as what Kennedy (1982) calls "working knowledge," described as the "array of beliefs, assumptions, interests, and experiences that influences the behavior of individuals at work" (p. 1–2).

Lastly, we must understand *who* uses research in educational decision-making. In the United States, districts and schools sit at the nexus of debates surrounding education research use. Much of the legislation that targets districts to utilize evidence in their decision-making was brought about by the passage of NCLB; for example, several provisions state districts are responsible for the timely collection and reporting of massive amounts of demographic and achievement data, for identifying scientifically based research on program effectiveness to inform adoption of programs and practices, and for conducting and utilizing evaluations in decisions about program improvement and funding. This is reiterated under ESSA in which districts must present plans for improving persistently low-performing schools, and those plans must meet at least one of the tiers of evidence previously described. Furthermore, school district central offices play an important role in district change, influencing the everyday work of school level educators. For example, central offices may restructure instructional programs, professional development, school leadership structures, or relationships with the community (Corcoran et al. 2001; Hightower 2002; Massell and Goertz 2002). Further, district central offices are critical actors in the use of research in education decision-making, both as users of research in decisions about curricular and instructional reform (Farley-Ripple 2008, 2012; Honig and Coburn 2008; Corcoran 2003; Penuel et al. 2016) and in supporting the role of research in school-based decisions (Finnegan et al. 2012; Honig and Venkatswaran, 2012). Accordingly, much of what we know about research use in the U.S. is focused on district central offices, though that literature remains sparse and in need of development, particularly in light of increasing expectations under accountability policy.

In contrast to advancements in our knowledge about the ways in which research is used in districts, relatively little is known about school-based use of research and use of research by individual practitioners such as teachers or school-administrators in the United States, in contrast to other nations which have explored this issue more systematically (Hemsley-Brown and Sharp 2003; Dagenais et al. 2012; Biddle and Saha 2006). Schools and school-based administrators are not specifically targeted in current accountability policy, but may, in fact, be important to consider as users of research evidence as many decisions impacting teaching and learning are situated at the school level. In one of a handful of studies, Drill et al. (2012) examined teacher's perspectives on education research and found that teachers occasionally review and apply education research, but under very specific circumstances. Teachers reported using peer-reviewed academic research when there was an immediate, pressing concern, but only after consulting with other, more "efficient" resources. Additionally, teachers reported a wide range of skepticism around research, but this skepticism was reduced when the information came from trusted sources and/or the findings worked in their classroom (Drill et al. 2012). Other studies have focused on how school based educators talk about research (Nicholson-Goodman and Garman 2007; Mirezky 2007), which suggest engagement with research in decision-making about practice but offer little insight into actual use.

Across districts and schools, use of research depends on a variety of factors, and knowledge use hinges on the intricacies of implementation at the local level. The complex nature of decision-making in education is well documented and understood to be multi-faceted where technical, political, and educational challenges abound (Fuhrman and Elmore 2004; Honig et al. 2014). Decision-maker goals vary, and pressure from a variety of key stakeholders can result in the devaluation of research evidence and increased emphasis on other forms of evidence or opinion (Asen and Gurke 2014). Ultimately, this means that there is a large disconnect between the expectations of research use in schools from a policy standpoint, and the actual use of research in school decision-making.

A review of what we know about research use in schools, with particular attention to the *who, what*, and *how*, reveals that the assumptions reflected in policy attempts to bridge research and practice may be flawed. We recognize that the types of research privileged by policy are not necessarily prioritized by decision-makers, and that a focus on the instrumental role of research in educational decision-making substantially underestimates the extent to which research can and does serve the public good. Further, the literature suggests that educators at all levels of the system – from teachers through central office administrators – are actors in decision-making and engage with research as part of their practice (Coburn et al. 2009; Daly et al. 2014; Farley-Ripple 2012; Finnigan et al. 2013; Hightower 2002; Honig and Coburn 2008; Honig and Venkateswaran 2012; Mac Iver and Farley 2003). This disconnect suggests that the top-down approach of improving the relationship between research and practice is not likely to be an effective one; research use cannot be oversimplified as only a dissemination issue, nor a lack of practitioner consumption. Rather, Lavis et al. (2003) describes the challenge as developing a "decision-relevant culture" among researchers and a "research-attuned culture" among decision-makers. Thus, we argue that the problem of the research-practice gap, and any proposed solution, is "bi-directional".

## A Bidirectional Perspective on Research and Practice

Improving the role of research in educational decision-making requires a bi-directional approach, rather than isolated shifts in the production of research or mandated changes in decision-making. Our current line of research seeks to better understand what it would take to better align or couple the research and practice communities. To do so, we must better understand the disconnect between the communities. We have adopted a comprehensive framework for rethinking research use in schools (Farley-Ripple, et al., under review), but attend here to some of the key areas in which a new model for research to practice ought to focus. We look to Dunn's (1980) five types of assumptions that underlie the "gap" between research and policy, which he articulates as contingent on products, inquiry, problems, structures, and processes. As we seek to understand differences between research and practice communities in the education context of the twenty-first century, we interpret these five categories, or gaps, as relating to assumptions and perspectives about: the usefulness of research products; the nature and quality of research; problems that research addresses; the structures, processes, and incentives surrounding research production and use; and the relationships between communities.

*Usefulness of Research Products* Building on the prior discussion of forms of research privileged by policy and those valued by practitioners, one critical gap that must be understood and addressed is differing assumptions about the usefulness of research products (Cousins and Simon 1996; Davidson and Nowicki 2012; Tseng and Nutley 2014). From the research community perspective, usefulness can be understood as the range of products produced, their intended audience, and how they are anticipated to be used. From the practitioner perspective, usefulness relates to frequently accessed resources and the preferences underlying those choices. The extent to which the products valued and produced by researchers intersect with those preferred by practitioners indicates the usefulness dimension of the gap.

*Nature and Quality of Research* This gap pertains to differences in how the two communities value different qualities of research, including issues related to internal and external validity as well as conclusiveness of findings. For example, the What Works Clearinghouse employs standards that place great weight on internal validity for drawing causal inference (i.e., randomized experiments). In contrast, school-based decision-makers often prefer evidence from organizations similar to their own, regardless of study design (Supovitz and Klein 2003; Corcoran et al. 2001; Finnegan et al. 2012), which suggests greater weight on external validity. These preferences raise questions about how practitioners value research methods (Broekkamp and Hout-Walters 2007; Coburn and Talbert 2006) or, alternatively, they suggest limited capacity to critically interpret research (Supovitz and Klein

2003; West and Rhoton 1994; Reichardt 2000; Coburn and Talbert 2006). The extent to which researcher standards and practitioner preferences are similar or different is an indication of the nature/quality dimension of the gap.

*Problems Addressed by Research* This dimension of the gap suggests that there may be issues related to the relevance of research. From the research community perspective, this concern relates to decisions about what should be researched and to what degree research is able to address current problems of practice (Maynard 2006). From the practitioner perspective, the characteristics of problems of practice, including both the issue (e.g. instructional, organizational) and the nature of the problem (e.g. identifying the range of potential solutions vs. choosing to adopt a specific solution) may influence the role of research in solving those problems (West and Rhoton 1994; Supovitz and Klein 2003; Hemsley-Brown 2009). The extent to which the evidence produced by the research community is timely and relevant to the problems confronting real schools is an indicator of this dimension of the gap.

*Structure, Process, and Incentives* This dimension of the gap is concerned with the context in which researchers and practitioners operate, what influences researchers to produce certain kinds of research, and what influences practitioners to use research or other evidence (Coburn and Turner 2012; Burkhardt and Schoenfeld 2003; Landry et al. 2001). A range of conditions influence use, including organizational structure and culture (Coburn and Talbert 2006; Corcoran et al. 2001; Honig 2003; Finnegan et al. 2012; Massel and Goertz 2012; Spillane 1998; Weiss 1995; West and Rhoton 1994). As contextual factors related to structures, processes, and incentives influence research use, it is important to understand when and to what degree these factors increase or reduce the gap between research and practice communities.

*Relationships Between Communities* Research use may be considered a function of the relationship between communities in the production of research and in education decision- making (Huberman 1990; Landry et al. 2001; Cousins and Simon 1996; Backer 1986; Honig and Venkateswaran 2012; Lavis et al. 2003; Coburn and Stein 2010; Louis 1992). Lavis et al. (2003) categorizes relations as producer pushed (e.g. dissemination), user-pulled (e.g. active search by users), and exchange (e.g. interaction between users and producers during key processes). Wentworth, et al. (2016) showcase an example of a productive, institutionalized relationship between a school district (San Francisco Unified School District) and a university (Stanford University) that is working to bridge the gap between research and local practice.

## What's Next?

We started this chapter with a discussion of current educational policy and the evolution of policy-driven efforts to unite research and practice – a relationship we argued promotes the public good. The "top down approach," currently embodied in federal efforts to improve the relationship between research and practice is logical on many levels. There have been large investments in the production of rigorous research on "what works" in schools, coupled with mandates and contingent funding mechanisms to hold districts and schools accountable for adopting evidence-based programs and interventions. Despite an intuitive appeal for such an approach, however, a significant body of education research reveals that the underlying assumptions are problematic and unlikely to meaningfully alter the role of research in decision-making. We argue the need to recognize the issue as bidirectional and offer a framework for understanding, and ultimately ameliorating, the gaps between research and practice communities.

So what is next for policy and practice in the United States? First, there needs to be significant investment in understanding research production and decision-making in schools. This investment has been realized in many ways by the recent investment in two knowledge utilization centers by the Institute for Education Sciences: the National Center for Research in Policy and Practice (NCRPP) and the Center for Research Use in Education (R4S). The goal of the Centers is to explore how and when practitioners use research evidence to make decisions, study the relationships between researchers and practitioners, and how existing education research can be made more relevant and useful to practitioners in state and local education agencies and individual schools (IES 2014). Additional support for the field has also come from the philanthropic community, notably the William T. Grant Foundation which as prioritized the role of research evidence in programs and policies affecting youth for almost a decade.

A second step forward is the investment in local and regional research partnerships, designed to improve the relevance and timeliness of research as well as engage practitioners in the process so that the results of research are useful to decision-makers. We note two advances on this point: Regional Education Laboratories (RELs) and the research practice partnership (RPP) movement.

*RELs* The U.S. Department of Education, in an effort to improve the translation of research evidence into schools nationally, launched a Regional Educational Laboratory (REL) program, sponsored by the Departments' Institute of Education Sciences (IES). According to the USDE the stated mission is to "help states and districts systematically use data and analysis to answer important issues of policy and practice with the goal of improving student outcomes." In effect, RELs are charged with producing and disseminating high quality, rigorous research. In 2012, the REL program launched a new effort to establish "alliances" – partnerships with state and local agencies across region – to inform the approaches and research undertaken by the RELs but also serve as a mechanism to build capacity to ask and study important questions. With over 70 research alliances across the nation, RELs have worked to produce research briefs on a myriad of topics including approaches to providing effective early education, best practices in identifying and retaining effective teachers and principals, how to adopt and implement rigorous standards and assessments, approaches to increase student readiness for college, and how to improve low-achieving schools. The approach represents a significant shift in effort and demonstrates recognition of the need for locally relevant research.

*RPPs* In the last 5 years, RPPs have proliferated across the U.S. Defined as "long-term collaborations, which are organized to investigate problems of practice and generate solutions for improving district outcomes" (Coburn et al. 2013), these arrangements vary in format, scope, and purpose. The longest standing model for RPPs is the University of Chicago Consortium on School Research, established in 1990. However, similar partnerships have emerged in Baltimore, Houston, San Francisco, and Philadelphia. Other partnerships utilize design-based research as a model for collaboration that advances both research and practice, such as the Middle-school Mathematics and the Institutional Setting of Teaching (MIST) housed at Vanderbilt University. While these represent larger efforts to partner with districts, dozens of smaller initiatives, including partnerships with smaller districts and even individual schools, are emerging in recognition of the need for researchers and practitioners to work more collaboratively throughout the research process. The success of these partnerships and the proliferation of this work nationwide reinforces the need for an alternative to top-down and dissemination focused efforts.

The third direction forward in shifting the relationship between research and practice are new models for translation and dissemination. Our prior discussion highlighted differences in how communities value particular products as well as the need for significant translation of research in order for findings to be useful to practitioners. Though translation and dissemination do not truly reflect the bidirectional nature of the research-practice gap, those efforts that recognize the needs of the practitioner community are worth noting here.

One well-recognized mechanism for making rigorous research available is the What Works Clearinghouse (WWC), established by the Institute for Education Sciences in 2002 to review, critique, and synthesize evidence of impacts of education interventions. Though initially criticized for excluding a good deal of available research due to its standards of evidence, at present, the clearinghouse currently includes several hundred intervention reports and practice guides based on reviews of more than 11,000 studies (IES 2016b). Further, management of the WWC has been responsive to critiques and to user needs, resulting in an evolving set of tools designed to make evidence readily available and useable to schools and practitioners. For example, the WWC now has 19 practice guides that offer specific recommendations for practice coupled with explanations about the level of evidence supporting those practices.

While the WWC is a notable effort, other strategies for translation have been adopted for particular content areas or policy issues. For example, another important translational effort which to date has been limited to the school lunchroom, represents how novel and incentive-based (rather than punitive) efforts have been used to improve use of strategies in the cafeteria known to support healthy selections by children (Hanks et al. 2013). Not unlike research done in the classroom or with school leaders, school health researchers examined efforts to incentivize children to consume healthier offerings in the cafeteria. A variety of approaches were tested first in a laboratory setting, then translated to specific tactics which were later tested in community schools. Research dissemination efforts were translated into an aspirational list of "to do's" yet presented in a way that allowed schools to feel rewarded with recognition rather than penalized.

Efforts to improve translation and dissemination fall not only with researchers, but with other organizations and individuals that serve to broker education research. For example, Penuel et al. (2016) find professional associations to be the most reported source of research. Farley-Ripple and Jones (2015) also find that professional development providers may be important translators for moving research into practice. More extensive work on brokering has been done in other contexts, such as Canada and the United Kingdom, but the role of brokers in translation and dissemination is garnering attention in the U.S. context and is likely to be the focus of research and policy in the future.

## Conclusion

Recognizing the role research can and often does play in the public good, along with efforts to better connect research and practice have been on the policy agenda in the U.S. for more than a decade and half. Although the results of those efforts are not yet well documented, the need for alternative approaches to bridge the gap are widely recognized in research and practice. Our purpose has been to highlight that need and to identify some key issues worth considering through a bi-directional lens. Moving forward, we hope to better understand those persistent gaps and resulting knowledge to leverage changes in the relationship between the research and practice communities. The examples we offer suggest that meaningful change is underway, but that continued efforts on the part of researchers, policymakers, and practitioners are needed to ensure improved educational opportunities and outcomes for all students.

## References

Asen, R., & Gurke, D. (2014). The Research on Education, Deliberation, and Decision-Making (REDD) project. In K. Finnigan & A. Daly (Eds.), *Using research evidence in education: From the schoolhouse door to Capitol Hill* (pp. 53–68). New York: Springer.

Backer, T. E. (1986). *Utilization: The challenge of transferring innovations in rehabilitation and special education*. Washington, DC: National Rehabilitation Information Center.

Backer, T. E. (1993). Information alchemy: Transforming information through knowledge utilization. *Journal of the American Society for Information Science, (1986–1998), 44*(4), 217.

Behrstock-Sherratt, E., Drill, K., & Miller, S. (2011). *Is the supply in demand? Exploring how, whey, and why teachers use research*. Washington, DC: American Institutes for Research.
Biddle, B. J., & Saha, L. J. (2006). How principals use research. *Educational Leadership, 63*(6), 72–77.
Birkeland, S., Murphy-Graham, E., & Weiss, C. H. (2005). Good reasons for ignoring good evaluation: The case of the drug abuse resistance education (D.A.R.E.) program. *Evaluation and Program Planning, 28*, 247–256.
Blake, S. C., & Ottoson, J. M. (2009). Knowledge utilization: Implications for evaluation. *New Directions for Evaluation, 124*, 21–34.
Bouffard, S. (2003). Doing what works: Scientifically based research in education. *The Evaluation Exchange, 9*(1).
Bransford, J. D., Stipek, D. J., Vye, N. J., Gomez, L. M., & Lam, D. (2009). *The role of research in educational improvement*. Cambridge: Harvard Education Press.
Brenchley, C. (2011, March 14). *It's time to fix no child left behind*. Retrieved from http://blog.ed.gov/2011/03/lets-fix-no-child-left-behind/
Broekkamp, H., & van Hout-Wolters, B. (2007). The gap between educational research and practice: A literature review, symposium, and questionnaire. *Educational Researcher, 32*(9), 3–14.
Burkhardt, H., & Schoenfeld, A. H. (2003). Improving educational research: Toward a more useful, more influential, and better-funded enterprise. *Educational Researcher, 32*(9), 3–14.
Caplan, N. (1979). The two-communities theory and knowledge utilization. *American Behavioral Scientist, 22*(3), 459–470.
Center for Research Use in Education. (2016). *About us*. Retrieved from research4schools.org
Coburn, S. E., & Stein, M. K. (2010). *Research and practice in education. Building alliances, bridging the divide*. Lanham: Rowman & Littlefield Publishers.
Coburn, C. E., & Talbert, J. E. (2006). Conceptions of evidence use in school districts: Mapping the terrain. *American Journal of Education, 112*(4), 469–495.
Coburn, C. E., & Turner, E. O. (2012). The practice of data use: An introduction. *American Journal of Education, 118*(2), 99–111.
Coburn, C. E., Toure, J., & Yamashita, M. (2009). Evidence, interpretation, and persuasion: Instructional decision making in the district central office. *Teachers College Record, 11*(4), 1115–1161.
Coburn, C. E., Penuel, W. R., & Geil, K. E. (2013). *Research-practice partnerships: A strategy for leveraging research for educational improvement in school districts*. New York: William T. Grant Foundation.
Corcoran, T. (2003). *The use of research evidence in instructional improvement (RB-40)*. Philadelphia: Consortium for Policy Research in Education, University of Pennsylvania.
Corcoran, T., Fuhrman, S. H., & Belcher, C. L. (2001). The district role in instructional improvement. *Phi Delta Kappan, 83*(1), 78–84.
Corcoran, T., McVay, S., & Riordan, K. (2003). *Getting it right: The MISE approach to professional development*. CPRE Research Reports. Retrieved from http://repository.upenn.edu/cpre_researchreports/42
Cousins, J., & Simon, M. (1996). The nature and impact of policy-induced partnerships between research and practice communities. *Educational Evaluation and Policy Analysis, 18*(3), 199–218.
Dagenais, C., Lysenko, L., Abrami, P. C., Bernard, R. M., Ramde, J., & Janosz, M. (2012). Use of research-based information by school practitioners and determinants of use: A review of empirical research. *Evidence & Policy: A Journal of Research, Debate and Practice, 8*(3), 285–309.
Daly, A. J., Finnigan, K. S., Jordan, S., Moolenaar, N. M., & Che, J. (2014). Misalignment and perverse incentives: Examining the politics of district leaders as brokers in the use of research evidence. *Educational Policy, 28*(2), 145–174.
Davidson, K., & Nowicki, E. (2012). An exploration of the utility of a knowledge utilization framework to study the gap between reading disabilities research and practice. *Alberta Journal of Educational Research, 58*(3), 330–349.

Davies, H.T., & Nutley, S. (2008). *Learning more about how research-based knowledge gets used.* Unpublished Working Paper. New York: William T. Grant Foundation.

Drill, K., Miller, S., & Behrstock-Sherratt, E. (2012). Teachers' perspectives on educational research. *American Institute for Research.* Retrieved from http://files.eric.ed.gov/fulltext/ED530742.pdf

Dunn, W. N. (1980). The two-communities metaphor and models of knowledge use. *Knowledge, 1*, 515–536.

Every Student Succeeds Act. (2015). S. 1177-114th Congress. Retrieved from https://www.gpo.gov/fdsys/pkg/BILLS-114s1177enr/pdf/BILLS-114s1177enr.pdf

Fabelo, T., Thompson, M. D., Plotkin, M., Carmichael, D., Marchbanks, M. P., & Booth, E. A. (2011). *Breaking schools' rules: A statewide study of how school discipline relates to students' success and juvenile justice involvement.* New York: Council of State Governments Justice Center.

Farley-Ripple, E. N. (2008). *Accountability, evidence and school district decision-making.* Unpublished doctoral dissertation, University of Pennsylvania, Philadelphia, PA.

Farley-Ripple, E. N. (2012). Research use in central office decision-making: A case study. *Education Management, Administration, and Leadership, 40*(6), 784–804.

Farley-Ripple, E. N., & Jones, A. (2015). Educational contracting, and the translation of research into practice: The case of Data Coach vendors in Delaware. *International Journal of Educational Policy and Leadership, 10*(2).

Farrell, C., & Coburn, C. E. (2016, April 8). *What is the conceptual use of research, and why is it important?* Retrieved from http://wtgrantfoundation.org/conceptual-use-research-important

Feldman, M. S., & March, J. G. (1981). Information as signal and symbol. *Administrative Science Quarterly, 26*(2), 171–186.

Finnigan, K.S., Daly, A.S., & Che, J. (2012). *Proceedings from AERA '12: The acquisition and use of evidence districtwide.* Vancouver, Canada.

Finnigan, K. S., Daly, A. J., & Che, J. (2013). Systemwide reform in districts under pressure. The role of social networks in defining, acquiring, using, and diffusing research evidence. *Journal of Educational Administration, 51*(4), 476–497.

Fuhrman, S., & Elmore, R. F. (Eds.). (2004). *Redesigning accountability systems for education* (Vol. 38). New York: Teachers College Press.

Hanks, A. S., Just, D. R., & Wansink, B. (2013). Smarter lunchrooms can address new school lunchroom guidelines and childhood obesity. *The Journal of Pediatrics, 162*(4), 867–869.

Hannaway, J. (1989). *Managers managing: The workings of an administrative system.* New York: Oxford University Press.

Hemsley-Brown, J. (2009). Using evidence to support administrative decisions. In T. J. Kowalski & T. J. Lasley II (Eds.), *Handbook of data-based decision making in education* (pp. 272–285). New York: Taylor & Francis.

Hemsley-Brown, J., & Sharp, C. (2003). The use of research to improve professional practice: A systematic review of the literature. *Oxford Review of Education, 29*(4), 449–470.

Hernandez, D. J. (2011). *Double jeopardy: How third-grade reading skills and poverty influence high school graduation.* New York: The Annie E. Casey Foundation.

Hess, F. M., & Rotherham, A. J. (2007). NCLB and the competitiveness agenda: Happy collaboration or a collisions course? *Phi Delta Kappa International, 88*(5).

Hightower, A. (2002). San Diego's big boom: Systematic instructional change in the central office and schools. *School districts and instructional renewal*, 76–93.

Honig, M. I. (2003). Building policy from practice: District central office administrators' roles and capacity for implementing collaborative education policy. *Educational Administration Quarterly, 39*(3), 292–338.

Honig, M. I., & Coburn, C. (2008). Evidence-based decision making in school district central offices: Toward a policy and research agenda. *Educational Policy, 22*(4), 578–608.

Honig, M. I., & Venkateswaran, N. (2012). School–central office relationships in evidence use: Understanding evidence use as a systems problem. *American Journal of Education, 118*(2), 199–222.
Honig, M., Venkateswaran, N., McNeil, P., & Twitchell, K. (2014). Leaders' use of research for fundamental change in school district central offices: Processes and challenges. In K. Finnigan & A. Daly (Eds.), *Using research evidence in education* (pp. 33–52). New York: Springer International Publishing.
Huberman, M. (1990). Linkage between researchers and practitioners: A qualitative study. *American Educational Research Journal, 27*(2), 363–391.
Institute of Education Sciences. (2014). *Funding opportunities*. Retrieved from http://ies.ed.gov/funding/ncer_rfas/randd_knowledge.asp
Institute of Education Sciences. (2016a). *Regional Educational Laboratory Program*. Retrieved from http://ies.ed.gov/ncee/edlabs/
Institute of Education Sciences. (2016b). *What works clearinghouse*. Retrieved from http://ies.ed.gov/ncee.wwc
Kennedy, M. M. (1982). Evidence and decision. In M. M. Kennedy (Ed.), *Working knowledge and other essays* (pp. 59–103). Cambridge, MA: The Huron Institute.
Knorr, K. (1977). Policymakers' use of social science knowledge: Symbolic or instrumental? In C. H. Weiss (Ed.), *Using social research in public policymaking*. Lexington: Lexington Books.
Labaree, D. F. (1997). Public goods, private goods: The American struggle over educational goals. *American Educational Research Journal, 34*(1), 39–81.
Landry, R., Amara, N., & Lamari, M. (2001). Climbing the ladder of research utilization evidence from social science research. *Science Communication, 22*(4), 396–422.
Lavis, J.N., Robertson, D., Woodside, J., McLeod, C., & Abelson, J. (2003). How can research organizations more effectively transfer research knowledge to decision makers? *The Milbank Quarterly*, 81(2). Retrieved from http://onlinelibrary.wiley.com/doi/10.1111/1468-0009.t01-1-00052/epdf
Louis, K. S. (1992). Restructuring and the problem of teachers' work. In A. Lieberman (Ed.), *The changing contexts of teaching* (Vol. I, pp. 138–156). *Ninety-first Yearbook of the National Society for the Study of Education*, Chicago, IL.
Mac Iver, M. A., & Farley, E. (2003). *Bringing the district back in: The role of the central office in improving Instruction and student achievement.* Center for Research on the Education of Students Placed at Risk.
March, J. G. (1994). *A primer on decision making*. New York: The Free Press.
Massell, D., & Goertz, M. E. (2002). District strategies for building instructional capacity. In A. M. Hightower, M. S. Knapp, J. A. Marsh, & M. W. McLaughlin (Eds.), *School districts and instructional renewal* (pp. 43–60). New York: Teachers College Press.
Massell, D., & Goertz, M. E. (2012, April). *State education department acquisition and use of research in school improvement.* Paper presented at the 2012 Annual Meeting of the American Education Research Association, Vancouver.
May, H., Sirinides, P., Gray, A., & Goldsworthy, H. (2016). *Reading recovery: An evaluation of the four-year i3 scale-up*. Philadelphia: Consortium for Policy Research in Education.
Maynard, L. M. (2006). The role of repetition in the practice sessions of artist teachers and their students. *Bulletin of the Council for Research in Music Education, 167*, 61–72.
Miretzky, D. (2007). A view of research from practice: Teachers talk about research. *Theory Into Practice, 46*(4), 272–280.
National Board for Education Sciences. (2008). *National Board for Education Sciences: 5-year report, 2003 through 2008*. (NBES 2009–6011). Washington, DC.
National Board for Education Sciences. (2015). *National Board for Education Sciences: 2014 NBES annual report, July 2013 through June 2014*. Washington, DC.
National Center for Research in Policy and Practice. (2016). *Our work*. Retrieved from http://ncrpp.org

Nicholson-Goodman, J., & Garman, N. B. (2007). Mapping practitioner perceptions of 'It's research based': Scientific discourse, speech acts and the use and abuse of research. *International Journal of Leadership in Education, 10*(3), 283–299.

No Child Left Behind Act. (2001). Pub. L. 107–110. 115 Stat. 1425- 107th Congress. Retrieved from http://www2.ed.gov/policy/elsec/leg/esea02/107-110.pdf

Ottoson, J. M. (2009). Knowledge-for-action theories in evaluation: Knowledge utilization, diffusion, implementation, transfer, and translation. *New Directions for Evaluation, 124*, 7–20.

Penuel, W. R., Briggs, D. C., Davidson, K. C., Herlihy, C., Sherer, D., Hill, H. C., Farrell, C., & Allen, A. (2016). *Findings from a national study on research use among school and district leaders.* Retrieved from ncrpp.org/pages/ourwork

Porter, R. W., & Hicks, I. (1997). Knowledge utilization and the process of policy formation: towards a framework for action. In D. W. Chapman, L. O. Mahlck, & A. E. M. Smulders (Eds.), *From planning to action: Government initiatives for improving school-level practice* (pp. 32–67). Paris: UNESCO International Institute for Educational Planning.

Reichardt, R. (2000). *The state's role in supporting data-driven decision-making: A view of Wyoming*. Aurora: Mid-Continent Research for Education and Learning.

Rich, R. F. (1977). Use of social science information by federal bureaucrats: Knowledge for action versus knowledge for understanding. In C. H. Weiss (Ed.), *Using social research in public policymaking* (pp. 199–211). Lexington: Lexington Books.

Short, E. C. (1970). *A review of studies on the general problem of knowledge production and utilization*.

Spillane, J. P. (1998). State policy and the non-monolithic nature of the local school district: Organizational and professional considerations. *American Educational Research Journal, 35*(1), 33–63.

Supovitz, J. A., & Klein, V. (2003). *Mapping a course for improved student learning: How innovative schools systematically use student performance data to guide improvement.* University of Pennsylvania: Consortium for Policy Research in Education.

Tseng, V., & Nutley, S. (2014). Building the infrastructure to improve the use and usefulness of research in education. In *Using research evidence in education* (pp. 163–175). New York: Springer.

U.S. Department of Education. (1983). *A nation at risk: The imperative for educational reform.* Retrieved from http://www2.ed.gov/pubs/NatAtRisk/index.html

U.S. Department of Education. (2011). *Secretary Duncan, Attorney General Holder announce effort to respond to school-to-prison pipeline by supporting good discipline practices.* Retrieved from http://www.ed.gov/news/press-releases/secretary-duncan-attorney-general-holder-announce-effort-respond-school-prison-p

Viadero. (2004). Ed. Dept. issues practical guide to research-based practice. *Education Week, 23*(16), 12.

Weiss, C. H. (1995). Nothing as practical as good theory: Exploring theory-based evaluation for comprehensive community initiatives for children and families. In J. P. Connell, A. C. Kubisch, L. B. Schorr, & C. H. Weiss (Eds.), *New approaches to evaluating community initiatives: Concepts, methods, and contexts* (pp. 65–92). Washington, DC: The Aspen Institute.

Weiss, C. H., & Bucuvalas, M. J. (1980). *Social science research and decision-making*. New York: Columbia University Press.

Wentworth, L., Carranza, R., & Stipek, D. (2016). A university and district partnership closes the research-to-classroom gap. *Phi Delta Kappan, 97*(8), 66–69.

West, R. F., & Rhoton, C. (1994). School district administrators' perceptions of educational research and barriers to research utilization. *ERS Spectrum, 12*(1), 23–30.

Wong, K. K., & Mid-Atlantic Lab. for Student Success, P. P. A (1998). *Laying the groundwork for a new generation of policy research: Commentary on "Knowledge utilization in educational policy and politics". Spotlight on student success No. 303*. Washington, DC: Office of Educational Research and Improvement.

# Chapter 6
# Assessing Students' Growth in Mathematics and English Language in Singapore: The Practice, the Evidence and the Perceptions

**Jonathan W.P. Goh, Ong Kim Lee, and Hairon Salleh**

**Abstract** This chapter provides a discussion on how the Singapore education system uses evidence from educational research conducted both locally and internationally, to shape policies and initiatives that can effectuate the "common good". In addition to research outcomes, the Singapore Ministry of Education also takes into consideration the various theories in the various aspects of education, specifically in teaching and learning (which includes curriculum matters, pedagogical issues and assessment practices). The common good referred to here are better positive outcomes to the relevant stakeholders (i.e., the students, parents, teachers and the school leadership) in the teaching and learning processes. Examples of earlier policy decisions that befit the conditions and situations of the education scenario of that time, are described. Focus for the current situation where policy decisions may be made that will impact on teachers' practices is research on assessment practices in schools. The common good with better assessment practices is the more accurate measures of student learning and growth, resulting in students knowing better where they stand, and teachers knowing better the areas and concepts where students lack clarity in, and what they are already clear about and have learnt well. With greater autonomy given to schools by the Singapore Ministry of Education, schools are encouraged to be innovative in their teaching and learning approaches and as such, schools may also decide on their own policies in teaching practices.

J.W.P. Goh • H. Salleh
National Institute of Education, Nanyang Technological University, Singapore, Singapore

O.K. Lee (✉)
Ohio University, Athens, OH, USA
e-mail: johnoklee@hotmail.com

 
M.Y. Eryaman, B. Schneider (eds.), *Evidence and Public Good in Educational Policy, Research and Practice*, Educational Governance Research 6,
DOI 10.1007/978-3-319-58850-6_6

## Introduction

The earliest record of the nationwide standardized testing dates back to 605AD during the Sui Dynasty in ancient China, where hopeful candidates applying for government positions had to take the imperial examinations to test their knowledge of Confucian philosophy and poetry (see Bodde n.d.). This is in stark contrast from the ancient Western world, where examiners favored giving essays in line with traditions of Socratic methods or *elenchus* (Fletcher 2009). The aim was for candidates to ask and answer questions to stimulate critical thinking and to surface perspectives and underlying presumptions. The Chinese imperial examination system however attracted much attention and greatly inspired political theorists in the West (Kracke 1957; Teng 1942–1943). In fact, many governments have since successfully implemented systematic, open, and competitive examinations in their respective countries (Wu 1982). Today, determining individuals' abilities through testing continues to be used in multiple different contexts (e.g., employment, and placement), most importantly in education. As school systems developed, testing began to be used in classrooms as a pedagogical tool. It helps teachers and instructors determine students' learning progress on subjects taught, as well as to provide feedback on the extent of students' understanding and learning difficulties, and also to indicate how effective their instruction has been. This in turn helps teachers modify their instruction to facilitate better student comprehension of what is being taught. This has been referred to as "formative evaluation" or sometimes as "assessment for learning". In contrast, testing for the determination of students' current ability status for purposes such as awards and promotions, is called "summative evaluation" or sometimes referred to as "assessment of learning".

Regardless of the purpose of evaluation, testing remains a critical process by which measurement is made of student learning. Measurement necessarily involves comparisons of some properties of an object – for example, length (i.e., shorter versus longer), height (i.e., lower versus higher), and ability (i.e., lower versus higher). Such comparisons must be made objectively and this can only be achieved if a common yardstick (or scale) is used for the variable being measured. Objectivity, in turn, requires linear scales to be used in the measurement process. The questions confronting educators on the accuracy and objectivity of testing used in schools thus include:

1. Are teachers using linear scales in measuring their students' ability in the subjects they teach and making interpretations of student performance accordingly?
2. What are their current measurement practices and how do they perceive the accuracy of such measurement?
3. What does research evidence show regarding the accuracy of teacher interpretations of students' test performance?

The purpose of this chapter is to address the above questions by examining data collected from Grade 5 students' performances in Mathematics and English Language in 28 primary (or elementary) schools in Singapore. It will provide a discussion on the assessment practices of a sample of teachers in these schools, and contrast the findings with accepted theoretical concepts of the measurement tools required for valid assessments. This will serve as part of the research inputs used by the Ministry of Education (MOE) in the overall changes that it makes for continuous improvement of the education system. The Singapore education system provides an excellent basis for such a study as it is built on the ideology of meritocracy that places great emphasis on academic performance of students for social mobility. Students' academic grades are considered as 'objective' measures of their abilities, regardless of social backgrounds. The MOE has in fact put in place mechanisms to help level up academically weaker students. The race toward excellence based on meritocratic educational achievements provides students and all other players in the education system, equal opportunities to succeed in life and in the long run, to create a just society (Heng 2015). It is in this context that this chapter describes the contributions to justice and equality as a public good by the Singapore education system, through the use of proper measurement systems, to obtain more accurate and therefore more meaningful comparisons of students' performance and growth. An objective view of student growth or the lack of it, provides the students, their teachers and their parents with a better understanding of the subsequent steps to take. At this point, it would be useful to provide a brief description on the development of education in Singapore and current assessment practices so as to contextualize our discussion on the findings of the study.

## A Brief Background on the Development of Education in Singapore

Since its independence, the development of Singapore has been described in three main phases (i.e., the "survival-driven phase" from 1959 to 1978, "efficiency-driven phase" from 1979 to 1996, and "ability-based and aspiration-driven phase" from 1997 onward) (OECD 2010; Mourshed et al. 2010). This development was holistic in nature with every segment of government developing in tandem, and included the system of governance, the economy, and the education system (Goh and Gopinathan 2006).

During the ***survival-driven phase***, student attrition was high with only a little more than half of students in primary (or elementary) schools moving on to secondary or high schools, and again with less than half of students graduating from secondary schools with what was considered as good grades in the Ordinary-level end-of-secondary school examinations. During the ***efficiency-driven phase***, the education system made major efforts to improve graduation rates. The path taken by students was no longer common for all. They were instead 'channeled' into the (i) academic stream, (ii) polytechnic stream or (iii) technical education stream. Within this phase alone, Singapore became the top performer in Trends in Mathematics and Science Study (TIMSS). In 2009 and 2012, Singapore was ranked second in the Program for International Student Assessment (PISA). These achievements have led many observers to conclude that Singapore has a top-performing education system (OECD 2011). In the ***ability-based and aspiration-driven phase***, the education system introduced the concept of "Thinking Schools, Learning Nation" (TSLN), one of the aims being to develop thinking skills among students. According to the then Prime Minister Goh Chok Tong, "our Ministry of Education is undertaking a fundamental review of its curriculum and assessment system to see how we can better develop the creative thinking skills and learning skills required for the future" (Goh 1997). Building on the policy of TSLN, Prime Minister Lee Hsien Loong introduced the "Teach Less, Learn More" (TLLM) initiative in 2005. The idea of TLLM was for teachers to be more creative and innovative in their teaching through which they will arouse interest in their students, sufficient for them to crave for more learning, and will proceed to do their own search for information and knowledge for which schools are to create what is referred to as "white space". Students will begin to take responsibility for their own learning and will reflect, analyze, make references to understand what they have learnt during the class sessions, and they need time to do this. This is in sharp contrast to teachers having to "complete the syllabus" irrespective of whether or not students have really learnt at the various stages. Following TLLM, the MOE introduced other initiatives and educational policies (e.g., reduction of content from syllabuses across the primary, secondary and pre-university levels; de-emphasis of rote learning; and introduction of discretionary admissions at lower primary, and tertiary levels) to promote holistic learning and development (e.g., creative and critical thinking; and the use of information technology and innovative pedagogies) (Heng 2013).

## Assessment in Singapore Schools

Through the phases of development of education in Singapore, invariably the system of assessment has to change alongside the other changes that were taking place. During the survival-driven phase, assessment in schools gave greater emphasis on content knowledge. The nature of test questions was more on recall and the assessment system was not so well organized. Assessment did not appear to be for formative or diagnostic purposes but more of being a task to be completed and to have a summative understanding of student status on each subject. During the efficiency-driven phase where streaming of students was introduced, the school assessment system appeared to be more established. School-based tests were of two major types administered to students in a regular fashion – (i) formative assessment [or Continual Assessment (CA)] which teachers administer to students as and when they see fit during the teaching and learning process, and (ii) summative assessment [or Semestral Assessment (SA)] which are administered to students at the end of each semester. Singapore schools run for two semesters in a year, each semester being about 22 weeks. In addition to these tests, teachers may give their own short quizzes to check on students' short-term progress. Teachers used the SA results summatively to assess content mastery although students with poor performance will be given remedial lessons but without the identification of specific individual problems in those subject areas. The remedial lessons were of the "one size fits all" type. During the ability-driven phase, there was greater emphasis given to thinking skills, and assessment items began to shift so as to be able to indicate levels of thinking skills students have developed. In addition, other skills such as team work were inculcated in students, and for this, project planning was given emphasis. For the development of collaborative work, the assessment was through project work that students had to carry out in teams.

At the end of primary education, Primary 6 (or Grade 6) students will sit for the *Primary School Leaving Examination* (a National achievement examination) – the results of which will determine which stream the students will be admitted into in secondary schools the following year. There are currently three streams for students in secondary school. One is the Express stream where students will take only 4 years to complete. Each student would typically be following between seven to eight subjects and at the end of the 4 years, will be sitting for the General Certificate of Education Ordinary Level (GCE "O" Level). Second is the Normal Academic stream where students will take 5 years to complete secondary school studying generally the same subjects as for the express stream but with a lower treatment. The examination they sit for at the end of 5 years require between five to eight subjects for them to qualify for the General Certificate of Education Normal Academic Level (GCE "N" Level). The third stream is the Normal Technical stream where, in addition to basic Science, Mathematics and the Humanities subjects, students also follow technical courses such as in computer networking, electrical technology and applications and mobile robotics. These students will sit for General Certificate of Education Normal Level examination (GCE "N" Level), typically offering between five and seven subjects (see MOE 2016). The students can also choose, subject to their achievement grades, to enroll in the International Baccalaureate (IB) program or the Integrated Program (IP) offered by some secondary schools.

## The Research

This study was conducted in 2015 over 5 months, and focuses on assessment practices in Singapore classrooms. It involved a total of 1,888 students, 88 English Language teachers and 93 Mathematics teachers from 28 primary schools in Singapore. The breakdown of students in terms of gender is shown in Table 6.1.

**Table 6.1** Number and gender of students in the study

| | | Frequency | Percent | Valid percent | Cumulative percent |
|---|---|---|---|---|---|
| Valid | Female | 862 | 45.7 | 50.2 | 50.2 |
| | Male | 856 | 45.3 | 49.8 | 100.0 |
| | Total | 1718 | 91.0 | 100.0 | |
| Missing | System | 170 | 9.0 | | |
| Total | | 1888 | 100.0 | | |

**Table 6.2** Item numbers of overlapping items for Tests 1–3

| Test | No. of items | Item numbers | Overlapping items | | |
|---|---|---|---|---|---|
| | | | Tests 1 and 2 | Tests 2 and 3 | Tests 1 and 3 |
| Math (1) | 20 | 1–20 | 3, 4, 9, 13, 17, 18, 19, 20 | | 19 |
| Math (2) | 20 | 3, 4, 9, 13, 17–32 | 3, 4, 9, 13, 17, 18, 19, 20 | 19, 21 23, 25, 26, 27, 29, 31 | |
| Math (3) | 20 | 19, 21, 23, 25–27, 29, 31, 33–44 | | 19, 21 23, 25, 26, 27, 29, 31 | 19 |
| Eng (1) | 20 | 1–20 | 1, 3 5, 6, 8, 10, 13, 16, | | 3, 10, 13 |
| Eng (2) | 20 | 1, 3, 5, 6, 8, 10, 13, 16, 21–32 | 1, 3 5, 6, 8, 10, 13, 16, | 3, 10, 13, 21, 23, 25, 26, 27 | |
| Eng (3) | 20 | 3, 10, 13, 21, 23, 25, 26, 27, 33–44 | | 3, 10, 13, 21, 23, 25, 26, 27 | 3, 10, 13 |

The teachers carried on with their normal lessons in English Language and Mathematics. The students were then tested at intervals of 2 months, using a total of three tests, Test 1, Test 2 and Test 3, for each of the two subjects. The English Language and Mathematics test items were developed by senior curriculum specialist from MOE academies – that is, the Academy of Singapore Teachers (AST) and the English Language Institute of Singapore (ELiS) respectively. Test 1 was administered in July, Test 2 in September and Test 3 in November. This enabled observations of growth after each two-month interval. The items within the three Mathematics tests and those within the three English Language tests were such that there were common (overlapping) items between them, deliberately made for the purpose of equating each set of three tests. The common items are shown in Table 6.2 and Fig. 6.1. This process of equating is called the "common items" approach in which the three sets of data from the three tests were arranged into a single large matrix of persons by items, with the common items aligned in their respective columns in the data set. In this way, the three tests are equated in a single step calibration process (see Chong and Popp 2005; Lee 2003). Likewise, the three English Language tests were equated using the same approach.

The study also determined the teachers' practices on assessment in their schools and they responded to questions as subjects in the study. They then collaborate with the researchers in administration of tests, continuing with their normal lessons, and subsequently follow the researchers' explanations on how the analyses will be done and why. When analyses are completed and interpretations made, they were presented to the educators of the participating 28 primary schools for them to understand the approaches and why they are more accurate in measurement of students' cognitive ability compared to scoring them using the traditional approach of "number correct" system.

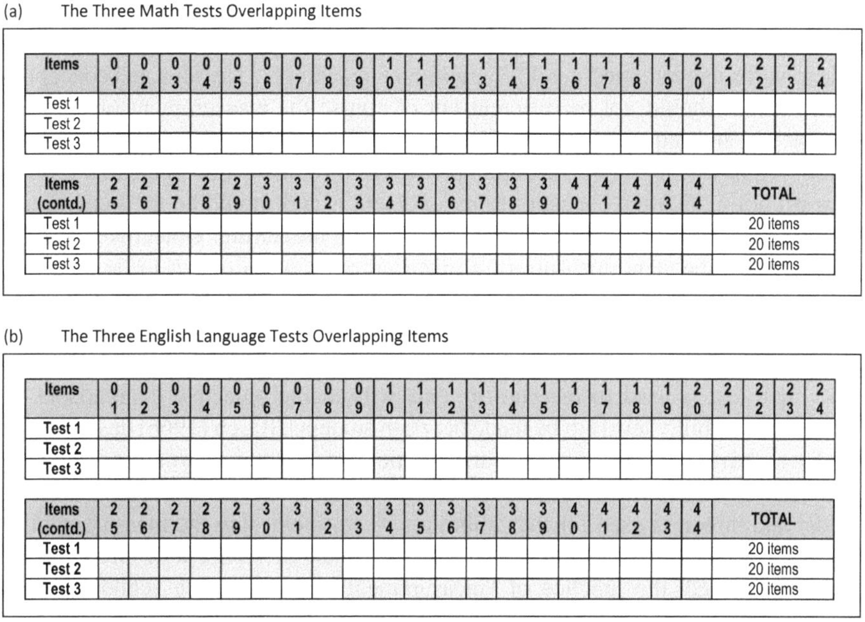


**Fig. 6.1** Overlapping items for three mathematics tests and three English language tests. (**a**) The three math tests overlapping items. (**b**) The three English language tests overlapping items

## The Research Evidence: Summary of Findings

In general, teachers were found to be using the classical theory in their analysis of test data and making interpretations from these analyses. The idea of this study is to show how the use of Rasch linearized measures instead of raw scores can provide more accurate comparisons and hence better understanding of student performance. This includes both comparisons between individual students in a single test administration as well as between two different time points for the same student.

### *The Concept of Measurement*

Measurement of any variable whether in the physical sciences or social sciences, should have the same conceptual meaning. Fundamentally, they all require the establishment and use of a linear scale – such as those of height and weight in physics, as described by Campbell (1920) (c.f., Wright 1997; Luce and Tukey 1964; Andrich 1988). As opposed to fundamental measurement, a derived measure such as volume, is defined as the product of three 'lengths' (i.e., length, width and height), while density is defined as the amount of mass per unit volume. The same fundamental measurement principles would be required to measure variables in the social sciences and in psychology, such as "perceptions of leadership skills", "attitude towards mathematics", and "commitment to achieve". The idea and concept of measurement should not be different but of course the measurement of different variables would require the establishment of different measuring instruments and scales, requiring the use of a different process in its construction and calibration. It is worth noting that the concept of measurement is and should be the same in any field. What differs is the process or method of the measuring. Objective measurement enables the same measure of a given property of an object to be obtained, independent of which specific instrument is used to measure that variable. Likewise, it is desirable to measure a student's Mathematics ability at a given time point and obtaining the same results (within measurement errors) independent of which specific math test is used to measure it. This will enable objective comparisons of Mathematics ability levels to be made between students. Rasch (1966) describes his model as having this particular characteristic, a property he termed as "specific objectivity". This term is further elaborated in Perline et al. (1979). The Rasch model and how it is used for the calibration of test items and the measurement of ability, is detailed in Wright and Stone (1979). While the concept of measurement may be clarified, the practice of "measurement" particularly in schools (where teachers often need to determine changes in students' abilities in the subject or subjects they teach), is still based on the classical theory approach. Perhaps, this preference for the use of raw scores may be driven by the (i) need for simplicity, or (ii) lack of sufficient understanding of measurement principles and failure to recognize the flaws of such practices. Educators in schools must not only be cognizant of the measurement principles but also interpretation of the results, to better inform how their students' are learning and the effectiveness of their own teaching practices and pedagogies.

## *The Scale*

Teachers are constantly measuring their students' learning progress and achievement using tests but they are not necessarily constructing the proper scaling for such measurement. A linear scale is one in which one unit on any part of the scale represents the same 'amount' of the variable being measured. This is not true of raw scores, as may be seen by the fact that if a student with a raw score of say, 55 % requires to put in an effort (increase in his or her ability) by say, 'b' units to score an additional 5 %, a student with a higher score of say, 85 % will need to put in an effort of more than 'b' to gain the additional 5% (see Fig. 6.2).

Besides the non-linearity issue, the meaning of how 'good' or 'how smart' a student is when he or she scores say, 100 % is not really clear. Was it because the student was smart to score a 100 % or was it because the test was too easy?

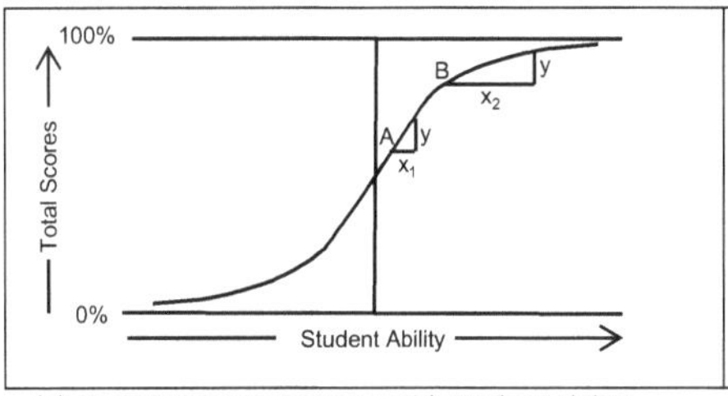


(a) How Raw Scores Increase with Student Ability

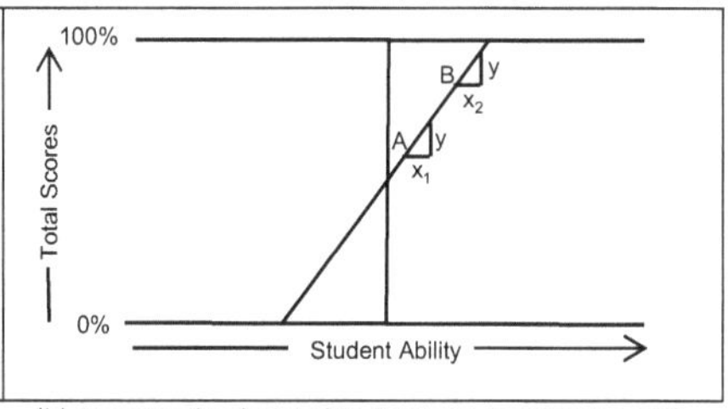


(b) Perceived Relationship Between Raw Scores and Student Ability

**Fig. 6.2** Actual and perceived relationships between raw scores and student ability. (**a**) How raw scores increase with student ability. (**b**) Perceived relationship between raw scores and student ability

Wright (1967) remarked in a humorous way during his presentation at an invitational conference on testing problems, that "sometimes we prayed for easier tests to make us smarter" (p. 85).

## *Problem with Ignoring the Non-linearity of Test Scores*

Almost every teacher in this study used raw scores (mainly in the form of "percent correct") to interpret and report on student performance as well as student growth in the respective subject areas. The findings also show that the teachers do what they do due to several reasons, some of which would appear to be logical assumptions for them to make, although erroneous. The fact that raw scores are not linear is not intuitive. The idea that a score of 60 % is 5 % more than 55 % is not different from a score of 95 % being 5 % more than 90 % may lead them to conclude that both additional "five percent" represent equal student effort.

The 'ogive' relationship between scores and student ability may easily be seen when considering the 'floor and ceiling' effects of the score 'scale' as depicted by Fig. 6.2a. When tests are scored ranging from a minimum of 0 % and a maximum of 100 % these become the natural 'floor and ceiling' of the test scores range. Hence no matter how much more able a student is beyond the test items' difficulty levels given by the teacher, the student's ability level is indeterminate when he or she scores 100 %. Likewise, a student who scores 0 % has an indeterminate weak ability level. In Fig. 6.2a, for a student at point 'A' to increase his or her score by 'y' points, he or she needs to put in an effort (additional ability) of $x_1$ while a student who is already at point 'B' needs to put in an effort of $x_2$ which is clearly much larger than $x_1$, in order to increase his or her score by the same amount of 'y' points. This fact is often missed due to the automatic assumption of teachers that the relationship between scores and ability levels is linear like that shown in Fig. 6.2b, resulting in the interpretation that $x_2$ is equal to $x_1$.

Every teacher in the research sample compared students' performances on different tests at different time points by comparing the magnitude of the test scores on those tests, where 'more is better'. It is very clear that the different tests given at different time points were assumed to be on the same difficulty scale. This misses the fact that the same score obtained on a harder test actually reflects a higher ability compared to that score on an easier test. The important implication here is that the tests given at the different time points should first be equated on to a common scale before such interpretations can be made legitimately. Equating tests enables each test item to be calibrated on a common difficulty scale so that all item difficulty levels are known quantities within their standard errors of measurement, and the relative difficulties between items are known.

Rasch analysis centers the zero point of the scale on the mean of the item calibrations. This means all test item difficulties start at the same "zero point". If this is not done, the three Mathematics tests will be on different scales and the same score on each of the tests would be on scales that start at different zero points. This is a common error and was made by all teachers in this study. This problem of comparing scales with different zero points was pointed out by Thorndike (1919):

> The influence of the zero point of a scale upon measurements made by that scale will alter the interpretation of, but not the method of making, measurements of things and conditions; But when things or conditions are *COMPARED*, that is, when measurements are made of difference, changes and relations, it is usually desirable to be able to use the "times as …" comparison. But such comparisons are subject to momentous misunderstandings unless the zero-point is absolute. One of the common fallacies in the mental sciences is to compare directly the amounts of measurements made from different zero points. Another is to use arbitrarily some point along the scale as if it were an absolute zero-point. (p. 17).

To illustrate the non-linearity of raw scores, we consider one of the outputs of the analysis which shows the students' raw scores and their corresponding measures. The 1888 students were entered into the data set for the three tests, giving a total of 1888 × 3 = 5664 'different' persons. Note that this a legitimate way of entering the data because each student who has changed the status of his or her ability level at the different time points, is essentially a 'different' person in as far at that variable (Mathematics or English Language) is concerned. For the analysis, students with invalid data were omitted, leaving a total of total of 5373 measured persons. Table 6.3 shows an extraction of a number of students with scores from 1 to 19 with their corresponding measures. Consider pairs of students with total scores having differences of 3, starting with the total score of 2, namely, 2, 5, 8, 11, 14, and 17. The corresponding measures on a linear scale in logits are −3.20, −1.83, −0.95, −0.19, 0.60 and 1.67. The differences between pairs of measures are calculated and shown in Fig. 6.3. Clearly, the measure differences in logits for persons with extreme scores (2 and 19), are much more than the measure differences for persons closer to the average scores although their score differences are uniformly at the same value of 3 throughout the range.

**Table 6.3** Segments of Math Person file in measure order for scores from 1 to 19

| ENTRY-ID | TEST | SEX | SCORE | COUNT | MEASURE | S.E. | MNSQ | ZSTD | MNSQ | ZSTD |
|---|---|---|---|---|---|---|---|---|---|---|
| 1244 | 1 | 1 | 1 | 20 | -4.07 | 1.09 | 1.34 | 0.70 | 3.87 | 1.50 |
| 1826 | 1 | 2 | 1 | 20 | -4.07 | 1.09 | 1.23 | 0.50 | 0.89 | 0.60 |
| 542 | 1 | 1 | 2 | 20 | -3.20 | 0.82 | 0.96 | 0.10 | 0.44 | -0.20 |
| 810 | 1 | 1 | 2 | 20 | -3.20 | 0.82 | 1.16 | 0.50 | 2.94 | 1.50 |
| 447 | 1 | 2 | 3 | 20 | -2.63 | 0.70 | 1.07 | 0.30 | 1.32 | 0.60 |
| 454 | 1 | 2 | 3 | 20 | -2.63 | 0.70 | 0.62 | -0.80 | 0.41 | -0.60 |
| 1361 | 1 | 1 | 4 | 20 | -2.19 | 0.63 | 0.79 | -0.50 | 0.69 | -0.30 |
| 1362 | 1 | 1 | 4 | 20 | -2.19 | 0.63 | 1.33 | 0.90 | 5.36 | 3.50 |
| 1720 | 1 | 2 | 5 | 20 | -1.83 | 0.58 | 1.49 | 1.40 | 4.30 | 3.60 |
| 1831 | 1 | 2 | 5 | 20 | -1.83 | 0.58 | 1.48 | 1.40 | 4.35 | 3.60 |
| 141 | 1 | 2 | 6 | 20 | -1.51 | 0.55 | 0.75 | -0.90 | 0.71 | -0.50 |
| 159 | 1 | 1 | 6 | 20 | -1.51 | 0.55 | 1.03 | 0.20 | 0.93 | 0.00 |
| 82 | 1 | 1 | 7 | 20 | -1.22 | 0.53 | 1.29 | 1.20 | 2.56 | 2.90 |
| 239 | 1 | 2 | 7 | 20 | -1.22 | 0.53 | 0.65 | -1.60 | 0.54 | -1.30 |
| 16 | 1 | 1 | 8 | 20 | -0.95 | 0.51 | 1.07 | 0.40 | 0.95 | 0.00 |
| 83 | 1 | 1 | 8 | 20 | -0.95 | 0.51 | 1.03 | 0.20 | 0.96 | 0.00 |
| 70 | 1 | 2 | 9 | 20 | -0.69 | 0.50 | 1.05 | 0.30 | 0.93 | -0.10 |
| 73 | 1 | 1 | 9 | 20 | -0.69 | 0.50 | 1.40 | 2.00 | 1.49 | 1.40 |
| 81 | 1 | 1 | 10 | 20 | -0.44 | 0.50 | 1.24 | 1.30 | 1.16 | 0.60 |
| 91 | 1 | 1 | 10 | 20 | -0.44 | 0.50 | 1.04 | 0.30 | 0.94 | -0.10 |
| 25 | 1 | 1 | 11 | 20 | -0.19 | 0.50 | 0.95 | -0.20 | 0.89 | -0.20 |
| 67 | 1 | 1 | 11 | 20 | -0.19 | 0.50 | 0.99 | 0.00 | 0.88 | -0.30 |
| 11 | 1 | 1 | 12 | 20 | 0.06 | 0.51 | 0.81 | -1.00 | 0.71 | -0.70 |
| 17 | 1 | 1 | 12 | 20 | 0.06 | 0.51 | 1.13 | 0.80 | 1.02 | 0.20 |
| 39 | 1 | 1 | 13 | 20 | 0.32 | 0.52 | 1.35 | 1.60 | 2.12 | 2.10 |
| 49 | 1 | 2 | 13 | 20 | 0.32 | 0.52 | 1.17 | 0.80 | 1.11 | 0.40 |
| 24 | 1 | 1 | 14 | 20 | 0.60 | 0.54 | 0.69 | -1.30 | 0.55 | -0.90 |
| 27 | 1 | 1 | 14 | 20 | 0.60 | 0.54 | 1.50 | 1.80 | 1.49 | 1.00 |
| 7 | 1 | 1 | 15 | 20 | 0.91 | 0.57 | 0.89 | -0.30 | 0.73 | -0.30 |
| 10 | 1 | 1 | 15 | 20 | 0.91 | 0.57 | 1.07 | 0.30 | 0.90 | 0.00 |
| 6 | 1 | 1 | 16 | 20 | 1.26 | 0.61 | 0.76 | -0.60 | 0.55 | -0.50 |
| 20 | 1 | 1 | 16 | 20 | 1.26 | 0.61 | 0.79 | -0.50 | 1.17 | 0.50 |
| 28 | 1 | 1 | 17 | 20 | 1.67 | 0.68 | 0.78 | -0.40 | 0.55 | -0.30 |
| 55 | 1 | 1 | 17 | 20 | 1.67 | 0.68 | 0.80 | -0.40 | 0.59 | -0.20 |
| 13 | 1 | 1 | 18 | 20 | 2.21 | 0.80 | 1.19 | 0.50 | 0.84 | 0.30 |
| 15 | 1 | 1 | 18 | 20 | 2.21 | 0.80 | 0.67 | -0.50 | 0.33 | -0.30 |
| 8 | 1 | 1 | 19 | 20 | 3.04 | 1.07 | 0.62 | -0.20 | 0.16 | -0.10 |
| 31 | 1 | 1 | 19 | 20 | 3.04 | 1.07 | 1.21 | 0.50 | 1.17 | 0.70 |

## *Test Preparation*

Like teachers in many education systems, the teachers in Singapore would usually plan their tests using a "table of specifications (TOS)" which is a test blueprint. Teachers recognize the usefulness of preparing a test blueprint, which includes the following:

1. The ability to set test items according to certain assessment objectives of each test item, generally stated in the form "students will be able to demonstrate the level of understanding of the concept of ..." or "students will be able to demonstrate the ability to apply the concept of ... to a different scenario", thereby enhancing construct validity of the test.

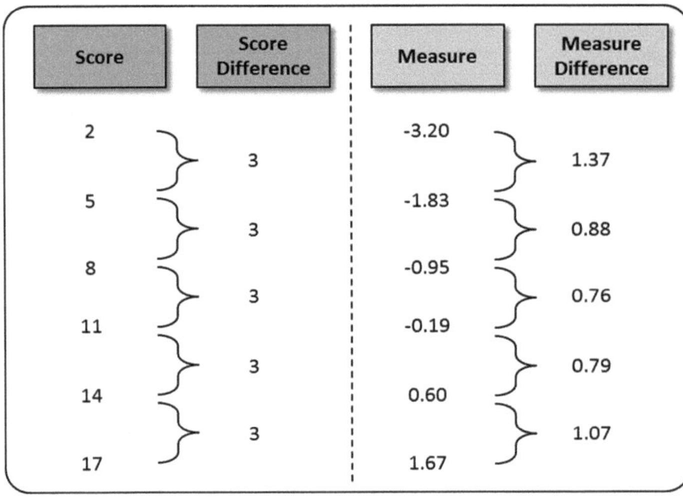


**Fig. 6.3** Comparing students' Math measure differences for score difference of 3

2. To enhance content validity of the test by ensuring a balance of the number of items by the proportion of emphasis on the different topics and subtopics as provided for by the syllabus, and the proportion of the number of items at each level of the taxonomy in the cognitive domain, namely, recall, comprehension, application, analysis, synthesis and evaluation levels. At the primary and secondary school levels, teachers often test up to as high as the analysis level and sometimes even up to the synthesis and evaluation levels, depending on the subject being tested.
3. In the event that the teacher who plans the test is unable to construct and set the test items, the task may be taken up by another teacher of the same subject by following the blueprint without deviating very much from what has been planned.

## *Interpretation of Student Performance Using Raw Scores*

Some teachers may not have heard of the Item Response Theory (IRT) of which the Rasch Model is a specific case with a single parameter. Teachers who are aware of Rasch analysis may also prefer to use raw scores and the classical theory for interpretations of performance, due to its simplicity. There are generally three main shortcomings in these interpretations.

(a) The comparisons made between students' performances on a given test do not take into consideration the standard error of measurement (even in terms of raw scores).

(b) Secondly, two different tests used at different time points to measure students' growth are not equated, and yet comparisons are still made between their raw scores at those two time points.
(c) Thirdly, raw scores are interpreted as if they are values on a linear scale. This means that the same raw scores on the three different tests would be interpreted as reflecting the same ability levels and the same raw score intervals on the three different tests would be interpreted as reflecting the same 'amount' of ability.

Clearly, measurement interpretations can be challenging if not impossible, without having a linear scale. Comparisons of students' performances across different time points can also be problematic if each test is independent of each other with their relative difficulty levels unknown. These challenges faced by teachers are elaborated upon below, using observations of teachers' practices from their perceptions of scales and test difficulty levels, and contrasting them with what theory says.

## *The Concept of Standard Error of the Measurement*

The standard error (s. e.) of a test may be understood by considering the idea of the 'observed score', $X_O$, of a student on that test, being made up of two components, namely, his 'true score' $X_T$ plus the 'error score', $X_E$.

$$X_O = X_T + X_E$$

which leads to the variance of the observed scores among all the students to be the sum of variances of the true scores and the error scores.

$$s_O^2 = s_T^2 + s_E^2$$

Note that the closer the variance of observed scores to the variance of the true scores, the more reliable the test. Hence the test reliability r may be appropriately defined as the proportion of variance of observed scores that is represented by the variance of the true scores, that is,

$$r = \frac{s_T^2}{s_O^2}$$

Since $s_T^2 = s_O^2 - s_E^2$, we may write the test reliability as:

$$r = \frac{s_O^2 - s_E^2}{s_O^2} = 1 - \frac{s_E^2}{s_O^2}$$

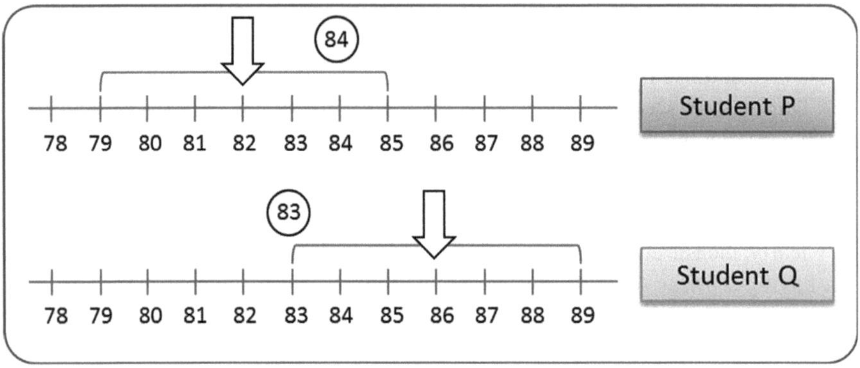


**Fig. 6.4** Student scores in standard error range

Rearranging and taking the square root, we have the standard error of measurement, $s_E$ given by:

$$s_E = s_O\sqrt{1-r}$$

The test reliability may be estimated by using the Kuder-Richardson formula or by means of parallel tests or test-retest while $s_O$ is the observed standard deviation of the distribution of test scores. Hence the standard error of measurement of the test may be estimated. The standard error of measurement should not be confused with the standard error of the mean (which is in fact the standard deviation of a sampling distribution of sample means $\sigma_{\bar{x}}$ ).

## *Problem with Ignoring the Standard Error of Measurement*

The usual practice of classroom teachers in ranking their students for various purposes would be to use 'the higher score is the better performance', disregarding the standard error of measurement. If we take into account the standard error, each score is actually a range of scores for a given student. Two adjacent scores may overlap and the uncertainty results in the teacher being unable to tell which of the two adjacent scores is actually showing better performance. Consider two students, P and Q who scored 82 % and 86 % respectively. Teachers would normally conclude that Q performed better than P. Suppose the test has a standard error of 3 raw score points. Then the range of possible scores for each student would be as shown in Fig. 6.4.

Taking into account the standard error of measurement, P's score may be anywhere from 79 % to 85 % while that of Q may be anywhere between 83 % and 89 %. If P's 'true' score is 84 % and Q's 'true' score is 83 %, then P has performed better than Q. Since the 'true' score is always an unknown (as no measure can be constructed that provides a perfect reflection of the 'true' score), these two students should be considered to have performed equally well.

## *Raw Scores on Different Tests*

We have stated earlier that when tests are not equated, the same score on the different tests will not represent the same ability level if the test difficulty levels are not the same. The problem of treating raw scores as being on a linear scale is further illustrated in Fig. 6.2. Consider an output of the analysis shown in Table 6.4 which shows extracted segments of persons with their scores and respective measures on the three tests. Persons marked A, B and C all scored 14 raw score points, but notice that their measures are 0.60, 1.39 and 1.41 logits respectively.

Rasch analysis also allows students to take tests of different lengths and would still determine their measures. Omitted items are not marked wrong but considered as not taken and hence the student has taken a shorter test. Consider the person marked P for Test 2 in Table 6.4 who also scored 14 raw score points but has omitted one item and the 'count' is 19 (responded to only 19 items). When compared to person B whose measures 1.39 logits, P measures 1.69 logits. These may not result in any excessive unfairness to students if the teacher's intention is to make students

**Table 6.4** Person scores and measures on three equated Math tests

| | ENTRY-ID | TEST | SEX | MEASURE | COUNT | SCORE | ERROR | IN.MSQ | IN.ZSTD | OUT.MS | OUT.ZSTD |
|---|---|---|---|---|---|---|---|---|---|---|---|
| | ... | ... | ... | ... | ... | ... | ... | ... | ... | ... | ... |
| Ⓐ→ | 41 | 1 | 1 | 0.60 | 20 | 14 | 0.54 | 1.16 | 0.71 | 2.03 | 1.74 |
| | 42 | 1 | 2 | 1.64 | 19 | 16 | 0.68 | 0.87 | -0.17 | 1.06 | 0.37 |
| | 43 | 1 | 1 | 1.26 | 20 | 16 | 0.61 | 1.19 | 0.61 | 1.54 | 0.88 |
| | 44 | 1 | 2 | 1.02 | 18 | 14 | 0.63 | 1.07 | 0.31 | 1.01 | 0.25 |
| | 45 | 1 | 1 | 0.60 | 20 | 14 | 0.54 | 1.06 | 0.30 | 0.95 | 0.06 |
| | 46 | 1 | 2 | 2.21 | 20 | 18 | 0.80 | 0.88 | -0.04 | 1.44 | 0.73 |
| | ... | ... | ... | ... | ... | ... | ... | ... | ... | ... | ... |
| Ⓟ→ | 2235 | 2 | 1 | 1.69 | 19 | 14 | 0.59 | 1.14 | 0.54 | 1.12 | 0.39 |
| | 2236 | 2 | 1 | 0.80 | 20 | 12 | 0.53 | 0.91 | -0.27 | 0.93 | -0.11 |
| Ⓑ→ | 2237 | 2 | 2 | 1.39 | 20 | 14 | 0.56 | 0.83 | -0.54 | 0.77 | -0.44 |
| | 2238 | 2 | 2 | 0.80 | 20 | 12 | 0.53 | 0.93 | -0.21 | 0.94 | -0.10 |
| | 2239 | 2 | 1 | -1.12 | 20 | 5 | 0.56 | 0.88 | -0.41 | 0.75 | -0.28 |
| | 2240 | 2 | 1 | 0.00 | 20 | 9 | 0.51 | 1.15 | 0.73 | 1.06 | 0.29 |
| | 2241 | 2 | 2 | 2.09 | 20 | 16 | 0.63 | 0.51 | -1.69 | 0.31 | -1.27 |
| | 2242 | 2 | 1 | 2.09 | 20 | 16 | 0.63 | 0.89 | -0.22 | 0.55 | -0.62 |
| | ... | ... | ... | ... | ... | ... | ... | ... | ... | ... | ... |
| | 3680 | 3 | 2 | 2.15 | 20 | 16 | 0.66 | 0.97 | 0.07 | 1.18 | 0.48 |
| | 3681 | 3 | 1 | 2.63 | 20 | 17 | 0.75 | 0.84 | -0.15 | 0.71 | -0.01 |
| Ⓒ→ | 3682 | 3 | 1 | 1.41 | 20 | 14 | 0.57 | 1.13 | 0.54 | 1.17 | 0.48 |
| | 3683 | 3 | 1 | -0.53 | 20 | 7 | 0.53 | 1.26 | 1.08 | 1.64 | 0.95 |
| | 3684 | 3 | 1 | 2.15 | 20 | 16 | 0.66 | 0.85 | -0.28 | 0.55 | -0.46 |
| | 3685 | 3 | 1 | 2.15 | 20 | 16 | 0.66 | 0.77 | -0.51 | 0.47 | -0.63 |
| | 3686 | 3 | 2 | 1.41 | 20 | 14 | 0.57 | 0.85 | -0.50 | 0.77 | -0.28 |
| | 3687 | 3 | 1 | 3.31 | 20 | 18 | 0.91 | 0.60 | -0.44 | 0.23 | -0.37 |
| | 3689 | 3 | 1 | 2.15 | 20 | 16 | 0.66 | 0.88 | -0.18 | 0.61 | -0.36 |
| | 3690 | 3 | 2 | 2.15 | 20 | 16 | 0.66 | 0.60 | -1.06 | 0.35 | -0.92 |
| | 3695 | 3 | 1 | 1.70 | 19 | 14 | 0.61 | 0.80 | -0.57 | 0.94 | 0.12 |
| | 3696 | 3 | 1 | 1.41 | 20 | 14 | 0.57 | 0.84 | -0.52 | 0.78 | -0.26 |
| | 3697 | 3 | 1 | 2.15 | 20 | 16 | 0.66 | 0.74 | -0.60 | 0.56 | -0.44 |
| | ... | ... | ... | ... | ... | ... | ... | ... | ... | ... | ... |

aware that they have room for improvement and to drive them towards excellence. However, it matters when such test performance comparisons are for purposes of selection or placement, or when the scores are on the borderline between the defined 'passing' and 'failing' grades. Students finding themselves in 'second' place may not be in a position that is 'truly second' if the standard error of measurement is not taken into consideration. Likewise, students who are within a standard error of measurement below the cut-off point for 'passing', need not have necessarily failed.

Before the use of IRT, the need for common scaling was already very much felt. In the classical theory of measurement, the need for comparability of performance on a common scale led to the use of norm groups. A test that has been constructed that is targeted at a certain level of students would be administered to a representative sample of the target population. The scores are distributed and normalized. From the normal distribution, the score cut-off points are determined for the various grades to be awarded, such as stanines, or other score-range descriptors (e.g., 'below expected', 'average', 'good', and 'excellent). From this norm group, all future students taking the same test (which is therefore standardized), will be given the same grades or descriptors for the same corresponding scores.

The problem with using norm groups is that the it can become outdated such as when the nature of students taking the test is no longer like that of the norm group or when the syllabus of the subject has been modified. In such cases, either a different form of the test will have to be planned and constructed, or the same test will need to be re-normed. This has been noted by Angoff (1960):

> Most of the test scales now in use derive their systems of units from data taken from actual test administrations, and thus are dependent on the performance of the groups tested. When so constructed, the scale has meaning only so long as the group is well defined and has meaning, and bears a resemblance in some fashion to the groups or individuals who later take the test for the particular purpose of selection, guidance or group evaluation. However, if it is found that the sampling for the development of a test has not been adequate, or that the group on which the test has been scaled has outlived its usefulness, possibly because of changes in the defined population or because of changes in educational emphases, then the scale itself comes into question. This is a serious matter. A test which is to have continued usefulness must have a scale which does not change with the times, which will permit acquaintance and familiarity with the system of units, and which will permit an accumulation of data for historical comparisons. (p. 815).

## *Perceptions and Practice of Test Equating*

In a given year, all students in Singapore will be taking two summative tests which are school-based, one at the end of Semester 1 and the second at the end of Semester 2. These are referred to as Semestral Assessments (SAs). A small percentage of the teachers of about 1–5 % (i.e., which we may not consider as significant) compare students' performance between two tests through normalizing the score distributions of the two tests and determining their normalized standard scores. To illustrate this, let us suppose that 150 students were given a summative test of 25 items at the

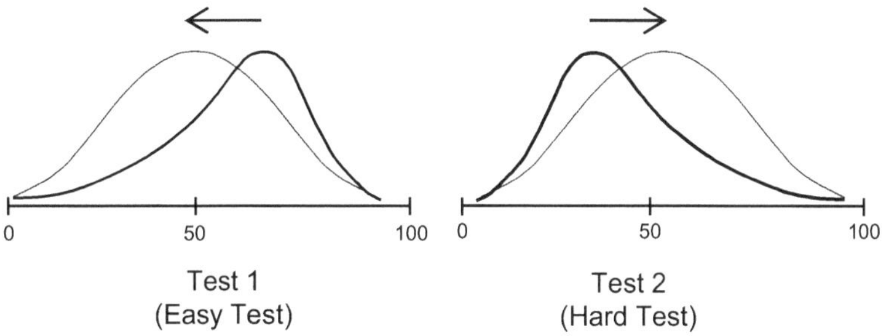


**Fig. 6.5** Example of distributions for easy and hard tests

end of the first semester (Test 1) and another 25-item summative test which is different from the first, at the end of the second semester (Test 2). Let us further suppose that the distributions of scores for these two tests are as shown in Table 6.4. It is clear from Table 6.4 that there are larger numbers of students with higher scores on Test 1 while larger numbers of students obtained lower scores on Test 2. This means that relative to the students' ability levels at the two time points, Test 2 is harder compared to Test 1. The distribution of scores on Test 1 is skewed to the left while the distribution of scores for Test 2 is skewed to the right. This is illustrated in Fig. 6.5 which also shows how 'pushing' the skewed curves into a unit normal curve each, enables the two distributions (and hence the relative positioning of the respective student scores) to be comparable.

To make the test scores comparable between the two tests, the standard score (z-score) for each possible score is first calculated. The standard score is then normalized by looking up the equivalent z-score on the unit normal curve, for the percentile rank that corresponds to the percentile rank of that score on the respective test score distributions. These equivalent z-scores are called the normalized z-scores. These were calculated for all the possible scores on the tests, and entered into Table 6.5. Students' performances are then compared by comparing their normalized z-scores.

As an illustration, suppose a student scored 17 marks on Test 1 at the end of the first semester and 13 marks on Test 2 at the end of the second semester. Teachers using raw score interpretations will fail to consider the different difficulty levels of the two tests and may make remarks such as, student has 'not shown improvement' or 'dropped in performance'. If the teacher goes one step further and calculates the student's z-scores, the student has obtained a z-score of −0.46 on Test 1 and again −0.46 on Test 2. The teacher's remark may have changed to student has 'stayed at the same level of performance'. Now, if the teacher takes yet another step and normalizes the z-scores, the student would have increased from a normalized z-score of −0.58 to −0.24. Now the teacher's remark to the student should be 'you have scored 17 points on Test 1 and 13 points on Test 2. Good, you have shown improvement!' This is a complete reversal of the conclusion the teacher arrives at by looking only at the raw scores.

**Table 6.5** Comparing student performance on two tests using normalized standard scores

| Test 1 scores (X) | Freq (f1) | Cum Freq (cf) | (x)*(f1) | z- scores | PR | Normalized z-scores | Test 2 scores (X) | Freq (f1) | Cum Freq (cf) | (x)*(f1) | z- scores | PR | Normalized z-scores |
|---|---|---|---|---|---|---|---|---|---|---|---|---|---|
| 25 | 2 | 150 | 50 | 1.85 | 99.33 | 2.48 | 25 | 2 | 150 | 50 | 2.64 | 99.33 | 2.48 |
| 24 | 5 | 148 | 120 | 1.56 | 97.00 | 1.88 | 24 | 2 | 148 | 48 | 2.38 | 98.00 | 2.05 |
| 23 | 8 | 143 | 184 | 1.27 | 92.67 | 1.45 | 23 | 3 | 146 | 69 | 2.12 | 96.33 | 1.79 |
| 22 | 13 | 135 | 286 | 0.98 | 85.67 | 1.06 | 22 | 4 | 143 | 88 | 1.87 | 94.00 | 1.56 |
| 21 | 18 | 122 | 378 | 0.69 | 75.33 | 0.69 | 21 | 5 | 139 | 105 | 1.61 | 91.00 | 1.34 |
| 20 | 25 | 104 | 500 | 0.41 | 61.00 | 0.28 | 20 | 6 | 134 | 120 | 1.35 | 87.33 | 1.14 |
| 19 | 19 | 79 | 361 | 0.12 | 46.33 | −0.09 | 19 | 6 | 128 | 114 | 1.09 | 83.33 | 0.97 |
| 18 | 13 | 60 | 234 | −0.17 | 35.67 | −0.37 | 18 | 7 | 122 | 126 | 0.83 | 79.00 | 0.81 |
| 17 | 10 | 47 | 170 | −0.46 | 28.00 | −0.58 | 17 | 9 | 115 | 153 | 0.58 | 73.67 | 0.63 |
| 16 | 8 | 37 | 128 | −0.74 | 22.00 | −0.77 | 16 | 9 | 106 | 144 | 0.32 | 67.67 | 0.46 |
| 15 | 9 | 29 | 135 | −1.03 | 16.33 | −0.98 | 15 | 12 | 97 | 180 | 0.06 | 60.67 | 0.27 |
| 14 | 6 | 20 | 84 | −1.32 | 11.33 | −1.21 | 14 | 15 | 85 | 210 | −0.20 | 51.67 | 0.04 |
| 13 | 4 | 14 | 52 | −1.61 | 8.00 | −1.40 | 13 | 18 | 70 | 234 | −0.46 | 40.67 | −0.24 |
| 12 | 3 | 10 | 36 | −1.90 | 5.67 | −1.59 | 12 | 22 | 52 | 264 | −0.71 | 27.33 | −0.60 |
| 11 | 3 | 7 | 33 | −2.18 | 3.67 | −1.79 | 11 | 17 | 30 | 187 | −0.97 | 14.33 | −1.07 |
| 10 | 2 | 4 | 20 | −2.47 | 2.00 | −2.05 | 10 | 8 | 13 | 80 | −1.23 | 6.00 | −1.55 |
| 9 | 1 | 2 | 9 | −2.76 | 1.00 | −2.33 | 9 | 3 | 5 | 27 | −1.49 | 2.33 | −1.99 |
| 8 | 1 | 1 | 8 | −3.05 | 0.33 | −2.72 | 8 | 2 | 2 | 16 | −1.75 | 0.67 | −2.48 |
| Sum | 150 | | 2,788 | | | | Sum | 150 | | 2215 | | | |
| | Mean | | 18.59 | | | | | Mean | | 14.77 | | | |
| | Variance | | 12.07 | | | | | Variance | | 15.03 | | | |
| | Std Dev | | 3.47 | | | | | Std Dev | | 3.88 | | | |

While this may appear to be a good way to proceed, there is still a problem due to the fact that the raw scores are still bounded in range, in this case, between the possible scores of '0' (i.e., the minimum mark) and '25' (i.e., the maximum mark). This gives rise to comparisons being made only between students within the group for both tests 1 and 2. The z-score of a given student depends on how other students who took the same test perform like in any norm-referenced test. Also, students at or close to the extreme scores (minimum and maximum), cannot be compared in terms of improvement (or otherwise) shown between the two tests.

## *Conjoint Measurement: Item Difficulty and Student Ability*

One of the key strengths in using Rasch analysis is it provides us with conjoint measurement (i.e., the investigation of the interaction between two attributes – student ability and item difficulty). As stated by Perline et al. (1979), the Rasch model is a "practical realization of conjoint measurement" (p. 237). It essentially facilitates teachers to make diagnostic interpretations of issues that students may have with certain items which in turn facilitate remedial actions by teachers.

As an illustration, consider another output of the analysis which shows the relative positioning of items and persons according to their calibrations and measures. This is shown in Fig. 6.6 for both Mathematics and English Language. The map shows that the most difficult Mathematics item is Item 35 while the easiest is Item 5, while the most difficult item for English Language is Item 40 and the English Language test items 4 and 12 are very easy items.

These maps are useful for a quick observation of the relative positioning. For actual calibrations of items and measures of persons, we may look at the respective item files and person files. Rasch model is a probabilistic model which uses the fact that if an item is at a difficulty level that is above a student's ability level, then the probability of that student getting that item correct is less compared to the probability of getting it right if the item difficulty is below the student's ability. Of course this does not mean that it is guaranteed that students will answer wrongly all the items that are above their ability level and vice versa. It would however be surprising if a student answering incorrectly items that are way below his or her ability level, or answering correctly items that are way above his or her ability level. For items that are more difficult than a given student's ability and for which the student has answered wrongly, the teacher can begin to investigate the difficulties that the student has, by starting with the items closer to the student's ability and move on outwards to the more difficult items. This provides for efficiency in diagnostic process. In Fig. 6.5 for example, suppose a student with ability level of 0.5 logits in Mathematics answered wrongly items 12, 40, 25, 27, 23 28, and 35 which are in ascending order of difficulty. It would make more sense for the teacher to investigate the student's problems with item 12 first followed by item 40, 25, and so on. These difficulties may range from the student being careless to having a complete misunderstanding of certain concepts.

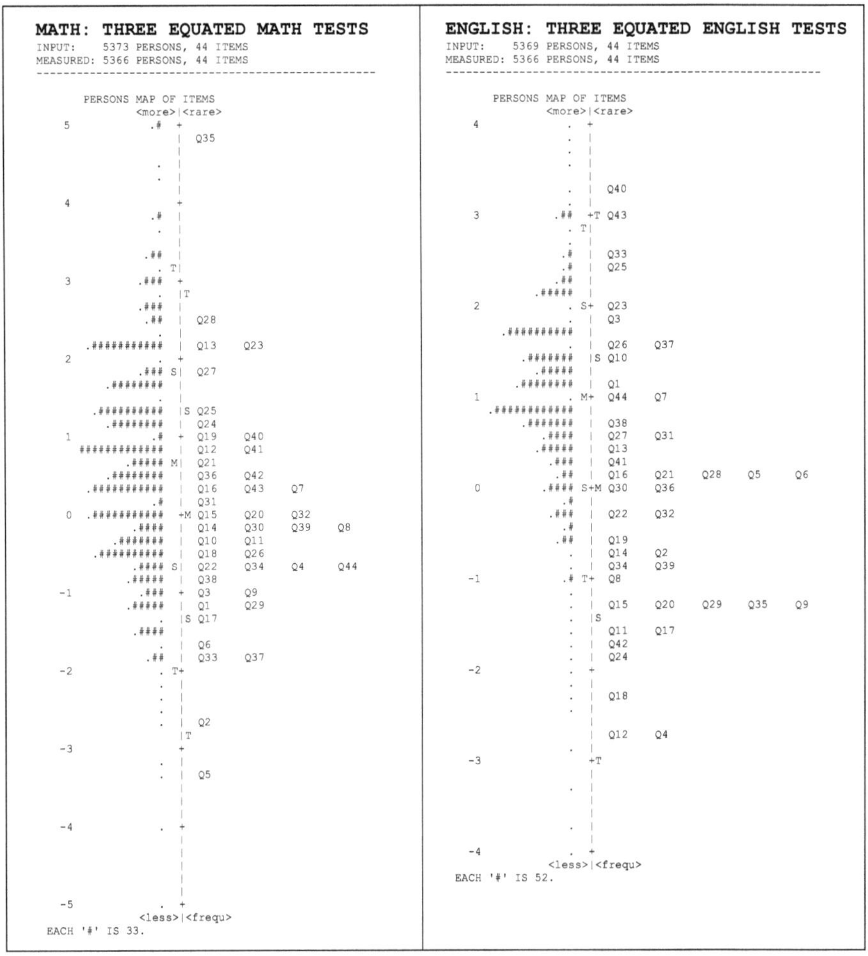


**Fig. 6.6** Distribution maps of persons and items for Mathematics and English Language

## *Interpretation of Student Growth Through Test Equating*

While classroom teachers generally do not have problems with test planning, their interpretations of student performance are often made without much attention to accuracy of "comparisons" between performances. The problems are when such interpretations are made without regard to the lack of scale linearity and changes in test difficulty levels given at different time points (Wright 1992, 1993a). A single-step equating of the tests using Rasch analysis will put the two tests onto a common scale, thus enabling proper comparisons of student ability measures and hence their performances across the different tests, and to check for growth. Rasch analysis calibrates items irrespective of the students who took the test (i.e., items' difficulty levels are determined independent of persons who took the test). Likewise, it also enables proper comparisons of person abilities independent of which test or test items they responded to. As noted earlier, Rasch (1966) referred to this characteristic of his model as "specific objectivity". Scale invariance is an important property of a measurement instrument such as the ruler for the measurement of length where 1 inch on the ruler remains the same length irrespective of what object it is measuring. If we calibrate a test item by using the proportion of persons who answered it wrongly as an expression of its difficulty, as is commonly used by teachers in this study, then we can be quite certain that the difficulty level will be different if the group of persons responding to that item is different. This will clearly result in the test being a fluctuating instrument of measure depending on what group of students it is measuring. Thurstone (1959) pointed this out, stating

> A measuring instrument must not be seriously affected in its measuring function by the object of measurement. To the extent that its measuring function is so affected, the validity of the instrument is impaired or limited. If a yardstick measured differently because of the fact that it was a rug, a picture, or a piece of paper that was being measured, then to that extent the trustworthiness of that yardstick as a measuring device would be impaired. Within the range of objects for which the measuring instrument is intended, its function must be independent of the object of measurement. (p. 228).

With the datasets arranged in the single matrix described earlier, Rasch analysis using Winsteps software program (Linacre and Wright 2000) was run on for the 5,373 respondents and a total of 44 different (unique) items with a certain number of overlapping test items between every pair of tests as shown in Table 6.2 and Fig. 6.1. The outcome of the analysis is that each test item is calibrated in logits and each person is measured also on the same logit scale. The scale runs from negative infinity to positive infinity, with the calibrations being centered on their mean as the zero point. This therefore results in items with positive and negative calibrations of item difficulty and students with positive and negative measures of ability. To work with only positive values, we may transform the ability measures using an appropriate multiplicative factor and an appropriate translational factor,

$$y = mx + c$$

where $y$ is the transformed measure, $x$ is the measure obtained from the analysis, m is the multiplicative factor and $c$ is the translational factor. Rasch analysis has converted the ordered non-linear raw scores into linear measures in logits and the equating process puts all the three tests on to one common logit scale. This inventive approach of test equating can be credited to Danish mathematician Georg Rasch. In 1953, he was approached to equate some reading tests and ended up devising a method for estimating item difficulties entirely free of the effects of the abilities of the students who happen to respond to the items. In other words, it is possible to estimate a student's probability of success on an item, and this probability of a right answer is governed by student's ability and the item's difficulty. He deduced this formula:

$$\log\left[\frac{probability\,of\ success}{probability\,of\ failure}\right] = ability - difficulty$$

From the equation, all elements can be represented as fixed positions along one straight line. The above expression is called log-odds (odds of success), and the units of measurement constructed are called 'logits'. This puts 'ability' (i.e., the strength of ability in answering an item correctly) and 'difficulty' (i.e., the difficulty of an item to be answered correctly) on a common interval scale, making them comparable. Students' measures from different tests can be combined and analyzed together, using some network of commonalities (in our case, the test items or common-items equating) linking the tests. This analysis provides a calibration, standard error and fit statistic for every item, and a measure, standard error and fit statistic for every person involved in any of the tests (Wright 1993b). These item calibrations and person measures are completely equated and expressed together on a common linear scale. Evidently, the Rasch's formula is perhaps the only practical way that addressed all eight test equating problems presented by Wright (1993b). These eight equating problems include:

1. *Test Length* – Do we insist that all tests have the same number of items or always use percentages?
2. *Test Difficulty* – What if test B is harder than test A?
3. Item Difficulty Distribution Problem – Can we match average P-values of tests to equate them?
4. *Sample Ability* – Do different sample ability distributions yield incomparable P-values?
5. *Linear Scale* – Can raw score equating methods provide the linear metric necessary for quantitative comparisons?
6. *Missing Data* – Most equating methods require complete data. Would this be an issue if students do not respond to all test items?
7. *Standard Error* – Are reliability coefficients (averaged over all candidates and all items – thus, it only provides one average value for the standard error of any score) adequate?
8. *Quality Control* – Are items or persons behaving properly? That is, are the items in the tests cooperating to measure the same variable in the same way, and persons performing in the same way across tests, and across items within tests?

By way of using a Rasch test equating approach, we are able to determine the learning growth of the Grade 5 students in Mathematics and English Language over time. These learning growths in the two subjects are depicted in Fig. 6.7. It is evident that growth in learning can be seen on the left side of each of the Distribution Maps [i.e., in Mathematics (a) and in English Language (b)]. The students' mean measures in Mathematics grew from 0.35 to 0.65 to 0.89 logits over time, and it was

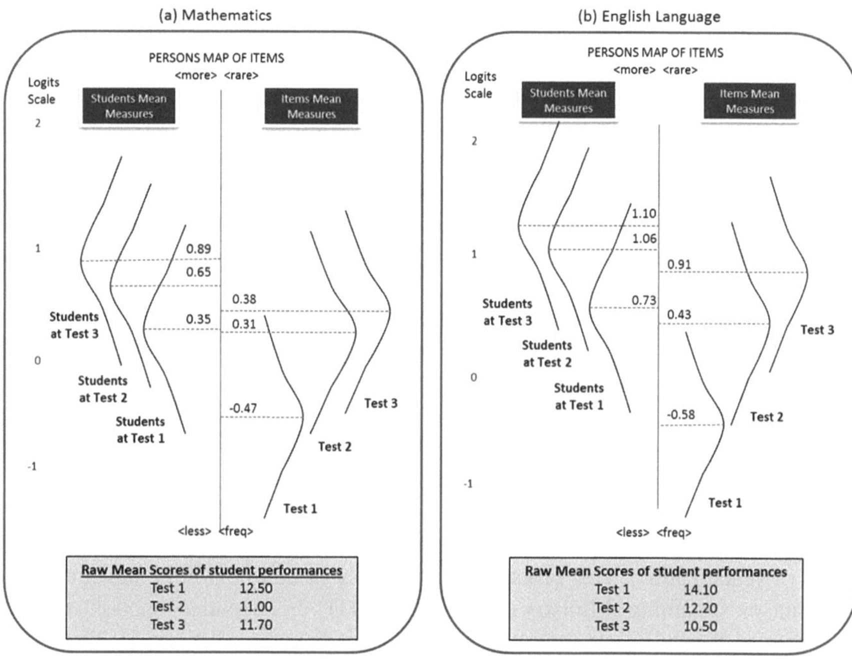


**Fig. 6.7** Comparing students' performances over three tests (Rasch Measures vs Raw Scores)

the same for English Language (i.e., growth from 0.73 to 1.06 to 1.10 logits). This growth was however not seen in the mean raw scores for the two subjects (i.e., 12.50, 11.00 and 11.70 for Mathematics, and 14.10, 12.20 and 10.50 for English Language).

From the mean item calibrations, we can see that for both Mathematics and English Language, the tests were increasing in difficulty from Test 1 to Test 3 as may be seen on the right side of the Distribution Maps in Fig. 6.7).

The item mean calibrations are −0.47 (for Test 1), 0.31 (for Test 2) and 0.38 (for Test 3) for Mathematics and −0.58 (for Test 1), 0.43 (for Test 2) and 0.91 (for Test 3) for English Language. Since the tests are not of the same difficulty level, and we should not be comparing students' performance scores (i.e., using raw scores) across tests if they are not equated. Some teachers may argue that they should be sufficiently experienced to tell difficult questions from easier questions, or simply keeping the 'structure' of the test questions and only changing certain numbers to ensure that the questions are equitable. Surely, we would agree that the square of 9 and 8 are not of the same difficulty level for students to answer. We conducted a simple experiment with the Grade 5 teachers from the participating schools for Mathematics and English Language, by asking them to identify and rank just three of the most difficult test items from Test 1 for the two subjects. The teachers were only partially correct as they identified items that were of medium difficulty as the most difficult questions (i.e., items that mostly calibrated around the mean difficulty of the 20 test items in Test 1).

## Conclusion

The Singapore education system is constantly ready to make policy adjustments based on sound research findings and literature, observations of other education systems around the world that are successful, as well as devising its own solutions to educational problems and issues, based on local expertise. The aim is for continuous improvements in student outcomes. As an example of policy adjustment, prior to 2004, primary school students used to be streamed into three different streams (i.e., EM1, EM2 and EM3 – 'English and Mother tongue' at first, second and third language respectively) as they progressed into primary 5 based on their performance on an examination administered at the end of primary 4. The rationale was to allow the teaching learning process to proceed at the students' pace. The top quarter of students will be placed in the EM1 stream, the middle 50 % will be placed in EM2 while the bottom quarter will be place in EM3. As of the end of 2004, the Singapore Education Ministry made adjustments to this policy of streaming and in effect collapsed EM1 and EM2 streams into one category without the earlier distinction between them, resulting in only two streams of students in the upper primary school levels of years 5 and 6. This gives primary schools greater flexibility and autonomy to decide on streaming (Ministry of Education 2004). In Secondary schools, there is also greater flexibility given to the Normal (Academic) and Normal (Technical) students to take subjects they are strong in at the Express level from Secondary 1 (Ministry of Education 2013). To do so, they have to do well in these subjects at the Primary School Leaving Examination (Ministry of Education 2015). Secondary schools also have greater flexibility to transfer these students to another course when they have shown evidence of abilities. Schools may also allow their top Normal (Academic) students to progress to Secondary 5 without taking the GCE 'N' Level examinations.

Another example is that the process and types of assessment itself have been undergoing changes in Singapore. Beyond only cognitive tests being used to measure student achievement, the need was seen for tests results to be more representative of actual student ability and skills which include thinking skills, calling for authentic assessment (for example Archibald and Newman 1988; Wolf et al. 1991). Authentic assessments are tasks given to students that resemble real world tasks that adults have to deal with in life, and from which students' knowledge and skills, creativity as well as the effectiveness of performance are then assessed. It is also referred to as alternative assessment. This mindset change was particularly evident after the MOE introduced its 'Innovation and Enterprise' policy initiative in 2004. The aim of this policy is to encourage the development of desired attributes such as intellectual curiosity, resilience, ruggedness and a willingness to contribute to the community (Wong 2005).

Research on school autonomy such as by Hanushek et al. (2013) and King and Ozler (2005), found that schools that are given the autonomy to make their own management reforms, were more effective in improving student performance. From many such inputs, international and local and through its own deliberations, the

MOE made the necessary adjustments to its policy and provided schools with greater autonomy and flexibility to construct tests whose results can exhibit the level of creative thinking in students, students' ability to perform a task using alternative assessment, portfolio assessment, and project work assessment, and the final achievement of a student be evaluated based on his or her performances on all relevant and different forms of assessment. The argument for a broader-based assessment is in line with theoretical arguments of the inadequacy of general achievement tests and standardized test that are measuring only the cognitive component of achievement, such as by Archibald and Newmann (1988). The ability to think may also be included the ability to perform. Wolf et al. (1991) argued compendiously that the importance and relevance of multidimensional performance assessment of students in order to capture and assess their skills in responding to issues in various contexts. For holistic development of the child, assessment has to be for all domains including cognitive, physical, emotional and character. We have seen in the research here, the focus has been on the measurement in the cognitive domain which requires an understanding of scales in measurement through the use of cognitive tests, and to accurately interpret how students have performed on the tests. In cases where student growth needed to be observed through comparisons of their performances on two or more tests over time, the tests have to be equated so as to be on a common scale.

This study provides the Singapore education system with a means to better measure students' growth and development so that teachers will be able to make more objective interpretations of their performance. However, the comparison of student performance on the international stage through TIMSS and PISA are still by means of standardized tests, mostly using multiple-choice type questions. Most if not all educators are aware of the limitations of objective tests. We know that many have argued that standardized tests are objective only in the scoring and that the test content limits the depth of students' thinking as well as the creativity of their answers. In this regard, it is also true that underlying the dimension of creative skills is cognitive skills, meaning that creativity is not possible without cognitive skills. Hence as a first measure, cognitive development is still an important contribution to students' overall development. There are also some positive qualities of standardized tests. They are typically shaped by established standards that provide teachers with a framework or guide for what is to be taught. Standardized testing has also been shown to have positive impact on improving the quality of the curriculum and improving student achievement (Yeh 2005). These positives can certainly help moderate the limitations to a certain extent. Hence there is hope yet for standardized tests, given that it is still a good proxy to future measures of creativity, and the fact that it is much more practical in its administration compared to the administration of tests of creative skills in the numerous fields of study.

**Acknowledgement** The data used in the chapter was obtained from a research funded by the Office of Educational Research, National Institute of Education (NIE), Nanyang Technological University, Singapore (Project Number & Title: OER 23/14 JG: An Investigation of the Impact of Leadership Practices on Student Learning Development Outcomes in Singapore Schools). The views expressed in this paper are the authors and do not necessarily represent the views of NIE.

## References


Andrich, D. (1988). Rasch models for measurement. *Series: Quantitative applications in the social sciences*, 68. Newbury Park: SAGE Publications Inc.

Angoff, W. H. (1960). Measurement and scaling. In C. W. Harris & M. R. Liba (Eds.), *Encyclopedia of educational research* (3rd ed., pp. 807–817). New York: Macmillan.

Archibald, D. A., & Newmann, F. M. (1988). *Beyond standardized testing*. Reston: National Association of Secondary School Principals.

Bodde, D. (n.d.). *Chinese ideas in the West*. Retrieved on April 25, 2016 from http://afe.easia.columbia.edu/chinawh/web/s10/ideas.pdf

Campbell, N. R. (1920). *Physics, the elements*. Cambridge: Cambridge University Press.

Chong, H. Y., & Popp, S. O. (2005). Test equating by common items and common subjects: Concepts and applications. *Practical Assessment, Research & Evaluation, 10*(4).

Fetcher, D. (2009). *Brief history – standardized testing*. Retrieved on April 25, 2016 from http://content.time.com/time/nation/article/0,8599,1947019,00.html

Goh, C. T. (1997). *Shaping our future: Thinking schools, learning nation*. Speech by Prime Minister Goh Chok Tong at the opening of the 7th International Conference on Thinking. https://www.moe.gov.sg/media/speeches/1997/020697.htm. Accessed on 5th Apr 2016.

Goh, C. B., & Gopinathan, S. (2006). *The development of education in Singapore since 1965*. Background paper prepared for the Asia Education Study Tour for African Policy Makers, June 18–30, 2006.

Hanushek, E. A., Link, S., & Woessmann, L. (2013). Does school autonomy make sense everywhere? Panel estimates from PISA. *Journal of Development Economics, 104*, 212–232.

Heng, S. K. (2013). *FY 2013 Committee of Supply Debate: 1st reply by Mr Heng Swee Keat*, Minister for Education: Hope – opportunities for all, available at: http://www.moe.gov.sg/media/speeches/2013/03/13/fy-2013-committee-of-supply-debate-first-reply.php. Accessed 20 Dec 2015.

Heng, S. K. (2015). *Pursuit of excellence 'need not lead to elitism': Heng Swee Keat*. Available at: http://www.channelnewsasia.com/news/singapore/pursuit-of-excellence/2067562.html. Accessed 9 May 2016.

King, E. M., & Ozler, B. (2005). *What's decentralization got to do with learning? School autonomy and student performance*. Available online at http://siteresources.worldbank.org/EXTGOVANTICORR/Resources/3035863-1291223960989/Nicaragua_Teacher_Staffing_Monitoring.pdf. Accessed 19 Dec 2015.

Kracke Jr., E. A. (1957). Region, family, and individual in the Chinese examination system. In J. K. Fairbank (Ed.), *Chinese thoughts & institutions*. Chicago: University of Chicago Press.

Lee, O. K. (2003). Rasch simultaneous vertical equating for measuring reading growth. *Journal of Applied Measurement, 4*(1), 10–23.

Linacre, J. M., & Wright, B. D. (2000). *A user's guide to Winsteps: Rasch model computer program*. Chicago: MESA Press.

Luce, R. D., & Tukey, J. (1964). Simultaneous conjoint measurement: A new type of fundamental measurement. *Journal of Mathematical Psychology, 1*(1), 1–27.

Ministry of Education. (2004). *Refinements to primary school streaming*. https://www.moe.gov.sg/media/press/2004/pr20040318.htm. Accessed on 9 May 2016.

Ministry of Education. (2013). *Workplan: Normal stream Sec 1 students from 12 schools can take express subjects*. http://www.straitstimes.com/singapore/moe-workplan-normal-stream-sec-1-students-from-12-schools-can-take-express-subjects. Accessed on 9 May 2016.

Ministry of Education. (2015). *Nurturing students – flexibility and diversity*. https://www.moe.gov.sg/education/education-system/nurturing-students. Accessed on 9 May 2016.

Ministry of Education. (2016). *Education, secondary*. https://www.moe.gov.sg/education/ secondary. Accessed on 7 Apr 2016.

Mourshed, M., Chijioke, C., & Barber, M. (2010). *How the world's most improved school systems keep getting better*. London: Mckinsey & Co. Available online at http://mckinseyonsociety.com/downloads/reports/Education/How-the-Worlds-Most-improved-School-Systems-Keep-Getting-Better_Download-version_Final.pdf. Accessed 20 Dec 2015.

OECD. (2010). *Singapore: Rapid improvement followed by strong performance*. Available online at http://www.oecd.or/countries/singapore/46581101.pdf. Accessed 20 Dec 2015.

OECD. (2011). *Strong performers and successful reformers in education: Lessons from PISA for the United States*.

Perline, R., Wright, B. D., & Wainer. (1979). The Rasch model as additive conjoint measurement. *Applied Psychological Measurement, 3*(2), 237–255.

Rasch, G. (1966). An item analysis which takes individual differences into account. *British Journal of Mathematical and Statistical Psychology, 19*, 49–57.

Teng, Ssu-yu. (1942–1943). Chinese influence on the Western examination system, *Harvard Journal of Asiatic Studies*, 7, 267–312.

Thorndike, E. L. (1919). *An introduction to the theory of mental and social measurements*. New York: Columbia University.

Thurstone, L. L. (1959). Attitudes can be measured. In L. L. Thurstone (Ed.), *The measurement of values* (pp. 215–233). Chicago: University of Chicago Press.

Wolf, D., Bixby, J., Glenn III, J., & Gardner, H. (1991). To use their minds well: Investigating new forms of student assessment. *Review of Research in Education, 17*, 31–74.

Wong, S. H.. (2005). *Title: Innovation, enterprise need daily nurturing*. https://www.moe.gov.sg/media/forum/2005/20050804.htm. Accessed on 9 May 2016.

Wright, B. D. (1967). Sample-free test calibration and person measurement. *Invitational Conference on Testing Problems*. ETS, Princeton.

Wright, B. D. (1992). Scores are not measures. *Rasch Measurement: Transactions of the Rasch Measurement SIG, American Educational Research Association, 6*(1), 208.

Wright, B. D. (1993a). Thinking with raw scores. *Rasch Measurement: Transactions of the Rasch Measurement SIG, American Educational Research Association, 7*(2), 299–300.

Wright, B. D. (1993b). Equitable test equating. *Rasch Measurement: Transactions of the Rasch Measurement SIG, American Educational Research Association, 7*(2), 298–299.

Wright, B. D. (1997). Fundamental measurement. *Rasch Measurement: Transactions of the Rasch Measurement SIG, American Educational Research Association, 11*(2), 558.

Wright, B. D., & Stone, G. N. (1979). *Best test design*. Chicago: MESA Press.

Wu, K. C. (1982). *The Chinese Heritage*. New York: Crown Publishers.

Yeh, S. S. (2005). Limiting the unintended consequences of high-stakes testing. *Education Policy Analysis Archives, 13*(43), 1–21.

# Chapter 7
# Evidence Informed Innovation of Education in the Netherlands: Learning from Reforms

**Theo Wubbels and Jan van Tartwijk**

**Abstract** In the Netherlands, between 1993 and 2002 the government introduced several reforms in secondary education. In one of these innovations, it was said that the student was at the centre of the teaching and learning process. Several Dutch educational researchers also advocated such approaches under the term "new learning". In this contribution, we will first describe the Dutch educational system, the reforms and the debates about these reforms. Then we will focus on the problematic relationship between educational research and practice and look at several proposals for improving that relationship. A next step in the collaboration between educational science and practice with the aim to stimulate evidence informed education might be the introduction of academic workplaces. In academic workplaces, schools, institutes for teacher education, and educational scientists work together on research, teacher education, teacher professional development, and educational innovation. In this innovation, Dutch policy makers pursued a better fit of education with the aim to improve social justice through and in education, and by doing so, contribute to the common good. However, they did so without relying on evidence that these innovations might indeed have positive effects on social justice.

## Setting the Stage: The Dutch Educational System[1]

In the Dutch educational system, primary schools provide education for children aged 4–12. The first 2 years are rather "play oriented". The more systematic schooling begins at age of 6. During primary school, the children's development is monitored using validated tests and teacher observations. The observations and tests together are used to underpin a teacher advice at the end of grade 8, about which secondary education stream will suit the child best. These streams in secondary education vary in the degree of academic difficulty and length of study. The largest stream, which more

[1] Parts of this section have been published previously in Hammerness et al. (2012) and Wubbels and van Tartwijk (in press).

T. Wubbels (✉) • J. van Tartwijk
Utrecht University, Utrecht, The Netherlands
e-mail: T.Wubbels@uu.nl



M.Y. Eryaman, B. Schneider (eds.), *Evidence and Public Good in Educational Policy, Research and Practice*, Educational Governance Research 6,
DOI 10.1007/978-3-319-58850-6_7

than half of the students attend, is a 4-year secondary education program that prepares students for secondary vocational education (VMBO; Preparatory Secondary Vocational Education). The second stream is a 5-year program preparing students for higher professional education, which is attended by about 30% of the students (HAVO; Higher General Secondary Education). The third stream is a 6-year program preparing students for university education and is attended by about one-fifth of the students (VWO; Preparatory Scientific Education). In all three streams in secondary education, students can choose a number of subjects, but mathematics, Dutch and English are obligatory. At the end of the final year, students are required to take final examinations in the form of nationally developed standardized tests in most of these subjects and in the compulsory subjects mathematics, Dutch and English. The results on these tests count for 50% of the final exam result. The other 50% is based on grades for tests, projects etc., which are developed and graded by the schools themselves. After secondary education, students can continue their education in specific types of tertiary education. VWO graduates typically enrol in a 3-year bachelor program at 1 of the 13 Dutch research universities that only admit students with a VWO or an equivalent foreign diploma. HAVO graduates typically enrol in a 4-year bachelor program in higher vocational education, which is provided for by 1 of the 37 universities of applied sciences. After their bachelor, most students at research universities will also take a 1- or 2-year master program. Most graduates of the universities of applied sciences will enter the labour market after their bachelors. VMBO students typically enrol in programs for middle level vocational education which are provided by 1 of the about 40 Regional Education Centres (ROC). These programs are usually 3 years in length. There are no national exams for tertiary education.

The national Inspectorate of Education monitors the quality of education, both public and private. It has the right to evaluate schools according to national standards regarding, among others, the quality of the lessons, the achievement levels of the students, and the internal quality assurance system of the school. In secondary schools, the exam results play an important role in these evaluations, but when evaluating these results, other factors are taken into account, such as the students' ability level and background and the number of students that leave the schools without a diploma or who would continue their education in a lower level of academic ability stream. When schools are evaluated negatively several times in a row, the government can close the school. In tertiary education, the quality of education is monitored by the Dutch-Flemish Accreditation Organization. When this organization concludes that the quality of programs is too low and no improvement in 1 or 2 years is shown, then the government will no longer fund the program and the institution is no longer allowed to grant the degree.

## Educational Reforms in Dutch Secondary Education

Between 1993 and 2002 the Netherlands witnessed three major reforms in secondary education. None of these reforms is considered successful nowadays, which has had a negative impact on how the public and politicians perceive and experience education and educational reform (Commissie Parlementair Onderzoek Onderwijsvernieuwing 2008).

## *The Reforms*

The first reform was referred to as the "basic curriculum" and was implemented from 1993 onwards. In this reform, 14 subjects were introduced with standardized goals that had to be covered in the first 3 years of secondary education for all students. The original goals of this reform were to pay more attention to the development of skills in the curriculum and to postpone the streaming of children at the age of 12 until 14. Both aims sought to strengthen the chances on good education for all students specifically those of parents with low Social Economic Status (SES). In this way, the innovation wanted to contribute to a more just society and thus contribute to the common good. However, the reform became the topic of a heated debate and only a weak version of the original plans was implemented: all students had to take the 14 subjects and reach the common goals, but they would do that *within* streams for which they were selected at the age of 12. The first element still contributed to realizing social justice goals, but the second in fact counteracted it because evidence shows that the earlier students are out into a specific track the more students from parents with a high SES are favoured (OECD 2013). The second reform, which was implemented in 1998, involved a reform of the curriculum in the last 2 years of HAVO and the last 3 years of VWO with the aim to better prepare students for studying in higher education. One element of this innovation was that schools could implement the "study house", which many schools did. The study house was a radical shift in the pedagogical approach in classes towards student independent and self-responsible learning and inquiry. For teachers, it meant a shift in their role from being the source of knowledge to act as a supervisor, coach and facilitator of learning. This approach was referred to as "new learning". Underlying this reform were theoretical notions derived from constructivism that aimed at active and self-regulative learning (Simons 2000; Simons et al. 2000). From a policy perspective, the main aim was to strengthen students' chances for completing higher education successfully, by providing a better preparation in secondary education. Such preparation might compensate for the difference in the support that parents of caretakers from high and low SES can provide their children with. Parents form high SES more than from low SES have completed higher education themselves in the Netherlands. Thus this innovation was in the politicians' eyes also a way for reducing social inequality. The third reform, in 1999–2002, involved a reorganization of the lower levels of secondary education, combining junior general secondary education (MAVO, Medium General Secondary Education) with lower vocational education in one stream with the aim to create more pathways for students in these schools. This combination is the current VMBO which we discussed above.

Despite the good intentions of these reforms, the implementation was problematic. The basic education in particular, met with much resistance and ultimately was abolished in 2006. When it was proposed, many school leaders and teachers were positive about the study house, but in practice it turned out hard to implement (e.g. van Veen et al. 2005). Furthermore, although schools were free to implement the study house or not, many teachers did not feel they had a say in if and how this reform was implemented (Commissie Parlementair Onderzoek Onderwijsvernieuwing 2008). The third reform, combining junior general secondary education with lower vocational education in one stream was the relatively most successful of the three reforms, although at first the image of the new VMBO-stream was rather negative because it was perceived as a school type for students who couldn't succeed in the other levels.

## *The Role of Evidence in the New Learning Reform*

The number and intensity of government introduced reforms led to critical responses from parents, students, teachers and educational scientists. National newspapers for instance, reported about students rebelling against "new learning" (NRC 2007). The association Better Education Netherlands [Beter Onderwijs Nederland] was founded in 2006 by a coalition of secondary teachers and university staff with the explicit goal to stimulate direct instruction and practicing skills under the supervisions of competent teachers as the dominant teaching approach in secondary classrooms because "this is, in principle, the most effective type of teaching if carried out properly and supported by the programme" (Beter Onderwijs Nederland n.d.). In a theme issue of the Dutch educational journal Pedagogische Studiën, educational scientists discussed vigorously about the research evidence underlying the "new learning" approach in the study house (Wubbels et al. 2006). In this discussion, Simons (2006), one of the educational researchers whose work had been the inspiration for the "new learning" appoach, made clear that his work (Simons 2000; Simons et al. 2000) at least partially had been misinterpreted by policymakers, practitioners and colleague educational researchers alike. This misinterpretation may have been caused by a widely felt need in society to better cope with the general perceived lack of motivation of students in secondary education (van der Werf 2006). This lack of motivation put heavy demands on schools and teachers and many teachers felt unable to improve student motivation. So, the idea to give students more choice and say in what and how had to be learned was seized upon as a last rescue in a situation that was experienced as quite hopeless. Student responsibility for their learning thus became a panacea to help improve student motivation. Such practical teaching actions unbalanced only employed one element of Simon's thinking. His reasoning started from the assumption that nowadays society needed other student outcomes and learning aims than in previous years and that therefore "new learning" was needed. So, his starting point was not the pedagogy but rather the aims of education such as being able to retrieve and apply knowledge, solve problems, handle the huge amount of available data, and working in groups. In order to reach these new aims, Simons and co-workers (Simons 2000; Simons et al. 2000) advocated other ways of teaching and learning and assessing learning. So, for them there was a new integrated approach to aims, pedagogy and assessment, whereas practitioners and policy makers focused primarily on the pedagogy: the how instead of integrating this how with the content, the what.

A second problem in the practice of new learning (and nowadays also in the educational research literature; e.g., Kilday et al. 2016) was the misinterpretation of social constructivism. Social constructivism originally is an epistemological theory on how people learn: they construct knowledge in interaction with others (which includes artefacts such as books) and which implies that learning is situated in particular contexts (e.g., Phillips 1995; Von Glasersfeld 1996). Often, this is described rightly by adding the word "actively" before constructing knowledge; rightly because construction indeed is an action of the learner, but in practice the word active often leads to misunderstandings. Active then is interpreted as the student having to be active in class as opposed to passively sitting and take in what a teacher is saying. This is quite a different interpretation of the word active, because students also can learn by sitting and listening: also then they construct knowledge as long as they are paying attention by listening. Thus, a false antithesis is created of knowledge transfer opposed to knowledge construction often implying that instruction is useless (e.g., Benbunan-Fich and Arbaugh 2006). In fact, constructivism as an epistemological theory doesn't say anything about how students should be taught and certainly not that direct instruction cannot be effective. It points to the risk of assuming that what a teacher presents to students is learned or memorised in exactly that way. That is not the case because, according to constructivism, what students learn also depends on the knowledge structures they already have at their disposal (e.g. Nathan and Sawyer 2014). In that sense transfer of knowledge is impossible: student construct knowledge from what is presented to them.

With respect to evidence based education, the discussion in Pedagogische Studiën focused on the empirical evidence for the effectiveness of new learning as opposed to direct instruction. Such a discussion followed from van der Werf's (2006) assumption that educational research should contribute to a knowledge base about how as many students can learn as much as possible. Because van der Werf (2006) did not include in her assumption explicitly what type of outcomes should be aimed for, the discussion with her critics revolved around whether the research she cited had been studying outcomes that are important. This discussion got momentum because the aims that are important in "new learning" are different from the traditional aims. A lot of the research on teaching effectiveness indeed had not studied specifically the intended outcomes of new learning approaches (Simons 2006) and therefore the evidence for the prevalence of direct instruction above new learning was limited. In fact, de Jong (2006) presented evidence supporting that some elements of new learning (inquiry learning and collaborative learning) outperformed direct instruction. He added that these forms of learning are only effective when appropriately supported by teachers, thus countering the conclusion of Kirschner et al. (2006) on the relative ineffectiveness of inquiry based learning.

Another line in the discussion was opened by Stevens (2006) who introduced theory about education and the educational process as missing elements in the discussion about effectiveness of new learning and direct instruction. He rejected the possibility to acquire evidence from psychological teaching experiments, because such experiments in his view cannot take the idiosyncratic processes into account that make every learning individually unique and highly dependent on the interaction and relationships between individuals, that is between students and their teacher. He considered such experiments as too simplistic to describe the complex educational processes and provided advice for teachers in practice who have to cope with these idiosyncrasies. These experiments cannot include sense making processes that in Stevens' (2006) view are essential for educational practices; processes that need to result in activities and environments that are perceived as meaningful by participants, both students and teachers. Experiments never can sufficiently take the practical teaching and learning situations into account which make these experiments (or quasi experiments) valid: ecological validity of the experiments is always poor. Stevens (2006) referred to an example: direct instruction might work for a motivated student but not for an uninterested one.

When analysing the discussions above from the perspective of evidence and the public good, it is striking that social justice and (in)equality were not mentioned at all. This is striking because for the policy makers at the base of all these discussions certainly promoting social equality was an issue (e.g., Commissie Parlementair Onderzoek Onderwijsvernieuwing 2008, p. 128). Evidence on the potential effects of the innovations on promoting the public good was not used at all.

## *Lessons About Reforms*

As a consequence of the criticisms on the three reforms and specifically the study house, politicians called for a parliamentary committee that was commissioned to investigate the implementation process and results of the reforms and to formulate guidelines for future governmental educational policies (Commissie Parlementair Onderzoek Onderwijsvernieuwing 2008). Based on the literature, their own research and hearings, this committee concluded that while there had been considerable political support for the innovations, the implementation of the reforms had been too much top-down, and that, as a consequence, many teachers felt that the innovations were forced upon them. The parliamentary committee recommended that these kinds of reforms should never be implemented again without support from the educational field and more specifically from the teachers. The committee also concluded that scientific evidence had only played a marginal role when developing the educational reforms and that the own experiences of the policy makers and their circles had often been more important. The committee pleaded for basing educational innovations on sound empirical evidence. If such evidence was not available, innovations should always be piloted on a small scale and be monitored and evaluated by scientific research.

## The Role of Educational Research in Dutch Educational Innovations

### *State of Affairs*

When educational innovations should only be implemented when there is sufficient empirical evidence to support the innovation, then the issue becomes important if educational research has supplied or can supply such evidence. This issue asks for a reflection on the merits and status of educational research (and broader educational sciences). In the period after the report of the parliamentary committee was published, and related to this report, a discussion started on the position of the educational sciences in the Netherlands. Aside from the report of the parliamentary committee, this discussion was also stimulated by the report of yet another committee, which was commissioned to develop a plan for the educational and learning sciences in the Netherlands (Commissie Nationaal Plan Toekomst Onderwijswetenschappen 2011). The committee called its report "National plan educational/learning sciences" to emphasise that educational science was too limited a description of the field of study that is important for improving the quality of education. A first conclusion of this committee on the educational and learning sciences was that the quality of Dutch research in this field is in general good and that it is appreciated by the international community of scientists. The committee however also produced a list of problems in the educational sciences:

- A continuity problem: The number of students in the teaching programs in educational sciences and university teacher education was low and this was threatening the viability of these programs.
- An activation problem: knowledge that is available in many disciplines and could be used to improve education wasn't used and part of the reason was that the grants for research were provided along disciplinary lines which hindered multi- and interdisciplinary approaches.
- A fragmentation problem: The educational research that the universities carried out from their own funds was fragmented, lacked coherence and there were many small programs.
- Chain failing: The current institutions did not succeed in making the knowledge from educational sciences available for practice and policy.
- A quality problem: Research that universities and other institutions carried out based on external grants lacked quality control and the money was provided without clear aims and guarantee for methodological rigour.
- Attraction of international journals: Because educational researchers were evaluated on their publications in scholarly journals, research lacked connection with practice and policy.
- Underuse of education research results: practitioners did not show sufficient interest in research results and the competence to use the results and develop research questions was lagging behind.

The discussion on the (lack of) impact of the educational sciences in practice gained further momentum when the Dutch Scientific Council for Government Policy [Wetenschappelijke Raad voor het Regeringsbeleid] published a report on the future of the Dutch economy with title "Towards a Learning Economy" (Wetenschappelijk Raad voor het Regeringsbeleid 2013). A central concept in this report is "knowledge circulation" for which the ability to notice, absorb and use existing knowledge is crucial. The role of education is crucial for knowledge circulation, but the Scientific Council was rather negative about the ability of Dutch education to innovate. New knowledge is not systematically used, also because schools and teachers are hardly encouraged to do so. The council made a plea for an innovation system that is comparable to systems that are used in healthcare, where research and educational institutions collaborate in local knowledge centres. It is remarkable that in these reports evidence mainly refers to effect of innovations on student learning and hardly to the effects of innovations on social equality or justice. This is the more important because Dutch policy makers often have improvement of the position of students from low SES as an aim in the back of their mind (Commissie Parlementair Onderzoek Onderwijsvernieuwing 2008, p. 128).

The community of educational scientists took all these recommendations to heart. The then existing program council for educational research of the Netherlands Organization for Scientific Research (NWO), the Netherlands Association for Educational Research and the Interuniversity Center for Educational Sciences (ICO: a nationwide organisation for training of educational researchers) collaborated to send the committee *Nationaal Plan Toekomst Onderwijswetenschap* a proposal for establishing a funding organisation that would bring together all money for education research with money for innovations, so that these budgets would be granted in connection to each other. The committee endorsed this proposal and incorporated it in its report. As a result the Netherlands Initiative for Education Research (NRO) was established in 2012 (https://www.nro.nl/en/about/). In this organization, indeed several sources of research money were brought together, but unfortunately no innovation money was granted to this organization.

The Netherlands Initiative for Education Research (NRO) has three tasks: facilitating the coherency of education research by providing direction at a national level, awarding grants for high quality research, and facilitating knowledge utilisation by improving the links between science and practice. NRO tries to connect research and practice e.g. through the involvement of practitioners and policy makers in the programming of research. The budget of NRO is divided in three parts. The largest part is for practice oriented research, that means research in which researchers and practitioners collaborate. Smaller amounts are available for fundamental and policy oriented research. This separation in three parts seems to hinder the development of comprehensive research proposals and therefore there are efforts to find ways to integrate the three perspectives. One of the strong points of establishing the NRO is the rigorous evaluation procedure that now is used for government funded research projects.

A few years later, under the supervision of the Association of Research Universities in the Netherlands (VSNU) educational scientists representing their own research university collaborated in a committee Discipline Plan for the

Educational Sciences (Commissie Sectorplan Onderwijswetenschappen, COS) on developing a plan for the Dutch educational sciences of the future. In this plan, a lot of attention was paid to improving the usefulness of the results of the educational research for practice. Education was presented as the power source for the Dutch Society and the educational sciences as an "auxiliary engine for education". "[The educational sciences] deliver the body of knowledge which is necessary for evidence informed innovation and improvement of education" (Commissie Sectorplan Onderwijswetenschappen 2014, p. 41). Educational sciences have to provide a body of knowledge for evidence informed approaches in education and have to train educational experts and have to contribute to the professionalization of teachers. The committee also concluded that, at the moment, the educational sciences in the Netherlands do not fulfill this function of auxiliary engine. In research, the committee argued, the overlap between programs in various universities should be diminished and small programs should cooperate more with other programs. A national agenda for research and innovation in education should be developed and all money for education research aside from the universities' own money should be granted via the NRO. The research of universities and universities of applied sciences should be integrated.

## Connecting Educational Research and Practice

After this chronological overview of discussions on the use of evidence for educational innovations in the Netherlands and the description of the failure to reach a good connection between the evidence provided by the educational sciences and educational practice, we move to potential measures to help bridge the gap between educational sciences and educational practice in order to make innovations more successful. Key for success of the educational sciences, according to the Commissie Sectorplan Onderwijswetenschappen (2014, p. 41), is a better connection between educational sciences and practice and policy. Therefore, renewing research and teaching programs in the educational sciences is not sufficient and the committee advocated that research projects should be more based on the problems that practitioners and policy makers experience. We discuss four approaches for bridging the gap: (1) making research results better usable in practice, (2) research by teachers, (3) a primary role for teachers in educational innovation and (4) intensive collaboration between researchers, teachers and teacher educators in academic workplaces.

### *Research for Practice*

The receptiveness for research in education is quite low compared with other domains. Slavin (2004) for example, mentioned a much better receptiveness for evidence from research (e.g. from randomized controlled experiments) in medicine, engineering and agriculture than in education. This receptiveness has led to tremendous improvement of the medical, engineering and agricultural practice. Olson (2004) however contended in a similar vein as Stevens (2006) that in education an inventory of results of experiments in specific contexts doesn't help practitioners because of the poor generalizability of the results of such experiments and the disputed causality of relations found in experiments. He advocates the development of theories that might help explain why particular interventions have particular effects. By understanding mechanisms in educational processes through a robust theory, research can be helpful to fine tune such theories and making these more specific for different contexts.

Olson (2004) suggested a different way of doing educational research than the randomized controlled experiments so that research might be of more value for practice by being better theoretically grounded. The Educational Council of the Netherlands (Onderwijsraad 2011) pointed to the whole chain of actions between doing educational research and using its results in practice. The council mentioned two traditional ways in which research can inform practice: the Research Development and Diffusion model and the Evidence Based Practise model.

In the classical Research Development Diffusion model (Broekkamp and van Hout-Wolters 2007; Burkhardt and Schoenfeld 2003; Guba 1967; Onderwijsraad 2003) the first step is research, specifically fundamental research, which is the starting point to create knowledge about education. In the phase of development, curricular interventions, learning materials, assessments et cetera are developed that can be used in education and are based on knowledge created in the first step. Through diffusion then these new materials are brought to the attention of teachers, school principals and policy makers. In the original version a phase of adaption was included (van Tartwijk 2011). The aim of this phase is: "Adapt and install the invention in a local school setting" (Guba 1967, p. 5). In the evidence based practice model fundamental research is also central but the results of that research should be tested in research in practice, preferably in (quasi) experimental designs. Only after such testing, development and diffusion can be the next steps to get results used in practice.

The Educational Council of the Netherlands (Onderwijsraad 2006) advocated a particular stepwise approach to educational research in order to help improve educational effectiveness: explorative research, practical oriented research and curriculum design and finally experiments, that is research to prove effects of specific interventions. Such a series of studies should be carried out in a stepwise process in order to learn from mistakes in the different steps through a learning attitude and respect for results of research and the research should be based on problems experienced in practice.

The approaches discussed above were criticised in the Netherlands by for instance Gravemeijer and Kirschner (2007). They contended that this way of working would be very expensive and impractical, and that it ignores the study of mechanisms as also mentioned by Stevens (2006), Olson (2004), and (Maxwell 2004). Gravemeijer and Kirschner (2007) advocated to produce evidence for insight in mechanisms instead of evidence about interventions thus emphasizing the explaining processes (how does it work) instead of causality between actions and results (what works) (Maxwell 2004).

By applying the approaches discussed in this section, the educational council (Onderwijsraad 2011) hoped that research can contribute to improving teachers' receptiveness for educational research. In particular for improving this receptiveness, very different approaches have been proposed, which we discuss in the next section.

## *The Teacher as Producer of Knowledge*

A second option for bridging the gap between research and practice puts the teacher in the role of producer of knowledge (either alone or in collaboration with university based researchers). In such models the role of teachers shifts from consumers of research results towards creators of evidence. More and more, in the literature teachers are seen as (co) creators of knowledge (e.g. Admiraal 2013; van Tartwijk 2011). According to Admiraal et al. (2014) literature on teacher research characterizes teacher research as small-scale, qualitative studies focused on describing and understanding teaching practice and evaluation of teaching by perceptions of teachers and students, with conclusions about and implications for the practice of the particular teacher doing the research. Less frequent are quantitative or mix-method studies using pre-test/post-test control group designs and test scores to deduce conclusions about effects of teaching interventions (e.g., Cochran-Smith and Lytle 2009; Admiraal et al. 2013; Anderson and Shattuck 2012). When teachers participate in educational research, this may contribute to their professional development (e.g. Zeichner 2003), but whether this also contributes to the quality of their teaching remains unclear. Admiraal et al. (2013) concluded from a literature review that results of research by teachers usually only apply for their own context and cannot or do not say very much for other contexts.

The most extreme proposal for teacher as researcher advocates the teacher as independent full fleshed researcher. For example, Admiraal (2013) advocated a scholarly teaching profession in which action research by teachers themselves is used to improve their own practice by systematically gathering data on that practice, analyse these data and try and improve that practice. This research should be rigorous so that it contributes to theoretical developments and can be published in international scholarly journals. Such a teaching profession would resemble the medical profession where physicians also contribute to the scholarly literature and their research helps improve the medical practice (Bulterman-Bos 2008). In the Netherlands it is already possible for a limited number of teachers to get a grant for doing a PhD from a very competitive program of the Netherlands Organisation for Scientific Research. This grant however also can be used for research that is not related to education and thus not always will connect educational research and practice.

A more mixed model advocates co-creation of evidence (Onderwijsraad 2006) in collaboration between teachers, school principals and researchers. It is assumed that by collaboration between teachers and researchers both parties develop a shared understanding and vision and such shared ideas are needed for successful educational innovation (Fullan 2007). There are already several examples of such collaborations in the Netherlands, for example a project in which teachers, school principals and researchers work together to use data that have been collected by researchers as feedback for teachers to help them improve their practice (Geijsel and Krüger 2005; Schildkamp et al. 2013). An even closer cooperation exists in data teams where the actors work together also in the gathering of the data (Schildkamp and Ehren 2013). Another example is design research that now is quite popular in the Netherlands (McKenney and Reeves 2013; Plomp and Nieveen 2010; van den Akker et al. 2006). In such research teachers and researchers collaboratively design new teaching and learning approaches. Plomp and Nieveen (2010) advocated a stepwise approach starting from a practical or theoretical problem, then a literature review and problem analysis followed by a repeated cycle of design, action (trial), evaluation and analysis and redesign, until a satisfying design has been reached.

## *Teachers as Innovators*

A third way to make innovations more successful through a better connection between research and practice, is focusing on the role of the teacher as innovator and create conditions to help teachers fulfill that role effectively. For teachers to innovate implies to act as an adaptive expert. Bransford et al. (2005) distinguish between routine experts and adaptive experts. Routine experts have a number of core competencies that they developed throughout their lives with growing efficiency, whereas adaptive experts are much more likely to change their core competencies and expand and restructure their expertise and are therefore more inclined to innovate. Routines are efficient but also can be risky, because they may become outdated when tasks change. In teaching, an example is the change of classroom teaching because of the use of computers, which would for instance make it difficult for the teacher to recognize the relevant cues in class environments. Adaptive expertise is described by Bransford et al. (2005) as balancing between innovation and efficiency. Innovation requires letting go off efficient routines, thus reducing efficiency in the short run (Bransford et al. 2005, p. 49). However, in innovations routine can also be helpful because appropriate levels of efficiency make room for innovation (Hammerness et al. 2005). According to Hammerness et al. (2005), teachers who are adaptive experts make preconceptions explicit and learn to take control of their own learning. This can be stimulated by "providing tools for analysis of events and situations that enable them to understand and handle the complexities of life in classroom" (p. 366). They should not only develop a strong foundation of factual and theoretical knowledge, but also should this knowledge be organized in such a way that retrieval and action are facilitated. Bransford et al. (2005)

emphasize that the processes of restructuring “often have emotional consequences that accompany realization that cherished beliefs and practices need to be changed”. These emotional consequences can explain the resistance of teachers towards educational change, in particular when they feel that their voice is not heard and their expertise is not valued (van Veen et al. 2005).

Participating in innovation implies deliberately improving performance through identifying suitable training tasks that are outside a teacher’s current realm of performance, but that he or she can master by concentrating on critical aspects and by gradually refining performance through repetitions and feedback. Ericsson (2006) and Ericsson et al. (1993) refer to this as deliberate practice. Bronkhorst et al. (2014) describe four characteristics that have been used in the literature to define deliberate practice: (1) it is designed for self-improvement, (2) it is repeated to enable successive refinement, (3) it is followed by immediate, informative feedback, and (4) it requires significant effort and concentration or motivation. Such practice might be important for the teacher’s innovating role.

One example of an activity in which teachers play an important innovating role is the lesson study strategy (cf. Dudley 2013, 2015). Lesson study originated in Japan more than a century ago and provides a well-developed set of principles and procedures providing teachers with the support needed for innovating their practice (Xu and Pedder 2014). Lesson study is associated with high student performance (Dudley 2015) and positive effects on teacher learning (cf. Dudley 2013; Xu and Pedder 2014). In lesson study, a team of teachers collaboratively designs a lesson. One team member then executes the lesson while the other team members gather data on student learning processes, including live observation. Collectively reflecting upon the data results in changed knowledge or ideas. The lesson is then revised and taught again (i.e. deliberate practice). A lesson study-cycle is concluded by reflecting on the learning outcomes and sharing the results with colleagues. Within one or more lesson study-cycles, teachers engage in guided and collaborative experiential learning activities. These learning activities provide challenges that go beyond the teachers’ current level of reliable performance, ideally in guided and collaborative learning contexts that allow immediate feedback and gradual refinement by repetition. Such activities then lead to innovated practices. The characteristics of the learning activities described above resemble essential aspects of learning environments that could foster adaptive expertise (Anthony et al. 2015; Bohle Carbonell et al. 2014).

## *Academic Workplaces*

As a way to integrate the three approaches that have been discussed above, establishment of “Academic Workplaces” has been proposed in the Netherlands in several reports in the last 7 years (Onderwijsraad 2011; Wetenschappelijk Raad voor het Regeringsbeleid 2013; Commissie Sectorplan Onderwijswetenschappen 2014). In such workplaces schools, institutes for teacher education, and universities collaborate. Educational scientists, teachers, and teacher educators meet each other and work on solving educational problems, developing curricula, educational innovations, preparing teachers and teacher professionalization and doing research (Commissie Sectorplan Onderwijswetenschappen 2014). At the basis of all these suggestions is the generally assumed importance of collaboration between educational research and practice for systematic improvement of educational quality. These workplaces are seen as a means to make research more practice oriented among others by generating research questions based on problems experienced in the educational practice: that is a form of research on demand. Further it is expected that close cooperation between practitioners and researchers will help making the results be of practical value. In academic workplaces, it is aimed to develop a research culture in which evidence informed working is the standard.

The educational council (Onderwijsraad 2011) suggests as most important mechanisms in such workplaces boundary crossing practices and knowledge communities. Akkerman and Bakker (2011, p. 133) defined boundaries as sociocultural differences between practices leading to discontinuities in action or interaction. Boundaries are at play in the use of research results in practice. Knowledge that has been developed in one context needs to transfer to another context (e.g., Broekkamp and Van Hout-Wolters 2007), and such boundary crossing is difficult by nature. People working in different contexts do not easily cross borders. An important role can be played by so called brokers, people who are engaged in practices that cross borders and so also themselves move from one institution to another and thus literally cross boundaries (Akkerman and Bakker 2011). In academic workplaces, students from teacher education institutions for example can be brokers when they follow their internships in school or when they participate in research of the university that is carried out in the schools. Similarly, teachers who participate in research or follow a program for a master degree or PhD at a university can be brokers.

The second element the educational council mentions is the knowledge community which is to develop in an academic workplace. This knowledge community resembles what in the literature is referred to with several concepts such as professional learning community (Fullan 2007; Stoll et al. 2006), community of practice (Wenger and Snyder 2000), or social networks (Moolenaar et al. 2010). In knowledge communities, knowledge is exchanged in structured collaborative arrangements (Onderwijsraad 2011) such as in professional development schools or in teams of teachers and researchers who collaboratively are carrying out research projects in the school. Also the earlier mentioned teams in lesson study projects can be considered professional communities. It has been shown for example that the structure of such networks is related the ability of schools to innovate (Moolenaar et al. 2010).

## Conclusion

There seems to be broad consensus in the Netherlands that we shouldn't strive for evidence based education but rather for evidence informed education. Making education evidence based places research in a too presumptuous position, because there are strong doubts if educational research will ever produce convincing "evidence" that will enable teachers and policy makers to give an absolute answer to the question what and how to teach. Educational research results on the one hand will always be detached from practical teaching situations and on the other be influenced by idiosyncrasies of the specific research context. Thus, it never can tell what works under many different circumstances. What is possible, however, is that evidence informs practice and specifically educational innovations. Evidence informed then means that practitioners use empirical and theoretical knowledge that has been developed in educational research and combine this knowledge with their practical wisdom, experiences and insights on a specific situation. Thus, they can use evidence and contextualise it for building local innovations. They choose what part of evidence might apply in their specific situation showing adaptive expertise.

In the Netherlands, the bad experiences with government initiated innovations has led to the conclusion that innovations should be initiated by teachers themselves and that if the government wants innovations, teachers have to be involved much earlier than was done in previous innovations. In this reasoning the link between education as a means to strengthen the common good is markedly missing. The quality of proposals for innovation could be improved when evidence that is available on the effects of innovations on the position of students from low SES would be incorporated.

To bridge the gap between educational research and practice for the benefit of the quality of education, academic workplaces in which researchers, teachers, student teachers and teacher educators collaborate seem a promising avenue to enter. Therefore, NRO now has selected three consortia of schools, universities and universities of applied sciences to carry out a pilot with these workplaces.

In the introduction of the Handbook of Implementation Science of Psychology in Education Kelly asks: "What is it about real-world contexts that makes measurable effectiveness so difficult to achieve?" (Kelly 2012, p. 6). The answer to this (fundamental) question is crucial for the ultimate success of evidence informed education.

## References

Admiraal, W. F. (2013). *Academisch docentschap: Naar wetenschappelijk praktijkonderzoek door docenten* [Academic leadership: Towards scientific research by teachers]. Leiden: ICLON, Leiden University.

Admiraal, W. F., Smit, B. H. J., & Zwart, R. C. (2013). *Academisch docentschap in het basis- en voortgezet onderwijs: Aard en betekenis van onderzoek van docenten naar hun onderwijspraktijk* [Academic teaching in primary and secondary education: Nature and meaning of teacher research into their own practice]. Leiden: ICLON, Leiden University.

Admiraal, W., Smit, B., & Zwart, R. (2014). Models and design principles for teacher research. IB *Journal of Teaching Practice, 2*, 1–7.

Akkerman, S., & Bakker, A. (2011). Boundary crossing and boundary objects. *Review of Research in Education, 81*(2), 132–169.

Anderson, T., & Shattuck, J. (2012). Design-based research: A decade of progress in education research? *Educational Researcher, 41*(1), 16–25.

Anthony, G., Hunter, J., & Hunter, R. (2015). Prospective teachers development of adaptive expertise. *Teaching and Teacher Education, 49*, 108–117.
Benbunan-Fich, R., & Arbaugh, J. B. (2006). Separating the effects of knowledge construction and group collaboration in learning outcomes of web-based courses. *Information Management, 43*(6), 778–793.
Beter Onderwijs Nederland. (n.d.). Over de Vereniging [About the association]. Retrieved from https://www.beteronderwijsnederland.nl/content/over-de-vereniging
Bohle Carbonell, K., Stalmeijer, R. E., Könings, K. D., Segers, M., & van Meriënboer, J. J. G. (2014). How experts deal with novel situations: A review of adaptive expertise. *Educational Research Review, 12*(1), 14–29.
Bransford, J., Derry, S., Berliner, D. C., Hammerness, K., & Beckett, K. L. (2005). Theories of learning and their roles in teaching. In L. Darling-Hammond, J. Bransford, P. LePage, K. Hammerness, & H. Duffy (Eds.), *Preparing teachers for a changing world: What teachers should learn and be able to do* (pp. 40–88). San Francisco: Jossey-Bass.
Broekkamp, H., & van Hout-Wolters, B. (2007). The gap between educational research and practice: A literature review, symposium, and questionnaire. *Educational Research and Evaluation, 13*(3), 203–220.
Bronkhorst, L. H., Meijer, P. C., Koster, B., & Vermunt, J. D. (2014). Deliberate practice in teacher education. *European Journal of Teacher Education, 37*(1), 18–34.
Bulterman-Bos, J. A. (2008). Will a clinical approach make education research more relevant for practice? *Educational Researcher, 37*(7), 412–420.
Burkhardt, H., & Schoenfeld, A. H. (2003). Improving educational research: Toward a more useful, more influential, and better-funded enterprise. *Educational Researcher, 32*(9), 3–14.
Cochran-Smith, M., & Lytle, S. L. (2009). *Inquiry as stance: Practitioner research for the next generation*. New York: Teachers College Press.
Commissie Nationaal Plan Toekomst Onderwijswetenschappen. (2011). *Nationaal Plan Onderwijs/leerwetenschappen* [National Plan Education/Learning Sciences]. Retrieved from Den Haag: http://www.rijksoverheid.nl/documenten-en-publicaties/rapporten/2011/02/10/nationaal-plan-toekomst-onderwijswetenschappen.html
Commissie Parlementair Onderzoek Onderwijsvernieuwing. (2008). *Tijd voor onderwijs*. [Time for education]. s-Gravenhage: Sdu.
Commissie Sectorplan Onderwijswetenschappen. (2014). *Sectorplan onderwijswetenschappen: Wetenschap voor het onderwijs* [Sectorplan educational sciences: Science for education practice]. Den Haag: VSNU.
de Jong, T. (2006). Nieuw leren en oude kennis: Over bestaande evidentie voor de effectiviteit van "nieuwe" en "gecombineerde" vormen van leren. [New learning and old knowledge: On existing evidence for the effectiveness of "new" and "combined" forms of learning]. *Pedagogische Studiën, 83*(1), 89–94.
Dudley, P. (2013). Teacher learning in lesson study: What interaction-level discourse analysis revealed about how teachers utilised imagination, tacit knowledge of teaching and fresh evidence of pupils learning, to develop practice knowledge and so enhance their pupils' learning. *Teaching and Teacher Education, 34*, 107–121.
Dudley, P. (2015). *Lesson study: Professional learning for our time*. Milton Park: Routledge.
Ericsson, K. A. (2006). The influence of experience and deliberate practice on the development of expert performance. In K. A. Ericsson, N. Charness, P. J. Feltovich, & R. R. Hoffman (Eds.), *The Cambridge handbook of expertise and expert performance* (pp. 683–704). New York: Cambridge University Press.
Ericsson, K. A., Krampe, R. T., & Tesch-Römer, C. (1993). The role of deliberate practice in the acquisition of expert performance. *Psychological Review, 100*(3), 363.
Fullan, M. (2007). *The new meaning of educational change* (4th ed.). New York: Teachers College.
Geijsel, F., & Krüger, M. (2005). Leren van onderzoek: De benutting van datafeedback ten behoove van schoolontwikkeling. [Learning from reserach: The use of data feedback for school development]. *Pedagogische Studiën, 82*(4), 327–342.

Gravemeijer, K. P. E., & Kirschner, P. A. (2007). Naar meer evidence-based onderwijs? [Towards more evidence based education?]. *Pedagogische Studiën, 84*(6), 463–472.
Guba, E. G. (1967). *Development, diffusion, and evaluation*. Paper presented at the conference on knowledge production and utilization in educational administration: Role emergence and reorganization, Portland OR.
Hammerness, K., Darling-Hammond, L., Bransford, J., Berliner, D. C., Cochran-Smith, M., McDonald, M., & Zeichner, K. (2005). How teachers learn and develop. In L. Darling-Hammond, J. Bransford, P. LePage, K. Hammerness, & H. Duffy (Eds.), *Preparing teachers for a changing world: What teachers should learn and be able to do* (pp. 358–389). San Francisco: Jossey-Bass.
Hammerness, K., van Tartwijk, J., & Snoek, M. (2012). Teacher preparation in the Netherlands: Shared visions and common features. In L. Darling-Hammond & A. Lieberman (Eds.), *Teacher education around the world: Changing policies and practices* (pp. 44–65). New York: Routledge.
Kelly, B. (2012). Implementation science for psychology in education. In B. Kelly & D. F. Perkins (Eds.), *Handbook of implementation science for psychology in education* (pp. 3–12). New York: Cambridge University Press.
Kilday, J. E., Lenser, M. L., & Miller, A. D. (2016). Considering students in teachers' self-efficacy: Examination of a scale for student-oriented teaching. *Teaching and Teacher Education, 56*, 61–71.
Kirschner, P. A., Sweller, J., & Clark, R. E. (2006). Why minimal guidance during instruction does not work: An analysis of the failure of constructivist, discovery, problem-based, experiential, and inquiry-based teaching. *Educational Psychologist, 41*(2), 75–86.
Maxwell, J. A. (2004). Causal explanation, qualitative research, and scientific inquiry in education. *Educational Researcher, 33*(2), 3–11.
McKenney, S., & Reeves, T. C. (2013). Systematic review of design-based research progress: Is a little knowledge a dangerous thing? *Educational Researcher, 42*(2), 97–100.
Moolenaar, N. M., Daly, A. J., & Sleegers, P. J. (2010). Occupying the principal position: Examining relationships between transformational leadership, social network position, and schools' innovative climate. *Educational Administration Quarterly, 46*(5), 623–670.
Nathan, M. J., & Sawyer, R. K. (2014). Foundations of the learning sciences. In R. K. Sawyer (Ed.), *The Cambridge handbook of the learning sciences* (2nd ed., pp. 21–43). New York: Cambridge University Press.
NRC. (2007). *Scholierenprotest tegen 'nieuwe leren*. [Student-protest against 'New Learning']. NRC.
OECD. (2013). *PISA 2012 results: What makes schools successful? Resources, policies and practices (Volume IV)*. PISA, OECD Publishing. http://dx.doi.org/10.1787/9789264201156-en
Olson, D. R. (2004). The triumph of hope over experience in the search for "What Works": A response to Slavin. *Educational Researcher 33*(1), 24–26.
Onderwijsraad. (2003). *Kennis van onderwijs: Ontwikkeling en benutting* [Knowledge on education: Development and use]. Den Haag: Onderwijsraad.
Onderwijsraad. (2006). *Naar meer evidence based onderwijs* [Towards more evidence based education]. Den Haag: Onderwijsraad.
Onderwijsraad. (2011). *Ruim baan voor stapsgewijze verbetering* [Clear the way for stepwise improvement]. Den Haag: Onderwijsraad.
Phillips, D. C. (1995). The good, the bad, and the ugly: The many faces of constructivism. *Educational Researcher, 24*(7), 5–12.
Plomp, T., & Nieveen, N. (Eds.). (2010). *An introduction to educational design research*. Enschede: SLO.
Schildkamp, K., & Ehren, M. (2013). From "intuition"-to "data"-based decision making in dutch secondary schools? In K. Schildkamp, M. K. Lai, & L. Earl (Eds.), *Data-based decision making in education* (pp. 49–67). Dordrecht: Springer.
Schildkamp, K., Lai, M. K., & Earl, L. (Eds.). (2013). *Data-based decision making in education: Challenges and opportunities* (Vol. 17). Dordrecht: Springer.

Simons, P. R. J. (2000). Towards a constructivistic theory of self-directed learning. In G. A. Straka (Ed.), *Conceptions of self-directed learning* (pp. 155–170). New York: Waxman.

Simons, P. R. J. (2006). Hoe je een karikatuur van het nieuwe leren om zeep helpt [How to kill a caricature of new learning]. *Pedagogische Studiën, 83*(1), 81–85.

Simons, P. R. J., van der Linden, J., & Duffy, T. (2000). New Learning: Three ways to learn in a new balance. In P. R. J. Simons, J. van der Linden, & T. Duffy (Eds.), *New learning* (pp. 191–208). Dordrecht: Kluwer Academic Publishers.

Slavin, R. E. (2004). Education research can and must address "what works" questions. *Educational Researcher, 33*(1), 27–28.

Stevens, L. (2006). Niet nieuw of oud, wel anders [Not new or old, but different]. *Pedagogische Studiën, 83*(1), 85–89.

Stoll, L., Bolam, R., McMahon, A., Wallace, M., & Thomas, S. (2006). Professional learning communities: A review of the literature. *Journal of Educational Change, 7*(4), 221–258.

van den Akker, J., Gravemeijer, K., McKenney, S., & Nieveen, N. (Eds.). (2006). *Educational design research*. London: Routledge.

van der Werf, G. (2006). Oud of nieuw leren? Of liever gewoon léren? [Old or new learning? Or rather just learning?]. *Pedagogische Studiën, 83*(1), 74–81.

van Tartwijk, J. (2011). *Van onderzoek naar onderwijs of de kunst van de toepassing* [From research to teaching or the art of application]. Utrecht: Universiteit Utrecht.

van Veen, K., Sleegers, P., & van de Ven, P. (2005). One teacher's identity, emotions, and commitment to change: A case study into the cognitive-affective processes of a secondary school teacher in the context of reforms. *Teaching and Teacher Education, 21*(8), 917–934.

von Glasersfeld, E. (1996). Footnotes to "The many faces of Constructivism". *Educational Researcher, 25*(6), 19.

Wenger, E. C., & Snyder, W. M. (2000). Communities of practice: The organizational frontier. *Harvard Business Review, 78*(1), 139–146.

Wetenschappelijk Raad voor het Regeringsbeleid. (2013). *Naar een lerende economie: Investeren in het verdienvermogen van Nederland*. [Towards learning economy: invest in the Dutch earnings]. Amsterdam: Amsterdam University Press.

Wubbels, T., & van Tartwijk, J. (in press). Dutch teacher and teacher education policies: Trends and ambiguities. In H. Niemi, A. Toom, A. Kallioniemi, & J. Lavonen (Eds.), *Teacher's role in changing global world: On resources and challenges related to the teaching profession*. Rotterdam: Sense.

Wubbels, T., de Jong, T., Simons, R. J., Stevens, L., & van der Werf, G. (2006). Discussie: Het nieuwe leren [Discussion: New learning]. *Pedagogische Studiën, 83*(1), 74–99.

Xu, H., & Pedder, D. (2014). Lesson study: An international review of the research. In P. Dudley (Ed.), *Lesson study: Professional learning for our time* (pp. 29–58). London: Routledge.

Zeichner, K. M. (2003). Teacher research as professional development for P–12 educators in the USA. *Educational Action Research, 11*(2), 301–326.

# Chapter 8
# The Evidence Agenda in Education: An International Perspective

**Tracey Burns and Rien Rouw**

**Abstract** In this chapter the authors provide an overview of the evidence-for-education landscape across countries. Although the importance of using evidence to inform policy and practice in education was identified over 20 years ago, many education systems are still struggling to make this a reality. The enormous expansion of publicly available data on education and its increased access by diverse stakeholders has only contributed to the complexity of the endeavour. In recent years it has become clear that providing data and research and promoting evidence-informed policy does not ensure that the knowledge will actually be used. Furthermore, data and research can and will also be misused, selectively used or even abused. Therefore, the appropriate use of knowledge should be a high priority on the evidence agenda in education. Illustrated by two country cases the authors argue for a systematic effort to promote appropriate use through building capacity at the local level and creating a culture of evaluation and self-reflection across the system. Peer learning networks and the engagement of a broader range of stakeholders can be powerful levers for establishing a holistic culture for the use of evidence.

## Introduction

In recent years a number of public crises have seized the attention of the world and required rapid responses from governments to ensure the health and safety of the public and maintain their confidence in policy makers. Climate change, for example, has emerged as a generally agreed upon public emergency after years of public debate. This debate has been in turns emotional and rational, with much of the disagreement about the nature and reliability of the evidence presented. We have now reached a new era where, superficially at least, the COP 21 agreement sets out the science in an uncontested manner, and provides a roadmap for action. The goal is of course to contain the substantial economic and societal losses projected from a rise

T. Burns (✉) • R. Rouw
Organisation for Economic Cooperation and Development (OECD), Paris, France
e-mail: Tracey.BURNS@oecd.org



M.Y. Eryaman, B. Schneider (eds.), *Evidence and Public Good in Educational Policy, Research and Practice*, Educational Governance Research 6,
DOI 10.1007/978-3-319-58850-6_8

in temperatures of over 2°, as well as ensure the future viability of our planet in the longer term.

This is one of the most dramatic and meaningful challenges facing our modern world. It is also an excellent study of the role of the use of research and evidence in decision making, and the potential of evidence to be used for the public good. This real-life example demonstrates the challenge facing policy makers of all stripes, including education, who must make swift, time-sensitive decisions based on the information they have available. Often the information that is readily available is not "perfect" research on the subject. This could be either because the rigorous research relevant to policy needs has not been conducted; or because there is a disjoint between policy and research communities such that the relevant information is not widely disseminated and so overlooked by the policy maker; or simply that the research that is available is contradictory and so does not suggest a single course of action that could be reflected in policy (OECD 2007). Yet clearly it is crucial that policy decisions be made with the best available evidence, as the decisions made can, as the climate change example demonstrates, have far-reaching impacts on all members of society.

## The Evidence Agenda in Education

Interest in and discussion on how educational policy is aided by research, and specifically on what kinds of evidence from research count or should count in policy and practice, have grown dramatically in the last decades. One of the reasons for this interest is the growing awareness that good or even excellent quality education is vital for the development of societies in general and for economic growth and prosperity in particular. Scientific research is believed to be one of the levers for the improvement of education. Discourse on the nature of scientific evidence, challenges for raising awareness of policy makers, and pleas to bring research into classrooms all trigger intense and sometimes heated debate on what constitutes "evidence-based" or "evidence-informed policy", the terms which have come to denote this field, and which we define as "the conscientious and explicit use of current best evidence in making decisions and choosing between policy options" (OECD 2007, p. 16).

Education systems struggle with the best way to integrate the various kinds of research and knowledge in policy and practice. This is an ongoing challenge that was highlighted 10 years ago in seminal work on evidence-informed policy in education (OECD 2007) and observed more than a decade previous (OECD 1995). The importance of this process has only increased in the 20 years since it was first identified: In fact, the increase in the availability of information has been one of the most dramatic transformations in our education systems.

This explosion of information is fuelled by two concurrent trends: (1) the rise of standardised tests (both national and international, for example PISA) and the resulting proliferation of available evidence and greater emphasis on testing and assessment; and (2) the increased access to information via the Internet and other technologies, which has enabled a multitude of actors to bring their own informed opinions to the discussion (OECD 2007).

The impact of this second point cannot be understated. Across the OECD, education governance has in general moved away from hierarchical governance systems towards more complex environments in which a multitude of actors collaborate through formal and informal channels. This broad diversity of actors, who are more informed and empowered due to the availability of performance data and other measures of education excellence, has in many countries reshaped the power and control of the education system (Burns and Köster 2016).

## *What Counts as Evidence?*

Performance data is only one source of evidence. Other forms include descriptive system data (on achievement, graduation, etc.), and research findings that can determine whether something is working, and why. Evidence also includes the wealth of expert practitioner knowledge available, both formal and informal. And, in the political realm, the power of a good anecdote overheard by the minister on the way to a meeting can be immense. Ideas which are generally perceived as "intuitively reasonable" gain power and support of public opinion. This is especially the case where they are promoted by the media, who often play a major role in shaping, or stunting, the policy agenda.

Some authors organise different types of knowledge into a hierarchy where quantitative scientific knowledge in general, and randomised control trials in particular, are considered the most robust (Sackett et al. 1996; Clarke et al. 2014). This is then followed in the hierarchy by knowledge obtained through quasi-experimental research, and then by that gleaned from qualitative study (e.g. case studies, focus groups, etc.). Presumably practitioner knowledge and expert knowledge of teachers is then placed lower in the hierarchy, if it is included at all. This then sets up a tension in the public discourse in terms of who has the power and expertise, and who has the right to make decisions based on what evidence.

In this chapter, quantitative scientific knowledge is not the only type of knowledge considered as valid, and no explicit hierarchy of evidence is used. As stated in OECD (2007): "…our basic proposition [is] that there is no single best method for or type of evidence-based policy research" (p. 24). The type of method required depends both on the type of question to be answered and what the data will be used for.

## *The Production and Use of Evidence in Education*

In an environment where different actors with different needs, cultures and perspectives need to share information with each other, what counts as evidence becomes an important point. There are also systemic challenges to both the production and use of evidence in education.

In terms of **production**, the key question is how public actors can steer research (e.g. defining go and no-go areas of research) and how the quality as well as the quantity of research can be enhanced. These questions are far from obvious, as the state and main research producing institutions are generally separated and, thus, issues of control and governance arise (Fuller 2000).

There is a range of policy instruments in the hands of decision makers to steer research production. Traditionally this has involved grants and grant making (e.g. sponsorship) and modification of the institutional setting of main research centres such as universities (Kogan 2007). As knowledge and research evidence in education have become commodified, the market of research producers and users has expanded accordingly. Government levers to steer education research production now typically target major independent research producers such as think tanks, independent research consortiums, and even some brokerage agencies (OECD 2007). In addition to targeting independent research providers, governments can also sponsor research arms of ministries and other government affiliated centres that have more independence than ministries but less than independent research centres (in fact, government affiliated research centres lie at the boundary between direct state knowledge production and facilitation of knowledge production).

Providing funding and support is one of the most common steering mechanisms. External funding generally involves stronger or weaker restrictions on research questions and objectives, methods of enquiry and publication and dissemination. Sponsorship is typically embedded in varying institutional settings ranging from (1) the autonomous model where researchers can determine all major aspects of scientific enquiry, (2) the partnership model where academics and funders define the elements and boundaries of the research jointly, and (3) the managed model where the important characteristics of the research project are defined by the funder, either public or private (Kogan 2007). The further one gets from the autonomous model, the more questions are posed regarding the impartiality and objectivity of the research and interpretation of results.

A clear area of tension lies in the different timescales of knowledge production (i.e. research) and governance and policy-making: while researchers take years to thoroughly investigate a particular question, governments are looking for immediate answers to practical policy questions. As a result, governments that are sophisticated users of research are increasingly funding and fielding calls for tender that provide rapid responses to their most pressing questions. The rise in the number of governmental research organisations and governmental organisations which engage in research is also part of this process. This co-determination and management of research projects can be and is often used as a policy lever (Wilkoszewski and

Sundby 2014), but it does raise the concern that the desired answer is provided with the question and that funding is used as a lever to "cherry pick" those research results which support a desired position. Thus as linking policy to research through funding and priority setting has become more popular among many OECD governments, thorny questions have arisen regarding the independence, impartiality and objectivity of scientific research especially under the managed model (Henkel 2000; Moss 2013).

In addition to those challenges, there is an underlying reality that any knowledge and evidence system must face. This is that increased access to data (via the internet and including media-friendly testing and assessment results which lend themselves so well to league tables and rankings) does not ensure that the quality of the information is consistently high. The Internet has effectively removed many of the established gatekeepers or quality controls that were traditionally put in place by research institutes and academic journals (Burns and Schuller 2008). As they argue: "More information is available, yes, but is it good information? And is it presented accurately and in an understandable fashion? Can the reader use it in a comprehensible and useful manner?" (p. 17).

In addition to the challenges connected to the production of evidence, there are also issues related to its **use**. The rich variety of evidence available (e.g. student achievement data, teacher assessment data, school budget data, teacher knowledge, school choices of parents etc.), and the sheer amount of that evidence, can inadvertently complicate the process.

Some challenges can be systemic. For example, there might be few incentives for collected data to be shared widely, especially if there is a concern that it could be used in a negative manner (for example, in systems where there is strong competition for students between schools, the weaknesses of a particular school might be disguised or otherwise presented to avoid injuring the reputation of the school). Moreover, information might be hard to find, little publicised, or produced without thinking that it may be useful and hence not passed onwards to other actors in the system. The 2011 report of the Swedish National Agency for Education illustrates these problems; municipalities were shown to focus their attention on their rankings rather than performance, and used only a small share of the available data in its decision-making process (Swedish National Agency for Education [*Skolverket*] 2011) as cited in Blanchenay and Burns 2016).

On the other hand, too much information can obscure information pertinent to decision-making and/or render it unusable by its sheer magnitude. Loeb and Plank (2008) illustrate this danger with the California Education Code, which includes more than 100,000 articles and more than 2000 pages. The abundance of information increases the difficulty with which stakeholders can learn about the existence of documents and then locate them. As O'Day (2002) points out, the abundance of information may even be counterproductive, as "teachers and schools may metaphorically and literally close the door on new information, shutting out the noise". It also raises the question of how all the information can be gathered and maintained in a way that can be used by the other parties. In a complex environment with multiple active stakeholders, harnessing all this heterogeneous data and ensuring that it reaches those who need it becomes an important challenge.

There is an underlying equity issue in the discussion of increasing the availability of evidence in order to increase transparency and accountability to a broader range of stakeholders. In most countries upper middle-class and middle-class families (or parent(s) with higher education, higher professional positions and higher income) are the ones that are most aware of how to actively use the education system for their own interest and benefit (Taylor 2009). They are also more likely to have the capacity to lobby and press for change in the educational system through policy and practice (van Zanten 2003).

In practice this means that in many OECD countries upper and middle-class parents are more likely than parents with lower socio-economic status to use school achievement and school performance data, when available, in order to place their child in the best-performing schools. If changing schools is not possible, middle and upper-class parents are more likely to demand (and successfully lobby for) change in the system. Parents with lower incomes (including, in many countries, high proportions of immigrant parents) are less likely to be aware of their rights regarding school choice and may often lack the capacity to use achievement and performance data, or indeed base their decisions on other factors, such as geographical proximity and the availability of public transport to access the school (Elacqua et al. 2006).

A similar argument can be made that some districts or municipalities might be more likely than others to fully use available data – perhaps those that care more about education quality, or those that have better capacity to analyse and interpret such data. These equity arguments are not trivial – indeed, any system motivated to provide full access to performance and achievement data in the name of transparency and efficiency cannot turn a blind eye to how and by whom those data are being used. In this sense there is a very real question whether evidence is being harnessed for the public good or not in education systems.

## The Evidence Agenda Revisited

Despite the excitement of the discourse around evidence-informed policy, it has become clear that *promoting* the use of evidence in policy making is not the same thing as *ensuring* its use. A number of realities intrude, including the limited time and capacity of policy makers and practitioners, the need to build consensus and incorporate public opinion, and the interaction among different forms of knowledge when determining the best course of action (OECD 2009; Burns and Köster 2016; Moss 2013). Limitations to the possible topics and scope of change due to the prevailing status quo are accompanied by limitations in the process of using knowledge itself. The distinction above between individuals, organisations and processes is an interesting way to analyse this issue.

On an individual level, policy makers' analytical experience and capacity is likely to be one of the main drivers of low levels of research utilisation, even in countries characterised by high overall quality of policy making (Davies et al. 2000). In a high-pressure and time-pressed environment, it is a rare policy-maker who has the capacity to access and interpret the relevant research at the precise moment it is needed; hence, organisational processes become crucial. The analytical capacity of organisations to use complex and multiple sources of information is likely influenced by institutional culture and the importance given to using research (including the role of media) (OECD 2007). For example, if there is an individual and organisational requirement or organisational norm that research knowledge is used during decision-making and implementation, and if access and capacity are sufficient in the organisation, there is a much higher likelihood that it will be used. However these capacities and requirements are very rarely built into governance systems, and are often the first elements of the process to be skipped when under time or budgetary pressure (OECD 2009; Burns et al. 2016).

Indeed a cynical corruption of the process does, unfortunately, occur: policy is formed, and then, with the expectation that it be based on research evidence, staff are tasked with finding the evidence that will support the already-developed policy. Although clearly subverting both the letter and spirit of the process, this behaviour makes clear that there are actually two discrete issues pertaining to the use of evidence: (1) the use of evidence in policy-making; and (2) the *appropriate* use of this evidence (Fazekas and Burns 2012).

The appropriate use of evidence for decision-making requires that administrators and educators themselves become experts in interpreting data and transforming it into knowledge. Schildkamp et al. (2014) identify three discrete categories of incorrect use of data: *non-use, misuse*, and *abuse:*

1. *Non-use*: data is not collected or capacity is lacking to allow for its use. This also includes actors choosing not to use data that is contrary to their argument or beliefs.
2. *Misuse*: data is poorly collected (quality concerns), incorrectly interpreted (analysis or capacity issues) or does not provide adequate answers to be useful for decision-making.
3. *Abuse*: sample or data are manipulated to yield particular results, or the data results in unintended consequences (for example, narrowing the curriculum to improve student scores on tested subjects).

These are serious issues. Appropriate use of evidence for decision-making requires that local administrators and educators themselves become experts in interpreting data and transforming it into knowledge. This also requires a governance structure that allows for proper circulation and collection of data and provides the correct incentives for its use. It also requires being able to combine this data with all other available evidence, including research as well as teacher professional knowledge. All of these elements: the capacity for use of data, the systemic mobilization of knowledge, and the ability to combine and make sense of multiple, varied sources of evidence, have in many senses been overlooked in the excitement and desire to provide the information and develop user-friendly web portals to display it. This human element has hitherto been an aspect that has not been fully addressed by current education systems (with the possible exception of the United Kingdom and the USA).

The next section will look at two cases of the use of evidence in action: Sweden and Flanders (Belgium).

## Use of Evidence in Action: Two Cases

### *Sweden*

Sweden set out an ambitious plan of education reform in the early 1990s, in which the responsibility for running public schools was decentralised to the municipalities (see Blanchenay et al. 2014, for the full case study). Taking place at the same time as a liberalisation of school choice, the decentralisation reform was intended to improve education and local education systems by increased demand sensitivity and competition. Schools were encouraged to compete for students by creating individual emphases in their curricula. The reform created a system in which national goals would be set and monitored by the central administration, while decisions and responsibilities on how to reach those goals would be left with municipalities. Teachers could fulfil the goals based on their own interpretation and adopt practices considering individual student's needs.

As part of this, a comprehensive system of data collection was developed and internet based portals were created to allow public access to achievement data (NAE 2009; Carlgren 2009). At the same time, Sweden also took part in international tests such as TIMSS and PISA, and published those results. This public availability of school data was meant to stimulate competition among schools as the public could hold the municipalities accountable based on these data. Similarly, the municipalities were meant to use the comprehensive data to inform decision-making and improve their educational practices. Interestingly, it is an example of the use of market mechanisms in order to improve the quality of public good (in this case, high quality and equitable education).

The sudden shift away from a traditionally centralised education system towards a decentralised one meant that municipalities had to quickly accommodate new responsibilities. Difficulties related to this shift were noticed early on by the central administration, particularly in terms of the capacity required to fill their new roles. These initial concerns were then confirmed by international surveys, in particular PISA, which revealed that the average student performance was deteriorating while the gap increased between and top- and bottom-performers.

The case study reveals that municipalities did not necessarily have adequate governance structures or the internal culture to implement collaborative decision-making and widen input into decision-making processes (see also Lewin et al. 2014). In addition, they did not receive or seek capacity building or training to make this possible. In many cases, local government was unclear about the changes in responsibilities the reforms entailed and did not provide adequate structures to facilitate the involvement of lower hierarchy levels in the decision-making process (see also NAE 2011). In turn, lower hierarchy levels did not want to be held responsible for poor performance because of decisions taken at higher levels of local government.

Part of the challenge for municipalities was that the decentralisation reform was accompanied by deregulation and the introduction of school choice, thus giving parents and students more power at the same time that local authorities were handed individual responsibility or education. To some extent, this interaction restricted what the municipalities could do, in the sense that they were also answerable to increasingly well-informed parents and in competition with a strong set of independent schools (see also Bunar et al. n.d). This has created a mismatch between knowledge and power. Being held accountable by parents and the broader community additionally generated tension with the traditional hierarchical accountability of the municipalities to the central administration.

Although the reform intended for municipalities to manage education based on regular assessment of their performance against nationally set goals and requirements, in practice, municipalities relied heavily on a limited set of data and evidence (see also NAE 2011). Particular forms of evidence were prioritised, for example, media-friendly rankings that were deemed important politically even though they did not represent the depth and breadth of information necessary for making strategic choices for the long-term development of education. Instead of carefully selecting and using indicators and research generated by the system, decision makers tended to prefer other sources of knowledge such as traditional spending choices, simple comparative measures (instead of holistic assessment of cause and effect). Although this was most marked in the smallest communities with the least capacity, it was, to some extent or other, present broadly across the entire system. In addition, this simplistic use of a limited type of evidence source was accompanied by a general lack of self-assessment, and indeed a lack of capacity for the efficient use of resources to enable the smooth functioning of the system.

The capacity to use available data for thorough reflection and strategic decisions about education is fundamental to establish accountability relationships across levels of the municipal administration and with community stakeholders. In order to understand the needs of the system, municipal authorities must use different sources of knowledge, including the experiences of local actors in defining and solving problems in schools and classrooms. This is a nuanced skill and process, which requires connections to relevant stakeholders, the forums and capacities to gather and use achievement and assessment data, and the ability to formalise and make explicit what is often tacit or procedural knowledge.

Using the lens of the evidence in education agenda, the Swedish case study (Blanchenay et al. 2014) revealed that simply making achievement data available did not immediately translate into stronger accountability regimes or indeed better achievement. Instead, truncated indicators were used and decisions did not sufficiently harness knowledge by stakeholders at grassroots level. The preference to prioritise media-friendly rankings over a more nuanced set of evidence reveals the challenge of evidence-informed decision making. When a wide range of data becomes available, individuals in charge might be tempted to select the indicators that will paint a more favourable picture for their (often short-term) goals (see also NAE 2011). As one interviewee in the case study stated, "*one cannot blame [the municipal leaders] for being rational*".

The case study suggested a number of recommendations, including the following:

- Increasing local accountability, making use of all publicly available data and research and including expert guidance as well as enhancing the involvement of parents, the community and citizens more broadly.
- Building local capacity to gather and use the wealth of achievement and assessment data available, with an emphasis on harnessing relevant expert knowledge, prioritising the creation of a broad and holistic culture of evaluation, and creating networks and mentoring relationships.
- Strengthening systemic strategic vision, including the appropriate use of data for strategic planning.

## *Flanders (Belgium)*

The Flemish education system is one of the most decentralised education systems and is characterised by a high degree of autonomy at the school level (see Rouw et al. 2016, for the full case study). The basis for school autonomy is the constitutional principle of "freedom of education," which gives any person the right to set up a school and determine its educational principles, as long as it fulfils the regulations set by the Flemish Government. Furthermore, parents are allowed to choose and are guaranteed access to a school of their choice within reasonable distance of their residence, with funding allocated to schools on a per student basis. School governing bodies – school boards – have the autonomy to determine their own learning plan, choose their educational approach and teaching methods, and appoint their own staff. At the same time, every child in the country is entitled to receive a good quality education no matter which school she attends, which means that the Flemish Government has the responsibility of ensuring high-quality provision of education across the system. Therefore attainment targets were from the onset seen as a vital element of quality assurance arrangements in Flanders.

Moreover in a decentralized system there is always a risk of fragmentation and a wide variation of performance between schools and students. The results in both national and international tests prove that this is not an imaginary risk. The PISA (Programme for International Student Assessment) 2012 assessment for example showed that the difference in performance between the highest and lowest-achieving students is the second largest among all surveyed regions (OECD 2013). That is why attainment targets are also seen as a means to secure equity in the system, to prevent schools from lowering their expectations for particularly children from a lower socioeconomic status background. In terms of this publication attainment targets are meant to serve at least the deliverance of two public goods, i.e. high-quality education and equity. For this reason schools that seek government recognition or public funding are required by the government to meet certain standards, among them not least the attainment targets.

Since the late 1990s, attainment targets have been applicable in primary and secondary education and adult education. Attainment targets are educational goals to be met by pupils in terms of knowledge, insight, attitudes and skills, both transversal to the curriculum and subject-related. Attainment targets must be included in the elaboration of learning plans developed by school boards or umbrella organisations – the organisations under which similar schools are grouped together. The Inspectorate oversees the completion of this task and also checks if students reach the attainment targets. Attainment targets are regularly renewed and expanded.

In terms of knowledge and evidence for practice and policy, there are two vital issues regarding the implementation of attainment targets. The first is if the system provides enough knowledge at all levels of the system but particularly at the school and classroom level to implement the attainment targets as intended. The second issue is if system players are provided with data and knowledge about the actual implementation of and achievement on attainment targets in order to learn and improve.

Within the Flemish education system there is a strong emphasis on the broad development of children. Many actors disapprove of system level standardised testing for fear of narrowing assessment and evaluation of achievement to a limited number of cognitive measures (see also Ministry of Education and Training and University of Antwerp Edubron Research Group 2010). This explains why the Flemish system has no standard national examinations at the end of primary and secondary education. Schools are also primarily responsible for the assessment of student achievement both on attainment targets and other goals.

The system thus relies strongly on the capacity of school leaders and teachers, on their knowledge of subject content and pedagogy but also their knowledge of the development of children and their observational skills. Our research showed that many teachers seemed to lack knowledge of the rationale and underpinnings of the attainment targets. Furthermore the knowledge and use of new, more interactive pedagogies and appropriate assessment was unevenly distributed across schools and teachers (Rouw et al. 2016). Even more importantly, there was no coordinated and systemic effort to provide knowledge and build capacity across the system. It seemed as if the coordination force needed for such an effort was lacking, support to schools was provided rather fragmented and also missing the sustainability needed for a thorough change of pedagogies (see also Commissie Monard 2014).

Something similar can be said about data literacy and evaluation capacity at the level of schools as a whole. In many schools a culture of evaluation was underdeveloped and a reasonable amount of school leaders appeared reluctant to use system data to benchmark the achievement of schools (see also Ministry of Education and Training and University of Antwerp Edubron Research Group 2010 and OECD 2011). This shows the vital role of beliefs in evidence based policy and practice.

It is not enough to provide schools with data and information, as the Flemish Ministry is doing. It is not even enough to build data and knowledge capacities, as long as beliefs about the usefulness of such data remain unchanged.

The knowledge function at system level seemed to be the most developed at the government level and at level of intermediate organisations operating as a mediator between the system and school level. Intermediary organisations hold a range of expertise and skills, from knowledge of policy processes to pedagogical knowledge. To measure system achievement a programme of national assessments has been in place delivering policy relevant information for quite some time. One of the perceived strengths of the National Assessment Programme is that it covers a variety of subjects, from mathematics and languages to citizenship. It is not confined to two or three core subjects as many other system assessments are. Over the years, it has resulted in a rich and more well-rounded picture of the system. The Inspectorate not only functions as a catalyst for improvement in schools, but also provides information on teaching and learning at an aggregated level.

That said, there is still room for improvement. The National Assessment Programme covers only two subjects each year. Consequently an annual picture of achievement in core subjects is missing just as insight in the development of achievement over a longer period of time. The Inspectorate does not report on achievement at student level but offers a more general picture on achievement at school level (see also Rekenhof 2011). Scientific research provides insights in beliefs and practices of teachers and school leaders, however not as up-to-date and comprehensive as necessary for a systematic and thorough knowledge of classroom practices. All-in-all it seems as if the relatively fast feedback cycles required in contemporary complex systems with unpredictable and unintended effects are missing across the Flemish system.

The way forward for Flanders lies in joining forces in a powerful and sustainable effort in capacity building, particularly in data literacy and evaluation capacity. This is one step in building a culture of evaluation and feedback by providing the necessary data and knowledge and even more questioning current beliefs and offering alternative stories of good education.

## Conclusions: The Evidence Agenda in Education (Reprise)

So what is the way forward? Just as the traditional policy cycle can no longer capture modern governance processes (Hallsworth et al. 2011), models of knowledge mobilisation and use must also be adapted for modern environments. This requires taking a step back to see how the various elements are being brought together, not just by researchers, but by decision-makers at all levels of the system. We argue that evidence-informed policy cannot be separated from the governance process, but rather must be seen as part of one ecosystem where the use and production of knowledge is linked to all elements of governance and decision-making for both policy and practice (Burns et al. 2016, see Fig. 8.1).

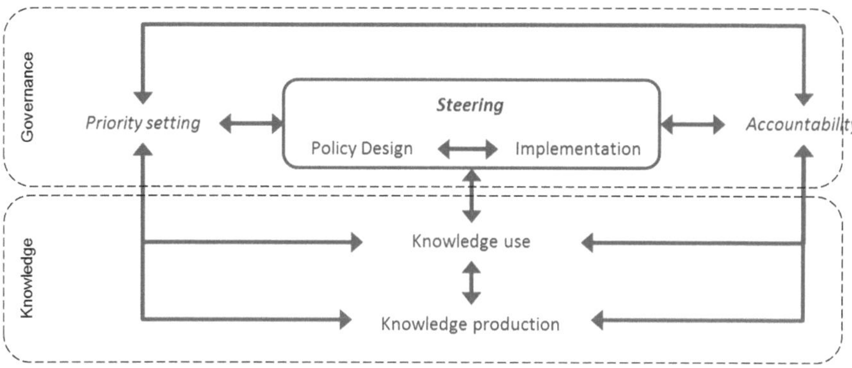


**Fig. 8.1** Analytical framework of governance and knowledge (Source: Burns et al. 2016)

Knowledge and evidence – in all their forms – can only lead to school improvement if they are relevant, available in adequate quantity, and properly interpreted (O'Day 2002). Thorny questions about how best to incorporate teacher expertise and practitioner knowledge with more quantitative data sources need to be addressed. One of the biggest challenges is how best to balance the various sources of information, especially if they are competing with each other (Nutley et al. 2007). Joining a broad set of literature, our work has identified a number of ways in which the use of evidence can be improved in educational decision-making: through building capacity at the local level in Germany (Busemeyer and Vossiek 2015), encouraging self-reflection and a culture of evaluation in Poland (Mazurkiewicz et al. 2014) and developing user-friendly platforms to access data in Sweden (Blanchenay et al. 2014).

Peer learning and networks can be a good way to build the capacity of the smallest municipalities and schools to use research knowledge and apply it in practice, as seen in Norway (Hopfenbeck et al. 2013). And having a clear and easy way to communicate the effectiveness of a school or system is a very powerful way to motivate a broad set of stakeholders around a school or community, as demonstrated in the Netherlands (van Twist et al. 2013). The Flemish case shows the potential of moving beyond performance metrics to develop a holistic evaluation of system progress (Rouw et al. 2016).

Despite the various challenges, it is important to get it right. The use of evidence in educational policy-making is important to ensure efficient and equitable school systems that work to serve the public good. Although there has been a great deal of research in the area, a number of important questions remain (Burns and Köster 2016):

- What type of data should be collected (in particular, what balance between qualitative and quantitative data)? At which level? By whom? And what for?
- How well does access to data enable better accountability, with more carefully crafted incentives and responsibilities better tailored to local context? How can it be combined with other sources of evidence from research, teacher expertise, etc.?

- What is the best way to create capacity for the use of evidence (among local decision-makers and central authorities, as well as school administrators and teachers)?
- Is it possible to have 'too much' evidence?

## References


Blanchenay, P., Burns, T., & Köster, F. (2014). *Shifting responsibilities – 20 years of education devolution in Sweden: A governing complex education systems case study* (OECD Education Working Papers, No. 104). Paris: OECD Publishing. http://dx.doi.org/10.1787/5jz2jg1rqrd7-en

Blanchenay, P., & Burns, T. (2016). Policy experimentation in complex education systems. In T. Burns & F. Köster (Eds.), *Governing education in a complex world* (pp. 161–186). Paris: OECD Publishing. http://dx.doi.org/10.1787/9789264255364-10-en.

Bunar, N., Barham, E., & Pater, C. (unpublished n.d.). *Market mechanisms in Swedish schooling, an explorative study of two Swedish municipalities*, Gävle and Västerås.

Burns, T., & Köster, F. (2016). Modern governance challenges in education. In T. Burns & F. Köster (Eds.), *Governing education in a complex world*. Paris: OECD Publishing. http://dx.doi.org/10.1787/9789264255364-3-en.

Burns, T., Köster, F., & Fuster, M. (2016). *Education governance in action: Lessons from case studies*. Paris: OECD Publishing. http://dx.doi.org/10.1787/9789264262829-en.

Burns, T., & Schuller, T. (2008). Evidence-informed policy in education: New opportunities and challenges. In R. Desjardins & K. Rubensen (Eds.), *Research of policy and research for policy in an era of transnational education policy making*. Aarhaus: Aarhaus University Press.

Busemeyer, M., & Vossiek, J. (2015). *Reforming education governance through local capacity-building: A case study of the 'Learning Locally' programme in Germany* (OECD Education Working Papers, No. 113). Paris: OECD Publishing. http://dx.doi.org/10.1787/5js6bhl2mxjg-en

Carlgren, I. (2009). The Swedish comprehensive school, lost in transition? *Zeitschrift für Erziehungswissenschaft, 12*(4), 633–649.

Clarke, B., et al. (2014). Mechanisms and the evidence hierarchy. *Topoi, 33/2*, 339–360.

Commissie Monard. (2014). *Evaluatie Pedagogische Begeleidingsdiensten, Permanente ondersteuningscellen en VZW Samenwerkingsverband Netgebonden Begeleidingsdiensten. Overkoepelend rapport* [Evaluation Pedagogical Advisory Services, Permanent Support Centres and Partnership Networked Advisory Services]. Brussels: Ministry of Education and Training.

Davies, H., Nutley, S., & Smith, P. (Eds.). (2000). *What works?: Evidence-based policy and practice in public services*. Bristol: The Policy Press.

Elacqua, G., Schneider, M., & Buckley, J. (2006). School choice in Chile: Is it class or the classroom? *Journal of Policy Analysis and Management, 25*(3), 577–601.

Fazekas, M., & Burns, T. (2012). *Exploring the complex interaction between governance and knowledge in education* (OECD Education Working Papers, No. 67). Paris: OECD Publishing. http://dx.doi.org/10.1787/5k9flcx2l340-en

Fuller, S. (2000). *The governance of science: Ideology and the future of the open society*. Buckingham: Open University Press.

Hallsworth, M., Parker, S. & Rutter, J. (2011). *Policy-making in the real world*. Institute for Government.

Henkel, M. (2000). *Academic identities and policy change in higher education*. London: Jessica Kingsley Publishers.

Hopfenbeck, T., et al. (2013). *Balancing trust and accountability? The assessment for learning programme in Norway: A governing complex education systems case study* (OECD Education Working Papers, No. 97). Paris: OECD Publishing. http://dx.doi.org/10.1787/5k3txnpqlsnn-en

Kogan, M. (2007). Modes of knowledge and patterns of power. In S. Sörlin & H. Vessuri (Eds.), *Knowledge society vs. knowledge economy: Knowledge, power, and politics* (pp. 35–52). New York: Palgrave Macmillan.

Lewin, L., et al. (2014). Staten får inte abdikera, om kommunaliseringen av den svenska skolan [The State must not abdicate on the municipalisation of the Swedish school system], *Statens Offentliga Utredningar SOU* 2014:5. Stockholm.

Loeb, S., D.N. Plank, (2008), Learning what works: Continuous improvement in California's education system, Policy Brief, 8 4, Policy Analysis for California Education, Berkeley.

Mazurkiewicz, G., Walczak, B., Jewdokimow, M. (2014). *Implementation of a new school supervision system in Poland* (OECD Education Working Papers, No. 111). Paris: OECD Publishing. http://dx.doi.org/10.1787/5jxrlxrxgc6b-en

Ministry of Education and Training and University of Antwerp Edubron Research Group. (2010). *OECD review on evaluation and assessment frameworks for improving school outcomes*, country background report for the flemish community of Belgium. www.oecd.org/edu/evaluationpolicy

Moss, G. (2013). Research, policy and knowledge flows in education: What counts in knowledge mobilisation. *Contemporary Social Science, 8*(33), 237–248.

NAE. (2009). What influences educational achievement in Swedish schools? In *A systematic review and summary analysis*. Stockholm: National Agency for Education (Skolverket).

NAE. (2011). *Municipal responsibility in practice; a qualitative study, Report 382*. Stockholm: National Agency for Education (Skolverket).

Nutley, S., Walter, I., & Davies, H. (2007). *Using evidence: How research can inform public services*. Bristol: Policy Press.

O'Day, J. A. (2002). Complexity, accountability, and school improvement. *Harvard Educational Review, 72*(3), 293–329. www.hepg.org/her-home/issues/harvard-educational-review-volume-72-issue-3/herarticle/_48.

OECD. (1995). *Educational research and development – trends issues and challenges*. Paris: OECD Publishing.

OECD. (2007). *Evidence in education: Linking research and policy*. Paris: OECD Publishing. http://dx.doi.org/10.1787/9789264033672-en.

OECD. (2009). *Working out change: Systemic innovation in vocational education and training*. Paris: Educational Research and Innovation, OECD Publishing. http://dx.doi.org/10.1787/9789264075924-en.

OECD. (2011). *School evaluation in the flemish community of Belgium, OECD Reviews of Evaluation and Assessment in Education*. Paris: OECD, Publishing. http://dx.doi.org/10.1787/9789264116726en.

OECD. (2013). *PISA 2012 results: Excellence through equity: Giving every student the chance to succeed* (Vol. II). Paris: PISA, OECD Publishing. http://dx.doi.org/10.1787/9789264201132-en.

Rekenhof. (2011). *Verslag van het Rekenhof over het toezicht op de kwaliteit van het onderwijs door de inspectie* [Report of the Court of Audit on the oversight of the quality of education by the Inspectorate]. Brussels: Vlaams Parlement.

Rouw, R., et al. (2016). *United in diversity – A complexity perspective on the role of attainment targets in quality assurance in Flanders: A GCES case study of Flanders (Belgium)* (OECD Education Working Papers No. 139). Paris: OECD Publishing.

Sackett, D. L., Rosenberg, W. M. C., & Gray, A. J. (1996). Evidence based medicine; what it is and what it isn't. *British Medical Journal, 312*, 71–72.

Schildkamp, K., Karbautzki, L., & Vanhoof, J. (2014). Exploring data use practices around Europe: Identifying enablers and barriers. *Studies in Educational Evaluation, 42*, 15–24.

Taylor, C. (2009). Choice competition, and segregation in a United Kingdom education market. *American Journal of Education, 115*(4), 549–568.
Van Twist, M., et al. (2013). *Coping with very weak primary schools: Towards smart interventions in Dutch education policy* (OECD Education Working Papers, No. 98). Paris: OECD Publishing. http://dx.doi.org/10.1787/5k3txnpnhld7-en
Van Zanten, A. (2003). Middle-class parents and social mix in French urban schools: Reproduction and transformation of class relations in education. *International Studies in Sociology of Education, 13*(2), 107–123.
Wilkoszewski, H., & Sundby, E. (2014). *Steering from the centre: New modes of governance in multi-level education eystems* (OECD Education Working Papers, No. 109). Paris: OECD Publishing. http://dx.doi.org/10.1787/5jxswcfs4s5g-en

# Chapter 9
# School Principals and Evidence Use: Possibilities and Problems for Preparation and Practice

**Jeffrey S. Brooks, Mark Rickinson, and Jane Wilkinson**

**Abstract** In this chapter, we review and critique the literature on school leadership preparation and evidence use. The chapter is organized into three sections. In "What is Evidence and What is evidence Use?" we explore distinctions in the ways that scholars and practitioners have come to conceptualize evidence use and consider the implications of various definitions for leadership practice. In the second section, "School Leadership Preparation and Evidence Use," we examine various ways that programs around the world approach training prospective or sitting school leaders in pre-service programmes. This includes university-based programs, district/department/state/national delivered programmes, those offered by private providers and partnerships between these various stakeholders. In doing so, we look both at program design and program outcomes. The third section, "Evidence in Use: How Principals Use Evidence to Make Decisions", we review and interrogate research that investigates this phenomenon, paying special attention to effective and ineffective strategies. The chapter concludes with recommendations for pre-service and in-service development in relation to leadership and evidence use for the public good.

## Introduction

In this chapter, we review and critique the literature on school leadership preparation and evidence use. The chapter is organized into three sections. In "What is Evidence and What is evidence Use?" we explore distinctions in the ways that scholars and practitioners have come to conceptualize evidence use and consider the implications of various definitions for leadership practice. In the second section, "School Leadership Preparation and Evidence Use," we examine various ways that programs around the world approach training prospective or sitting school leaders

J.S. Brooks (✉) • M. Rickinson • J. Wilkinson
Faculty of Education, Monash University, Clayton, VIC, Australia
e-mail: jeffrey.brooks@monash.edu



M.Y. Eryaman, B. Schneider (eds.), *Evidence and Public Good in Educational Policy, Research and Practice*, Educational Governance Research 6,
DOI 10.1007/978-3-319-58850-6_9

in pre-service programmes. This includes university-based programs, district/department/state/national delivered programmes, those offered by private providers and partnerships between these various stakeholders. In doing so, we look both at program design and program outcomes. The third section, "Evidence in Use: How Principals Use Evidence to Make Decisions," we review and interrogate research that investigates this phenomenon, paying special attention to effective and ineffective strategies. The chapter concludes with a discussion of conclusions and recommendations for pre-service and in-service development in relation to leadership and evidence use for the public good. In a sense, our chapter advance a conceptual argument based on a review of extant literature rather than case examples that illustrate key concepts. Our rationale for this approach is grounded in our belief that the field of educational leadership needs to reframe its orientation toward evidence use. As such, we feel our chapter constitutes a necessary contribution toward the end of thinking more deeply about evidence use in the preparation and practice of school administration.

## What Is Evidence and What Is Evidence Use?

Any exploration of the issues surrounding school principals and evidence use needs to start with a careful consideration of what is meant by 'evidence' and what is involved in its 'use'. In debates about evidence use, conceptual starting points are significant. How one answers the question 'What counts as evidence?' and, more importantly, 'What counts as good evidence?', will have an important bearing on how one frames ideas about evidence in leadership preparation and practice. Similarly, how one conceptualises 'evidence use' and the processes and skills involved in 'using evidence' will fundamentally shape how one approaches the challenge of supporting school leaders to improve evidence use in schools.

### *Views on Evidence*

As a starting point, it is important to be clear that what counts as evidence is a complex, contested and often politicised issue. As Nutley et al. (2007: 25) explain:

> The attaching of labels such as 'evidence' or 'research' to particular types of 'knowledge' are in fact political acts. [...] Assessing 'what counts as evidence' or 'what counts as research' involves not just technical objective judgements but also subjective and contextualised assessments.

With this in mind, we want to flag up two ways in which 'evidence' can be conceptualised too narrowly within debates about education and schools. In short, our argument is that efforts to enhance schools' and school leaders' use of evidence need to work from an understanding of evidence as broader than 'research' and not limited to 'data'. In addition, on the question of evidence quality, we want to stress the importance of judging quality in connection with the intended use, rather than as an absolute in isolation. Each of these three points – evidence as broader than research, evidence as more than data, evidence quality as connected with intended use – are now considered in turn.

Evidence as broader than research is about recognising that 'research evidence' is one type of evidence. While researchers may think of and speak about 'research' and 'evidence' interchangeably, studies of research users have shown that for school leaders, teachers and decision-makers 'evidence' often includes more than 'research'. Writing about educational policy-makers in the UK, for example, Sebba (2004) outlined three types of evidence that are used: *data* collected through national surveys for monitoring, evaluation and/or forecasting; *inspection data* generated through school inspections; and *research evidence* usually collected through externally commissioned research projects or programs. In a US study of evidence use within local school boards, Asen et al. (2013: 40) investigated six different types of evidence: research, experience, testimony, data, example, and law/policy. And in the concluding chapter of an edited volume on *Leading the Use of Research and Evidence in Schools*, Earl (2015: 148) emphasises how using evidence in schools can involve 'attending to published research, gathering local data, referring to experts, considering personal experiences, social network analysis and big data analytics, just to mention a few'. Taken together, the common point that these studies flag up is that evidence in use can involve a number of different types in addition to research evidence.

Similarly, though, if seeing evidence and research as synonymous can be unhelpful then so too can seeing evidence and data as one and the same. Developments around terms such as 'data-based decision-making' and 'data-led school improvement' have led to a very strong focus on the analysis and use of performance data within and across schools and school systems. In the US context, for example, 'the use of data in educational decision making is expected to span all layers of the education system – from the federal to the state, district, school and classroom levels' (Means et al. 2009: vii). One consequence of this focus on data use has been a tendency in some quarters to see no real distinction between evidence use and data use. In an exploratory study involving interviews with 54 educators in a mid-sized US school district, for example, Finnigan et al. (2015: 140) found that:

> Staff had narrow views of evidence, almost exclusively focusing on test scores or other administrative records and outcome data [...] In fact, several interviewees equated 'evidence' and 'research evidence' with standardized test scores.

Findings like this lead us to stress the importance of recognising that performance data and other types of data are one form of evidence. In other words, discussions about school leaders and evidence use should not be restricted to analysis and use of data but also encompass engagement in and with other forms of evidence, including research evidence.

So evidence needs to be understood in broad terms that include but go beyond 'research evidence' on the one hand, and are not restricted solely to 'performance data' on the other hand. But added to this, any consideration of evidence also needs to take into account questions surrounding evidence quality. It is clear that one of the pre-requisites for evidence use in educational practice is educators with skills in the critical evaluation of evidence in its many forms:

> Educationalists at all levels need to be able to: retrieve and read evidence competently and undertake critical appraisal and analysis of that evidence according to agreed professional and scientific standards. (Davies 1999: 109)

> It is important for school leaders [...] to have mechanisms for determining the sources, credibility and technical adequacy of the evidence before they use it. (Earl 2015: 149)

One of the responses to this need has been the promotion of evidence hierarchies as a way to distinguish between different kinds of research evidence based on study design. There are many examples of these hierarchies all with slight differences but their common pattern is that 'randomised experiments with clearly defined controls (RCTs) are placed at or near the top of the hierarchy and case study reports are usually at the bottom' (Nutley et al. 2013: 10). The value and appropriateness of evidence hierarchies within education and other social science fields has been the topic of considerable debate (see, for example, Nutley et al. 2013: 11–14). While much of this discussion goes beyond our purposes here, there is one criticism that is highly pertinent to evidence use in schools. That is, the argument that evidence hierarchies do not take sufficient account of how the evidence will be used. In other words, they pre-suppose a very particular type of use (evidence about what programs/practices are effective i.e. what works) and grade different types of evidence on that basis. But as Davies et al. (2008: 188) make clear the needs of practitioners and policy-makers can go well beyond questions about what works:

> As well as knowledge about what works we need, for example, knowledge about the scale, source and structuring of social problems; practical knowledge to support effective programme implementation in different contexts; and insights into the relationships between values and policy directions.

So, as argued by Nutley et al. (2013: 6), 'What counts as good evidence [...] depends on what we want to know, for what purposes, and in what contexts we envisage that evidence being used'. This takes us beyond the question of how we view 'evidence' to the equally important issue of how we understand 'evidence use'.

## *Conceptions of Evidence Use*

It is easy for evidence use to be viewed as a relatively straightforward process, which fails to take account of the complexity and richness that it can involve. Nutley et al. (2007) in their analysis of how research is used across a range of social policy areas show how certain understandings of research use provide a better basis than others for developing strategies to promote research use. As they explain:

> Our view is that interactive, social and interpretive models of research use – models that acknowledge and engage with context, models that admit roles for other types of knowl-

> edge, and models that see research use as being more than just about individual behavior – are more likely to help us when it comes to understanding how research actually gets used, and to assist us in intervening to get research used more. (Nutley et al. 2007: 319–320)

Building on this perspective, we want to underline the importance of nuanced understandings of evidence use. A helpful starting point for this is to recognise that evidence can be used in different ways. One well-established categorisation of evidence use within the knowledge utilization literature, for example, draws distinctions between:

- **Instrumental evidence use** – which 'implies a concrete application of research, where the research has often been translated into a material or usable form' and 'is used to direct specific decisions and/or interventions';
- **Conceptual evidence use** – where 'research may change one's thinking but not necessarily one's particular action … In this kind of research utilization, research informs and enlightens the decision-maker'; and
- **Symbolic evidence use** – which 'involves the use of research as a persuasive or political tool to legitimate a position or practice' (Estabrooks 2001: 283–4).

This categorization helps to flag up an important source of complexity in how evidence can be used, in that evidence can be used in ways that are more instrumental (evidence providing answers), more conceptual (evidence raising questions) and/or more symbolic (evidence as ammunition). However, this is not the only source of complexity in how evidence gets used. Empirical and conceptual work on evidence use within and beyond education suggests that efforts to improve evidence use in practice need to recognise not only its varied purposes, but also its multiple scales, indirect character, active processes and demanding nature (Table 9.1).

Taken together, these various complexities of evidence use convey a process that at its heart is about sophisticated professional learning rather than 'merely bringing new information about what works to bear on professional practice' (Cordingley 2004, p. 80). In other words, evidence use needs to be understood as 'a pedagogic problem' rather than a transmission problem (Bell et al. 2002, no page number). This takes seriously the idea that evidence does not speak for itself but needs to be engaged with, interpreted and contextualised for different professional settings and needs.

In connection with this reality, we find the notion of *'evidence-informed'* leadership more helpful than that of *'evidence-based'* leadership because of its recognition that evidence works to complement, not replace, professional judgement and expertise. Evidence-informed practice, then, is about: 'integrating professional expertise with the best external evidence from research to improve the quality of practice' (Sharples 2013: 7). As such, it can be argued to represent 'a more nuanced [view of] the link between research, policy, and practice' (Biesta 2007: 5), based on a clear understanding that 'judgements will always be needed about how to use the evidence derived from evaluative research' (Chalmers 2005: 36, cited in Chalmers 2005: 229).

**Table 9.1** Complexities of evidence use

| | |
|---|---|
| **Varied purposes** i.e. purposes that can be instrumental, conceptual and/or symbolic | 'Much attention [...] has been focused on instrumental uses of research, where research evidence has a concrete and demonstrable impact on the actions and choices of policy-makers and practitioners. However, we know that, on the ground, research and other forms of knowledge are often used in more subtle, indirect and conceptual ways: bringing about changes in knowledge and understanding, or shifts in perceptions, attitudes and beliefs' (Davies et al. 2008: 189) |
| **Multiple scales** i.e. actions not only by individuals but also by institutions and groups of institutions | 'The dominant model of research use [...] envisages individual policy makers and practitioners [...] applying the evidence [...] in their day-to-day work. [...] The potential roles that research may play at the organisational and system levels thus remain relatively unexplored, although the evidence we have suggests such uses of research may well be important' (Nutley et al. 2007: 302) |
| **Indirect character** i.e. connections and interactions are indirect rather than direct | 'Most of the connection [between researchers and research users] happens through third party mediation. The connections also run to varying degrees in both directions; that is, research production and mediation are also influenced by contexts of use' (Levin 2004, p. 7) |
| **Active processes** i.e. active engagement and learning rather than passive reception and transfer | 'Practitioners/policy-makers must not be thought of as passive receptacles patiently waiting to receive advice and insight from research and researchers. For too long the literature on research utilisation and dissemination has implied a straight transmission model' (Figgis et al. 2000, p. 347) |
| **Demanding nature** i.e. requiring skills and capacities that are relational as well as technical | 'Productive evidence-informed conversation [are] more than conversations with some attention to evidence [...] The qualities that are required in these kinds of conversations are having an "inquiry habit of mind", considering a broad range of "relevant evidence" and engaging in "learning conversations" [based on relationships of respect and challenge]' (Earl and Timperley 2009: 3) |

In summary, then, we are arguing that efforts to improve schools' and school leaders' use of evidence need to be clear that:

- Evidence is broader than 'research' and not limited to 'data';
- Evidence quality depends on its intended use as well as its methodological rigour, and;
- Evidence use is a complex, interactive and skilled process that informs (rather than replaces) professional judgement and expertise.

## School Leadership Preparation and Evidence Use

School leadership preparation and professional development programs have traditionally included fairly basic instruction in statistical procedures and techniques (Murphy 2001). In the early and mid-twentieth century, these skills were largely applied to school finance and a variety of management systems related to personnel issues (Murphy and Vriesenga 2006). From the early 1980s onward, preparation and professional development programs for school administrators became gradually more concerned with connecting leadership to learning (Brooks and Miles 2006). As a result, preparation and professional development programs increasingly tried to develop the ability of principals to generate, interpret and design programs, interventions and supports related to student achievement outcomes and the curricular and pedagogical processes that undergird this work (Black and Murtadha 2007). This emphasis has ushered in a still-emerging era wherein school leaders ostensibly engage in data driven decision-making, practice leadership for learning and act as informed instructional and curricular leaders who have the information in hand to ensure that every child receives an equitable and excellent education. Sadly, numerous studies indicate that very few classrooms, schools and school systems actually provide this sort of education. In order to better understand issues related to the practice of school leadership in relation to evidence use, it is instructive to examine research that describes how they are prepared and trained.

## *Leadership Preparation Program Design*

Although there are no universally accept approaches to pre-practice programming, several countries have formalized principal preparation and research indicates that school systems benefit from such activity (Darling-Hammond et al. 2007; Orr and Orphanos 2011; Orr 2007). Typically, the providers for such programs are universities, school districts/departments, private providers or some partnership of these groups working together (Brooks et al. 2010). School leadership preparation programs are routinely criticized for their "lack of connection between the nature of educational administration preparation programs and the crisis conditions facing many school administrators" (Cambron-McCabe 1999, 217). That said, Brooks et al. (2010) note that there are a variety of suggestions as to what should be done to decrease this gap. Some suggestions include:

- Leadership preparation standards linked to organizational efficiency, teaching and learning (Murphy 1990c)[1];
- More stringent selection, entrance and certification requirements (Murphy 1990a, b, c, d);
- A focus on research-based best practices. There are those who claim we already know what effective principals do (Hattie 2015; Leithwood et al. 2008; Marzano et al. 2005)[2];

[1] Alternately, some have argued for doing away with standards entirely (English, 2001, April; English 2003, Spring).

[2] Others contend that we do not know what makes leaders "effective" or "successful," and that leadership practice is instead idiosyncratic, context-bound and co-constructed among leaders and followers in an organization (Brooks 2006; Wolcott 1970).

Put simply, the knowledge base of educational administration, if indeed there is 'a' knowledge base, is the subject of great and ongoing debate (Brooks and Miles 2006; Donmoyer et al. 1995).

Still, some scholars suggest that there are certain distinctive features of excellent leadership preparation programs. Jackson and Kelley (2002) identified several practices of exceptional and innovative programs in educational leadership:

- Clear vision drives program decisions and guides the development of coherent programs.
- Identifies, screens, and selects students based on leadership potential using a variety of criteria and sources to collect screen applicants.
- Offer a clear, well-defined curriculum based on the knowledge base needed to perform effectively in the administrator's first years as a principal.
- Programs are developed through strong partnerships with local school districts/ departments. Districts help identify and screen applicants, provide in-kind support for maintenance of program operations.
- Instructional strategies are selected with students' needs/characteristics and knowledge base in mind. Courses are often team taught with careful assignment of faculty to courses.
- Field experience is the primary tool for learning – coursework supports fieldwork. Internships are longer, typically 600 or more hours
- Program structures develop stronger connections between students and between students and faculty members. Almost all are cohort-based.
- Programs are forums that explicitly discuss the values and decision-making processes that underlie leadership.

But how much are aspiring principals trained to generate, analyse and use evidence in their programs? While there is little research that addresses this specific question, Hess and Kelly (Hess and Kelley 2005) collected 210 course syllabi from 56 programs in the United States and examined instructional activities during 2,424 course weeks. Three of their findings shed light on the topic:

- Just 2% of 2,424 course weeks addressed accountability in the context of school management or school improvement and less than 5% included instruction on managing school improvement via data, technology, or empirical research;
- Eleven percent of 2424 course weeks made mention of or reference to statistics, data, or empirical research in some context, and;
- Eleven percent of course weeks dealt with instructional management issues like curriculum development, pedagogy, classroom management, and learning theory.

Though this is a small sample and an imperfect way to analyse leadership preparation programs, it is alarming to see how little time and attention is devoted to evidence use. Notably, the study does not take capstone projects into account, which typically employ a variety of qualitative and quantitative research approaches and use school-level data (Larson and Murtadha 2002).

Finally, it is also important to consider the philosophical foundations of leadership, and ask – what is the purpose of evidence use? Should school leaders be prepared like researchers, so that they can conceptualize and conduct their own studies at the school, classroom or grade level? Should they play a primary role in assisting teachers to generate and interpret evidence in their classrooms? Should evidence be used for professional development, assessment of learning and teaching, for longitudinal examination of performance over time? Should evidence be used for compliance or performance measures? The answers to each of these questions, individually and collectively has implications for leadership preparation and practice.

Importantly, many scholars have argued that leadership preparation is not a value-free proposition, and must instead address the public good by seeking to orient aspirant leaders to a social justice perspective (Brooks and Brooks 2015; DeMatthews 2016). This means that as aspirant leaders are learning the skills, dispositions and knowledge that will ungird their subsequent work in the field, they must also be taught that evidence and evidence use have ethical dimensions, and that they can work toward equity in schools or exacerbate inequity (Johnson 2002). Thus, it is critical that those who prepare school leaders emphasize the notion that the purpose of evidence and evidence use is in the interest of the public good – that is, that it is there – to promote an equitable and excellent education for all children (Scheurich and Skrla 2003).

## Evidence in Use: How Principals Use Evidence to Make Decisions

### *Principals Shape the Way Data Are Used in Schools*

An increasing body of research is emerging in regard to the critical role played by principals in shaping and influencing how data and other forms of evidence and research are used in schools (Earl and Timperley 2009; Finnigan and Daly 2014; Hallinger and Murphy 2012; Levin 2010). That this should be the case is unsurprising given the significant body of evidence that has amassed over the past three decades which suggests the crucial nature of the principalship in driving school improvement. Key practices of principals that have been identified as supporting school improvement include: promoting and participating in teacher learning and development; planning, coordinating and evaluating teaching and the curriculum; establishing goals and expectations; strategic resourcing; and ensuring an orderly and supportive environment (Robinson 2007). For school improvement to be sustained over time, however, requires "active skillful instructional school leadership" by both principals and teachers (Hallinger and Murphy 2013, p. 6). In this sense, instructional leadership is not an individual capacity possessed solely by the hero leader but is a collective process. Furthermore, it suggests an indirect "mediated effects" model of leadership, that is, an "influence process through which leaders identify a direction for the school, motivate staff, and coordinate school and classroom-based strategies aimed at improvements in teaching and learning" (Hallinger and Murphy 2013, p. 7).

The impact of government policies mandating educational reform such as *No Child Left Behind* or *Race to the Top* in the USA, along with similar policy moves in Anglophone nations such as England, Canada and Australia has refocused the gaze on the principal as key instructional leader. As such instructional leadership is no longer an optional extra but an imperative for principals and in Anglophone nations at least, is being driven by increasingly vigorous accountability regimes such as the adoption of principal standards (Hallinger and Murphy 2013). The use of a variety of forms of evidence including a range of data and research can inform school improvement in relation to how both students and teachers are performing. It can identify schools' weaknesses and strengths and inform decisions about where best to locate resources (Fullan 2016). In essence, the effective use of data/evidence and research to inform school improvement changes is now considered to be a foundational aspect of instructional principals' educational 'toolkit'. The broader policy imperatives which underpin principal data use suggest that how data are employed and shaped by principals in steering school-wide instructional programs is not solely about thoughtful, evidence-informed professional practice. It also calls attention to the reality that such practice is highly politicised, contested and complex and is invariably a "political act…" (Nutley et al. 2007, p. 25).

In relation to shaping the way data, research and other forms of evidence are used in schools, the principal's role is crucial for a number of reasons. Principals play a critical role in guiding professional conversations about changed teaching practices so that dialogue remains clearly focused on evidence of student learning (e.g., through performance student data) rather than slipping into a deficit mode which focuses on what teachers cannot control such as out-of-school factors (Earl 2009). Principals as leaders play a key role in nurturing or disrupting how research is used in schools depending on how they conceive of what constitutes valid evidence (Coburn and Talbert 2006, as cited in Levin 2010, p. 491). Small practices send crucial messages in schools about how a principal regards research. Regular timetabling of discussion of research implications at staff meetings, for instance, sends a powerful message about the utility of research and can increase staff receptivity (Levin 2010). Despite principals' and districts' increasing awareness of the importance of research (Cooper and Levin 2013), it is still uncommon to have a nominated person whose job it is to source important and relevant research for schools and districts (Levin 2010). Yet the existence of designated roles for research and data use was "one of the strongest factors distinguishing school districts in the US with higher levels of such use" (Coburn et al. 2009, as cited in Levin 2010, p. 312).

The use of a range of data such as "district standards, report cards, and classroom observations" by principals and districts can assist educators to more effectively identify and target the professional development needs of staff (Messelt 2004 as cited in Young Yoon 2016, p. 3). Principals' use of a variety of forms of credible data and research with teachers, can enhance teachers' understanding of students' learning progress, thus increasing teacher buy-in and support for undertaking new reforms (Young Yoon 2016). Increasing teacher buy-in is a crucial element in enhancing students' learning with a recent study of students' reading achievement in high poverty elementary schools finding that schools which had a higher level of teacher buy in had students who performed significantly better in their reading compared to schools with lower levels of teacher buy in (Young Yoon 2016). Administrative support was crucial for teacher buy in (Young Yoon 2016).

## *Utopia Versus Reality Versus Dystopia*

There is an increasing body of research suggesting the importance of the principals' role in shaping how data is used in schools, and the links to effective data, research and evidence use and school improvement. However, there remains a disconnect between the messy reality of current principal and district practices in relation to data, research and evidence use and the ideals and drivers behind current accountability systems. In other words, there is a significant "knowing-doing gap" between principal, school and district practices and evidence use systems on the one hand, and accountability systems on the other hand (Ball 2012, as cited in Sheard and Sharples 2016, p. 669).

The reasons for this gap lie in a number of major barriers and challenges to principals' effective use of data in school improvement efforts. First of all, schools and principals are not islands. They do not work in isolation but in the USA and many other national systems are part of educational districts and systems. Recent research into the role of districts in regard to school principals and evidence use suggests that district "brokers" such as area superintendents in the USA were key mediators of state and federal policies and played a "critical role in selecting evidence, developing knowledge, and supporting the use of data" for schools and principals (Finnigan and Daly 2014, p. 14). Worryingly, the study suggested that access and use of evidence to drive school improvements was inconsistent across and within districts, with principals of low performing schools gaining the least amount of access to district evidence (Finnigan and Daly 2014).

A further study of research use by leaders in Canadian educational districts found that principals used research when devising their school annual plans and improvement plans as part of their growing awareness of the importance of research (Cooper and Levin 2013). However, with one exception, districts had fairly poor processes and systems for locating relevant and credible research, and for sharing and using such research with their schools (Cooper and Levin 2013). There was a "modest use of research in meetings and events" (Cooper and Levin 2013, p. 8). Research was extensively drawn on in professional development of principals but educational leaders reported that professional development had less of an impact on their practices than "personal experience and interaction with colleagues" (Cooper and Levin 2013, p. 8).

Other barriers to effective evidence use by principals and schools include avoidance strategies in which principals (but also system leaders and teachers) "wished the data away" (MacBeath 2001, as cited in Timperley and Earl 2009, p. 126). However, when support is provided to build the capacities required by principals and other leaders to thoughtfully analyse and employ data and other forms of evidence to shape improvement strategies, these kinds of avoidance strategies disappeared (Timperley and Earl 2009). The time to lead learning versus attending to the myriad of daily management tasks required of principals was also a significant barrier (Hallinger and Murphy 2013). This is where professional development for principals is crucial.

## *Professional Development*

A number of suggestions emerge from the research in regard to how principals use evidence to make decisions. They focus on the importance of professional development and training that is not 'one-off' or formulaic. Moreover, they highlight the tight nexus between efforts to build the capacity of principals to engage thoughtfully and strategically with evidence and district improvement initiatives. Firstly, principals' practices in using evidence to make decisions are tightly coupled with the practices of education districts in which they and their schools are nested. Hence, at district level, research suggests the need for districts to focus on a small number of top priorities, with mechanisms by which schools are networked with one another, rather than schools and principals working in isolation from one another (Cooper and Levin 2013). Secondly, professional development for principals in developing the skills to distinguish between what counts as legitimate evidence and what is suspect is crucial (Earl and Timperley 2009). However, developing these skills along with training in how to move from "evidence to meaningful and targeted action based on the analysis of multiple and sometimes conflicting data sources" is a "very steep learning curve" (Earl and Timperley 2009, p. 11). This is where districts and system-wide support is required so that principals can be provided with the necessary opportunities to learn and practise these skills so that they become part of their inquiry disposition.

Levin (2010) argues that a key characteristic of all professional development should be discussion of research, particularly in terms of determining the current state of play in regard to knowledge and how that knowledge can be incorporated into schools and districts in regard to what needs to be done differently. Such strategies, combined with the building of relationships with researchers that subject research to interrogation and debate, along with educators sharing their learning from graduate programs should become essential features of school and district professional practices (Levin 2010). These strategies would help to foreground the pedagogical nature of evidence use in ways that would support, rather than undermine, educational leaders' efforts to develop evidence-*informed*, rather than evidence-*driven*, practices.

## Implications, Recommendations, Conclusions

It is important to recognize that the way school leaders use evidence is based on their philosophical assumptions, their training and their context. In some ways, the fields of both scholarship and practice have been slow to embrace the potential of thoughtful evidence use and have an impoverished view of the topic that emphasizes a few poorly understood outcomes. As such, it is critical for school leaders and those who train and study them to begin developing a more nuanced perspective on both evidence and on school leadership. In particular, we argue that school leadership and evidence use should be considered as a continuum of knowledge and skills that spans the entire range of preparation and practice. If school leaders acquired foundational skills and knowledge in pre-service preparation programs and were taught a nuanced perspective on evidence use that included more than simple input-outcome relationships, their practice would be greatly enhanced.

In sum, we argue that if principals are to act in the public good, they must understand that evidence and evidence use are highly politicized, and that they have the potential to facilitate a more (or less) equitable education for students (Brooks et al. 2007; DeMatthews 2016; Jean-Marie et al. 2009). To be sure, subsequent empirical studies need to explore these issues in both preparation programs and in practice. We hope that in some ways we have helped lay a conceptual foundation for these studies. Leaders, and those who prepare them, must understand that a social justice orientation toward the teaching and practice of leadership is necessary in order to address systemic inequities in school and society (Brooks et al. 2016; Brooks and Brooks 2015; Normore and Brooks 2014).

## References


Asen, R., Gurke, D., Conners, P., Solomon, R., & Gumm, E. (2013). Research evidence and school-board deliberations: Lessons from three Wisconsin school districts. *Educational Policy, 27*(1), 33–63.

Biesta, G. (2007). Why "What works" won't work: Evidence-based practice and the democratic deficit in educational research. *Educational Theory, 57*(1), 1–22.

Bell, M., Cordingley, P., Curtis, A., Evans, D., Hughes, S., & Shreeve, A. (2002). *Bringing research resources to practitioner users via web technology: Lesson learned to date*. Paper presented at the British Educational Research Association Annual Conference, University of Exeter, 12–14 September. http://www.leeds.ac.uk/educol/documents/00002175.htm. Accessed 21 Oct 2015.

Black, W. R., & Murtadha, K. (2007). Toward a signature pedagogy in educational leadership preparation and program assessment. *Journal of Research on Leadership Education, 2*(1), 1–29.

Brooks, J. S. (2006). *The dark side of school reform: Teaching in the space between reality and utopia*. Rowman & Littlefield Education: Lanham.

Brooks, J. S., & Brooks, M. C. (Eds.). (2015). *Urban educational leadership for social justice: International perspectives*. Charlotte: Information Age Publishing.

Brooks, J. S., & Miles, M. T. (2006). From scientific management to social justice and back again? Pedagogical shifts in educational leadership. *International Electronic Journal for Leadership in Learning, 4*(1), 2–15.

Brooks, J. S., Normore, A. H., Jean-Marie, G., & Hodgins, D. (2007). Distributed leadership for social justice: Influence and equity in an urban high school. *Journal of School Leadership, 17*(4), 378–408.

Brooks, J. S., Havard, T., Tatum, K., & Patrick, L. (2010, October). It takes more than a village: Inviting partners and complexity in educational leadership preparation reform. *Journal of Research on Leadership in Education, 5*(12.4), 418–435.

Brooks, J. S., Normore, A. H., Jean-Marie, G., & Brooks, M. C. (2016). Social justice. In *Oxford bibliographies*. http://oxfordbibliographies.com/view/document/obo-9780199756810/obo-9780199756810-0172.xml?rskey=Dibawa&result=17&q=Jeffrey+Brooks+Social+Justice#firstMatch. New York: Oxford University Press.

Cambron-McCabe, N. H. (1999). Confronting fundamental transformation of leadership preparation. In J. Murphy & P. B. Forsyth (Eds.), *Educational administration: A decade of reform* (pp. 217–227). Thousand Oaks: Corwin Press.

Chalmers, I. (2005). If evidence-informed policy works in practice, does it matter if it doesn't work in theory? *Evidence and Policy, 1*(2), 227–242.

Cooper, A., & Levin, B. (2013). Research use by leaders in Canadian school districts. *International Journal of Educational Policy & Leadership, 8*(7), 1–15.

Coburn, C. E., & Talbert, J. E. (2006). Conceptions of evidence-based practice in school districts: Mapping the terrain. *American Journal of Education, 112*(4), 469–495.

Coburn, C. E., Toure, J., & Yamashita, M. (2009). Evidence, interpretation, and persuasion: Instructional decision making at the district central office. *Teachers College Record, 111*(4), 1115–1161.

Cordingley, P. (2004). Teachers using evidence: using what we know about teaching and learning to reconceptualize evidence-based practice. In G. Thomas & R. Pring (Eds.), *Evidence-based practice in education* (pp. 77–87). Maidenhead: Open University Press.

Darling-Hammond, L., LaPointe, M., Meyerson, D., & Orr, M. T. (2007). *Preparing school leaders for a changing world: Lessons from exemplary leadership development programs*. School Leadership Study. Executive Summary. Stanford Educational Leadership Institute.

Davies, P. (1999). What is evidence-based education? *British Journal of Educational Studies, 47*(2), 108–121.

Davies, H., Nutley, S., & Walter, I. (2008). Why "knowledge transfer" is misconceived for applied social research. *Journal of Health Services Research & Policy, 13*(3), 188–190.

DeMatthews, D. (2016). Social justice dilemmas: Evidence on the successes and shortcomings of three principals trying to make a difference. *International Journal of Leadership in Education*, 1–15.

Donmoyer, R., Imber, M., & Scheurich, J. J. (1995). *The knowledge base in educational administration: Multiple perspectives*. Albany: SUNY Press.

Earl, L. M. (2009). Leadership for evidence-informed conversations. In L. M. Earl & H. Timperley (Eds.), *Professional learning conversations* (pp. 43–52). Dordrecht: Springer.

Earl, L. M. (2015). Reflections on the challenges of leading research and evidence use in schools. In C. Brown (Ed.), *Leading the use of research and evidence in schools* (pp. 146–152). London: Institute of Education Press.

Earl, L. M., & Timperley, H. (2009). Understanding how evidence and learning conversations work. In L. M. Earl & H. Timperley (Eds.), *Professional learning conversations* (pp. 1–12). Dordrecht: Springer.

Estabrooks, C. A. (2001). Research utilization and qualitative research. In J. M. Morse, J. M. Swanson, & A. J. Kuzel (Eds.), *The nature of qualitative evidence*. London: Sage.

Figgis, J., Zubrick, A., Butorac, A., & Alderson, A. (2000). Backtracking practice and policies to research. In DETYA (Ed.), *The impact of educational research*. Canberra: DETYA.

Finnigan, K. S., & Daly, A. J. (2014). *Using research evidence in education*. Dordrecht: Springer.

Finnigan, K. S., Daly, A. J., Hylton, N. D., & Che, J. (2015). Leveraging social networks for educational improvement. In C. Brown (Ed.), *Leading the use of research and evidence in schools* (pp. 137–145). London: Institute of Education Press.

Fullan, M. (2016). *The new meaning of educational change* (5th ed.). New York: Teachers' College Press.
Hallinger, P., & Murphy, J. F. (2012). Running on empty? Finding the time and capacity to lead learning. *NASSP Bulletin, 97*(1), 5–21.
Hallinger, P., & Murphy, J. F. (2013). Running on empty? Finding the time and capacity to lead learning. *NASSP Bulletin, 97*(1), 5–21.
Halverson, R., Grigg, J., Pritchett, R., & Thomas, C. (2007). The new instructional leadership: Creating data-driven instructional systems in school. *Journal of School Leadership, 17*, 159–194.
Halverson, R., Grigg, J., Prichett, R., & Thomas, C. (2015). The new instructional leadership: Creating data-driven instructional systems in school. *Journal of School Leadership, 25*(3), 447–481. Retrieved from http://go.galegroup.com.ezproxy.lib.monash.edu.au/ps/i.do?id=GALE%7CA424532364&v=2.1&u=monash&it=r&p=AONE&sw=w&asid=8ead134fb60960d92c51ee77e4d30d91.
Hattie, J. (2015). High-impact leadership. *Educational Leadership, 72*(5), 36–40.
Hess, F., & Kelley, A. (2005). *Learning to lead? What gets taught in principal preparation programs*. Cambridge, MA: Kennedy School of Government: Program on Education Policy and Governance.
Jackson, B. L., & Kelley, C. (2002). Exceptional and innovative programs in educational leadership. *Educational Administration Quarterly, 38*(2), 192–212.
Jean-Marie, G., Normore, A. H., & Brooks, J. S. (2009). Leadership for social justice: Preparing 21st century school leaders for a new social order. *Journal of Research on Leadership in Education, 4*(1), 1–31.
Johnson, R. S. (2002). *Using data to close the achievement gap: How to measure equity in our schools*. Thousand Oaks: Corwin Press.
Larson, C. L., & Murtadha, K. (2002). Leadership for social justice. *Yearbook of the National Society for the Study of Education, 101*(1), 134–161. Chicago.
Leithwood, K., Harris, A., & Hopkins, D. (2008). Seven strong claims about successful school leadership. *School Leadership & Management, 28*(1), 27–42. doi:10.1080/13632430701800060.
Levin, B. (2004). Making research matter more. *Education Policy Analysis Archives, 12*, 56.
Levin, B. (2010). Leadership for evidence-informed education. *School leadership and managerment, 30*(4), 303–315. doi:10.1080/13632434.2010.497483.
Marzano, R. J., Waters, T., & McNulty, B. A. (2005). *School leadership that works: From research to results*. Alexandria: Association for Supervision and Curriculum Development.
Means, B., Padilla, C., DeBarger, A., & Bakia, M. (2009). *Implementing data-informed decision making in schools: Teacher access, supports and use*. Washington, DC: U.S. Department of Education.
Murphy, J. (1990a). The educational reform movement of the 1980s: A comprehensive analysis. In J. Murphy (Ed.), *The reform of American public education in the 1980s: Perspectives and cases* (pp. 3–55). Berkeley: McCutchan.
Murphy, J. (1990b). Improving the preparation of school administrators: The National Policy Board's story. *The Journal of Educational Policy, 5*(2), 181–186.
Murphy, J. (1990c). Preparing school administrators for the twenty-first century: The reform agenda. In B. Mitchell & L. L. Cunningham (Eds.), *Educational leadership and changing contexts of families, communities, and schools* (pp. 232–251). (the 1990 NSSE yearbook). Chicago: University of Chicago Press.
Murphy, J. (1990d). The reform of school administration: Pressures and calls for change. In J. Murphy (Ed.), *The reform of American public education in the 1980s: Perspectives and cases* (pp. 277–303). Berkeley: McCutchan.
Murphy, J. (2001). The changing face of leadership preparation. *The School Administrator, 58*(10), 14–17.
Murphy, J., & Vriesenga, M. (2006). Research on school leadership preparation in the United States: An analysis. *School Leadership and Management, 26*(2), 183–195.

Normore, A. H., & Brooks, J. S. (Eds.). (2014). *Educational leadership for ethics and social justice: Views from the social sciences*. Charlotte: Information Age Publishing.
Nutley, S., Walter, I., & Davies, H. T. O. (2007). *Using evidence: How research can inform public services*. Bristol: Policy Press.
Nutley, S., Powell, A., & Davies, H. (2013). *What counts as good evidence?* London: Alliance for Useful Evidence.
Orr, M. T. (2007). *How preparation influences school leaders and their school improvement: Comparing exemplary and conventionally prepared principals*. School Leadership Study: Developing Successful Principals. Stanford Educational Leadership Institute.
Orr, M. T., & Orphanos, S. (2011). How graduate-level preparation influences the effectiveness of school leaders: A comparison of the outcomes of exemplary and conventional leadership preparation programs for principals. *Educational Administration Quarterly, 47*(1), 18–70.
Robinson, V. (2007). *School leadership and student outcomes: Identifying what works and why, Australian Council for Educational Leaders Monograph Series Number 41*. Winmalee: Australian Council for Educational Leaders.
Scheurich, J. J., & Skrla, L. (2003). *Leadership for equity and excellence: Creating high achievement classrooms, schools, and districts*. Thousand Oaks: Corwin Press.
Sebba, J. (2004). Developing evidence-informed policy and practice in education. In G. Thomas & R. Pring (Eds.), *Evidence-based practice in education* (pp. 34–43). Maidenhead: Open.
Sharples, J. (2013). *Evidence for the Frontline*. London: Alliance for Useful Evidence.
Sheard, M. K., & Sharples, J. (2016). School leaders' engagement with the concept of evidence-based practice as a management tool for school improvement. *Educational Management and Leadership, 44*(4), 668–687.
Timperley, H., & Earl, L. (2009). Using conversations to make sense of evidence: Possibilities and pitfalls. In L. M. Earl & H. Timperley (Eds.), *Professional learning conversations* (pp. 121–126). Dordrecht: Springer.
Wolcott, H. F. (1970). An ethnographic approach to the study of school administrators. *Human Organization, 29*(2), 115–122.
Young Yoon, S. (2016). Principals' data-driven practice and its influence on teacher buy-in and student achievement in comprehensive school reform models. *Leadership and Policy in Schools*. doi.org/10.1080/15700763.2016.1181187

# Chapter 10
# Guiding Principles for Evaluating Evidence in Education Research

**Sarah Kay McDonald and Barbara Schneider**

> *Mistaking no answers in practice for no answers in principle is a great source of moral confusion – Sam Harris*

**Abstract** Based on their experiences from their work with two national initiatives designed to reform educational practice in U.S., the authors present seven guiding principles of evidence-based/informed educational policy and research to lay the foundation for making rigorous and comprehensive judgments about what evidence and scientific research designs should be taken into account when scaling-up educational reforms to serve the public good. The authors further provide case examples from US with a clear potential to both utilize and generate evidence in the public interest including educational research studies that seeks to support underrepresented groups in preparing for and achieving successful transitions to postsecondary education and careers, in STEM and other fields. The authors conclude that educational researchers have a critical role to play in providing decision-makers with the tools to judge the evidence to serve public good.

The improvement of the education system has been a constant concern to educators and policymakers both within the U.S. and abroad and it has assumed a position of national and international significance unparalleled in previous decades. Never before have we seen so much attention by governments, philanthropic

S.K. McDonald
National Science Foundation, Arlington, VA, USA

B. Schneider (✉)
College of Education, Michigan State University, East Lansing, MI, USA
e-mail: bschneid@msu.edu



M.Y. Eryaman, B. Schneider (eds.), *Evidence and Public Good in Educational Policy, Research and Practice*, Educational Governance Research 6,
DOI 10.1007/978-3-319-58850-6_10

organizations, and social media directed at the transformation of school organizations, teacher evaluation systems, instruction, and assessments. In the U.S. alone, in 2010, President Obama awarded over $4.5 billion dollars for education reform through the American Recovery and Reinvestment Act. That same year the Bill & Melinda Gates Foundation awarded an additional half a billion dollars to early learning and college-ready education initiatives.[1]

Why is education drawing such attention and resources? Two major problems continue to plague many world-wide educational systems. First, is the continuing achievement gap between more socially advantaged students and those with fewer social and economic resources in elementary, secondary school, and higher education (Duncan and Murnane 2011; Chmielewski 2014). In some countries, these achievement gaps are also confounded by race and ethnicity and immigration status (OECD 2015). For several decades in the U.S. the average performance of white students has surpassed that of blacks and Hispanics.[2] Recent projections indicate that these trends are likely to persist at least in the near future (Reardon 2011).

Second, is differential access to quality schools, postsecondary education, and job training. In the U.S. the number of minorities in low-paying, non-skilled jobs continues to be disproportionately higher than that of whites (U.S. Department of Labor 2011). These trends reflect, in part, the lower numbers of minorities completing postsecondary degrees compared to whites (National Science Foundation 2010). Similar to the U.S., many countries throughout the globe have also been challenged with improving secondary school completion rates and access to higher education and training among all students regardless of their family characteristics. Problems of inequity of educational access and opportunity are also predicted to escalate with the increases in immigrants seeking refugee from political unrest in the Middle East and several African nations (OECD 2015).

Educational developers and researchers have responded to these problems by designing interventions that create new pedagogical tools, instructional content, and assessments to narrow the achievement gap. One area of particular emphasis has been teacher quality including reforms such as alternative routes to teacher certification, merit-pay, and evaluation practices. Other types of reforms for enhancing access include changes in school structure and programs that offer a more successful transition into postsecondary education and the labor market, including national initiatives such as the Knowledge is Power Program (KIPP) and local initiatives such as the Chicago-based Urban Prep Academies.[3] Considerable investments have also been

[1]American Recovery and Reinvestment Act. (Pub.L.11-5); Gates Foundation: http://www.gatesfoundation.org/united-states/Pages/measures-of-effective-teaching-fact-sheet.aspx

[2]Results of the 2009 NAEP for U.S. high school seniors found no significant changes in the gap between white and black students' reading scores from 1992 to 2009, and no significant change between white and black or Hispanic students' mathematics scores from 2005 to 2009 (NCES 2011).

[3]KIPP (http://www.kipp.org/) is "based around high expectations for student achievement; commitment to a college preparatory education by students, parents, and faculty; devotion of time to both educational and extracurricular activities; increased leadership power of school principals; and a focus on results through regular student assessments" (U.S. Department of Education, Institute of Education Sciences, What Works Clearinghouse 2010). Urban Prep is a Chicago-based

made in leveraging the power of technology to support student learning (e.g., through data visualization tools, online learning communities, intelligent tutoring systems, and computer games and virtual environments) and access to postsecondary education.[4] Despite the large number of initiatives being piloted, some have proved disappointing when adopted at scale, while others have had a more successful trajectory.

One major innovation that has been successfully scaled is Success for All (SFA), a comprehensive whole-school reform approach to improvement that incorporates research-based curriculum materials, professional development, assessment and data-monitoring tools, and activities that facilitate family involvement and community support. First implemented in a single school in Baltimore, Maryland, 25 years later the Success for All Foundation serves over 2000 schools in 46 U.S. states and offers assistance to projects in five other countries.[5] In 2010, the Foundation was the recipient of a $50 million grant from the U.S. Department of Education's Investing in Innovation program to scale-up the program to reach over half a million additional elementary school students. Key to the success of SFA has been the robust evidence of its positive impact on student learning. Multiple evaluations have been conducted on SFA including an independent study that showed it met the criteria for the strongest evidence of effectiveness, indicating significant positive effects and replication in multiple contexts including schools likely to adopt and implement SFA (Borman et al. 2003, 2007). Other more recent independent positive evaluations of SFA include an assessment of major comprehensive education reforms by Rowan et al. (2009) and another by MDRC funded by the U.S. federal government showing that SFA was especially effective in schools with students having low preliteracy skills (Quint et al. 2015).

While not without its critics, the SFA program is notable both for its acknowledged impacts and for its commitment to amassing a rich and deep research base that has informed its development and implementation. Few interventions have such a track record of evidence warranting scale-up. Rather, the educational research landscape remains heavily populated by small studies with disparate findings and less rigorous evaluations. This uneven evidential base of research might explain why educational studies have had such a limited role in formulating public policy. Scholars have argued that strong evidence on its own is rarely sufficient to explain how public policy agendas are shaped and enacted (Weiss 1989; Stevenson 2000). Their position has been that research, whether in the U.S or in other countries, rarely provides definitive answers or prescribes specific policies (see, e.g., Weiss 1982; U.K., House of Commons

initiative operating in the only all-male public schools in the state of Illinois to "provide a comprehensive, high-quality college preparatory education that results in graduates succeeding in college" (see http://www.urbanprep.org/about/historvlindex.asp).

[4] See, Dynarski and Scott-Clayton (2007) and Hoxby (2007). Other examples of online resources on the college selection and application processes in the U.S. include the National Center for Education Statistics College Navigator (http://nces.ed.gov/collegenavigator) and the American Council on Education, Lumina Foundation for Education, and Ad Council's KnowHow2GO (http://www.knowhow2go.org/).

[5] See the Success for All Foundation's 'Our Story', retrieved February 22, 2011 from http://www.successforall.org/About/story.html

2006). Instead, research often plays a 'framing' function, shaping discourse, conceptualizations, and the ways problems and potential solutions are formulated.

Times have changed, however, and whereas policy makers may once have discounted educational research, that does not seem to be the case today. Policymakers now value reforms like SFA that produce statistically sound results that can be used to inform educational decisions. In the U.S. this press for evidence accountability encompasses the entire educational system from the federal government to local school districts. The most obvious example of this was the enactment of the No Child Left Behind Act (NCLB) (Public Law 107–110), with its reliance on data to sanction schools based on their lack of academic performance. State and local school districts were mandated to collect, validate, and transmit massive amounts of student, school, and teacher performance data on the effectiveness of their educational systems.

NCLB had a rocky road of implementation, caught in a net of local and state dissatisfaction and bipartisan political conflict all of which delayed reauthorization of the next bill for over a decade. Finally, in 2015, a new federal education bill the, Every Student Succeeds Act (Pub. L. 114–95), was ratified. While permitting states more flexibility in determining standards for measuring school and student performance, the general public and its legislatures, continued to press for testing, reporting, and accountability on the progress of all students and their schools. This emphasis on testing and accountability, although somewhat more relaxed than the previous legislation, corresponds to a more world-wide movement to measure the status and improvement of student learning and teacher and school effectiveness.

This trend toward amassing data for purposes of decision making has been augmented by a number of activities, one of which is the development of research organizations and associations designed to highlight experimental and quasi-experimental studies and methods. Some of these organizations include the Society for Research on Educational Effectiveness (SREE, https://www.sree.org), the What Works Clearinghouse in the U.S., and the Campbell Collaboration (which includes health, social sciences and education), all of which compile lists of robust studies that rely on evidence for decision-making.[6] Older, more established education associations both in the U.S. and around the world are also revamping and professionalizing their organizations to reflect these new demands for rigorous education research. Organizations such as the American Educational Research Association (AERA, https://www.aera.org) have and continue to be committed to these goals and exercise leadership in these areas, including assisting in the formation of the World Education Research Association (WERA, https://www.wera.org), an international society with a similar purpose.

[6] The What Works Clearinghouse is an initiative of the U.S. Department of Education's Institute of Education Sciences which 'develops and implements standards for reviewing and synthesizing education research' (http://ies.ed.gov/ncee/wwc/aboutus). The Campbell Collaboration is an 'international research network that produces systematic reviews of the effects of social interventions' (http://www.campbellcollaboration.org/aboutus/index.php). The Society for Research on Educational Effectiveness seeks to advance and disseminate research on the causal effects of education interventions, programs, and policy (http://www.sree.org/pages/mission.php).

Even though there has been a general sentiment for more rigorous research within the education community, there has been considerable attention regarding the methodology and criteria for determining what works and what does not (National Research Council 2002; Walters et al. 2008), with some critics arguing against standards for evaluating educational programs and practices. Policymakers have strongly pressed for only making investments in education reforms, particularly those with public resources, on robust evidence. However, the field's ability to produce such an evidence base seems incompatible with many reform timelines. One exception to speed the process of evidence-informed reform is being tested at The Carnegie Foundation for Teaching and Learning.

Spearheaded by its President, Anthony Bryk, the Foundation is working on implementing reforms using the modified 90-day cycle for researching and assessing innovative ideas employed by the Institute for Healthcare Improvement (see Bryk 2015). Bryk began by using this model to explore whether math-intensive programs can move students in community colleges out of developmental math courses (Yamada and Bryk 2016) and has now applied the model to other reforms that can be quickly implemented in educational systems. The intent of Bryk's plan is to re-engineer educational research to one that promotes an improvement science that addresses the complexity and variability in school performance within a shorter more productive time frame (Bryk 2015).

One of the most beneficial outcomes of efforts to truncate the research and development cycle may be embracing more realistic expectations regarding the roles educational research can and should play for informing reform. This chapter is designed to define some of the principles for making sound judgments about research quality and what evidence should be taken into account in making decisions regarding educational practices and policies, especially for those interventions designed for scale-up. At issue is not just the strength of evidence that can be attributed to specific interventions (determining what works), but establishing the contexts (e.g., classroom, school, neighborhood) and populations (e.g., demographic characteristics) for which it is likely to work equally well (e.g., generalizability of effects). The principles here reflect current work being conducted by social scientists working in diverse national and international settings and our work with two U.S. national initiatives designed to articulate what considerations need to be taken into account when bringing promising interventions to scale (Schneider and McDonald 2007; Milesi et al. 2014). Principles are merely touchstones; even if scientifically grounded, their use is subject to the will of decision makers. Our intent is simply to lay the foundation for making sound judgments about the nature of evidence that should be taken into account when scaling-up educational reforms.

## Principle 1: Gauging the Impact on Learning

One of the first issues to consider in weighing the value of evidence is its potential impact on advancing knowledge of learning and instruction. Whether studying pedagogy, redesigns of school organizations, or new technologies, the fundamental issue is if the intervention impacts learning outcomes. It is important to consider the theory upon which the intervention is based, how it has been tested over time, and how it affects different populations in diverse settings. One example that meets these criteria is the Carnegie Learning Cognitive Tutor®, developed by John R. Anderson and colleagues.

For decades, psychological experiments have generated data about humans' attention to and perceptions of their external environment, including reasoning, memory, problem solving, and decision-making. Anderson integrated these ideas into a single unified theory of cognition which models how humans perceive, organize, think about, and act upon knowledge.[7] This blueprint of human information processing suggested opportunities to stimulate learning through intelligent computer-based tutoring systems. Critical to the model is the notion that knowledge is strengthened with use. This is the theory upon which he developed a tutoring system that focuses on active engagement with and use of knowledge (see Ritter et al. 2007a). Initial field tests suggested that the tutors were more successful with some teachers than others, a finding that led the investigators to focus more closely on the enacted curriculum (i.e., what was actually occurring in classrooms). Consequently, the team expanded on its work to develop a curriculum that could be embedded within the tutor.

Over time, Carnegie Learning's Cognitive Tutors have been tested in studies using some of the most rigorous designs supporting causal inference, with numerous student and teacher populations and outcome measures. The methodological approach here is a randomized control trial in which the treatment condition is measured against a control condition taking into account potential assignment counterfactual conditions (Holland 1986; Imbens and Rubin 2010; Rubin 2005). Positive impacts of the tutor on students' mathematics learning and achievement have been found in numerous middle-school, secondary school, and higher education settings in California, Colorado, Florida, Oklahoma, Ohio, Pennsylvania, Texas, Washington, and Wisconsin. Controlled comparison field trials (utilizing matched control groups and quasi-experimental designs) and other robust statistical analyses demonstrate significant improvements in student learning attributable to the Cognitive Tutor of student learning (e.g. SAT, Iowa Algebra Aptitude Test, and problem situations and multiple representations tests). On the positive side, an independent evaluation that met the What Works Clearinghouse evidence standards found significant increases in first semester grades and other learning measures including scores on the ETS Algebra I end-of-course exam.[8] But even with these successful evaluations, a U.S. Department of Education study found no significant differences between the Cognitive Tutor versus a control condition (see Campuzano et al. 2009). Should we discount this evidence or recognize that there will be instances where results will not replicate?

[7]Anderson's original Adaptive Control of Thought (ACT) theory of human cognition was first described in Anderson, 1976; elaborated in 1983; and refined into the ACT-R (Adaptive Control of Thought-Rational) theory for understanding and stimulating cognition, 1993, which is the foundation of the Cognitive Tutor software.

[8]For additional information see Ritter et al. (2007a, b). For a review of this study, see the WWC July 2009 Intervention Report on the Cognitive Tutor® Algebra I available online at http://ies.ed.gov/ncee/wwc/pdf/wwccogtutor072809.pdf

Reproducibility of studies, especially ones like this with multiple conditions and unusual contextual factors, including implementation procedures are part of conducting work in classrooms *not laboratories*. There are no silver bullets for improving *all students'* mathematical learning at this time. Nevertheless, we should continue to investigate different designs especially those that take advantage of emerging technologies. The important message here is the value of solid theoretically driven interventions that allow for strategic iterative evaluations which identify factors that influence their success and the contextual conditions that undermine their effectiveness.

## Principle 2: Knowing What to Measure

Having established a study's potential to improve our knowledge base regarding learning, it is important to consider how the outcomes of interest should be measured. At issue is whether the metrics proposed are calibrated to detect meaningful change. From the investigator's perspective, key considerations include: how well the metrics capture constructs of interest; whether the process of assigning values to measure change is sufficiently transparent to enable replication; and whether the costs of developing, collecting, coding, and analyzing proposed metrics will yield information of commensurate value. From the perspective of the decision maker, the key criterion is whether what is being measured is the relevant outcome for observing, assessing, and enabling a policy change.

An example of educational research that underscores the importance of employing assessments to detect specific changes in learning is the BioKIDS: Kids' Inquiry of Diverse Species intervention developed by Nancy Songer and colleagues. Like the Cognitive Tutor, BioKIDS integrated new curricular units with innovative technologies (in this case, handheld devices for students' use). Focusing on elementary and middle school students in high-poverty urban classrooms, BioKIDS fostered the development of inquiry thinking skills while providing instruction in life science content. Using their schoolyard environments, students explored biodiversity, tracking animals and logging data on personal digital assistants (PDAs). The students' observational data were explored through a carefully scaffolded series of activities designed to foster inquiry-based science learning.[9]

The Songer team recognized the inadequacy of standard science assessments to detect the outcomes targeted by the BioKIDS intervention. Evaluating students' ability to engage in complex reasoning about scientific ideas required alternative forms of assessment. Developing an assessment that identified and calibrated students' reasoning capacity became central to measuring the impacts of the intervention. The BioKIDS team partnered with researchers on the Principled Assessment Design for Inquiry (PADI) project to develop high quality assessments of science

[9] For additional information on BioKIDS see the project's web site at http://www.biokids.umich.edu/

inquiry aligned with the goals of the intervention and informed by emergent thinking regarding the science and design of assessment.[10]

With the new metric, Songer's team disentangled "students' content knowledge from their complex reasoning abilities," vital for developing students' capacity not only to master content knowledge but also to interpret data and formulate scientific explanations. More generally, empirical evaluations of the BioKIDS intervention and its assessment system enhanced the development of both curricular units and the assessments, while demonstrating statistically significant and substantively meaningful improvements in student achievement (see e.g., Songer et al. 2009, 2007; BioKIDS, University of Michigan 2005). Impressive as student standardized achievement tests were, Songer singled-out the insensitivity of standardized tests to evaluate complex thinking about science' as "perhaps the most important aspect of this work" (Songer et al. 2009: 628).

Importantly, the challenges of assessing rich and multi-faceted effects of interventions that seek to improve content knowledge and deeper thinking skills are not unique to BioKIDS. Standardized tests are often poorly aligned with innovative curricula and are insensitive to changes new interventions seek to foster (see e.g., Pellegrino et al. 2001, 2014) For this reason, it is unwise to dismiss interventions incapable of producing higher scores on existing metrics; instead, it is important to ask whether existing metrics are misaligned with the interventions designed to attain them. Critical questioning of metrics is a natural component of any improvement process. Defaulting to traditional measures is unlikely to prove helpful in advancing new knowledge and skill sets. Weighing evidence, then, it is always important to ask "are we measuring what we ought to measure?", and to consider when it may be necessary to augment the assessment repertoire with new metrics for gauging impacts on learning.

## Principle 3: Employing Standards of Scientific Design

There are many types of study designs, all of which have important roles to play in understanding educational phenomena. In deciding among them a key consideration is how confident the investigator needs to be in examining the nature of relationships she posits or observes among educational outcomes and other variables of interest. Important differences in individual research objectives notwithstanding, any study which aims to generate evidence to inform educational policy or practice fundamentally strives to illuminate potentially causal connections. How secure we need to be in our assessments of these connections varies at different stages in the

[10] The Principled Assessment Designs for Inquiry (PADI) project builds on developments in measurement theory, technology, cognitive psychology, and science inquiry, implementing the evidence-centered assessment design (ECD) framework (see http://padi.sri.com). For additional information on the BioKIDS/PADI collaboration and details of the assessment system, see Songer et al. (2009), and Gotwals and Songer (2006).

research and development cycle. The first stage of the research cycle is to provide proof of concept for innovations. Initial proof of concept tests may tolerate some ambiguity, but by the time we move to the next stage of the experimental cycle (establishing efficacy trials), gaps in logic models cannot be overlooked. By the time one is testing a fully scaled intervention with an effectiveness trial, the design should provide solid evidence of cause and effect.

Scientific design standards are invaluable for constructing investigations that yield evidence for eventually meeting requirements for scale-up. Properly applied, they increase the likelihood that robust and credible evidence rather than compelling stories will provide the foundations for policy initiatives. Likelihood is not, however, certainty; even the best designs may yield evidence of questionable value – for example, when plagued by circumstances (such as attrition) beyond the investigator's control, or when concerns with establishing the cause of an effect overwhelm attention to moderators which may condition and constrain impact.

An example of a program of educational research that over a decade employed a wide range of robust designs to establish causal connections was conducted by Barbara Foorman and colleagues. Working in Texas and Florida, Foorman developed, piloted, refined, tested, and scaled two evidence-based reading interventions. The first intervention was designed for teachers to establish appropriate learning objectives for each student and provide individualized instruction enabling students to read at or above grade level. Targeting children in the primary grades, they developed the Texas Primary Reading Inventory (TPRl) to align with new state standards and research evidence on the development of reading skills. The second intervention was the Florida Assessments for Instruction in Reading (FAIR) to assist teachers in their instructional decision-making. Both TPRl and FAIR use diagnostic, classroom-based assessments to identify those students at risk of developing reading problems with more intensive, targeted diagnostic inventories.

Each of these interventions uses technology (e.g., in the case of TPRI, internet and handheld devices; in the case of FAIR, computer adaptive testing) that provides ancillary supports to assist teachers in adapting and targeting instruction that focuses on skills the students have not yet mastered. Both of these interventions have been tested with rigorous validity and reliability evaluations of the assessment instruments and their impact for supporting assessment-driven instruction. On the basis of this evidence each has been scaled for use with students and teachers across the state. In Texas, TPRI is used with students in Kindergarten through the third grade; in Florida, FAIR is used at no charge in public schools with students in grades K-12.[11]

While both the TPRI and FAIR evolved through a careful progression from development to evaluations establishing effectiveness and achieved widespread adoption, each was further developed with ongoing testing of the assessments and the targeted

[11] For additional information on the TPRI see Foorman et al. (1998) and Foorman et al. (2007); and the web site at http://www.childrensleaminginstitute.org/ourprograms/program-overview/TPRI/. For information on FAIR see Foorman and Petscher (2010) and Foorman et al. (2009); and the web site at http://www.fcrr.org/fair/index.shtm

instruction they facilitate. A 2008–2009 development study was designed to assess and improve the validity and reliability of the entire TPRI (CLI/TIMES 2014: 4) based on material tested with approximately 3000 students. Similarly, investigators at the Florida Center for Reading Research continued to leverage data from FAIR to explore and develop activities that enhanced reading skills (see Foorman and Petscher 2010), and conduct research on the development and evidence from the assessment system, including causal effects of individualized instruction.[12]

The TPRI and FAIR initiatives highlight the iterative refinement of effective interventions, the partnerships required to enact robust designs in the classroom, and the importance of continued R&D commitments long after efficacy and effectiveness is established. Exemplary interventions moved to scale should not be regarded as sacrosanct but instead as appropriate responses to particular problems in given situations which, given the ever-evolving standards for instruction and expectations regarding student achievement, will continue to shift over time. From an evidentiary perspective, scale-up signals confidence that robust evidence of meaningful change warrants widespread adoption. Scalable interventions are not, however, dead-end products of an R&D process from which further movement is neither possible nor desirable. Continual examination of exemplary interventions is vital to ensure their continued viability.

This is the case for interventions warranted by the sequential 'proof-of-concept to efficacy to effectiveness trial' experimental model of evidence generation, but also for those whose positive effects are established in other ways. Consider the secondary analyses that provide the evidence warranting various grade retention and remedial instruction policies. Analyses of administrative records can yield incontrovertible evidence of the benefits of ending social promotion policies, but periodic re-analyses to establish the veracity of these conclusions can change as new student populations move through the education system. In thinking about the standards of scientific design necessary to warrant the adoption of new educational policies and practices, it is critical to remember that science must evolve if only to ensure static outcomes in dynamic contexts.

## Principle 4: Recognizing Magnitudes of Change

Even when designs support causal inference, care needs to be exercised in interpreting their import. Critical is distinguishing statistically significant from substantively meaningful changes. When findings are statistically significant, we can be confident (within specified boundaries, e.g., 95% of the time) that observed results are not likely due to chance. However, statistical significance is not always substantively meaningful, signaling important differences meriting attention or action.

---

[12] For a complete listing of current research projects being conducted by research faculty at the Florida Center for Reading Research, see http://www.fcrr.org/centerResearch/centerResearch.shtm

Some results (e.g., an increase in scores on a test of student achievement following exposure to an intervention) provide clear indications of changes which are meaningful and worth replication. In such cases, the metrics employed to measure the results are unambiguously aligned with our educational objectives. Unfortunately, not all primary effects (e.g., changes in test scores) are inherently meaningful, and there are wide variations in metrics and measurement scales. To address these difficulties in interpreting primary findings, researchers increasingly report the size of an effect (i.e., change attributed to an intervention) not only in absolute terms (e.g., the number of points scored on a test of basic skills) but also on a common scale which facilitates comparisons of outcomes (see, e.g., Hedges 1981).

Such 'effect size' metrics are invaluable in assessing the practical import of changes that follow exposure to interventions. Yet even when confidence is high that observed changes following implementation of an intervention are both real (statistically significant) and substantively meaningful (in absolute or effect size terms), questions often remain regarding the implications of study findings for particular individuals in specific contexts. For example, an intervention that boosts academic achievement in mathematics by a third of a grade level may produce important benefits for students near the middle of a test-score distribution, yet have far less import for students at the bottom of the distribution. When average growth is 1 year of schooling, it is vital to consider whether an intervention is likely to help a student who starts the school-year more than a year behind her grade-level peers. Given how much of the variation in academic performance is accounted for by external factors outside the classroom, it is important to establish parameters within which it is reasonable to expect a single teacher to help raise student performance over the course of an academic year. Even evidence of large effects may not be sufficient to warrant support for an intervention in all circumstances or contexts.

The importance of context and its impact on magnitude is particularly evident with respect to efforts to improve student achievement by reducing class size. Tennessee was one of the first states to undertake a statewide class-size reduction initiative, the Student/Teacher Achievement Ratio (STAR) project. Implemented in 1985, the STAR project was designed to study the effects of reduced class sizes on kindergarten through third grade. Students were randomly assigned to one of three classroom size conditions (a 'small' class of 13–17 students per teacher, a 'regular class' of 22–25 pupils, and a 'regular-with-aide' class of 22–25 students with a full-time teacher's aide), and remained in the same classroom size from kindergarten through third grade. Data were collected from 79 schools and over 7000 students throughout the state, with outcome data including the Stanford Achievement Test (SAT), the Basic Skills First (BSF) performance tests (starting in first grade), and the SCAMIN self-concept and motivation scales (see Word et al. 1990).

Overall results from the STAR program showed that students uniformly benefited from smaller classes, scoring significantly higher on standardized tests of reading and math across grades and regardless of whether the small classes were in urban, suburban, or rural schools. Students in small classes outperformed students in classrooms with full-time teacher aides, the only exception being when aides were in regular first grade classrooms. Despite some concerns regarding student attrition and movement between classrooms, and the inability to generalize results to very small or ethnically diverse schools, the experimental results of Project STAR held up under considerable scrutiny (Schanzenbach 2006).

So impressive were the results from the STAR program that the research was used to justify a similar effort in California. In the mid-1990s elementary schools in California averaged 29 students per classroom, the highest in the country. Regional economic prosperity provided tax revenues, over $1 billion per year that allowed bringing all K-3 classroom sizes down to 20 or fewer students. However, when class size reduction was implemented in California the outcome was quite different from that experienced in Tennessee.

The 1996 California class size reduction initiative affected over 1.6 million public school students in kindergarten through the third grade (see Bohrnstedt et al. 2000). This ambitious reform was carefully chronicled and evaluated by a research consortium whose members included the American Institutes for Research (AIR), RAND, WestEd, Policy Analysis for California Education (PACE), and EdSource. Key outcomes assessed in this 4-year, non-experimental evaluation of the California program included not only impacts on student achievement but also the quality of the state's teaching corps (Bohrnstedt and Stecher 2002). Since there was no random assignment of students to classrooms and the program was being implemented statewide, analyses of achievement gains relied on controlling for student and school characteristics and tracking cohorts of students with varying exposures to class size reduction.

Despite these methodological limitations, based on analyses of state data supplemented with information (including internal evaluation reports and specially-prepared student and teacher data sets) from school districts, the evaluators ultimately concluded that the relationship of the program to student achievement was inconclusive and attribution of gains in scores to the program was not warranted. One possible reason for this contrary finding is that rapid statewide implementation greatly increased the demand for teachers the year before the program was implemented. The demand for new teachers was met, in part, by hiring teachers not yet fully credentialed. In addition, most California districts also lacked sufficient funds to fully implement the program, often leading to a reallocation of resources from other programs and services.

The California experience suggests that policies that work in one place may not work in another, and moving to a statewide reduction in class size may have been premature. Importantly, recommendations arising from the California experience underscored the need to consider potential unanticipated consequences, contextual differences, and local adaptations that may be necessary to successfully bring to scale interventions that previously had produced meaningful change. The Tennessee STAR class size reduction project embraced scientific research principles, in both its design and its evaluation, and achieved impressive, substantively meaningful results. Results of a similar magnitude were not achieved, however, when an, on the face of it, quite similar reform was implemented in another context. The student populations were similar (K-3 public elementary school students) but critically the instructional work force with whom these students now had the opportunity to come into closer daily contact was not. Tennessee's and California's different experiences with class size reduction policies underscore the need when making judgments about evidence that is statistically significant and substantively meaningful, that salient contextual factors in this case the quality and experience of the teacher can make major differences in results.

## Principle 5: Judging the Evidence for Scale-Up

Questions about context are central to efforts to 'scale-up' interventions, extending the reach of policies and taking promising practices to larger diverse populations. Since the late 1990s, the scale-up model's stage-wise progression from innovation and proof of concept to widespread implementation of effective interventions has attained considerable traction in the U.S. among both policymakers and researchers as a framework for accumulating evidence in support of reform. Scale-up has become the implicit end-game of many R&D initiatives, the ultimate goal of a research and development process that begins with proving the concept behind an intervention, moves on to establish efficacy in ideal then document effectiveness in 'real world' contexts, all the while accumulating a body of knowledge as the foundation for judgments regarding the possibility (or undesirability) of scaling things that 'work' (with one population, in one context to others). Increasingly it has also become an explicit standard guiding research funding decisions. Embraced by governmental and philanthropic organizations alike, the scale-up heuristic underscores key differences in the aims and strategies of generating evidence to inform educational reform, providing a framework that guides study design and focuses attention on the types of evidence it is reasonable to demand before implementing largescale systematic reforms.

Importantly, with this emphasis on the pathways to devising largescale solutions, the question shifted from the straightforward (if not always straightforward to answer) 'what works?' to the more nuanced 'what works when, for whom, under what conditions?' Answers to these more finely-grained questions are critical if both human capital and financial resources are to be targeted efficiently and effectively to improve educational outcomes. But to answer them often requires substantial resources and a shortened timeline to implementation. Leveraging the wealth of administrative and accountability data can be a seedbed for designing and implementing future reforms. Properly mined, such data hold the potential to identify teachers, classrooms, schools and districts which, on the face of it, appear to be 'over-performing' (e.g., in comparison to population norms). Such outliers can then be examined more closely to see if their success are identifiable and potentially replicable in other settings.

Secondary analyses of major national datasets can also be invaluable in suggesting and monitoring the effects of strategies for implementing sound educational practices at scale. An example is research conducted by Richard Ingersoll to establish the prevalence and correlates of out-of-field teaching in U.S. public elementary and secondary schools. Drawing on personal insights and experience as a secondary school teacher in Canada and the U.S., Ingersoll (1998) observed first-hand meaningful differences in student performance when teachers were assigned to offer instruction in subjects in which they were not specifically trained. Beginning with the U.S. Schools and Staffing Survey (SASS) that surveyed teachers, principals, and district administrators to comprehensively learn the characteristics of the instructional workforce; conditions in schools; and other related issues, he analyzed this administration survey data from several decades.[13] Ingersoll and colleagues found substantial proportions of high school teachers taught classes for which they were not adequately qualified, a problem exacerbated by teacher turnover. Subsequent analyses continued to document meaningfully high levels of outof-field teaching, leading Ingersoll to characterize the problem nearly a decade later as "chronic and widespread" (Ingersoll 2004: 14).

The data on the prevalence of out-of-field teaching (and subsequent replications of Ingersoll's findings) began to shape discourse and strategies for addressing the larger issue of what it takes to ensure equal access to high quality instruction (see, e.g., Ingersoll 1999). Particularly powerful was the inclusion in the No Child Left Behind Act of 2002 (U.S. Pub. L. 107-110) in its definitions of 'highly qualified' public elementary or secondary school teachers specific requirements for demonstrating competence in all academic subjects taught. These requirements included holding advanced degrees and passing state tests or graduate coursework in specific areas. However, knowledge of subject matter does not, of course, guarantee quality teaching, or even qualified teachers (Ingersoll et al. 1995). Such implicit choices and tradeoffs (e.g., devoting resources to placing more qualified teachers in classrooms versus expending the same resources to redress more fundamental socioeconomic inequalities, or calculating the moderating effect of the latter on investments in the former) underscore the important role judgment is likely to continue to play in decisions regarding the desirability of enacting laws and issuing regulations to address perceived shortcomings in the educational system, and reaching conclusions more generally regarding the scalability of interventions.

The intuitive appeal of evidence documenting the prevalence of 'poorly qualified' teachers is considerable; at some level, the evidence of out-of-field teaching has face validity so powerful that protracted testing to confirm this problem seems unwarranted. A counterargument however, could be made that one cannot be assured resources allocated to placing more highly qualified teachers in classrooms will prove more effective than resources devoted to better diagnostic assessments, computerized tutoring, and more offerings in online learning opportunities. Rich longitudinal national and state datasets coupled with sophisticated analytic procedures hold great promise for identifying potentially troubling characteristics of underperforming classrooms, schools, and districts, and for suggesting corrective actions for achieving best practices at scale. Ingersoll's important work on the prevalence of

[13] For a detailed description of the Schools and Staffing Survey, including copies of instrumentation administered in 1987–1988 m 1990–1991, 1993–1994, 1999–2000, 2003–2004, and 2007–2008, see the National Center for Education Statistics online at http://nces.ed.gov/surveys/sass/index.asp

out-of-field teaching, while not causal, presents robust evidence that underlie our judgments regarding which practices are indeed 'best' and strongly related to desired outcomes.

The availability of finely-grained data and efforts to support cultures of data sharing and data linkage suggest we may well be moving towards having the information necessary to document and weigh such tradeoffs, but it is unclear whether other obstacles to evidence-based education will ever be overcome. Reverse engineering exemplary practices already in the field (e.g., as identified through data mining that focuses attention upon districts, schools, and classes in which unusually large achievement gains are made over the course of a school-year) may help short-circuit the time intensive research and development process. But randomized control trials to ensure these outlier effects are replicable may take years to produce results. It is thus unlikely – and indeed would arguably be wrong to insist – that experimental evidence will ever become the sole basis for reform. Innovation and evidence generation will continue to proceed side-by-side, and important education policy decisions will continue to be made absent the most robust evidence scientific education research can provide. Moreover, judgment will always come in to play in weighing evidence. The task for educational researchers is to provide frameworks in which reasonable judgments can be made regarding the risks and likely benefits of supporting change with more and less of an empirical base.

## Principle 6: Accumulating Knowledge for Generalizability

It is important in weighing evidence to consider whether or not study findings are applicable to a broader population. If every member of a population were affected equally by an intervention – i.e., if treatment effects were homogeneous – then results of any well-designed study would be generalizable to the population in its entirety. Typically, however, we expect that specific individuals (e.g., students, teachers) and organizations (e.g., schools, districts) will be differentially affected by interventions. Specifically, we expect populations themselves to be heterogeneous and anticipate key characteristics of population elements (e.g., the developmental trajectory of students in a classroom, the experience of instructors teaching in a particular field, the social organization of a school) will moderate interventions' impacts, resulting in heterogeneous intervention effects.

One way to enhance the generalizability of study findings is to address such variations (or covariates) at the design stage, specifying procedures for drawing the sample that will be investigated. For example, individuals might be randomly selected from the population to constitute the study sample and members of the sample might then be randomly assigned to receive or not receive an intervention. Alternatively, when distinct segments of the population share characteristics known (or hypothesized) to affect the outcome of interest and/or the likelihood of having a positive response to an intervention, these subgroups may constitute strata from which sample members may be selected purposively.

Leveraging information regarding subgroup characteristics is valuable not only in designing representative samples but also to an alternative strategy for estimating the generalizability of findings. Specifically, information on covariates and the probability these covariates predict selection into the study sample can be utilized to identify the inferential population to which the sample applies (i.e., the population of which the sample is representative), and to estimate average treatment effects for that subpopulation. In this way, we can be more confident of the broader applicability of findings found in studies of samples which are underrepresented either by design or as a result of implementation problems (such as inability to secure cooperation or attrition).

The Scaling Up SimCalc project conducted by Jeremy Roschelle and colleagues, integrates technology, curriculum, and teacher professional development to support middle school students in learning key mathematical concepts.[14] In the scale-up project, two large-scale randomized controlled trials and a quasi-experiment were conducted with middle-school teachers in Texas. These studies, found statistically significant and meaningful treatment effects on student learning (see Roschelle et al. 2007). As random assignment to treatments was not feasible, the investigators had to seek alternative methods to estimate the generalizability of study findings (Tipton 2011).

Utilizing data on 26 covariates (including school-level achievement, aggregated student and teacher demographics, and school funding and structure), analysts were able to identify a subpopulation characterized by the 78 schools in the study sample – i.e., a population to which the study sample generalizes (see Tipton 2011; and Roschelle et al. 2010b).[15] Subsequent re-analyses of the SimCalc data (Tipton 2011) suggested this line of inquiry proved promising. Both at the design stage and as sampling strategies are implemented and studies unfold, educational research frequently explores impacts of interventions within non-representative samples. We are not advocating that this is the ideal situation, but realize it is one that often occurs in education studies as researchers work toward studying interventions anticipating the likelihood of scale-up.

The SimCalc work illustrates the possibility of generalizing appropriately findings of even those studies which are not at the design stage devised to represent the population of ultimate interest. This is not to say that efforts to conduct studies of the impacts of interventions upon representative samples of populations should be abandoned, but as the example illustrates it may be possible to draw sound conclusions regarding the extendibility or potential broader impacts of a particular set of study findings. These researchers' innovative use of statistical techniques to create

[14] For information about the SimCalc intervention and the scaling-up SimCalc study, see the Kaput Center for Research and Innovation in STEM Education (http://www.kaputcenter.umassd.edu/projects/simcalc), the SRI International Scaling Up SimCalc project website (at http://math.sri.com/index.html), and Roschelle et al. (2010b).

[15] Specifically, using a method and a propensity score sub classification estimator introduced by O'Muircheartaigh and Hedges reduced "bias in the estimate of a population average treatment effect" and identified "the portion of a population for which an experiment can generalize with fewer costs in terms [of] bias, variance, and extrapolation" (Tipton 2011: 4).

their representative population shows great promise for assessing the impact of an intervention and generating broadly generalizable findings (Hedges 2013; O'Muircheartaigh and Hedges 2014; Tipton et al. 2014; Tipton 2014).

This cutting-edge approach leveraged information derived from extant data collections to define a population to which it is reasonable to generalize the SimCalc findings, underscoring the research value of state and federal data systems and supporting a culture of data sharing (with appropriate privacy and confidentiality safeguards).

Administrative data are increasingly being used to assess state level interventions including changes in curricular requirements, teacher effectiveness, and scholarship programs to enable postsecondary attendance. Federal compliance and state data systems not only have key roles to play in administering and ensuring accountability across educational systems, but can also (when shared and linked) be used for a variety of analytic purposes, including deriving and testing hypotheses regarding factors that contribute to and impede instruction, learning, and achievement, and addressing issues such as small sample size, unrepresentative samples (e.g., due to the challenges of recruiting study participants, differential attrition) and other statistical problems that plague educational research. As the SimCalc example shows, working with administrative data can ease the process of generating evidence that warrants the move from intervention development to scale-up. Critically, strengthening the elements of the state and federal data systems, and the mechanisms and cultures for linking these with primary data from studies such as the SimCalc evaluation, provide new opportunities to appropriately contextualize single-study findings, assisting practitioners, policymakers, and educational researchers in making principled judgments regarding the generalizability of their findings.

## Principle 7: Conducting Research for the Public Good

An important goal of educational research in an era of evidence-informed decision-making is to promote the utilization of knowledge resulting from scholarly inquiry in support of the public good. Research conducted for the public good tackles issues of broad social interest. Striving to ensure research results in the greatest possible good for the largest number of individuals brings us back full circle to the importance of investigating issues that matter. Issues highly salient to only a small number of individuals merit exploration, but it is critically important for investigators and funders alike to ask themselves at every step of the educational research process 'who benefits from this work?' and 'do the potential implications of the evidence warrant the resources required to support the inquiry?'

A common appeal to motivate interest in educational research is to link education and learning with future economic competitiveness (for the individual and/or nations and society more generally). Examples include educational research that seeks to support underrepresented groups in preparing for and achieving successful transitions to postsecondary education and careers in STEM and other fields. One such study is an intervention designed to facilitate the successful entry of minority youth into health research careers, Training Early Achievers for Careers in Health (TEACH) research, directed by Vineet Arora M.D. The TEACH intervention was itself the product of research on an important social issue: factors affecting low-income urban high school students' matriculation to college. Informed by extensive analyses of longitudinal observational data and a resulting theory regarding the importance of aligning students' knowledge, attitudes, and behaviors to attain their ambitions (see Schneider and Stevenson 1999), the TEACH program was designed to foster 'aligned ambitions' (educational expectations in sync with occupational aspirations) for Chicago area high school students interested in preparing for health research careers. TEACH enabled students to engage in realistic health career experiences (e.g., internships and opportunities to observe clinical rounds) and to receive mentoring support from a multi-tiered structure of peers that includes high school student peers, undergraduate students, medical school students, and clinical research faculty.[16]

Drawing on lessons learned from the TEACH experience and with evidence of the efficacy of that intervention behind them, in 2009 a team of researchers from Michigan State University's College of Education collaborated with a sample of central Michigan high schools to launch the College Ambition Program (CAP), a school-wide initiative that like TEACH seeks to align ambitions and "give students the support system they need to make it to, and in, postsecondary education" (Schneider 2015). CAP investigators seek evidence on the merits and limits of their intervention striving to make changes for the public good (in this case improving the educational opportunities for low-income and minority children). In practice this means not only employing research designs capable of yielding evidence of meaningful change at the end of the 3-year study period, but ensuring those not selected to be part of the CAP treatment condition are not disadvantaged by serving in the controlled comparison group (for example, a wide range of online resources to support students in planning to attend postsecondary institutions are publicly available through the study website).[17]

## Applying These Principles for Educational Research

Another dimension of what it means to conduct research for the common good is to ensure access and improve the communication of research findings. Data upon which analyses are based and the measures employed in collecting them should be seen as public goods, and appropriately documented, archived, and made available for confirmatory or secondary analyses. A commitment to data sharing is critical to

[16] For additional information on the TEACH (Training Early Achievers for Careers in Health) Research program see http://chess.uchicago.edu/TEACH

[17] For additional information on the College Ambition Program and the NSF-supported Transforming Interests in STEM Careers (TISC) study evaluating its impacts see the program website at http://collegeambition.org/

facilitate the replications that increase confidence in findings. It is also vital to leverage investments in often costly primary data collections and encourages careful training in and application of best practices for recording and tracing provenance, and documenting the coding, re-coding, and data transformation decisions to create archival-quality data for secondary study. A corollary to a commitment to data sharing is access. Whether research entails primary data collection or relies on secondary data analyses, investigators have moral and legal obligations to handle (e.g., collect, store, analyze, and report) data responsibly and in accordance with provisions governing the protection of human subjects.

In education, individual studies and larger programs of research are designed not only to generate new evidence on what works to improve instructional practice, educational attainment, and lifelong learning but to inform practice and policy. With these broader goals in mind the criteria we have presented here encourage researchers to consider the intrinsic value of the topic being explored, the capacity to recognize and measure meaningful change, the broader applicability (scalability and generalizability) of findings, and how the research aligns with larger public interest objectives.

Although there are many criteria for assessing the quality of educational research, establishing standards for them is challenging, in part because of the tradeoffs inherent among them. Different stakeholders are likely to attach more or less importance to individual criteria at each stage in the research process. In education as in other fields it is not only the evidence educational science generates but assessments of its quality are often socially constructed and subject to disagreement. Evidence is meant to inform, and some does it better than others. Educational researchers have a critical role to play in providing decision-makers with the tools to judge the evidence before them. Ultimately, however, judgments will need to be made. Our goal is to identify a set of principles for interrogating the quality of evidence especially for studies conducted in the public interest that are designed to inform educational reform.

**Acknowledgement** This material is based upon work supported by the National Science Foundation under awards: No. DRL-131672 (CAP), No. OISE-1545684 (PIRE), and No. DRL-0815295 (ARC).

## References

American Educational Research Association (AERA). (2016). Retrieved from homepage: https://www.aera.org

American Recovery and Reinvestment Act of 2009 (ARRA). (2009, February 19). Pub. L. No. 111–5, 123 Stat. 115, 516.

BioKIDS: Kids' Inquiry of Diverse Species. (2005). Retrieved from http://www.biokids.umich.edu

Bohrnstedt, G. W., & Stecher, B. M. (2002). *What we have learned about class size reduction in California*. Sacramento: California Department of Education.

Bohrnstedt, G., Stecher, B., & Wiley, E. (2000). The California class size reduction evaluation: Lessons learned. In *How small classes help teachers do their best* (pp. 201–226). Philadelphia: Temple University Center for Research in Human Development and Education.

Borman, G. D., Hewes, G. M., Overman, L. T., & Brown, S. (2003). Comprehensive school reform and achievement: A meta-analysis. *Review of Educational Research, 73*(2), 125–230. doi:10.3102/00346543073002125.

Borman, G., Slavin, R. E., Cheung, A., Chamberlain, A., Madden, N. A., & Chambers, B. (2007). Final reading outcomes of the national randomized field trial of success for all. *American Educational Research Journal, 44*(3), 701–731. doi:10.3102/0002831207306743.

Bryk, A. S. (2015). Accelerating how we learn to improve. *Educational Researcher, 44*(9), 467–478.

Campbell Collaboration: Vision, Mission, and Key Principles. (2016). Retrieved from https://www.campbellcollaboration.org/vision-mission-and-principle/explore/our-key-principles

Campuzano, L., Dynarski, M., Agodini, R., & Rall, K. (2009). *Effectiveness of reading and mathematics software products: Findings from two student cohorts*. NCEE 2009–4041. National Center for Education Evaluation and Regional Assistance.

Children's Learning Institute (CLI) at The University of Texas-Houston Health Science Center and the Texas Institute for Measurement, Evaluation, and Statistics (TIMES) *Technical Report TPRI* (2010–2014 Edition). Retrieved from: http://tpri.org/resources/documents/20102014TechnicalReport.pdf

Children's Learning Institute: TPRI Early Reading Assessment. (2015). Retrieved from https://www.childrenslearninginstitute.org/resources/tpri-early-reading-assessment

Chmielewski, A. K. (2014). An international comparison of achievement inequality in within-and between-school tracking systems. *American Journal of Education, 120*(3), 293–324.

College Ambition Program. (2016). Retrieved from homepage: http://collegeambition.org

Duncan, G. J., & Murnane, R. J. (Eds.). (2011). *Whither opportunity?: Rising inequality, schools, and children's life chances*. New York: Russell Sage Foundation.

Dynarski, S., & Scott-Clayton, J. E. (2007). The feasibility of streamlining aid for college using the tax system. In *National Tax Association papers and proceedings* (vol. 99, pp. 250–262).

Every Student Succeeds Act of 2015, S. 1177, 114th Cong. (2015). Washington, DC: US Department of Education. Public Law 114–95.

Florida Center for Reading Research. (2008). Retrieved from homepage: http://www.fcrr.org/centerResearch/centerResearch.shtm

Foorman, B. R., & Petscher, Y. (2010). Development of spelling and differential relations to text reading in grades 3–12. *Assessment for Effective Intervention, 36*(1), 7–20.

Foorman, B. R., Fletcher, J. M., Frances, D. J., Carlson, C. D., Chen, D., & Mouzaki, A. (1998). *Technical report: Texas primary reading inventory* (1998th ed.). Houston: Center for Academic and Reading Skills and the University of Houston.

Foorman, B., Santi, K., & Berger, L. (2007). Scaling assessment-driven instruction using the internet and handheld computers. In B. Schneider & S. K. McDonald (Eds.), *Scale-up in education* (pp. 68–90). Plymouth: Rowman & Littlefield Publishers.

Foorman, B., Torgesen, J., Crawford, E., & Petscher, Y. (2009). Assessments to guide reading instruction in K-12: Decisions supported by the new Florida system. *Perspectives on Language and Literacy, 35*(5), 13–19.

Gates Foundation. (2016). Retrieved from homepage: http://www.gatesfoundation.org

Gotwals, A. W., & Songer, N. B. (2006). Measuring students' scientific content and inquiry reasoning. In *Proceedings of the 7th international conference on learning sciences* (pp. 196–202). International Society of the Learning Sciences.

Harris, S. (2016). Retrieved from homepage: https://www.samharris.org

Hedges, L. V. (1981). Distribution theory for Glass's estimator of effect size and related estimators. *Journal of Educational and Behavioral Statistics, 6*(2), 107–128.

Hedges, L. V. (2013). Recommendations for practice: Justifying claims of generalizability. *Educational Psychology Review, 25*(3), 331–337. doi:1040-726X.

Holland, P. W. (1986). Statistics and causal inference. *Journal of the American Statistical Association, 81*(396), 945–960.

Hoxby, C. M. (Ed.). (2007). *College choices: The economics of where to go, when to go, and how to pay for it*. Chicago: University of Chicago Press.
Imbens, G. W., & Rubin, D. B. (2010). Rubin causal model. In S. N. Durlauf & L. E. Blume (Eds.), *Microeconometrics* (pp. 229–241). New York: Macmillan.
Ingersoll, R. M. (1998). The problem of out-of-field teaching. *The Phi Delta Kappan, 79*(10), 773–776.
Ingersoll, R. M. (1999). The problem of underqualified teachers in American secondary schools. *Educational Researcher, 28*(2), 26–37.
Ingersoll, R. M. (2004). *Why do high-poverty schools have difficulty staffing their classrooms with qualified teachers?* Center for American Progress, Institute for America's Future.
Ingersoll, R. M., Han, M., & Bobbitt, S. (1995). *Teacher supply, teacher qualifications, and teacher turnover: 1990–1991* (pp. 95–744). Washington, DC: U.S. Department of Education, Office of Educational Research and Improvement, National Center for Education Statistics, NCES.
Kaput Center for Research and Innovation in STEM Education. (2016). University of Massachusetts, Dartmouth. Retrieved from: http://www.kaputcenter.umassd.edu/projects/simcalc
KIPP: About KIPP. (2016). Retrieved from homepage: http://www.kipp.org
KnowHow2Go. (2013). Retrieved from homepage: http://www.knowhow2go.org
Milesi, C., Brown, K., Hawkley, L., Dropkin, E., & Schneider, B. (2014). Charting the impact of federal spending for education research: A bibliometric approach. *Educational Researcher, 43*(7), 361–370. doi:10.3102/0013189X14554002.
National Center for Education Statistics. (2011a). *College Navigator*. Retrieved from http://nces.ed.gov/collegenavigator
National Center for Education Statistics. (2011b). *The nation's report card: Reading 2011 (NCES 2012–457)*. Washington, DC: Institute of Education Sciences, U.S. Department of Education.
National Center for Education Statistics. (2016). *Schools and Staffing Survey (SASS)*. Washington, DC: Institute of Education Sciences, U.S. Department of Education. Retrieved from: http://nces.ed.gov/surveys/sass/index.asp.
National Research Council. (2002). Scientific research in education. Committee on Scientific Principles for Education Research. In R. J. Shavelson & L. Towne (Eds.), *Center for education, division of behavioral and social sciences and education*. Washington, DC: National Academy Press.
National Science Foundation. (2010a). *Preparing the next generation of stem innovators: Identifying and developing our nation's human capital*. National Science Foundation. Retrieved from: https://www.nsf.gov/nsb/publications/2010/nsb1033.pdf
National Science Foundation. (2010b). *Research and Evaluation on Education in Science and Engineering (REESE). Program Solicitation.* Retrieved from: http://www.nsf.gov/pubs/2010/nsf10586/nsf10586.pdf
No Child Left Behind Act of 2002, S. 1115, 107th Cong. (2002). Washington, DC: US Department of Education. Public Law 107–110.
O'Muircheartaigh, C., & Hedges, L. V. (2014). Generalizing from unrepresentative experiments: A stratified propensity score approach. *Journal of the Royal Statistical Society, Series C, 63*(2), 195–210. doi:10.1111/rssc.12037.
Organization for Economic Co-operation and Development, OECD/EU. (2015). *Indicators of Immigrant Integration 2015: Settling In*, OECD Publishing, Paris. 1–348. doi:http://dx.doi.org/10.1787/9789264234024-en
Pellegrino, J. W., Chudowsky, N., & Glaser, R. (Eds.). (2001). *Knowing what students know: The science and design of educational assessment*. Washington, DC, National Academies Press.
Pellegrino, J. W., Wilson, M. R., Koenig, J. A., & Beatty, A. S. (Eds.). (2014). *Developing assessments for the next generation science standards*. Washington, DC: National Academies Press.
Principled Assessment Designs for Inquiry. (2003). Retrieved from homepage: http://padi.sri.com
Quint, J., Zhu, P., Balu, R., Rappaport, S., & DeLaurentis, M. (2015). *Scaling up the success for all model of school reform: Final report from the investing in innovation (i3) evaluation*. New York: MDRC.

Reardon, S. F. (2011). The widening academic achievement gap between the rich and the poor: New evidence and possible explanations. In R. Murnane, & G. Duncan (Eds.), *Whither opportunity? Rising inequality and the uncertain life chances of low-income children*. New York: Russell Sage Foundation.
Ritter, S., Anderson, J. R., Koedinger, K. R., & Corbett, A. (2007a). Cognitive Tutor: Applied research in mathematics education. *Psychonomic Bulletin & Review, 14*(2), 249–255.
Ritter, S., Kulikowich, J., Lei, P. W., McGuire, C. L., & Morgan, P. (2007b). What evidence matters? A randomized field trial of Cognitive Tutor Algebra I. *Frontiers in Artificial Intelligence and Applications, 162*, 13.
Roschelle, J., Tatar, D., Shechtman, N., Hegedus, S., Hopkins, B., Knudsen, J., & Stroter, A. (2007). Can a technology-enhanced curriculum improve student learning of important mathematics. *Results from 7th grade, year, 1*.
Roschelle, J., Shechtman, N., Tatar, D., Hegedus, S., Hopkins, B., Empson, S., Knudsen, J., & Gallagher, L. P. (2010a). Integration of technology, curriculum, and professional development for advancing middle school mathematics three large-scale studies. *American Educational Research Journal, 47*(4), 833–878.
Roschelle, J., Tatar, D., Hedges, L., & Shechtman, N. (2010b). Two perspectives on the generalizability of lessons from scaling up SimCalc. *Society for Research on Educational Effectiveness*.
Rowan, B., Correnti, R., Miller, R., & Camburn, E. (2009). School improvement by design: Lessons from a study of comprehensive school reform programs. *Consortium for Policy Research in Education*, 1–62. doi:10.12698/cpre.2009.sii.
Rubin, B. (2005). Bayesian inference for causal effects. In C. R. Rao & D. K. Dey (Eds.), *Handbook of statistics, volume 25: Bayesian thinking: Modeling and computation* (pp. 1–16). Amsterdam: Elsevier.
Schanzenbach, D. W. (2006). What have researchers learned from Project STAR? *Brookings Papers on Education Policy, 9*, 205–228.
Schneider, B. (2015). 2014 AERA Presidential Address, The College Ambition Program: A realistic transition strategy for traditionally disadvantaged students. *Educational Researcher, 44*(7), 394–403.
Schneider, B., & McDonald, S. K. (2007). Scale-up in practice: An introduction. In B. Schneider & S. K. McDonald (Eds.), *Scale-up in education: Vol. 2: Issues in practice* (pp. 1–12). Lanham: Rowman & Littlefield.
Schneider, B., & Stevenson, D. (1999). *The ambitious generation: America's teenagers, motivated but directionless*. New Haven: Yale University Press.
SimCalc, the mathematics of change. (2011). Retrieved from: http://math.sri.com/index.html
Society for Research on Educational Effectiveness (SREE): Mission. (2010). Retrieved from https://www.sree.org/pages/mission.php
Songer, N. B., Myers, P., & Gotwals, A. W. (2007). *DeepThink: Fostering and measuring learning progressions focused on deep thinking about biodiversity*. Poster presented at the Principal Investigators Meeting of the National Science Foundation, Washington, DC.
Songer, N. B., Kelcey, B., & Gotwals, A. W. (2009). How and when does complex reasoning occur? Empirically driven development of a learning progression focused on complex reasoning about biodiversity. *Journal of Research in Science Teaching, 46*(6), 610–631.
Stevenson, D. L. (2000). The fit and misfit of sociological research and educational policy. In M. T. Hallinin (Ed.), *Handbook of the sociology of education* (pp. 547–563). Springer US.
Success for All Foundation: Our Story. (2005). Retrieved from http://www.successforall.org/who-we-are
The Center for Health and the Social Sciences. (2016). *High school students: Training early achievers for careers in heatlh (TEACH)*. The University of Chicago. Retrieved from: http://chess.uchicago.edu/TEACH
Tipton, E. (2011). *Improving the external validity of randomized experiments using propensity score subclassification*. Working Paper.

Tipton, E. (2014). How generalizable is your experiment? An index for comparing experimental samples and populations. *Journal of Educational and Behavioral Statistics, 39*(6), 478–501.

Tipton, E., Hedges, L. V., Borman, G., Vaden-Kiernan, M., Caverly, S., & Sullivan, K. (2014). Sample selection in randomized experiments: A new method using propensity score stratified sampling. *Journal of Research on Educational Effectiveness, 7*(1), 114–135. doi:10.1080/19345747.2013.831154.

U.K., House of Commons. (2006). *Science and technology committee: scientific advice, risk and evidence based policy making* (Vol. 1). House of Commons.

U.S. Department of Labor. (2011). *A profile of the working poor, 2009.* U.S. Department of Labor, U.W. Bureau of Labor Statistics. March 2011. Retrieved from: http://www.bls.gov/opub/reports/working-poor/archive/workingpoor_2009.pdf

Urban Prep Academies: History. (2012). Retrieved from: http://www.urbanprep.org/about/history-creed

Walters, P. B., Lareau, A., & Ranis, S. (Eds.). (2008). *Education research on trial.* Taylor & Francis.

Weiss, C. H. (1982). Policy research in the context of diffuse decision making. *The Journal of Higher Education, 53*, 619–639.

Weiss, C. H. (1989). Congressional committees as users of analysis. *Journal of Policy Analysis and Management, 8*(3), 411–431.

What Works Clearinghouse. (2009). Intervention report: Cognitive tutor algebra I. Retrieved from https://www.mbaea.org/documents/filelibrary/pdf/cognitive_tutor/WWC_CogTutor_Report_July2009_B2A3C279D0481.pdf

What Works Clearinghouse. (2010). *What works clearinghouse: Quick review of the report "Student Characteristics and Achievement in 22 KIPP Middle Schools.* U.S. Department of Education, Institute of Education Sciences. Retrieved from: http://ies.ed.gov/ncee/wwc/Docs/QuickReview/kipp_092110.pdf

What Works Clearinghouse. (2016). What we do. Retrieved from: http://ies.ed.gov/ncee/wwc/WhatWeDo

Word, E., Johnston, J., Bain, H., Fulton, B. D., Zaharias, J. B., Achilles, C. M., Lintz, M. N. Folger, J. & Breda, C. (1990). The State of Tennessee's student/teacher achievement ratio (STAR) Project. *Tennessee Board of Education.*

World Education Research Association (WERA). (2016). Retrieved from homepage: https://www.wera.org

Yamada, H., & Bryk, A. S. (2016). Assessing the first two years' effectiveness of statway® a multi-level model with propensity score matching. *Community College Review*. 0091552116643162.

# Chapter 11
# Evidence-Based Policy and Practice in Turkish Education System

**Selahattin Turan and Derya Yılmaz Kılıçoğlu**

**Abstract** The Turkish education system is highly centralized. All educational policies, such as curriculum development and appointment of teachers and administrators, have been formulated by its central structure since the establishment of the Republic of Turkey in 1923. Many reform policies and change initiatives can be seen in a Turkish context and different parties have imposed various policies with underlying ideological and political purposes in different periods. Therefore, it is possible to identify conflicting implementations and policies. As the aim of National Education is to promote the welfare and happiness of citizens and Turkish society, to support and accelerate economic, cultural and social development as well as national unity and cohesion, large-scale educational reforms and policies for public good supported by the EU have been launched. However, these reforms, which are not based on evidence, are also ineffectively put into practice. Thus, it can be concluded that there is a culture of disconnectedness in research, policy and practice in the Turkish education system. From this point of view, the aim of this study is two-fold: (1) to provide evidence about what is necessary for public good in a Turkish context, and (2) to offer evidence-based recommendations for practice and policy makers.

## Introduction

The concept of evidence-based policy and practice in education has been gaining currency over the last two decades (Segone 2004; Pring and Thomas 2004). By means of this interest, governments have a chance to improve the quality of decision making in the policymaking process. Thus, expectations about the practical role of research provide governments the idea of evidence-based education implicitly. Evidence-based practice presents an understanding about the role of research in educational practice and offers opportunities for participation in educational decision making. Well-informed decisions related to educational policies, programs and

S. Turan (✉) • D.Y. Kılıçoğlu
Eskisehir Osmangazi University, Eskişehir, Turkey
e-mail: selahattinturan2100@gmail.com



M.Y. Eryaman, B. Schneider (eds.), *Evidence and Public Good in Educational Policy, Research and Practice*, Educational Governance Research 6,
DOI 10.1007/978-3-319-58850-6_11

projects can be done with the best available evidence from a wide range of sources in policy development and implementation process (Davies 1999). In contrast to *opinion-based policy*, which merely depends on selective use of evidence through the lens of ideological standpoints, prejudice, or speculative conjecture of individuals or groups, not all sources are sufficiently sound to form the basis of policymaking in evidence-based education (Davies et al. 2000). Rather, evidence-based policy and practice are based on information produced by historical experience, a comprehensive monitoring and evaluation system, academic research and *"good practices"* (Segone 2004). Actually, evidence-based education has come to the forefront in several countries in the wake of critical reports on education. These national and international reports investigated the quality and effectiveness of education by providing the lagging aspects of education systems in nationwide. Therefore, quality and relevance of educational research are considered by policy makers and educational practitioners (Biesta 2007).

While developing an agenda based on evidence, decision- and policy-makers are needed to understand what constitutes evidence and in what context, and the role of research vis-à-vis other sources of information. Evidence-based policy and practice changes depend on evidence from different sources, namely systematic reviews, single studies and evaluations, pilot studies and case studies, experts' evidence and internet evidence. *Systematic reviews,* which use research and evaluation evidence, include systematic search, critical appraisal and rigorous analysis of the existing evidence by accounting for the variability of similar studies (Cooper and Hedges 1994). *Single studies* and *evaluations,* which are more commonly used to support government policy and practice, provide the total available evidence on a particular topic or policy issue in specific context. *Pilot studies* and *case studies* are the other sources of evidence for policymaking and policy implementation that justify the use of whatever evidence is readily available. *Experts' evidence* is a commonly used source of evidence that supports government policy and practice depending on the knowledge and expertise of advisory groups or special advisers. *Internet evidence* provides uneven access to information and knowledge related to any topic via the internet (Segone 2004).

Even though the nature of evidence is need for the comprehension of evidence-based policy in educational organizations, policymaking process is a political issue developed and delivered by the use of power. Authority and power influence policymaking and implementation in education. Besides, the power of the governments is held by politicians with advisers and agents in many countries. However, the major goal of evidence-based policy is to guarantee policymaking that integrates the experience, expertise and judgment of decision-makers with the best available evidence gathered from systematic research (Segone 2004). Unfortunately, decision making in the highly centralized Turkish educational system does not depend on evidence, experience or expertise. Rather, policymaking is in the hands of people with authority and power in Turkey.

Some national and international reports can be considered as the sources of evidence since they systematically review the existing situation of education, critically appraise it and provide evaluations for educational practitioners and policy makers.

In this context, even though there are numerous national or international reports related to education, educational practitioners and policy makers do not meticulously consider these reports while developing and implementing educational policies in Turkey. Specifically, despite a range of changes and implementations performed in Turkish education system throughout the years, there has been no effort made by policy makers or practitioners to narrow the gap between research, policy and practice. From this point of view, the aim of this study is twofold: (1) to provide information about what is evidence for public good in a Turkish context, and (2) to offer evidence-based recommendations for practice and policy makers.

## Turkish Education in Context: What Is Evidence for Public Good?

Education, like other basic public services such as justice, security and health, is provided under the supervision and inspection of the Turkish government. The right to education for all citizens is secured by the Constitution of the Republic of Turkey. Additionally, Turkish education is organized under the guidance of law, including the Law on the Organization and Duties of the Ministry of National Education (MoNE) and the Basic Law of National Education. Further direction is provided by Development Plans, Government Programs, and Decisions of National Education Councils, which are regarded as basic policy documents, and other legislation regulating the principles related with the type, level and function of education.

According to the 1973 Basic Law of National Education numbered 1739, the MoNE is commissioned with the duty of reaching the general aims set for Turkish National Education on behalf of the state. The general aims of the MoNE are as follows:

- To raise individuals who are committed to Ataturk's principles and reforms, and to Ataturk's nationalism as defined in the Constitution of the Republic of Turkey, who adopt, protect and develop the national, ethical, spiritual, historical and cultural values of the Turkish nation, who love and elevate their families, homeland and nation, who are aware of their duties and responsibilities to the Republic of Turkey;
- To bring up individuals who physically, mentally, morally, spiritually and emotionally have a moderate and healthy personality and mentality, independent and scientific thinking power, a wide world view;
- To prepare individuals for life by ensuring that they have professions which will make them happy and contribute to the welfare of society through equipping them with the necessary knowledge, skills, attitude and habit of working cooperatively in line with their own interests, talents and abilities.

Thus, the aim of National Education is to promote the welfare and happiness of Turkish citizens and society, to support and accelerate economic, cultural and social development in national unity and cohesion, and finally to make the Turkish Nation a constructive, creative and distinguished partner of contemporary civilization (Prime Ministry 2009; MoNE 2005, pp. 16–17).

To realize these general objectives, Turkish National Education adopted some basic principles such as: generality and equality; meeting the needs of the individual and society; orientation; ensuring that everybody enjoys the right to basic education; providing equal opportunities; continuity; democracy education; secularism; the scientific approach; planning; coeducation; school-family cooperation; and education everywhere (Prime Ministry 2009; MONE 2005, pp. 17–18).

Based on general objectives and basic principles, numerous laws, regulations, directives, general written notifications and circulars related to education, and many projects and campaigns were carried out by the MoNE. Moreover, it is obvious that there have been many fundamental changes, reform initiatives and restructuring plans made in Turkish education since the establishment of the Republic of Turkey. These reform policies and implementations have been seriously criticized by the public as they reflect the various ideological and political purposes in different periods. That is, different policies are implemented by different parties. In this context, educational reforms and policies supported by the European Union (EU) are launched with the aim of becoming a member of the EU. To provide equal opportunities for all students and enhance equality in education, the following actions were implemented: *bussed primary education, free textbook implementation,* and *establishment of regional primary boarding schools.* In addition, the projects and campaigns conducted towards the above goals were*: Support for Basic Education Project, Project on Education for All, Child Friendly Learning Environments, Preparing Primary School Children for Life* and *Vocational Guidance, Withdrawing Working Children from Industrial Areas, Supporting Regional Primary Boarding Schools, Promotion of Lifelong Learning, Increasing Enrollment Rates Especially for Girls Operation, Promotion of Gender Equality in Education Project, Struggle Against Violence Towards Children Project, Democratic Citizenship and Human Rights Education, Support Campaign for the Schooling of Girls,* and *100% Support Campaign for Education* (MoNE 2015).

Although most of these reform initiatives have been effective in sight, implementations in schools have gained little success in reality. The main reason for this failure is the lack of rigorous research related to education, and the attempts to impose these policies with no or limited evidence or research. Whether the government centered the design and implementation of educational policies on evidence is a controversial issue. There is an obvious gap between educational research and practice (Biesta 2007; Vanderlinde and van Braak 2010). In the current Turkish context, a broader range of evidence is required to inform policy and practice, and scientific knowledge could be used as evidence for rational policymaking (Sanderson 2002, 2003). However, implementing policy and practice in the Turkish education system is nothing more than rhetoric. Several specific indicators such as academic performance, ability to meet targets or proven effectiveness are used as evidence for policymaking in many countries. What actually counts as evidence today are examples of good practice and indicators of exceptional performance. To illustrate, scores from international assessment studies, especially PISA (The Programme for International Student Assessment) are acceptable ways to measure performance and provide information about the quality of schooling (Simons 2015), since examination systems provide motivation for educational change and can be used to set policy targets (Fitz-Gibbon 2000). Besides, student achievement in international studies provides evidence on what happens in education and how this performance is related to individual income as well as economic well-being (Hanushek and Woessman 2011).

Though it is clear that education is a public good for all Turkish citizens, designing and implementing policies based on evidence is a major governmental weakness. In this context, recommendations for practice and policy makers is offered based on reports created by the Turkish Educational Association's think tank institution (TEDMEM), a well-established organization that compiles and evaluates huge amounts of data related to education in Turkey.

## What Constitutes Evidence in Turkish Education Reports?

To evaluate the changes and reform initiatives carried out in the Turkish education system, and thus comparing with other nations and producing policy recommendations, three most comprehensive reports of TEDMEM were selected. These reports are as follows: *PISA 2012: Evaluations and Recommendations on Turkey, Evaluations on the 19th National Education Council Meeting,* and *2015 Education Evaluation Report.*

In recent years, PISA has been recognized as the most comprehensive assessment system measuring knowledge and skills, and the most reliable international performance evaluation index for education systems. Moreover, it aims to capture the current states of education systems and provide opportunity for stakeholders to monitor the development and changes of their respective countries, as well as offering an opportunity to compare performance among countries. Therefore, a TEDMEM report related to PISA 2012 was chosen for review. The evidence in *PISA 2012: Evaluations and Recommendations on Turkey Report* is quite remarkable, as 510,000 students from all countries participated in PISA 2012; 4848 students from 170 schools in Turkey, representing nearly one million students, participated. These results revealed that Turkey is located below the OECD (Organization for Economic Co-Operation and Development) average scores in all skill areas. More specifically, Turkey was 32nd out of 34 OECD countries. Of the 65 participating countries, Turkey was 44th with 448 points in mathematics skills, 43rd with 463 points in science skills, and 41st with 475 points in reading skills (OECD 2013a, b, c, d, e; Şirin and Vatanartıran 2014; TEDMEM 2014a).

The National Education Council is the council that provides suggestions for the improvement of Turkish education system and meets every 4 years. At the 19th National Education Council Meeting, suggestions for *curriculum and weekly schedule*, *enhancing teacher quality*, *enhancing educational administrators quality* and *school safety* were discussed (TEDMEM 2014b).

The overall function of the Turkish education system is evaluated through key indicators on education in the *2015 Education Evaluation Report*. Developments in education regarding governance and funding; policies to improve quality, teacher training and professional processes; Turkey in international context; basic and secondary education; vocational and technical education; special needs education; student guidance systems; and private education are topics evaluated in the report (TEDMEM 2015). In this report, developments in governance, migration and education, teacher assignment and relocation regulation, and recruitment and assignment of teachers, are the conspicuous issues evaluated and recommendations for which are offered.

## Evidence-Based Recommendations for Practice and Policy Makers

Evidence-based policies have great potential to transform the practice and use of research within education. In fact, evidence-based policies provide nations with the opportunity to set their education system on track for progressive improvement. Specifically, solid evidence of effectiveness behind national programs and practices in schools assure generational progress in education (Slavin 2002). Furthermore, scientific knowledge with the measurement of educational outcomes is emphasized to influence policy decisions. Thus, evidence-based practice is believed to affect educational policies as well as improve educational practices (Simons 2003). From this point of view, reports providing information about the Turkish education system that depend on evidence and solid output are examined and necessary recommendations are offered for practice and policy makers. Hence, the question of "what is being done in education and is it being done in the best possible way?" (Davies 1999) is answered through evaluations and recommendations based on research evidence. Therefore, the relationship between research, policy and practice in Turkish educational context is highlighted through presenting the evidence and policy recommendations.

### *PISA 2012: Evaluations and Recommendations for Turkey*

Though PISA provides significant information about worldwide education systems and an opportunity to compare global student achievement, for the purposes of this study, the most striking results for Turkey were evaluated to develop the necessary evidence-based policy suggestions. The main results examined were: the effect of pre-school education on mathematics scores, the effect of socio-economic background of parents on student achievement, the low level of students' cognitive and behavioral skills, the difference between socio-economically advantaged and disadvantaged students, the success of academic resistant students, differences between schools on success, and the effect of parental education level on student success (OECD 2004, 2013a, b, c, d, e; TEDMEM 2014a). PISA 2012 results revealed that students with a pre-school education are a step ahead of other peers in mathematics. These students also earned 62 points more in mathematics compared with their non-pre-school educated peers in Turkey; while students in OECD countries increased 52 points more. Indeed, students with a pre-school education are 1 year ahead compared with those students at the same grade level who have not received a pre-school education (OECD 2013a, b, c, d, e; TEDMEM 2014a).

**Policy Recommendation 1** Pre-school enrollment rate must be increased by providing students with increased opportunities to recieve pre-school education. In fact, the Turkish 12-year compulsory education system (4 + 4 + 4 education stages) should be rearranged, with the inclusion of pre-school education. Thus, developmental skills that are given importance in PISA such as language, social, thinking, problem solving and reasoning should be proposed for consideration in the first grades (OECD 2013a, b, c, d, e; TEDMEM 2014a).

**Policy Recommendation 2** Not only the quality of education, but also the socio-cultural background and human development level of the country are important for increasing student success. Therefore, practices for the good of disadvantaged groups may be increased in nationwide. The disadvantage of students resulting from their lower socio-economic backgrounds may be partly eliminated through strengthening the as yet incomplete 2011 MoNE project "Every Child Can Achieve." Additionally, the progress of Turkey regarding support for students with lower socio-economic status needs to be investigated through longitudinal research or establishment of educational research centers to effectively develop evidence-based policies about this issue (OECD 2004, 2013a, b, c, d, e; TEDMEM 2014a).

**Policy Recommendation 3** Assessment and measurement centered education and development of students' skills just for examination rather than learning should be abandoned. Instead, a learning-centered approach, which makes learning meaningful and is based on thinking, interpreting, and questioning skills rather than fulfilling program requirements should be constructed. That is, policy makers need to reconsider necessary curriculum elements, how to assess students, and what kind of skills students need in the twenty-first century. Furthermore, research- and problem-based learning is necessary additions to the national curriculum.

The difference between socio-economically advantaged and disadvantaged students in Turkey declined by 60 points in PISA 2012, whereas this difference was a further 100 points in PISA 2003. This situation indicates the descending effect the socio-economic level of parents has on the success of students; this particular case highlights that inequality in education is reduced in Turkey. Despite the difficult conditions, the number of successful students–academic resistant students–has increased in Turkey. Indeed, the performance of girls and boys living in difficult conditions has increased 59 points in PISA within 10 years (OECD 2004, 2013a, b, c, d, e; TEDMEM 2014a). Increase in the success of academic resistant students indicates reduction in inequality in education caused in part by initiation of MoNE projects such as "100% Support for Education" in 2003, "Increasing Enrollment Rates Especially for Girls Operation, Phase I" in 2009, "Increasing Enrollment Rates Especially for Girls Operation, Phase II" in 2011, "Promotion of Gender Equality in Education Project" in 2010 and an albeit small amount of financial assistance provided for economically disadvantaged families from the Social Assistance and Solidarity Foundations.

**Policy Recommendation 4** Further support from projects or campaigns of public partnerships or foundations is necessary to continue to support disadvantaged students and their parents in Turkey. Appropriate regulations need to be prepared for social welfare foundations to support deprived families and their disadvantaged students.

PISA 2012 results also indicated differences between schools regarding success in Turkey. In fact, a student's success is determined by the school they attend, represented by a 62% change in success based on whether a student goes to a successful or unsuccessful school. The success difference between schools in Turkey is among the highest compared to OECD countries. However, success difference observed within the same school is the lowest in Turkey compared with other countries, which indicates that students with similar characteristics attend the same school and have the same success owing to an exam-centered education system, especially the transition exams performed in Turkey (OECD 2004, 2013a, b, c, d, e; TEDMEM 2014a).

**Policy Recommendation 5** Rather than enrolling and ranking students based on exam scores, an address-based registration system should be embraced. To decrease success difference between schools, the classroom and teacher shortage in Turkey also needs to be addressed. Successful and experienced teachers should be encouraged to work long-term at schools in disadvantaged areas to provide educational opportunities for those students. Teachers working at central school districts should also be subjected to rotation to provide them with the chance to study and contribute to other schools.

PISA 2012 results indicated that Turkey has the lowest parental education level among OECD countries. The average parental education level is 8.7 years in Turkey, whereas this average is 13.5 years in other OECD countries. The effect of parental education level on student success is also considered in PISA examination. PISA exam scores for students with parents who have the highest education level attainable showed a 59 point difference compared with students with parents who have the lowest education level. Moreover, PISA 2012 results indicated that eight out of ten students who have the lowest parental education level attend socio-economically disadvantaged schools, while only one out of ten students with the highest parental education level go to these schools (OECD 2004, 2013a, b, c, d, e; TEDMEM 2014a).

**Policy Recommendation 6** As it is expected that an increase in the level of parental education will cause an equivalent increase in student success, parental education level must be increased in Turkey. This may be accomplished through a new policy of providing educational support for parents via lifelong learning or distance education programs. For parents with the lowest education levels, classroom teachers may also be given opportunities to support these individuals by preparing adult certification programs. Through these programs, parents can get necessary information or procedures t about their or children's education.

Among the countries participating in PISA, Turkey is the last country in terms of autonomy both in deciding curriculum content, course materials and auxiliary sources. The most autonomous countries in terms of curriculum, such as Japan, South Korea, Shanghai and Hong Kong, are the most successful countries in PISA (OECD 2004).

**Policy Recommendation 7** Autonomous schools, which determine the curriculum, the criteria for school success, and the course books, need to be expanded. This can be done gradually by giving more power and responsibility to school administrators at the national level. However, pilot implementations should first be performed in certain school groups and school districts.

Even as the PISA Exam increases its influence on educational discourse and educational policies in participating countries, some researchers criticize PISA international evaluations because of methodological limitations such as: an inconsistent rationality, problematic statistics, opaque sampling, flawed evaluative design, lack of transparency, questionable instrument validity, and problematic presentation of findings (Fernandez-Cano 2016; Kreiner and Christensen 2013). Additionally, PISA has been criticized for how results appear to shape the image of the education quality, universalize national institutions such as a country's school system, promote competition on the global scene, lead to complications, and influence the development of standardized skills and knowledge. Therefore, national educational policies should not be based solely on PISA findings. National curricula, values, traditions, and priorities should not be pushed aside (Sjøberg 2015).

## *Report on Evaluations from the 19th National Education Council Meeting*

At first, a national education goal and a proposed human and society model need to be drawn clearly and systematically, followed by establishment of macro teaching plans. More specifically, the mission, goals and targets for the curriculum need to be re-imagined, away from popular concepts. Owing to the transformation to a skills-based approach that considers the needs of the twenty-first century, subject based program approach is abandoned in the curriculum. In place of it, skills based approach is adopted in spiral education structure. However, providing students lower level of skills, and teachers' incompetency about high level questioning and critical thinking in classroom activities are striking points in the curriculum. Moreover, individual differences are not emphasized in learning activities and the number of attainment targets is still too high currently. The number and distribution of basic and optional courses in the weekly schedule is another issue. Selection and classification of these courses and their content are set based on the upper limit of the normal distribution, especially for students with higher economic status, social support and academic qualifications. Thus, there is a mismatch between the course contents and student characteristics and qualifications (TEDMEM 2014b).

**Policy Recommendation 8** Students should be given opportunities to transition to other fields and but should not be required to take 'must' courses out of their fields. Elective course selection can be given to students to prevent withdrawal from those such as sports, arts and other social courses. The curriculum quality should be increased and a skills-based approach should be effectively embraced. Different educational programs and weekly schedules should be designed depending on the students' needs in pilot schools.

Enhancing teacher quality is only achieved by focusing on pre-service and in-service teacher training, rather than the undergraduate training provided to teachers in universities. Furthermore, direct and indirect variables such as public perception towards the teaching profession, characteristics of teacher candidates and the teaching staff in universities, program content, research and practice competency of the trained faculty, school environment where teaching practice is performed, relations with colleagues, and attitudes of school administrators affecting teacher quality should receive less amount of attention. Moreover, policies related to teachers are only shaped through assignment, quotas and employability. In fact, teacher qualifications should not only be affected by technical and organizational regulations. However, structural requirements need to be addressed in the system. Besides, possessing only one type of teacher training prevents innovative approaches and, thus, the existing structure force teachers only to transfer the gained knowledge to their students. The issue of teacher training issue falls within those of the system of higher education and is considered the problem of the Council of Higher Education rather than the MoNE (TEDMEM 2014b).

**Policy Recommendation 9** Teacher quality should be assessed with a multidimensional approach rather than as a bureaucratic operation between the MoNE and Council of Higher Education. Development of supportive and motivating policies for teaching is necessary to increase the attractiveness of this profession and to change public perception of teaching. A multi-dimension evaluation system based on written and oral examinations, and having degree in the related field should be implemented during teacher assignment. The only type of teacher training institutions needs to be differentiated by changing the provided training system and establishment of research universities.

In Turkey, school administrators are generally responsible for completion of administrative duties, school operation, and human resource management. However, some emerging problems include how these people should be trained, what qualifications they need, what tasks they are expected to fulfill, and how they should be selected for their positions. Therefore, it is necessary to establish national and regional selection criteria, as well as expected performance standards, for school administrators (TEDMEM 2014b).

**Policy Recommendation 10** Nationally determined qualifications, competencies, expectations and responsibilities of school administrators should be set. In fact, expected standards and qualifications of school administrators must be scientifically determined and school administration should be professionalized. Assignment, promotion and a career system should be established for school administration by considering professional proficiency, standards, and competencies in school leadership.

Research done about school safety in recent years revealed that security level of the schools in Turkey has significantly declined. As of now, stakeholders and society perceive schools as unsafe. In the Turkish education system, the term "safe school" is usually discussed in the context of physical safety and security. However, physical safety includes both that of students within and outside of school. Thus, safety on the way to school and school health also need to be considered (TEDMEM 2014b).

**Policy Recommendation 11** Providing opportunities to students for being education-oriented, increasing students' potential and academic achievement, strengthening the relationship between school and stakeholders, creating an education system based on common values, principles, expectations, responsibilities and rules may help form students' sense of belonging. Because of this, students may perceive that they are in a safe environment and exhibit safe behaviors in the school. Hence, the construction of positive and healthy school environment can reinforce school safety and security.

## *2015 Evaluation Report on Education*

An issue in the governance of the Turkish education system is the constantly changing regulations on designation of educational institution administrators. Based on the Regulation on Designation and Relocation of Educational Institution Administrators (Prime Ministry 2013), school principals were evaluated by their written and oral exam scores and designated by the governor after receiving the proposal of the provincial education director. Before this, assignment of the school principals was done through written exam results and awards attained; further points for consideration were attainment of a graduate degree and having academic studies (Kılıçoğlu and Yılmaz 2015). This regulation underwent additional changes on 10 June 2014; the written exam was excluded during designation of the administrators. Because of a lack of objectivity and worthiness criteria during designations, the number of case records increased. Thus, loss and acquisition of rights came forward and legal processes were initialized in Turkey. These regulations changed again on 6 October 2015. Now, according to the Regulation on Assignment of Administrators in Ministry of National Educational Institutions, written and oral exams are included in the assignment procedure. Indeed, written exam results are considered for candidate assistant administrators and oral exam results are reviewed for candidate administrators with an uncertain evaluation and selection technique by the new arrangement (Prime Ministry 2015a; TEDMEM 2015).

**Policy Recommendation 12** The Ministry urgently needs an assignment and designation model for educational institution administrators rather than a constantly changing system that often discourages individuals. However, it is important to assert that the steps of the designation model should be well-evaluated by professionals and academics in the field, should not change very often, should be supported by regulations and should have maximum validity. The evaluation criteria in the exams should be meticulously discussed, and exams should be systematic. In addition, obtaining a graduate education degree in the field of educational administration can also be the part of the evaluation process.

According to United Nations High Commissioner for Refugees, 2.2 million Syrian refugees are under temporary protection in Turkey as of November 2015. Of this population, 54.2% comprises children under the age of 18, and 34.2% of them are school age (5–17 years old) which means that approximately 750,000 children are expected to take part in the Turkish education system, as is their right. According to data shared on 30 November 2015 by the Ministry of Interior Directorate General of Migration Management, 25 temporary refugee shelters were established in 10 cities and 263,241 refugees live in these shelters. There are 6857 students at a pre-school level, 421,191 primary school students, 20,051middle school students and 9308 secondary school students in these temporary shelters. That is, 78,707 students receive their basic education needs from these refugee shelters. Syrian curriculum, with minimal changes, is being taught in these shelters along with 6 h of Turkish lessons. As well as basic education services, 13,936 people attend adult courses and 61,749 people have already completed these courses. In total, 300,000 students benefit from these education services, but a remaining 400,000 people do not have access to education for various reasons, as the MoNE states (TEDMEM 2015).

**Policy Recommendation 13** Voluntary Syrian teachers in temporary education shelters should be provided educational support and incentives by the Ministry and UNICEF. To avoid issues of space and to meet the needs of Syrian students, the MoNE should perform necessary actions to continue education with a half-day education system. In addition, projects and campaigns need to be created and initiated to prevent problems regarding Syrian adaptation to school and society. However, it is necessary to consider a long-term and comprehensive strategy not only for ensuring attendance of these asylum-seekers and refugees to basic education, but also to higher education.

A significant change to the teacher assignment system was carried out in the Amendment of the Regulation on Teacher Assignment and Relocation, dated 28 January 2015 and the Regulation on Teacher Assignment and Relocation, dated 17 April 2015, which stated that the "40 year old condition" be removed for first-time teaching applicants. Additionally, an emphasis was placed on performance evaluation criteria for teacher candidates (Prime Ministry 2015b, c). After working at least 1 year and receiving three positive performance evaluations, candidate teachers have right to take written and oral or written exam. These exams include topics such as laws and regulations (50%) and teaching practices (planning, learning environments, classroom management, teaching methods and techniques, assessment and measurement, 50%). If candidate teachers are successful in these exams, they can transition to teaching. However, if they are not successful, they will be assigned to another educational institution, then re-subjected to performance evaluation and oral or written exam. If they fail the exams or performance evaluation again, they lose their title and official duty.

**Policy Recommendation 14** There is no model followed during assignment or relocation of teachers, everything progresses based on existing regulations. Steps for becoming a teacher need to be clarified by MoNE. In addition to evaluating teachers' theoretical understanding of regulations and their cognitive skills, the emotional and psychological characteristics of teachers should be considered. Performance evaluation should be used not only for candidate teachers but also for all other teachers in the education system, as there are no existing criteria for evaluating teachers throughout their career. Uncertainty about the oral exam in the regulation should be addressed by clearly expressing in which conditions this method should be used, how impartiality and expertise should be ensured, how to maintain the transparency of the exam, and how objection processes should be performed. Moreover, the structure, content and methods for national teacher qualifications in the teacher training process need to be determined.

In Turkey, the Teaching Knowledge Test has been used in the Public Personnel Selection Exam since 2013 to measure candidate teachers' knowledge about their fields. According to data presented by the Measurement, Selection and Placement Center, only 9.2% of candidate teachers had an average score above 30 points on Teaching Knowledge Test in 2015. Specifically, Turkish language teachers have the highest average score (30.809) while biology teachers have the lowest score (12.899) on this exam. In February and September 2015, teacher assignment was carried out twice. The quota of February assignment was determined as 15,000 while the quota of September assignment was 37,000. According to information given by the Ministry, 75,962 candidate teachers applied for February assignment from 108 different fields of expertise, whereas 150,934 candidate teachers applied for September assignment from 105 different fields of expertise. Mostly English, primary school, religious education and primary mathematics teachers were recruited in both February and September assignments. Philosophy, clothing technology, information technologies and history teachers were recruited with the highest minimum exam scores in February assignment while special education, music and guidance teachers were recruited with the lowest minimum exam scores. Likewise, philosophy, history, information technologies, mathematics and information technologies teachers were recruited with the highest minimum exam scores in September assignment whereas child development and education, Arabic and music teachers were recruited with the lowest minimum exam scores (TEDMEM 2015).

**Policy Recommendation 15** The evidence indicates that teacher qualifications have not possessed by the candidate teachers in practice and expected qualifications are mainly based on theoretical knowledge in the teachers' field of expertise and pedagogical content knowledge. Rather than just focusing on theoretical knowledge in the exam, aspects such as professional dedication; techno-pedagogical knowledge; planning and practice of instruction; evaluation and monitoring student development; effective communication in the learning environment; managing student behaviors; working in collaboration with other teachers, parents and school personnel; and awareness of job-related tasks, principles and procedures should be included to assess teacher qualifications. In addition, the supply-demand balance should be urgently considered during recruitment of teachers and teacher employment policies must be rethought because some are easily recruited, while others are not. Furthermore, the planning of higher education should also be reconsidered. Indeed, higher education programs and quotas should be reviewed and new employment models need to be developed.

## Discussion and Conclusion

Even though many reform policies and change initiatives can be seen in Turkey, different parties imposed regulations with varying ideological and political purposes in each period since the establishment of the Republic of Turkey in 1923. Therefore, it is possible to recognize conflicting implementations and policies that are not based on evidence. In addition, large-scale educational reforms and policies for public good supported by the EU (such as Support for Basic Education, Capacity Building Support Project for Ministry of National Education, and Democratic Citizenship and Human Rights Education) were launched during the process of joining the EU. However, these implementations were not put into practice effectively. Even though the 19th National Education Council Meeting is the most comprehensive national meeting in which educational experts, academics, researchers, and politicians participate and provide recommendations concerning educational problems faced in Turkey, a great majority of the proposed suggestions were not put into practice. Despite being shared with the public, other change initiatives, campaigns and projects of the government were also ineffectively implemented. Thus, it can be concluded that te Turkish education system is highly centralized and all educational policies, such as curriculum development, and appointment of teachers and administrators, have been formulated by the central structure. Moreover, there is a culture of disconnectedness in research, policy and practice in the Turkish education system. Specifically, problems facing in policymaking and further suggestions are provided as follows:

*Quality of Research for Policymaking* Research- or evidence-based practices are not embraced in the context of the Turkish education system. Although there is a wealth of ongoing experimental, correlational or descriptive research, the information yielded is limited and not add up to school reform or policy development. However, studies such as narrative, case studies, interviews or observational studies, which emphasize daily problems of students and teachers, can contribute to reaching professional practice decisions (Simons 2004). Both qualitative and quantitative studies involving a range of evidence need to be considered in the context of evidence-based practice to inform policy and practice (Sebba 1999; Davies 1999). That is, multiple studies need to be compiled systematically to assess relevant findings in education, as a variety of sources such as expert knowledge, national and international research, statistics, stakeholder consultation, evaluation of previous policies, secondary sources and new research count as evidence for good quality policymaking (Nutley and Webb 2000).

*Sharing Evidence and Cooperation* There is a general willingness to use evidence, but a lack of resources, as this approach it contradicts entrenched positions of policy makers (Sager and Ravlum 2005). In other words, political decision-makers gather information and do not use it while policymaking (Krizek et al. 2009; March 1994). This is the case in Turkey. Even though MoNE keeps information about any issue related to schools, teachers and students in Turkey, it does not share any necessary information with the public or academics for developing educational policy. Thus, it is obvious that there is a problem of transparency and accountability in the Turkish education system. Therefore, public framework and legal grounds for evidence-based policymaking are needed since every implementation is based on legitimacy in Turkey. Access to knowledge pools and government research programs should be shared with the public. Although the Turkish government has a role in supporting tools for effective practice, it may be counterproductive if the government is too close to the work of practitioners and policymakers (Baron 2016). Besides, policy makers and practitioners should form regulations using evidence and work together to improve practice in education. That is, researchers and analysts should cooperate with the government to provide evidence-based policy advice.

*Research Centers or Institutes for Providing Evidence* Although there are some think tanks and non-profit organizations in Turkey to conduct research and evaluate schooling outcomes and policies, the number of them is limited. Research centers and special research observatories tied to universities need to be set up for research-based knowledge and to compile large amounts of data professionally in national reports. Using these centers, national evaluations and data-gathering based on scientific methods can be carried out. These research centers or institutions should be legal entities in their own right that foster academic and independent research by controlling their own budget. Likewise, there is a real need to increase the number of national reports based on evidence in different subject areas as there are limited studies investigating current problems in education. Indeed, specific research topics concerning educational issues such as generality and equality, social justice, and democracy are necessary to research before developing specific policies.

*Adaptation of International Educational Practices and Policies* Educational policies and reforms performed in Turkey are mostly adapted from European and American contexts. Thus, they do not provide effective solutions for educational problems faced in Turkey. That is, it can be concluded that evidence or research-based policymaking is not effectively embraced in Turkey. Therefore, evidence and education models peculiar to Turkish culture need to be emphasized because it is obvious that "better evidence and better research yield better policy" (Baron 2016) and evidence provides a major policy lever for systematic improvement in education (Alton-Lee 2011).

In this chapter, facts regarding evidence-based practice and policy in a Turkish context were discussed. Depending on three comprehensive reports, changes and reform initiatives in the Turkish education system were evaluated and policy recommendations were offered.

Suggestions are provided for Turkish policymaking regarding the quality of performed research, sharing evidence, collaborative professional research and knowledge-building in the education system, as well as the establishment of research centers or institutions.

## References

Alton-Lee, A. (2011). (Using) evidence for educational improvement. *Cambridge Journal of Education, 41*(3), 303–329.

Baron, K. (2016). *Better evidence and beter research yield beter policy*. Carnegie Foundation fort he Advancement of Teaching. Retrieved from https://www.carnegiefoundation.org/blog/better-evidence-and-better-research-yield-better-policy/

Biesta, G. (2007). Why "What Works" won't work: Evidence-based practice and the democratic deficit in educational research. *Educational Theory, 57*(1), 1–22.

Cooper, H. M., & Hedges, L. V. (1994). *The handbook of research synthesis*. New York: The Russell Sage Foundation.

Davies, P. (1999). What is evidence-based education. *British Journal of Educational Studies, 47*, 108–121.

Davies, H. T. O., Nutley, S. M. & Smith, P. C. (2000). *What works? Evidence-based policy and practice in public services*. UK.

Fernandez-Cano, A. (2016). A methodological critique of the PISA evaluations. *RELIEVE, 22*(1), 1–16.

Fitz-Gibbon, C. (2000). Education: Realising the potential. In H. T. O. Davies, S. M. Nutley, & P. C. Smith (Eds.), *What works: Evidence-based policy and practice in public services* (pp. 69–92). Bristol: The Policy Press.

Hanushek, E., & Woessman, L. (2011). The economics of international differences in educational achievement. In E. Hanushek, S. Machin, & L. Woessman (Eds.), *Handbook of the Economic of Education* (Vol. 3, pp. 89–200). North-Holland: Elsevier.

Kılıçoğlu, G., & Yılmaz, D. (2015). Change interventions of the Ministry of National Education: An evaluation from an organizational perspective. *Journal of Teacher Education and Educators, 4*(1), 78–103.

Kreiner, S., & Christensen, K. B. (2013). Analyses of model fit and robustness: A new look at the PISA scaling model underlying ranking of countries according to reading literacy. *Psychometrika, 79*(2), 210–231.

Krizek, K., Forysth, A., & Slotterback, C. S. (2009). Is there a role for evidence-based practice in urban planning and policy? *Planning Theory and Practice, 10*(4), 459–478.

March, J. (1994). *A primer on decision making*. New York: Free Press.

MoNE, Ministry of National Education (2005). *Basic education in Turkey: Background report*. Turkish Ministry of National Education.
MoNE, Ministry of National Education (2015). Directorate of European Union and Projects Coordination Group.
Nutley, S., & Webb, J. (2000). Evidence and the policy process. In H. T. O. Davies, S. M. Nutley, & P. C. Smith (Eds.), *What works: Evidence-based policy and practice in public services* (pp. 13–42). Bristol: The Policy Press.
OECD, Organization for Economic Cooperation and Development. (2004). Learning for tomorrow's world. PISA, OECD Publishing.
OECD, Organization for Economic Cooperation and Development. (2013a). PISA 2012 results: What students know and can do – student performance in mathematics, reading and science I. PISA, OECD Publishing.
OECD, Organization for Economic Cooperation and Development. (2013b). PISA 2012 results: Excellence through equity: Giving every student the chance to succeed. II PISA, OECD Publishing.
OECD, Organization for Economic Cooperation and Development. (2013c). PISA 2012 results: Ready to learn – students' engagement, drive and self-beliefs. III, PISA, OECD Publishing.
OECD, Organization for Economic Cooperation and Development. (2013d). Education at a glance 2013: OECD indicators. PISA, OECD Publishing.
OECD, Organization for Economic Cooperation and Development. (2013e). PISA 2012 results: What makes schools successful? Resources, policies and practices. IV, PISA, OECD Publishing.
Prime Ministry. (2009). Basic Law of National Education. *Official Gazzette*, No: 27284.
Prime Ministry. (2013). Regulation on designation and relocation of Educational Institution Administrators. *Official Gazette*, No: 28728.
Prime Ministry. (2015a). Regulation on assignment of administrators in Ministry of National Educational Institutions. *Official Gazette*, No: 29494.
Prime Ministry. (2015b). Amendment of the regulation on teacher assignment and relocation. *Official Gazette*, No: 29250.
Prime Ministry. (2015c). Regulation on teacher assignment and relocation. *Official Gazette*, No: 29329.
Pring, R., & Thomas, G. (2004). *Evidence-based practice in education*. New York: McGraw-Hill Education.
Sager, T., & Ravlum, I. A. (2005). The political relevance of planners' analysis: The case of a parliamentary standing committee. *Planning Theory, 4*(1), 33–65.
Sanderson, I. (2002). Evaluation, policy learning and evidence-based policymaking. *Public Administration, 80*(1), 1–22.
Sanderson, I. (2003). Is it "what works" that matters? Evaluation and evidence-based policymaking. *Research Papers in Education Policy and Practice, 18*(4), 331–347.
Sebba, J. (1999). *Developing evidence-informed policy and practice in education*. Paper presented to the British Educational Research Association Conference, University of Sussex Brighton, 2–5 Sept 1999.
Segone, M. (2004). Evidence-based policymaking and the role of monitoring and evaluation within the new aid environment. In M. Segone (ed.), *Bridging the gap: The role of monitoring and evaluation in evidence-based policymaking* (pp. 16–45). UNICEF.
Simons, H. (2003). Evidence-based practice: Panacea or over promise. *Research Papers in Education, 18*(4), 303–311.
Simons, H. (2004). Utilizing evaluation evidence to enhance professional practice. *Evaluation, 10*(4), 410–429.
Simons, M. (2015). Governing education without reform: The power of the example. *Discourse: Studies in the Cultural Politics of Education, 36*(5), 712–731.
Şirin, S. R., & Vatanartıran, S. (2014). *PISA 2012 değerlendirmesi: Türkiye için veriye dayalı eğitim reform önerileri [PISA 2012 evaluation: Evidence-based reform suggestions for Turkey]*. İstanbul: TUSİAD, TÖDER.

Sjøberg, S. (2015). PISA and global education governance – a critique of the project, its uses and implications. *Eurasia Journal of Mathematics, Science & Technology Education, 11*(1), 111–127.

Slavin, R. E. (2002). Evidence-based education policies: Transforming educational practice and research. *Educational Researcher, 31*(7), 15–21.

TEDMEM. (2014a). *PISA 2012: Türkiye üzerine değerlendirme ve öneriler [PISA 2012: Evaluations and Recommendations on Turkey]*. Ankara: TEDMEM.

TEDMEM. (2014b). *19. Milli Eğitim Şurasına ilişkin değerlendirmeler [Report on Evaluations on 19th National Education Council Meeting]*. Ankara: TEDMEM.

TEDMEM. (2015). *2015 Eğitim değerledirme raporu [2015 Evaluation Report on Education]*. Ankara: TEDMEM.

Vanderlinde, R., & van Braak, J. (2010). The gap between educational research and practice: Views of teachers, school leaders, intermediaries and researchers. *British Educational Research Journal, 36*(2), 299–316.

# Index





M.Y. Eryaman, B. Schneider (eds.), *Evidence and Public Good in Educational Policy, Research and Practice*, Educational Governance Research 6,
DOI 10.1007/978-3-319-58850-6

MIX
Papier aus verantwortungsvollen Quellen
Paper from responsible sources
FSC® C105338

If you have any concerns about our products,
you can contact us on
**ProductSafety@springernature.com**

In case Publisher is established outside the EU,
the EU authorized representative is:
**Springer Nature Customer Service Center GmbH**
**Europaplatz 3, 69115 Heidelberg, Germany**

Printed by Libri Plureos GmbH
in Hamburg, Germany